p. 393- 436 missing
cl .... AT

6 · 30

9

ΰ : JUI

# DEVELOPMENT

5

The Scott, Foresman/Little, Brown Series
in Comparative Politics

*Under the Editorship of*

**GABRIEL A. ALMOND**

**LUCIAN W. PYE**

643139

# Understanding
# POLITICAL
# DEVELOPMENT

*General Editors*

Myron Weiner

Samuel P. Huntington

*Contributors*

Gabriel A. Almond
Ali Banuazizi
Robert H. Bates
Walker Connor
Winston Davis
Jorge I. Domínguez
Peter B. Evans
Samuel P. Huntington
Joel S. Migdal
Joan M. Nelson
Eric A. Nordlinger
Myron Weiner

HarperCollins*Publishers*

17/11/92

**Library of Congress Cataloging-in-Publication Data**

Understanding political development.

(The Little, Brown series in comparative politics)
Includes index.
1. Developing countries—Politics and government.
I. Weiner, Myron.   II. Huntington, Samuel P.   III. Series.
JF60.U52   1987          320.9.72′4          86-27411

Library of Congress Catalog Card No. 8627411

ISBN 0-673-39489-1

9  8  7  6  5

MV

Printed in the United States of America

# Preface

THIS VOLUME IS an effort to assess the state of contemporary scholarly thinking on the study of political change in the third world. The occasion for this retrospective and prospective look was the twentieth anniversary of the Harvard–M.I.T. Joint Seminar on Political Development. The seminar—known in Cambridge by its acronym, JOSPOD—was first convened in 1964–65 by Samuel P. Huntington of the Government Department at Harvard and Myron Weiner of the Political Science Department at M.I.T. Participants in the seminar, which has been meeting monthly for twenty years, are faculty members and visiting scholars from the various colleges and universities in the Cambridge–Boston area.

During these twenty years, the central theme for each year's monthly seminars was chosen from a variety of topics. The themes have included: the peasantry in developing countries, ethnicity and development, external and international influences on political development, religion and development, population and development, the politics of income distribution, generational change, the role of democratic institutions and processes in the third world, regional powers in the third world, the role of Marxist–Leninist ideologies, the role of the state in development, the political economy of development, neotraditionalism, security problems and military institutions, and the transition to democracy and/or market economies in the third world. At these seminars many pioneers in the study of political change in the third world have presented their work, among them, Daniel Lerner, David

McClelland, Everett Hagen, Dankwart Rustow, Lucian Pye, Al Stepan, S. N. Eisenstadt, Albert Hirschman, Karl Deutsch, Alex Inkeles, Martin Lipset, Warren Ilchman, Ithiel de Sola Pool, Charles Lindblom, Frances Sutton, Fred Frey, Sidney Verba, and Fred Riggs.

For this reassessment the organizers of the seminar commissioned studies by nine scholars. Each scholar was asked to assess the scholarly work in his or her area of special interest and to point to promising new directions. In addition, three regular seminar participants, Myron Weiner, Jorge Domínguez, and Samuel P. Huntington, contributed papers.

The editors' first appreciation must be extended to the other members of the JOSPOD planning committee, Professors Lucian Pye, Jorge Domínguez, and Lisa Anderson, for making this volume possible. They were instrumental in helping to choose both the topics and the speakers. We are especially grateful to Professor Anderson for serving as cochairperson of the seminar while Samuel Huntington was on leave. Catherine Boone, an M.I.T. graduate student and executive secretary of the seminar, did much of the organizational work to make the seminar possible and provided the contributors and seminar participants with carefully prepared summary transcripts of the discussions. Jesse Janjigian of the M.I.T. Center for International Studies was a patient and splendid editor of the manuscript. We also wish to express our appreciation to the sixty-seven members of the Cambridge–Boston academic community who joined the seminar, particularly those members who served as formal discussants of the papers: Professors Peter Smith, Sidney Verba, John Powell, John Field, Lucian Pye, and Stephen Haggard. We are also grateful to the Ford Foundation for a grant that made it possible for us to invite the contributions in this volume.

From the very inception of the Joint Seminar on Political Development, the M.I.T. Center for International Studies and the Harvard Center for International Affairs have provided administrative and financial support, for which the editors continue to be grateful.

Myron Weiner
*Massachusetts Institute of Technology*

Samuel P. Huntington
*Harvard University*

# Contents

MYRON WEINER

# Introduction

The subject matter of the political-development literature has always been a matter of contention. For some scholars it is the politics and policies that facilitate economic growth in developing countries. For other scholars it is the study of new regimes, the increased role of the state, the expansion of political participation, and the capacity of regimes to maintain order under conditions of rapid change and competition among political groups, classes, and ethnic groups for power, status, and wealth. For still other scholars it is how revolutions occur, particularly the conditions for the replacement of capitalist by socialist systems. Political scientists and sociologists studying the politics of Asia, Africa, and Latin America have wrestled with definitions ("modernization," "development," "political order," "integration," "legitimacy"), invented new concepts ("political institutionalization," "social mobilization," "political culture," "dependency"), and debated the question of what methodologies are appropriate. They have been motivated by intellectual curiosity, by idealism, and by their involvement in policy making by governments and foundations. Their thinking has also been influenced by political and ideological debates in the United States and the Western world, as well as by the events in the developing countries themselves.

The central concern of the essays in this volume is whether the various theories and concepts that scholars have invented have proven useful for understanding the enormous changes that have taken place in developing countries over the past two decades. Three major themes are explored. In Part I, the question of the relationship between theory and reality in the study of political change in the third world is explicitly addressed. The essays in Part II explore the changing relationship between society and development, focusing on the kinds of changes that have taken place, their determinants, and political consequences. The essays in Part III consider the changing role of the state in the third world, what determines its strengths and weaknesses, its autonomy, and its impact on economic development and social change. A concluding essay by Gabriel Almond brings us back to some of the fundamental debates among scholars concerning the relationship between theory and reality.

In the opening essay to Part I, Samuel P. Huntington provides an overview of the major issues in the study of political development in the past twenty years and the major points of contention. He traces the evolution of scholarship from the 1950s through the 1980s, from theories that focus on the compatability of development goals to current theories that emphasize conflicts among goals and the possibilities of their reconciliation. Huntington asks why it is that some countries have been so successful in achieving many of these apparently conflicting goals, while others have failed. He suggests that the answer may lie in the relationships between cultures and development, a theme to which we shall return.

In an essay on the major processes of political change in Asia, Africa, and the Middle East, Myron Weiner is particularly concerned with how adequate various theories of development have been in explaining and anticipating political changes. He examines five major areas of political change, then asks which ones were or were not anticipated, and whether some developments anticipated by scholars failed to materialize. The rapid modernization of East Asia and portions of Southeast Asia, the growth of autocratic regimes in much of Africa, the emergence of fundamentalism as a major political force in the Middle East, and the failure of class-based movements to replace ethnic movements were among the major political changes not anticipated by most scholars. By narrowly focusing on the economic determinants of political development, Weiner suggests, scholars have persistently undervalued critical social, cultural, and psychological determinants of political change.

Jorge Domínguez focuses on the growth of the state in Latin America and the paradox of strong states but weak regimes. He describes the emergence of bureaucratic authoritarian regimes, their domination over the economy, their repressive capabilities, and their role in excluding previously mobilized social forces from political power. A central concern of his analysis is the relationship between economic performance and the legitimacy of the regimes, and the impact that economic structures have had upon their emergence and decline. After exploring these and other economic/political relationships, Domínguez concludes that "two decades of scholarly research have ended with a great deal less certainty on these matters than they began." The differences in political development between the English-speaking Caribbean and the Spanish- and Portugese-speaking states of Latin America, he writes, suggest that factors other than rates and levels of economic development or even the impact of the global economy need to be given more attention.

The Weiner and Dominguez essays both note that, civil conflicts notwithstanding, states have proved to be more resilient than expected. Social mobilization has increased political participation in some regions, but state power has led to a decline in political participation elsewhere. The capacities of states to dominate economies have grown as have their repressive capabilities, but whether these changes have led to economic growth, equity, or political stability has varied greatly. The essays point to how international factors—changes in the global economy and international political conflicts—have affected internal political developments, but both also emphasize the primary importance of internal politics and the choices made by governments in dealing with the international environment.

Political participation—its determinants, the forms it takes, and its consequences—remains a central concern in the analysis of political development. Joan Nelson introduces the section on society and development with a retrospective look at what we have learned. She notes that there has been a great deal of departicipation in much of the third world, especially in Africa, as a consequence of the end of nationalist movements and the rise of authoritarian regimes. She finds that, Latin America aside, class has proved to be less salient as the unit of political participation than many expected. The industrial working class and the urban poor have proved, with few exceptions, to be politically less important than anticipated, and peasant revolutions, which some regarded as the most likely pattern of development in the third world, have not materialized. What has been particularly important politically are three units of social action: territorial groupings (such as region, village, and neighborhood), ethnicity (language, tribe, and caste), and religion. Nelson concludes that we have learned a great deal about the *determinants* of mass political participation (though it is easier to recognize determinants in hindsight than to predict when and where new mass movements will emerge) but know far less about the *consequences* of mass participation. How increasing political participation affects efficient government decision making, the capacity of the state to accumulate resources and to create the infrastructures for development, and the impact of mass participation on political stability remain among the most contentious areas of social inquiry.

The next two essays demonstrate contrasting perspectives on how to study political participation. Robert Bates emphasizes the need to look at peasants in third-world politics as "rational actors" engaged in "collective choice," to study peasants as pressure groups, and to examine the behavior of peasant elites rather than the social psychology of peasant behavior. In considering how and why peasants become politicized, Bates contrasts two approaches: one focuses on the impact of the international economy on the peasantry, the other focuses on the domestic political economy. While he does not minimize the impact on peasants of the international economy (such as a drop in the price of commodities or a rise in the price of energy), Bates points to the role of governments dominated by the urban elite (especially in Africa) in turning the terms of trade against the rural areas by their control over exchange rates and input prices and by government procurement policies, often with devastating effects on government productivity. Bates suggests that in many countries conflicts between peasants and the state may be more important than landlord–peasant conflicts.

In contrast with Bates's rational-actor model, Walker Connor reviews what we have learned about ethnic groups in politics and points to the emotional depth of ethnonational identities and the importance of culture and belief systems in determining political behavior. He writes that explanations of ethnic politics based on analyses of pressure groups, elite ambitions, and rational choice are unsatisfactory. A central issue in understanding the forms and consequences of ethnic politics (accommodative or secessionist) is the conditions under which ethnic groups develop loyalty to the state. Connor suggests a typology of states based not on types of authority, but on various configurations of ethnicity. He argues that such a typology is essential to a dynamic view of how states and nations develop.

The papers by Winston Davis on religion and Ali Banuazizi on social-psychological modernity return to a classic set of issues in the study of the determinants of political behavior and, more broadly, "modern" social and economic behavior. In the late sixties and early seventies, it was fashionable for many scholars of the third world to reject contemptuously "culture," "tradition," and "psychology" as determinants of behavior. Even among those who were not explicitly Marxists, there was a return to a materialist view of politics, one that emphasized interests as defined by place in the class structure and viewed culture (and, as Connor notes, ethnicity as well) as an epiphenomenon, a "superstructure" (in Marx's language) largely determined by the modes of production. This latter view may still dominate much scholarly writing, but with the emergence of Islamic fundamentalism as a political force, there are indications of a renewed concern with the impact of culture and values on political behavior.

Davis turns to the classic question of whether a country's "ethos" can impede or facilitate behavior conducive to economic development and the tasks of governance. Did the Confucian examination system, with its emphasis on meritocracy, moral tutelage, and state guidance make possible a political system that simultaneously emphasized achievement-oriented behavior and accommodation to political authoritarianism? How about the famed work ethic of the East Asians: Is it "embodied" in the traditional values of the family and the community? Davis argues that how a people interpret what they consider essential in their tradition is how they set normative rules of behavior. The Japanese, he notes, have taken from their tradition those values conducive to their conception of what it takes to be modern. But, he continues, their conceptions of modern institutions and behavior (paternalistic organizations, consensual rather than adversary behavior, conformity to family, peers, and organizations, for example) are often quite different from those of most Western societies. To Davis, it is important not to view religion as a given but to look at its internal transformation. There is no need, he writes, for a disenchantment with religion. The Japanese experience demonstrates that religion and even magic can exist side by side with and be supportive of the most rational forms of industrial behavior as long as we also understand that there are different forms of "rational" behavior.

Ali Banuazizi writes that the cultural and social structural perspectives—the former pointing to the determinative role of traditional values and culture, and the latter to the role of schools, factories, urbanization, mass media, and modern institutions and processes as creating modern men and women—are two important streams in the social-psychological literature on development. He persuasively argues that it is necessary to distinguish psychological factors that are preconditions to development from those that are concomitants or consequences. The social-psychological approach to development, he argues, is more appropriate when it treats psychological values as concomitants and consequences of social change instead of as determinants.

In his analysis of the role of tradition in development, Banuazizi notes that scholars have modified the earlier view (one argued by Davis for Japan) that traditions are adaptable to the present view that there can also be a strident reassertion and radicalization of tradition against modernization, as in the case of Islam in Iran. It follows from this observation that changes in social structure do not necessarily bring about a modern consciousness. Banuazizi goes on to question some of the basic premises on which the field of social psychology has approached the study of development, most notably its emphasis on individual attitudes to the neglect of the corporate and collectivist traditions within which individuals in most of the world's cultures live.

The Davis–Banuazizi analyses leave a fundamentally unresolved question: Why is it that in Japan there was, to quote Davis, an "internal transformation and pragmatic accommodation (of religion) with the spirit of capitalism, science, and technology," but that no such transformation has taken place within Islam? Is it adequate to examine the political and economic changes in Islamic countries as they differ from those in Japan? Shouldn't we also look at the structure and content of the Islamic and Buddhist–Shinto traditions?

Political scientists have not done particularly well in linking culture to patterns of political development. As Huntington writes, all too often "culture" is a residual category, a "soft" (nonquantifiable and nongeneralizable) explanation when "hard" ones do not work. There has been a reluctance to attribute policy choices by elites to their values, to explain differences among countries in the relationship between elites and masses in terms of culture, or to consider differences in responses to the West and to development as shaped by traditional beliefs. How does one explain, for example, why one government opts for military expansion, another for internal development? Why one government pursues an autarchic set of choices, while another actively internationalizes its economy? Why one government wants to enhance its national power to achieve equality with other states, while another emphasizes internal equalitarianism? Why one country borrows readily from others that it considers more advanced, while another consciously rejects external influences? And why one country tolerates divergent public viewpoints, while another considers dissent and public conflict disruptive? Neither a dependency perspective nor the kind of "world system" school of thought put forth by Immanuel Wallerstein explains why developing countries differ so much in the choices they make. The current emphasis on political economy approaches and rational-choice models does not deal with the fundamental questions of which values or preferences (or what economists refer to as "tastes") are chosen, how, and by whom. What is clearly needed is a cultural theory of preferences, one that is not deterministic but rather enables us to understand why the menus from which choices are made differ and why various groups within cultures, apart from instrumental considerations, prefer one set of choices over others.

Part III turns to the issue of the state and development. The "rediscovery" of the state has been a central theme of much of the recent political-development literature, but it is not always clear what is meant by the "state." Is there a difference between the "state" and the "government"? Does the "state" include elected officials, the bureaucracy, the police, the military, the judiciary? If so, is it useful to speak of the state as an undifferentiated actor with interests and preferences? How do we assess whether a state is "autonomous," acting in accordance with its own interests and preferences, or influenced by forces outside the state? How do we know whether a state is "weak" or "strong," or, in Gunnar Myrdal's language, "soft" or "hard"? Given the wealth of studies of the military, the bureaucracy, the police and paramilitary, one-party states, and monarchies in the politics of the third world, how correct is it to say that scholars of political development have neglected to study the state? Or is the concern with the state, particularly by Marxists, an indirect way of viewing class struggle as the engine of change, with the state perceived as the "apparatus" for domination by particular social classes?

All these issues are raised by a reading of the three papers that make up the section "The State and Development." Peter Evans turns to a question central to the dependency approach to the study of development: To what extent do international actors and institutions, namely, transnational corporations, affect the capacity of states in the third world "to facilitate, impede, or redirect the process of capital accumulation?" Evans takes issue with the fundamental assumptions of many dependency theorists that there is a zero-sum situation with regard to the development and control of resources for capital accumulation and that transnational corporations (especially in extractive industries) reap the benefits of growth at the cost of the third-world economies. Evans reviews recent case studies to demonstrate that where multinationals are present, government revenues increase, indigenous entrepreneurial activities grow, governments develop a bureaucrat apparatus to monitor foreign corporations, and the state itself begins to play a more active role in the industrial sector. In time the state may take over foreign-owned enterprises, especially if the multinationals do not conform to developmental goals set by the government. Evans makes the particularly interesting point that the nationalization of foreign-owned extractive industries is not limited to socialist regimes but seems to be independent of the character of the political regime. He also notes that as the power of the state over the economy expands indigenous entrepreneurs fall under the regulatory arm of the state. The subsequent pattern of state involvement in the economy varies, depending in part on the timing of multinational entry, the strength of local capital, and the attitudes of the government itself. Evans rejects the *dependencistas* view that multinationals limit the role of the state. "Third-world states," he concludes, "have clearly not been crushed by the fact that their economies are increasingly permeated by transnational capital. . . . Instead our survey of the literature has suggested that the state apparatus in a number of third-world countries has widened its role as a result of its interaction with transnational capital." Evans thus takes issue with a fundamental argument of those who adhere to the dependent development model, but he explicitly leaves open the other pillar of the model, that this pattern has "negative welfare consequences." He also leaves open the question of why the patterns of economic and political development have been so different in East Asia and Latin America, in spite of the presence of multinationals in both regions, a difference most economists attribute in large part to the export-oriented policies in the first region and the import-substitution policies in the second. The presence of multinationals may deepen the role of the state in the economy, but what form that intervention takes is a matter of political choice with profound consequences for the economy and the polity.

Eric Nordlinger turns our attention to the issue of why and how states develop "autonomy" from society, that is, whether a state "translates its own preferences into authoritative actions." (A narrower Marxist definition, notes Nordlinger, is that the state is autonomous "when it overcomes the opposition of the capitalist class that is taken to be dominant within civil society.") Nordlinger's starting point is the distinction between society-centered and state-centered explanations and under what conditions one or the other is more useful. Too often, he notes, analysts attribute the actions or inactions of government to constraints or influences from pressure groups, when government is actually acting in accordance with its own interests, ideologies, and values. Nordlinger argues that it is not only authoritarian, centralized, and bureaucratized states that are autonomous, but democratic states as well. In all political systems, says Nordlinger, it is important to look at the values, interests, and goals of public officials and to consider various properties of the state itself, its malleability, insulation, resilience, and vulnerability.

There can be little quarrel with Nordlinger's notion that members of the state (some would prefer to say "government") often act in terms of their own preferences and that, in developing countries in particular, major decisions affecting national development are often made by the civil or military bureaucracy over the preferences of various groups in society. But the notion of "autonomy" presents some serious conceptual problems. As Sidney Verba has pointed out, to speak of state "preferences" is to reify the state, minimize the importance of conflicts of preferences within the state, and fail to take into account that state actors often adjust their preferences to what they think they can accomplish.

Joel Migdal focuses on the strong state–weak state dichotomy. For Midgal the interesting question is not whether the state acts autonomously but whether it is able to implement what its leaders set out to do. Migdal notes that state officials are members of their society and therefore may side with societal forces to limit the state. Migdal defines the weak state as one that lacks resources and capabilities to carry out intended policies. In an effort to create stronger states and to strengthen their own authority, says Migdal, government leaders need to build institutions of authority (such as the military), which in turn may threaten governmental leaders. Migdal outlines the various strategies available to governing elites to strengthen their own authority in what he calls "the politics of survival." A major dilemma is that while some of these strategies increase the political survivability of governing elites, they do so at the cost of limiting the capacity of government to act. For example, by accommodating local strong men, landlords, *Caciques*, bossses, and moneylenders, government elites increase their chances of political survival, but at the cost of expanding the capabilities of the state. Many third-world countries appear to have "strong" rulers and to be authoritarian, but in fact, concludes Migdal, they have limited capabilities, few resources, and lack the political support essential for playing any innovative reshaping role. Migdal's analysis stimulates thinking about whether there are alternative elite strategies for political survival that could also enhance the capacity of government to adopt and implement policies.

The final paper in the volume is by Gabriel Almond, whose pioneer work in the fifties and sixties was a major stimulant to the study of political development. In his paper Almond examines the attacks by dependency theorists on what he regards as the mainstream political-development literature. He argues that the dependency literature has been largely a diversion, since its concern with international factors and political-economy considerations can also be found in the mainstream development literature but with less ideological baggage. He particularly criticizes the reification of the concept of the state, the return to class conceptions of politics, ideologically guided conceptions of the relationship between equality and development, and, to Almond, the most serious weakness of the dependency literature, the failure of its advocates to subject its hypotheses to rigorous empirical tests. He also believes that dependency writers have attacked the "mainstream literature by misrepresenting its content and meaning" and that they have sought to undermine the goal of an empirically based, value-free social science. Almond's views are not likely to be acceptable to some Latin Americanists who argue that the *dependencistas* have raised important questions about the impact of the global economy on economic and political development and normative questions about the effects of U.S. policies in the third world. His views are more congenial, however, to most Asianists who regard the internationalization of the economies and the outwardlooking orientation of the leaders of East and Southeast Asia as a key to their development. Once again it is worth noting the regional variations in the utility of different approaches (as we have seen in the differences between Davis and Banuazizi), which reflect in part the different "data bases" of scholars of development.

In any assessment of the determinants and consequences of political change in the third world, it is important to recognize that events themselves must lead to a change in our assessment. For example, the reemergence of democratic regimes in Latin America (the debt crisis notwithstanding) must invariably lead to a rethinking of the conditions for democratic pluralism in the third world. So too must the persistence of authoritarian regimes in the economically prosperous East Asian countries. The persistence of monarchies in the Gulf states (in spite of the disintegration of the monarchy in Iran), kinship succession in countries as diverse as India, Taiwan, Singapore, Haiti, Cuba, and North Korea, and the disintegration and strife that have beset what were once relatively stable regimes in Lebanon, Sri Lanka, Kampuchea, and Afghanistan suggests how little we still know about political institutionalization or political breakdowns. The quest for theory must continue, because theory provides us with a lens for looking at and interpreting a changing reality. But where reality no longer fits the theory, it is time to reconsider theory. One is reminded of Lord Maynard Keynes's reply to criticism that he had changed his position: "When my information changes, I alter my conclusions. What do you do, sir?"

Neither developmental nor dependency theorists have been able to anticipate or explain many of the changes (or lack of change) in the third world. Although both insist that they reject determinism and unilinear patterns of development, neither has been free of such tendencies. Some of the early development theorists—most notably, W. W. Rostow and Daniel Lerner—espoused unilinear and deterministic positions, though few have followed in their track. Even now many dependency theorists continue to argue that developing countries have no margin for decision making and that their political and economic development (or lack of development) is the inevitable consequence of their dependent and "peripheral" status. Both schools accept the notion that late development is very different from early development; nonetheless, neither has done particularly well in anticipating new patterns of change. Each school is, in a sense, a prisoner of history as well as its own framework for analysis. Over the next decade or so, what should we be looking at, what new forces for change and conflict might we anticipate? Any list is bound to be incomplete, but without such a list of "anticipations" scholars of political development are likely to be one step behind the journalists. Here is one scholar's idiosyncratic list:

—If capital flows from the developed countries to the third world continue to decline, will governments in the third world turn their attention to increasing the rate of domestic savings and investment (or as the Marxists say, "the primitive accumulation of capital"), or will they turn instead to the problem of how to increase returns on investment? If the latter, will governments in the third world promote the private sector (because returns are higher than in the public sector), encourage partnerships between local capital and multinationals, and even privatize portions of the public sector? If so, then the role of the state in the economy of many developing countries may prove to be quite different in the remaining years of this century from what it has been over the last several decades.

—What are the likely social and political consequences of the infusion of new communications technologies into the third world? In the past it was assumed that communications technologies strengthen attempts by authoritarian governments to influence and control their populations. But as the late Ithiel de Sola Pool pointed out, a characteristic of the new communications technologies—cassette tapes, VCRs, personal computers, satellite TV, wireless telephones—is that citizens acquire a greater capacity to communicate among themselves and to choose what they wish to receive. Government control over radio and television and censorship of the press may no longer be as effective in controlling dissidents. Moreover, dissidents operating outside their own country may play a more active role in effecting internal political changes than in the past. In an era of global communication, the political exile (Ayatullah Khomeini, Benigno and Corazon Aquino, Benazir Bhutto, Kim Dae Jung) can no longer be regarded as having been removed from the political scene.

—What are the likely consequences of the current diffusion of political ideas and movements from the advanced industrial countries to the less developed countries? Women's organizations, population-control groups, environmentalist groups, and civil liberties and public-interest legal groups have sprung up in a number of third-world countries. What they choose as their issues and how they relate to the local social structure, culture, and political system, however, are often quite different than in the West. How will these movements fare in comparison with the earlier movements that originated in the West, such as liberalism, secularism, and socialism? To what extent will they remain confined to the modern sector, and what impact, if any, will they have on policies and politics? What are the prospects, for example, of the women's movement in countries with strong Islamic revivals? Or public-interest legal groups in countries with government-controlled judiciaries?

The diffusion of political ideas and movements, it should be noted, is not only from the West to the less developed countries, but from among the developing countries as well. Within the developing world itself there is now an active diffusion process: the ideas of Islamic fundamentalism and liberation theology migrate from one country to another as does terrorism as a philosophy of political action. One striking feature of the new ideologies and movements, compared with the older ones, is the lack of explicit class content. The units of social action propagated by these new movements are (with the exception of liberation theology) multiclass: women, religious groups, ethnic groups, and "moral" groups with "post-materialist" values.

—What are the political implications of changing demographic patterns? In the past the major demographic patterns have been high fertility and declining mortality rates, high dependency ratios, large families, and, most important, large youth cohorts. As fertility rates decline, family size is reduced (with one-child families increasing in China), and the proportion of older people increases. What effects, if any, will a change in the age structure of populations and family size have on intergenerational conflict and on the demands made on governments? Another demographic development that needs to be explored is the political effects of population movements from developing to developed countries and the growth within developed countries of politically organized migrants concerned with their home countries. Dissident ethnic and religious minorities (for example, secessionist movements) often turn to their diaspora populations for financial and political support, with consequences not only for the domestic politics of developing countries but also for relations between developed and developing countries. Will diaspora populations from the third world to advanced industrial countries retain their ties to their countries of origin? If so, what political and economic role will they play?

—What are the possibilities that cultural traditions other than Islam will take an anti–Western turn? Xenophobic sentiments (the word "xenophobic" is imprecise because what is at issue is a reaction against not only foreigners but also imported foreign cultures) may affect other societies during periods of rapid development and modernization. It could turn out, for example, that the open-door policy currently pursued by the People's Republic of China will be accompanied by a degree of Western cultural penetration ("cultural pollution" to some), which could lead to a reaction against the present policies. Are these reactions shaped by the particular relationship between a country and the West and by the history of its colonial relationship? Or is it part of a country's development as its people seek to disentangle what is "modern" from what is Western? Are these reactions likely to emerge in some cultural traditions more than in others?

These "anticipations" are only suggestive of the kinds of changes that need to be watched, though it is not always clear how well they fit into existing theories. They remind us, however, that in many societies fundamental transformations are under way, driven by demographic factors, new technologies, changing international flows of both capital and people, the diffusion of political ideas and movements, and the ways in which particular cultures respond to the sharp differences in power and wealth between developing countries and the Western world. Social transformations shape the characteristics of states, and states in turn shape those social transformations. Time and again one is struck by the constraints on government elites and their opponents; time and again one is also struck by the capacity of political leaders to influence the shape of their societies and their governments. Theories of development, political or economic, must take into account both the constraints and the opportunities for choice. To put these obvious conclusions in the form of an epigram, we might say that nothing that has happened necessarily had to happen, but not everything is possible.

# PART I

# Political Change in the Third World

SAMUEL P. HUNTINGTON

# The Goals of Development

## THE DEVELOPMENT OF DEVELOPMENT GOALS

A point is often reached in the evolution of a body of theoretical and empirical scholarship when work about the work in the field eclipses work about the field. In the development of Marxism, for instance, writing about industrial conditions, class conflict, wages, and profits over time became secondary to writing about the history, varieties, contradictions, and interpretations of Marxist thought on these subjects. What came to matter was not so much the extent to which Marxist theory explained empirical reality, but rather the way in which Marxist theory could be explained. The theory displaced the thing as the primary focus of inquiry.

The study of development, at least of political development, appears to have reached this point. While I have no quantitative data to support the proposition, it seems not unlikely that the number of studies applying developmental theory to concrete cases has leveled off and quite probably declined during the past decade. Simultaneously, the number of studies not of development but of ideas about development has mushroomed. These studies focus not on the harsh facts of economic stagnation in Africa, religious conflict in the Middle East, authoritarianism in East Asia, or social turmoil in Latin America, but rather on "political development theory," "theories of development," "the idea of political development," "developmentalism," and "Modernization" and "Development" (capitalized and referring to "a specialized body of

3

literature"). Their concern is more with the politics of the Social Science Research Council than with the politics of the third world. Many of these studies vigorously critique the existing literature; a few hopefully suggest the possibility of a "revised theory of political development," a "new agenda for Third World studies," or a "new vitality in the field."[1] For political development, the era of introspection and retrospection had clearly arrived by the early 1980s.

The first portions of this essay do not depart from this pattern. They attempt to summarize briefly the development of the goals that have been thought important for development and to discuss theories concerning the relations among those goals. The conclusion, however, suggests an alternative explanation for the varied ways in which countries have and have not achieved these goals and urges the need for a return to empirical analysis of subjects that have not received much attention since the mid-1960s.

Both scholars concerned with development and leaders of developing countries have articulated a wide range of goals toward which the processes of development are presumably directed. These include, among others, such goals as national integration, governmental effectiveness and penetration of society, and military power. This essay, however, will focus on five other goals that have played key roles in the development literature: two economic, two political, and one both economic and political.

The initial goal for the third world set forth by economists was, of course, economic growth. The centrality of this goal was perhaps articulated most explicitly by Arthur Lewis in 1955 when he stated that "our primary interest is in analysing not distribution but growth," that is, "growth of output per head of population."[2] The emphasis on economic growth, defined primarily in terms of increases in per capita gross national product, remained the central concern of economists for about a decade. Many third-world economies did grow significantly, and the third world as a whole achieved the target set for it by development agencies of a 5 percent annual increase in GNP during the 1960s. By the late 1960s, however, it also became clear that economic growth alone was not necessarily improving the living conditions for millions of people in the third world. "Brazil is doing well," as its president put it, "but Brazilians are doing poorly." As a result, questions of distribution or equity came to the fore. The desire for equity focused on two subgoals, often but not necessarily related to each other: (1) reduction in absolute poverty, that is, in the proportion of the population living below a specified minimum level of material well-being (defined in terms of either income or consumption), and (2) reduction in inequality, that is, in the differences in income and/or wealth among population groups. By the early 1970s, equity had clearly joined growth as a central goal of developmental economists.

Meanwhile, a similar if somewhat reverse development occurred in the study of developmental politics. In the late 1950s and early 1960s, scholars in this area were primarily concerned with the preconditions for democracy and the development of democracy, democracy defined almost exclusively in terms of Western models. In the later 1960s, as many observers have pointed out, political scientists working on development became more preoccupied with the problems of political order and stability. This concern remained dominant for the better part of a decade, until in the early 1980s the problem of transitions to democracy again came to the fore.

During the 1960s and 1970s, the trends in the economics and politics of development thus tended to move in opposite directions. In economics the shift was from aggregation (that is, the creation of wealth) to distribution. In political science, the reverse shift occurred, from the problem of distributing power to achieve democracy to the problem of aggregating power to achieve political order, democratic or otherwise. The shift back to a focus on democracy in the early 1980s, in turn, paralleled the changing emphasis in developmental economics from planning to the market and an implied greater willingness to accept the skewed income distribution that the operation of market forces might bring.

Meanwhile, of course, the late 1960s and early 1970s had also seen the emergence of the dependency approach to development. Largely the work of Latin American social scientists, this approach differed from the theories developed in North America and Europe in stressing the international context of the developing country. In effect, the dependency theorists proclaimed the need to break the bonds the global capitalist order imposed on less developed countries and to achieve what may perhaps best be called the goal of national autonomy.

By the mid-1970s, substantial bodies of literature thus existed elaborating the importance of growth, equity, democracy, stability, and autonomy for developing societies and analyzing the ways in which those societies might best make progress toward those goals. Implicit in the widespread acceptance of these goals was also the acceptance of an image of the Good Society: wealthy, just, democratic, orderly, and in full control of its own affairs, a society, in short, very much like those found in Western Europe and North America. A backward society was poor, inequitable, repressive, violent, and dependent. Development was the process of moving from the latter to the former.

Individual scholars, of course, valued these individual goals differently and devoted their energies to analyzing and promoting different goals. They also, quite independently, had different ideas as to the relations that existed among these goals and the extent to which progress toward one goal helped or hindered progress toward another. In general, three broad approaches dominated the thinking about these relations. The first approach assumed the inherent compatibility among the goals. The second approach emphasized the intractable conflicts among the goals. The third approach stressed the imperative need for policies to reconcile those contradictions.[3]

### THE COMPATIBILITY ASSUMPTION

Compatibility theories in American social science essentially had their roots in the concept, elaborated by Karl Deutsch, Daniel Lerner, and Cyril Black, among others, of modernization as a comprehensive, systemic process in which societies changed fundamentally and across the board from an approximation of the traditional model to an approximation of the modern model. The various components of modernization were associated together, and changes from tradition to modernity in one sector or dimension were related to and reinforced by comparable changes in other sectors. To social scientists such as Deutsch, Lerner, and Black, it was perfectly clear that while modernization might be all of a piece, it was not necessarily all of a *good* piece; inevitably it involved stresses, strains, dislocations, upheavals. It was very easy for others, however, to move from the concept of modernization as a coherent process to the concept of development as a coherent process to a concept of the coherence and compatibility of the widely accepted goals of development. A society could and, indeed, almost had to make progress toward all these goals simultaneously; they were not only compatible with one another but also, in many cases, supportive of one another. This viewpoint, of course, had its roots in the fact that the societies of Western Europe and North America were, by and large, modern across the board; it may also have rested on the conclusion from a too-cursory survey of Western history that the progress of these societies toward wealth, equity, stability, democracy, and autonomy had been generally harmonious and linear.

This assumption that "all good things go together" is generally wrong and easy to criticize. It clearly does not describe developments in the third world between 1955 and 1985. Yet it would also be wrong to dismiss it entirely. Some countries, indeed, are good cases of what could be called "negative compatibility": that is, they equally failed to make progress toward any of the goals of development. A much smaller number of countries, less than a handful, recorded significant progress toward achievement with respect to all five goals. In Asia, Japan obviously did so, but was it a developing country or a recovering country after World War II? Of countries whose developmental status cannot be questioned, perhaps Costa Rica was the most obvious case of substantial success with respect to all five goals. Following their 1948 revolution, Costa Ricans established a stable democratic regime that endured for decades. From the 1960s through the mid-1970s, their country achieved a very high rate of economic growth that brought it into the "upper middle class" of Latin American countries.[4] Land ownership was, comparatively speaking, relatively equal. From the 1960s to the 1970s, the proportion of the population living in absolute poverty declined dramatically, and overall equality in income distribution increased. At the same time, however, the relative position of the poorest 20 percent in terms of income shares also decreased, as did that of the richest 10 percent, reflecting the gains of the middle class (a phenomenon that in a democracy could have been predicted). In terms of autonomy, Costa Rica was heavily dependent on international trade, but during the 1960s and 1970s its agricultural exports expanded and diversified. All in all, Costa Rica comes close to being a success story in terms of both progress toward and achievement of the goals of development.

Other success stories undoubtedly exist. There are not, however, many of them. The compatibility thesis, at least in its positive version, has not been borne out by events. Under one circumstance, however, the compatibility assumption may be more valid than it is otherwise, that is, when societies are at war or under the sustained imminent threat of war. Setting apart the physical destruction that may be caused by war, wars are generally periods of extremely intense economic growth. They are also, as Albert Hirschman pointed out, "frequently the condition for achieving a *peaceful* redistribution of income within the country."[5] This was certainly the case with Great Britain in World Wars I and II and with the United States in World War II. While antiwar dissent will be ruthlessly suppressed, political participation often expands in a variety of ways. Crime rates and civil disorder decline, unless it becomes clear that the war is being lost. National autonomy, of course, becomes identical with the pursuit of the war. It is, consequently, easy to understand why both Russians and Americans look back to World War II as "the best years of our lives"[6] and perhaps also why developing countries like South Korea, Taiwan, and Israel that confront an immediate and continuing security threat may have greater success than other countries in making simultaneous progress toward two or more developmental goals. The proponents of compatibility do not, however, argue for war as the engine of developmental progress, and, as the example of Vietnam demonstrates vividly, sustained war is in itself no guarantee of such progress.

Despite its dubious validity, the compatibility assumption has, as Robert Packenham showed, informed much of U.S. policy, particularly in economic aid, toward the third world.[7] It surely provided the central core of the Alliance for Progress, with its triple commitment to economic growth, structural reform, and political democratization. "These goals were, in theory," Arthur Schlesinger has observed, "mutually dependent. Structural change and political democratization were deemed indispensable in order to assure more equitable distribution of the gains of growth. The implication was that U.S. economic assistance would be conditioned on, or at least associated with, performance in social and political reform." Five years after the alliance was inaugurated, Senator Robert Kennedy similarly defined its goals as involving "economic progress, . . . social justice, political freedom, and democratic government." Eventually, however, even the alliance's most devoted advocates had to admit that the relations among these goals had not worked out as they had hoped. "We understood," concluded Schlesinger, "that in the short run there might well be conflict among these objectives. We also supposed, or hoped, that in the long run they were mutually reinforcing. This was evidently, in the middle run at least, an illusion."[8]

The impetus to assume the compatibility of these goals, however, remained present in U.S. policy toward Latin America. In 1984 the Kissinger Commission on Central America argued that "the requirements for the development of Central America are a seamless web" and defined U.S. goals for Central America in almost the identical words used two decades earlier in the Alliance for Progress:

> Elimination of the climate of violence and civil strife.
> Development of democratic institutions and processes.
> Development of strong and free economies with diversified production for both external and domestic markets.
> Sharp improvement in the social conditions of the poorest Central Americans.
> Substantially improved distribution of income and wealth.[9]

The assumption that political democracy was compatible with social reform was concretely evident in the policies the Carter Administration and the Reagan Administration pursued in El Salvador. Both administrations pushed both for land reform and for early elections to a national legislative assembly, apparently oblivious to the well-documented fact that elected legislatures in developing countries are almost invariably hostile to land reform. The 1982 legislative election in El Salvador, a product in part of the policies of both administrations, once again demonstrated that point, with voters returning a legislature dominated by opponents of the land reform that both U.S. administrations had been supporting.

The compatibility assumption is undergirded by two very natural human inclinations. The first is to believe that all good things will, in some way, go together and hence that it will be possible to avoid a difficult choice, such as that between democratic legislative elections and effective land reform. The second natural inclination is to believe that the elimination of one obvious, clear-cut evil will automatically lead to the elimination of the other principal social evils. Phrased another way, it is easy to see a particular goal as the critical one and progress toward that goal as performing a "locomotive" function and bringing progress toward other goals in its train. In the 1950s and early 1960s, for instance, it was widely assumed by some African nationalists and sympathetic Westerners that the granting of independence would usher in a new era in which the other goals of development could be relatively quickly achieved. "Seek ye first the political kingdom," as Kwame Nkrumah put it, "and all things will be added unto it."

In the postindependence world, three "locomotive" theories played major roles. One theory assumed that economic growth would perform the locomotive function and make possible a more equitable distribution of income and wealth, provide an indispensable precondition to the development of democratic institutions, reduce social conflict and hence undergird political order, and enable the society to stand independently on its own. This set of assumptions, which might be termed the liberal model of development, implicitly underlay much American scholarly and official thinking on the problems of development. For a traditional Marxist, the revolutionary overthrow of the existing social-political order in an underdeveloped society and its replacement by a more equitable system would lead to economic growth, true democracy, social harmony, and real independence. The dependency theorist, on the other hand, expected to achieve the same result by starting on the international scene, breaking the chains of dependence drastically, and freeing the society from the international capitalist order. Once this was achieved, democracy, equity, growth in the sense of true development, and social stability would necessarily follow. In effect, each of these theories focused on one single source of evil — poverty, injustice, dependency — the removal of which would almost inevitably lead to the elimination of other evils that flowed from it. Significantly, perhaps, all three theories — liberal, Marxist, and dependency — identified the preeminent evil as economic. No significant body of development theory argued that the replacement of dictatorial regimes by democratic ones or the achievement of political order (however desirable these might be in themselves) was likely to produce the wondrous effects resulting from the elimination of poverty, inequity, or dependency.

**CONFLICT THEORIES**

By the 1970s, the demonstrated limits of the compatibility assumption generated increased awareness that good things often did not and could not go together. A new body of literature emerged, sobering and somber in its message and emphasizing the necessity for choice among goals. The works of the 1960s on development usually had words like "development," "nation-building," or "modernization" in their titles, which conveyed a sense of hopeful movement: *The Passing of Traditional Society* (1958), *The Politics of the Developing Areas* (1960), *The Politics of Modernization* (1965), *The Dynamics of Modernization* (1966), *The Stages of Economic Growth* (1960), *Nation-Building and Citizenship* (1964), *Nation-Building* (1963). The titles of the new wave of the 1970s conveyed a different message: *The Cruel Choice* (1971), *Pyramids of Sacrifice* (1976),

*No Easy Choice* (1976), *Choice and the Politics of Allocation* (1971), *Crisis, Choice, and Change* (1973), *The Cruel Dilemmas of Development* (1980). As these titles suggest, the analyses of the 1970s were couched in terms of dilemmas, choices, trade-offs, crises, and even vicious circles. They particularly stressed the conflicts between growth and equity and between growth and freedom. In the mid-1980s, one scholar could quite legitimately conclude that "the conventional wisdom of the sixties and early seventies held that, except in the very long run, rapid development and human rights are competing concerns."[11]

At the simplest level, ten bilateral relationships can be conceived as possible among the five goals of development. In the 1960s and 1970s, significant bodies of thought and writing developed that saw at least six of these relations as at least in part conflictual. Four of these conflicts involved the relations of economic growth to social-economic equity, political stability, political democracy, and national autonomy. Other conflicts were identified between democracy and equity and between stability and equity.

In various forms, the growth versus equity conflict had, of course, been a staple of economics for some while. Simon Kuznets focused the attention of mid-twentieth-century developmental economists on it, however, with his 1950s argument that a U-shaped curve relationship existed between level of economic development and income inequality. Based on cross-sectional analysis, this argument implied, of course, that, as countries moved from the low to middle levels of economic development, economic inequality would initially increase before decreasing as still higher levels of economic development were reached. Subsequent evidence has borne out this relationship.[12] Other economists carried the argument further. Not only was there a curvilinear relationship between the levels of wealth and equity, there also was a significant negative relationship between the rate of economic growth and income equality. "Higher rates of industrialization, faster increases in agricultural productivity, and higher rates of growth all tend to shift income distribution in favor of the higher income groups and against the low income groups.

The dynamics of the process of economic development tend to work relatively against the poor; the major recipients of the rewards of economic development are consistently the middle class and the highest income groups.[13] Standard economics texts made the same point. A sizable literature on the "Green Revolution" emphasized how the benefits from increased agricultural productivity accrued primarily to well-off peasants rather than to the poor and landless. Some writers saw the contrast between growth and equity strategies epitomized in the cases of Brazil and China. "In the dichotomy of capitalist and socialist models of development, Brazil and China regularly appear as polar opposites.... Brazil is today the largest and most dynamic case of capitalist development in the Third World, as China is the most important case of the socialist alternative ... each model has been deemed a success *in its own terms.... Both ... models assume the sacrifice of at least a generation for the achievement of their respective goals.*"[14]

The liberal model of development assumed that political instability was associated with poverty. A whole series of studies soon showed, however, that the relationship between level of economic development and political instability was a curvilinear one, like that between wealth and equity. The highest levels of instability are associated with middle levels of development. The causes of instability were similarly found in the processes of economic growth. The conflict between these goals was summed up in the title of an early article by Mancur Olson, "Rapid Growth As a Destabilizing Force."[15] This and other works challenged the assumption of the liberal model of development that poverty was the source of instability. Political instability and civil violence were instead seen as the result of economic and social modernization and development. In some cases, it was argued, simple growth itself destabilized. In other cases, the culprit was seen as the slackening or ending of growth, which left unfulfilled expectations (the "J-shaped curve" hypothesis). In still other cases, imbalanced development, such as social mobilization (narrowly defined) outpacing economic development (narrowly defined), was held to be the source of instability. In still others, economic growth was the ultimate source of instability, but the proxi-

mate source was the heightened economic inequality produced by growth.[16] In virtually all these cases, efforts were
made to establish a general relationship between some aspect
or consequence of economic growth and one or more forms
of political instability.

In the two conflict theories just discussed, economic growth
is seen as undermining equity and stability. It is not clear that
rapid economic growth would necessarily have deleterious
effects on democracy, except insofar as it tended to produce
instability. It could then be argued, however, that a democratic
system might be better able than an authoritarian one to cope
with and moderate such instability. The conflicts between
growth and democracy are of a somewhat different sort. In
the first place, it was argued, and some evidence exists, that
rapid economic growth and social change may complicate and
even undermine the democratization of an undemocratic political system. As one analyst argued with respect to two indices
of economic change: "Successful attempts to introduce democracy are accompanied by more moderate change in urbanization and agricultural employment, while unsuccessful
attempts are accompanied by more rapid change."[17] More
basically, Guillermo O'Donnell's theory of bureaucratic authoritarianism challenged the proposition set forth in the late
1950s by Seymour Martin Lipset and others that higher levels
of economic development were associated with the prevalence
of democratic political systems. At least in Latin America,
O'Donnell argued, beyond a certain point a conflict existed
between economic development and democracy; democracy
was associated with intermediate levels of economic development; and "the higher levels of contemporary South American modernization are not associated with political democracies."[18]

In a more general sense the conflict between growth and
democracy is seen in terms of what Jack Donnelly calls "the
liberty tradeoff."[19] The argument is that if a less developed
country is going to achieve high rates of economic growth, it
will have to have a development-oriented authoritarian government. Democratic governments will simply be too "soft"
and hence unable to mobilize resources, curtail consumption,

and promote investment so as to achieve a high growth rate. Many analyses have probed the relations between political system and economic development and come up with varying answers. In general, however, it appears that democratic states almost never achieve very high rates of economic growth, while authoritarian states may have extremely high growth rates, moderate growth rates, and abysmally low growth rates. One careful analysis of ninety-eight countries did come to the conclusion that "among the poor nations, an authoritarian political system increases the rate of economic development, while a democratic political system does appear to be a luxury which hinders development."[20] In 1979 Soedjatmoko could sadly come to the conclusion that "a majority of western development theorists seem to have come to accept, with some regrets to be sure, the seeming inevitability of development to be accompanied by authoritarian government."[21] Interestingly enough, while those analysts concerned with the growth versus equity conflict focused on Brazil and China, those concerned with growth versus democracy have tended to zero in on India.

The conflicts between growth, on the one hand, and equity, stability, and democracy, on the other, tended to undermine the harmony assumptions underlying liberal theories of development. The harmony among goals posited by the dependency theorists also was challenged. One such challenge involved the high correlation existing between political stability and the absence of autonomy, this, of course, resulting from the fact that foreign investment and manifestations of dependency blossom under conditions of political stability. A more serious conflict involves the relation between various forms of dependency and economic growth. This issue has been explored in numerous studies focused in large part on Latin America that have come up with differing results. One of the more careful analyses came to the cautious conclusion that "there was a positive relationship between dependency and economic growth in Latin America in the 1960s."[22] It was still possible, however, that this economic growth might, as some dependency theorists argued, be distorted, and that in the longer run more-dependent states might grow at slower rates than less-dependent ones.

The prevailing Western approaches to development tended to see a mutually reinforcing relationship between equity and democracy. The creation of a democratic political system depended, in some measure, on the absence of great social-economic inequalities, and, once created, the functioning of that system would tend to produce movement toward greater equality. Data on nineteenth-century Western Europe tended to support these propositions. Yet one could also raise the question as to whether the movement toward greater equality in income distribution was produced primarily by higher levels of economic development or by the functioning of democracy. Conflict theorists could also point to the extent to which major inequalities in economic wealth persisted in democratic societies. More specifically, conflict theorists could and did make two arguments. First, the creation of a democratic political system in a country at a fairly low level of social mobilization, and hence with political participation effectively limited to a fairly small middle class, was likely to promote less economic equality. Second, while at higher levels of social mobilization democratic political systems might promote greater income equality, democratic political systems at any level of development were generally unable to bring about significant redistribution of economic assets. Hence at lower levels of development in particular, when issues such as land reform are likely to be more salient and any democratic system would involve political participation by only a limited portion of the population, an authoritarian system is more likely than a democratic one to be compatible with greater economic equality.

Finally, challenging liberal and reformist models of development, radical theorists argued that a high level of instability — that is, revolution — may be necessary in order to achieve a minimum degree of equity. Revolutionary theorists are, in this respect, generally right, at least in the short run. A major revolutionary upheaval will normally produce greater equality in income and wealth, at least among those whom the revolution neither exiles nor executes. In time, however, new patterns of inequality are likely to emerge, not necessarily any less inequitable than those that were destroyed by the revolution.[23]

The four conflictual relationships between economic growth and equity, stability, democracy, and autonomy exemplify what can perhaps best be termed the "rate/level paradox," that is, the condition in which a high level of Variable A is associated with a high level of Variable B but a high rate of increase in Variable A is associated with no increase or a negative rate of increase in Variable B. Globally high levels of economic wealth are associated with high levels of equity, stability, democracy, and autonomy. Yet, seemingly, high rates of economic growth also have negative consequences for movement toward these other goals. If this relationship existed in the past, one has to confront the following question: How did the developed countries of Western Europe and North America arrive at their present benign position blessed with high levels of all five good things?

One plausible answer to this question is that the rate/level paradox did not operate in Western development as it does now because the rate of economic change was so much lower then. During the years 1870–1913, for instance, the gross national products of the major European countries grew at annual rates varying from 1.4 percent for Italy to 2.8 percent for Germany. Among Western industrializing countries, only the U.S. economy, with an annual rate of 4.3 percent, grew at more than 3 percent a year. The average growth rate for current developing countries, on the other hand, was 4.8 percent in the 1950s, 5.2 percent in the early 1960s, and 5.9 percent in the late 1960s. Many individual countries, of course, achieved growth rates of 7–10 percent, which in some cases were sustained for several years. The relative success of the current developing countries in achieving historically high rates of economic growth may thus be the source of the rate/level paradox. The relatively slow processes of development in the West may have made possible their current high levels of goal achievement. Rapid economic growth in the presently developing countries may be the principal reason for the relevance of the conflict theories to the relations among developmental goals.

## RECONCILIATION POLICIES

The conflict theories posited general relationships between goals: the opposition between growth and equity, for instance, was conceived to be a universal one. At times, also, some conflict theorists seemed almost to revel in the difficulty and unpleasantness of the choices and dilemmas that they saw as unavoidable. Inevitably, however, the elaboration of these "cruel" alternatives generated a third body of development literature, devoted to exploring the ways in which development goals could be reconciled with one another. Assumed compatibility, in short, was undermined by the perceived pervasiveness of conflicts, which in turn gave birth to the psychological and political desire to resolve these conflicts. Emphasis on the cruel necessity for choice was replaced by emphasis on the urgent need for reconciliation. The issue became this: through what policies can developing societies expect to make progress toward two or more developmental goals? In varying ways, attention seemed to focus on policies concerning *sequences* in the choice of development goals, institutional *structures* for reconciling development goals, and governmental *strategies* to promote the simultaneous achievement of development goals.

If simultaneous progress toward several development goals is difficult or impossible, conceivably progress could be made toward them sequentially by first emphasizing one goal and then another. In one sense, some form of sequencing is inevitable: no government could hope to pursue all five goals simultaneously with equal intensity. The imperatives of politics and the requirements of bureaucratic implementation, at the least, would lead some goals to get priority over others. Beyond this, however, there is the question from a developmental viewpoint as to whether progress toward all goals will be affected by the sequence in which goals are pursued. Some sequences, conceivably, may be more productive than others and, conversely, giving early priority to one goal could conceivably preclude subsequent progress toward other goals. Or, to state the issue more formally: If progress toward Goal A at Time $T_1$ is incompatible with progress toward Goal B at Time $T_1$, does progress toward Goal A at Time $T_1$ aid or obstruct progress toward Goal B at Time $T_2$ and, conversely, does progress toward Goal B at Time $T_1$ aid or obstruct progress toward Goal A at Time $T_2$?

Much has been written on developmental sequences. By and large, consensus seems to exist on the most appropriate sequence to maximize achievement of political goals but not economic ones. Dankwart Rustow sums up much of the thinking when he says that "the most effective sequence" is the pursuit of national unity, governmental authority, and political equality, in that order. Eric Nordlinger and Samuel Huntington emphasize the importance of developing effective governmental institutions before the emergence of mass participation in politics. Robert Dahl similarly highlights the desirability of establishing patterns of contestation before expanding political participation.[24] Overall, the political science literature tends to urge the temporal priority of order over democracy.

In contrast, no agreement seems to exist among economic analysts as to whether growth or equity should have priority. Some argue that a heavy emphasis on rapid growth is essential to expand the economic pie to the point where some measure of equity becomes possible. This was, of course, the articulated policy of Delfim Neto during the years of the Brazilian "economic miracle." It was also explicitly followed in other countries. "In my view," a top Korean official said in 1975, "the first stage is getting the economy going; the next stage is to consider [social] welfare. First growth and efficiency, then equity."[25] Others, of course, argue the contrary view that a growth-first strategy will not work and that skewed patterns of income distribution that become fixed during periods of rapid growth are very resistant to subsequent change. Or, as one writer put it, if the "trickle down" theory were valid, in the early 1980s in Brazil the benefits of development "should be not merely trickling, but cascading, down to the poor. They are not. Likewise, according to the conventional wisdom, income inequality should be declining. It is not."[26] To the contrary, such analysts argue, redistribution should come first, particularly the more equitable distribution of assets, such as land, and then rapid economic growth will follow. By and large this view seems to prevail among academic analysts while practitioners often espouse the opposing sequence.

Policy choices can also promote or obstruct the development of particular institutional structures that may facilitate the reconciliation of goals. A strong two-party political system rather than a multiparty system, for instance, may be better able to reconcile expanded political participation with political stability, and both of these with the institutional means for promoting national autonomy. Limitation of the role of the state sector in the economy may encourage both economic growth and the development of an indigenous bourgeoisie supportive of democracy, although it may also obstruct progress toward greater social-economic equity. In the mid-1970s, economists also were increasingly publishing books with titles like *Redistribution with Growth*, analyzing the conflict between growth and equity, and setting forth strategies that would reconcile these goals.[27] Among the strategies frequently mentioned were extensive investment in education to develop human capital on a broad basis, promotion of labor-intensive rather than capital-intensive industries, priority to agriculture over industry, and early redistribution of economic assets, particularly land reform. Economists also identified strategies that did not seem to work: progressive taxation, expanded political participation, government ownership of productive enterprises. In their efforts to find out how growth and equity could be reconciled, economists rushed to analyze the experiences of those countries where, in some measure, it had been achieved: Japan, Costa Rica, Singapore, Israel, South Korea, Taiwan. The two latter countries, indeed, became the favorite cases of the reconciliation economists. They showed how to escape the cruel choice between Brazil and China posed by the conflict theorists.

As this brief discussion suggests, the efforts at reconciliation tended to involve either political scientists attempting to reconcile stability and democracy or economists attempting to reconcile equity and growth. Rarer were cross-disciplinary efforts to show how the achievement of economic goals might be reconciled with the achievement of political ones. One such effort was that by Ikuo Kabashima to show how democracy, growth, and equity could be reconciled. Joan Nelson and I had argued that more advanced developing countries often had to choose between (1) a populist "vicious circle," involving expanded political participation, more socioeconomic equality, slower economic growth, and intensifying class conflict leading to a military coup and a participation "implosion" and (2) a technocratic "vicious circle," often starting with a military coup, and involving suppression of political participation, rapid economic growth, and increased socioeconomic inequality, leading to mounting popular discontent and a participation "explosion" against the regime. "Not necessarily so," said Ikua Kabashima. Japan, he argued, was a case where "supportive" political participation enhanced the stability of the government, which in turn made possible rapid economic growth, which in turn made possible redistribution of income from more privileged to less privileged, which, in turn, reinforced the supportive participation. The "primary implication" of the Japanese case "for theories of development," he said, "is that political participation by the have-nots is not *necessarily* a cost to economic development, as Huntington and Nelson have argued." Japan may or may not be unique, but it does show that "participation by have-nots, rapid growth, and economic equality *can be* compatible. . . ."[28] The question, however, is: Can they be compatible outside Japan? If not, why not?

## THE CULTURES OF DEVELOPMENT

The conflict theorists effectively disposed of the assumption of universal or even general harmony among goals. The proponents of reconciliation showed that conflicts among goals were not necessarily unresolvable. They did not demonstrate, however, that any particular reconciliation policies could be successfully applied on a universal basis. Like harmony and conflict, reconciliation is not inevitable. Through some combination of sequencing, structural innovations, and appropriate strategies, some countries could and did make progress

toward two or more goals. Other countries did not. What
worked in Korea did not work in Brazil. What was possible
in India was not possible in Nigeria. By the 1980s, for instance,
economists were arguing that "there seems to be no clear
relationship between the rate of economic growth and either
(a) the degree of inequality at a point in time or (b) the trend
of inequality over time. Fast growers include both equal and
unequal societies; they also include societies that have been
growing more, and less, unequal. The same is true, also, of
slow growers."[29]

The question thus becomes: How can these and other differences in progress, achievement, and reconciliation be explained? Why were Korea and Taiwan but so few other
countries able to make simultaneous progress toward growth,
equity, and stability? Why was Japan able to achieve not only
these goals but democracy and autonomy also? Why did Brazil
do well first at growth and then at democratization but not
so well in terms of equity, stability, and autonomy? Why, generally, did South American countries seem to oscillate between
democracy and authoritarianism? How was Sri Lanka able to
reconcile equity and democracy for so long? Why did so many
African countries record so little progress toward any goals?
Why did India develop a stable democracy while no Islamic
country did? How can one explain, as Lawrence Harrison
asked, the contrasts in political and economic development
between Costa Rica and Nicaragua, Haiti and Barbados, Argentina and Australia?[30] As one economist observed, the differences among countries in achieving growth, equity, both,
or neither depend on "the environment in which growth occurs and the political decisions taken."[31] To explain why reconciliation, like harmony and conflict, is not universal, one is
forced back to things unique to the particular countries. These
include natural resources, geographical location, character of
the population, and, of course, historical experience. In terms
of explaining different patterns of political and economic development, however, a central independent variable is culture
— that is, the subjective attitudes, beliefs, and values prevalent
among the dominant groups in the society.

The concept of culture is a tricky one in social science because it is both easy and unsatisfying to use. It is easy (and also dangerous) to use because it is, in some sense, a residual category. If no other causes can plausibly explain significant differences between societies, it is inviting to attribute them to culture. Just exactly how culture is responsible for the political and economic differences one is attempting to explain is often left extraordinarily vague. Cultural explanations are thus often imprecise or tautological or both, at the extreme coming down to a more sophisticated rendering of "the French are like that!" On the other hand, cultural explanations are also unsatisfying for a social scientist because they run counter to the social scientist's proclivity to generalize. They do not explain consequences in terms of relationships among universal variables such as rates of economic growth, social mobilization, political participation, and civil violence. They tend, instead, to speak in particulars peculiar to specific cultural entities.

Culture can be thought of at a variety of levels. Within nations significant cultural differences may exist among regions, ethnic groups, and social classes. Even greater differences in culture usually exist among nations, and the nation and the nation-state are probably the most important units for the analysis and comparision of culture and its effect on development. Beyond the nation, however, exist a number of broad cultural families or groupings, often including several nations that often share much in terms of common race and ethnicity, language, religion, and history. At least nine such cultural families can be identified (see Table I.1).

These nine cultural groupings do not, obviously, encompass all the world's countries. Some national societies may include groups reflecting two or more traditions (e.g., Malaysia, South Africa). Some countries may not fit neatly into any of these categories; consider, for instance, Hungary, Poland, Rumania, Israel, Turkey, Iran, Pakistan, Afghanistan, Burma, Sri Lanka, Thailand, Cambodia, Laos, Bolivia, and Guatemala. At least 85 percent of the world's population, however, is in national societies that fit reasonably well into one of these categories. It consequently makes sense to ask whether each of these cultural groupings may not have its own particular

TABLE I.1 *Cultures and Regions*

| Culture | Principal Religion | Region/Countries |
|---------|--------------------|------------------|
| Nordic | Protestantism | Northwest Europe, British settler countries |
| Latin | Catholicism | Southern Europe, Latin America |
| Arab | Islam | North Africa, Middle East |
| Slavic | Orthodox | Eastern Europe, Soviet Union |
| Indian | Hinduism | India |
| Sinic | Confucianism | China, Taiwan, Korea, Singapore, Vietnam |
| Japanese | Confucianism/ Buddhism/Shinto | Japan |
| Malay | Islam/Buddhism/ Catholicism | Malaysia, Indonesia, Philippines |
| African | Christianity/ Paganism | Africa south of the Sahara |

pattern of political and economic development and of goal achievement. If one wanted to predict the probable pattern of development of a Country X and could be given only one piece of information concerning X, would not its cultural identity be the information to ask for? Would not that be the single most important factor in predicting the extent to which X was likely to achieve growth, equity, democracy, stability, and autonomy?

Major differences obviously exist among countries within particular cultural groupings; often one country may deviate strongly from the prevailing cultural pattern (e.g., Costa Rica in Latin America). Yet by and large significant differences do exist among these cultural groupings in terms of the extent to which their countries have made progress toward their developmental goals. The fact of the matter, as we all know, is that Islamic, Sinic, African, Latin, and other societies have developed in very different ways. It is hard to see much convergence among them in their patterns of development between the 1950s and the 1980s or between any one of them and the commonly accepted Western pattern (which is largely a Nordic pattern). In 1962, for instance, Ghana and South Korea had virtually identical economies in terms of per capita

GNP, sector sizes, and exports. Twenty years later they could hardly have been more different.[32] Looking at the economic and political variables in those countries in 1962, one could never have predicted that divergence. If one had thought at that point in terms of the differences between West African and Korean cultures, however, that divergence in development might not have been so surprising.

Widespread agreement appears to exist among scholars and practitioners on the desirability of societies becoming wealthy, equitable, democratic, stable, and autonomous. These goals, however, emerge out of the Western and particularly the Nordic experience. They are Western goals, as is, indeed, the concept of development itself. The articulated support for them by political and intellectual elites throughout the world may simply be tribute to the intellectual dominance of Western ideas, the extent to which non-Western elites have been indoctrinated in Locke, Smith, Rousseau, Marx, and their twentieth-century disciples. These ideas may find little support in the indigenous culture. In contrast to the Western model, another culture's image of the good society may be of a society that is simple, austere, hierarchical, authoritarian, disciplined, and martial.

The image of the developed Western society — wealthy, equitable, democratic, stable, autonomous — thus may not constitute a meaningful model or reference group for a modern Islamic, African, Confucian, or Hindu society.[33] Throughout the non-Western world, societies have judged themselves by Western standards and have found themselves wanting. Maybe the time has come to stop trying to change these societies and to change the model, to develop models of a modern Islamic, Confucian, or Hindu society that would be more relevant to countries where those cultures prevail. In some measure, of course, this process has been under way for some time as third-world intellectuals have spun out theories of "African socialism" and "Islamic democracy." The useful models, however, are less likely to come from the normative theorizing of intellectuals than from the historical experience of societies. The need is to generalize from the East Asian experience and derive from that experience a developmental model of a society that is authoritarian, stable, economically dynamic, and equitable in its income distribution. The South American model might be one of class stratification, inequality, moderate growth, political conflict, economic penetration, and alternating democratic and authoritarian regimes. Obviously, future development may change the model, and any theorist must be sensitive to that. Yet the construction of a Latin American model of development and the explanation of why in terms of culture and other variables Latin American experience approximates that model surely is a worthy scholarly undertaking. O'Donnell's theory of bureaucratic authoritarianism was a first approximation of such a model and is, in a sense, a prototype of the sort of region- and culture-specific theoretical model that is desirable. O'Donnell's theory threw needed light on the Latin American experience, and, interesting to note, efforts to apply it outside Latin America to East Asia or elsewhere have not been notably successful.

The relevance of culture to explaining different patterns of development may also be enhanced by once again emphasizing the distinction between modernization and Westernization. In theory these concepts were always distinguishable; in application, however, they seldom were distinguished. In many respects they overlapped. With respect to the non-Western world, the two usually went together no matter how much non-Western elites might attempt to differentiate technology and material processes, on the one hand, from basic values and norms, on the other. More recently, however, in a variety of ways in many different circumstances, non-Western values, attitudes, beliefs (religious and otherwise) have reasserted themselves. As Western colonial rule fades into history, as elites are increasingly the product of their own culture rather than that of Paris, London, or New York, as the masses in their societies, never much exposed to Western culture, play an increasingly important role in politics, as the global influence of the principal Western powers continues its relative decline, the indigenous cultures naturally become more important in shaping the development of these societies. The partnership between modernization and Westernization has been broken. While continuing to pursue modernization, the third world is also, in some measure, deeply involved in and committed to a process of de-Westernization.

In the 1950s, the systematic study of comparative politics developed apart from and partly in opposition to area or regional studies. Area specialists believed the explanation lay in the particular, that in order to understand and explain what happened politically in a society one had to have deep knowledge of its history, language, culture, and social institutions. The comparative politics scholars, on the other hand, believed the explanation could be found in empirical generalizations, that in order to understand and explain what happened politically in a society one had to have a broad knowledge of how social, economic, and political variables interacted generally and then had to apply the appropriate generalizations to the particular case. Area specialists and comparative scholars thus went their separate ways. In the late 1950s and 1960s, the study of comparative politics tended to subdivide further, as those specializing in development and developing countries became detached from those specializing in industrial societies. (Those specializing in the principal Communist societies, the Soviet Union and China, never fully escaped being area specialists.) The "developmentalists" and the "industrialists," with a few exceptions (e.g., corporatism), employed different concepts and had different foci of interest. The industrialists also worked fairly closely with the more traditional area specialists dealing with Western Europe. The developmentalists were more likely to be distant from and at odds with traditional specialists on the Middle East, Latin America, and East Asia.

The scholars of comparative politics would gain nothing by going back to the extreme parochialism of the traditional area specialists, in many cases so totally blind to any way in which the phenomena they studied might be illuminated by comparative generalizations. If, however, the study of development leads back to a focus on culture and the differences among major cultural traditions and country cultures, then the time is perhaps appropriate for closer links between the comparative politics scholars (developmentalist subbranch) and area specialists.[34] If the differences in the present and future development and goal achievement of East Asia, Latin America, and sub-Saharan Africa are to be found in the different values and beliefs of East Asians, Latin Americans, and Africans, then surely a primary place has to be accorded the comparative analysis of culture, how and why it develops, how it is transmitted, what patterns it forms, how its various dimensions can be defined and measured, and how and under what circumstances it changes. For those who wish to explain the extent to which different countries have made differing progress toward achieving the goals of development, such an approach becomes almost indispensable. Culture and its impact on development cry out for systematic and empirical, comparative and longitudinal study by the scholars of political development.

**NOTES**

1.  See Richard A. Higgott, *Political Development Theory: The Contemporary Debate* (London: Croom Helm, 1983); Ronald H. Chilcote and Dale L. Johnson, eds., *Theories of Development: Mode of Production or Dependency* (Beverly Hills, Calif: Sage, 1983); Harry Eckstein, "The Idea of Political Development: From Dignity to Efficiency," *World Politics* 34, no. 4 (July 1982):451–86; Tony Smith, "Requiem or New Agenda for Third World Studies," *World Politics* 37, no. 4 (July 1985):532–61; Irene L. Gendzier, *Managing Political Change: Social Scientists and the Third World* (Boulder, Colo.: Westview Press, (1985); Joel S. Migdal, "Studying the Politics of Development and Change: The State of the Art," in *Political Science: The State of the Discipline*, edited by Ada W. Finifter (Washington, D.C.: American Political Science Association, 1983), 309–38.

2.  W. Arthur Lewis, *The Theory of Economic Growth* (Homewood, Ill.: Richard D. Irwin, 1955), 1.

3.  At the simplest level, each of the five goals of development can be conceived as possibly having a relationship with the other four, for a total of ten bilateral relationships. The picture can be further complicated, however, if these are thought of in terms of relations in which each goal could be either the independent variable or the dependent variable. This would multiply the number of possible relations to twenty. Finally, if a distinction is made between relations involving the *level* of each variable and the *rate* of change of each variable, eighty possible

relations exist between pairs of variables. Many of these potential relationships would be meaningless or totally unascertainable. For purposes of discussion here, we will focus on the ten simple relationships, incorporating whatever references seem to be appropriate to the direction of the flow of influence and to the components of rate and level.

In evaluating third-world evolution, it is also desirable to distinguish between progress and achievement with respect to these five goals. Progress is measured by the rate of change of conditions with respect to that goal; achievement, by the level obtained or the extent to which the goal is realized. To take a simple example, if Country A increases its literacy from 10 percent to 30 percent of the population in five years, while Country B increases its literacy from 30 percent to 40 percent, clearly Country A has a higher rate of progress with respect to literacy, but Country B has a higher level of achievement. The distinction between progress and achievement, between rates and levels, of course, is particularly important in economic development, where progress is normally measured by rates of growth of GNP and of GNP per capita and achievement is measured by GNP per capita. Similar distinctions between rates and levels are at times useful with respect to other goals of development. The distribution of income in a society can be measured at a particular point in time and changes in that distribution over time, if reliable date are available (which is not often the case). In a similar manner, levels of stability (or, more likely, instability) can be measured and perhaps in some measure rates of change in stability can be identified over time. Countries can also be compared as to how democratic they are, and where democratization (or its opposite) takes place over time at least some qualitative measurement can be made of rates of change. The more common phenomenon, however, is a discontinuous break involving a rapid change of regime in a short period of time. Thus one speaks far more frequently of levels of democracy than of rates of democratization or its reverse. With respect to national autonomy, on the other hand, quantitative data as to some indices of both rates and levels are available, most notably with respect to trade, investment, loans, and foreign aid.

4.  Gary S. Fields, *Poverty, Inequality, and Development* (Cambridge: Cambridge University Press, 1980), 185.

5.  Albert O. Hirschman, *Journeys toward Progress: Studies of Eco-

*nomic Policy-making in Latin America* (New York: Twentieth Century Fund, 1963), 137.

6.  See Geoffrey Perrett, *Days of Sadness, Years of Triumph* (Baltimore, Md.: Penguin, 1974); Mark Jonathan Harris, Franklin D. Mitchell, and Steve J. Schechter, *The Homefront: America during World War II* (New York: Putnam, 1984); John Morton Blum, *V Was for Victory: Politics and American Culture during World War II* (New York: Harcourt Brace Jovanovich, 1976); and, on the Russians, Hedrick Smith, *The Russians* (New York: Quadrangle/New York Times, 1976), 302–3. The extent to which crime and civil violence increase or decrease during war is in dispute. See Arthur A. Stein, *The Nation at War* (Baltimore, Md.: Johns Hopkins University Press, 1980), and Michael Stohl, *War and Domestic Political Violence: The American Capacity for Repression and Reaction* (Beverly Hills, Calif.: Sage, 1976).

7.  Robert A. Packenham, *Liberal America and the Third World: Political Development Ideas in Foreign Aid and Social Science* (Princeton, N.J.: Princeton University Press, 1973), 123–29.

8.  Arthur Schlesinger, Jr., "The Alliance for Progress: A Retrospective," in *Latin America: The Search for a New International Role,* edited by Ronald G. Hellman and H. Jon Rosenbaum (New York: Wiley, 1975), 57–92.

9.  *The Report of the President's National Bipartisan Commission on Central America* (New York: Macmillan, 1984), 48, 60 ff.

10. See Packenham, *Liberal America,* passim, and Samuel P. Huntington and Joan M. Nelson, *No Easy Choice: Political Participation in Developing Countries* (Cambridge, Mass.: Harvard University Press, 1976), 17–21.

11. Jack Donnelly, "Human Rights and Development: Complementary or Competing Concerns?," *World Politics* 36, no. 2 (January 1984), 255.

12. Simon Kuznets, "Economic Growth and Income Inequality," *American Economic Review* 45, no. 1 (March 1955):1–28; Fields, *Poverty, Inequality, and Development,* 59–77, 122; David Morawetz, *Twenty-five Years of Economic Development 1950–1975* (Washington, D.C.: World Bank, 1977), 38–40.

13. Irma Adelman, "Summary, Conclusions, and Recommendations," Part I, Final Report, Grant AID/csd/2236, Northwestern University, Evanston, Ill., (12 February 1971), 6.

14. Peter L. Berger, *Pyramids of Sacrifice: Political Ethics and Social Change* (Garden City, N.Y.: Doubleday Anchor, 1976), 151. See also Sylvia Ann Hewlett, *The Cruel Dilemmas of Development:*

*Twentieth-century Brazil* (New York: Basic Books, 1980), 215–18.

15. Mancur Olson, Jr., "Rapid Growth as a Destabilizing Force," *Journal of Economic History* 23, no. 4 (December 1963):529–52, and, for a summary of the early conflict literature on this point, Samuel P. Huntington, *Political Order in Changing Societies* (New Haven, Conn.: Yale University Press, 1968), 39–59.

16. For a general review of research on the causes of instability, see Ekkart Zimmerman, *Political Violence. Crises, and Revolutions: Theories and Research* (Cambridge, Mass.: Schenkman, 1983).

17. William Flanigan and Edwin Fogelman, "Patterns of Democratic Development: An Historical Comparative Analysis," in *Macro-Quantitative Analysis: Conflict, Development, and Democratization,* edited by John V. Gillespie and Betty A. Nesvold (Beverly Hills, Calif.: Sage, 1971), 487.

18. Guillermo A. O'Donnell, *Modernization and Bureaucratic-Authoritarianism: Studies in South American Politics* (Berkeley: Institute of International Studies, University of California, 1973), 49–52, 114.

19. Donnelly, "Human Rights and Development," 257–58.

20. Robert M. Marsh, "Does Democracy Hinder Economic Development in the Latecomer Developing Nations?," *Comparative Social Research* 2 (1979):244.

21. Soedjatmoko, "Development and Freedom," Ishizaka Memorial Lectures, unpublished manuscript, 2–3.

22. James Lee Ray and Thomas Webster, "Dependency and Economic Growth in Latin America," *International Studies Quarterly* 22, no. 3 (September 1978):432.

23. See Jonathan Kelley and Herbert S. Klein, *Revolution and the Rebirth of Inequality* (Berkeley: University of California Press, 1981), especially chaps. 1 and 8.

24. Dankwart A. Rustow, *A World of Nations: Problems of Political Modernization* (Washington, D.C.: Brookings Institution, 1967), 120–32, 276; Eric A. Nordlinger, "Political Development: Times Sequences and Rates of Change," *World Politics* 20, no. 3 (April 1968):494–520; Huntington, *Political Order in Changing Societies,* 78–92; and Robert A. Dahl, *Polyarchy: Participation and Opposition* (New Haven, Conn.: Yale University Press, 1971), 33 ff. See also Leonard Binder et al., *Crises and Sequences in Political Development* (Princeton, N.J.: Princeton University Press, 1971).

25. Deputy Prime Minister Nam Duck Woo, *Time* 106 (22 December 1975):40.

26.    Donnelly, "Human Rights and Development," 260.

27.    Hollis Chenery et al., *Redistribution with Growth* (New York: Ox-
       ford University Press, 1974). It is striking how often efforts to
       reconcile growth and equity were spoken of as "strategies." See,
       for example, Irma Adelman, "Growth, Income Distribution
       and Equity-oriented Development Strategies," in *The Political
       Economy of Development and Underdevelopment,* edited by Charles
       K. Wilber, 2d ed. (New York: Random House, 1979), 312–23,
       and Francis Stewart and Paul Streeten, "New Strategies for
       Development: Poverty, Income Distribution, and Growth," in
       Wilber, *Political Economy of Development and Underdevelopment,*
       390–411.

28.    Ikuo Kabashima, "Supportive Participation with Economic
       Growth: The Case of Japan," *World Politics,* 36, no. 3 (April
       1984):309–38.

29.    Morawetz, *Twenty-five Years of Economic Development,* 41.

30.    See Lawrence E. Harrison, *Underdevelopment Is a State of Mind:
       The Latin American Case* (Cambridge, Mass.: Center for Inter-
       national Affairs, Harvard University, and University Press of
       America, 1985). Harrison makes the argument that the dif-
       ferences in development within Latin America can be explained
       only in cultural terms.

31.    Fields, *Poverty, Inequality, and Development,* 94.

32.    Keith Marsden, "Why Asia Boomed and Africa Busted," *Asian
       Wall Street Journal,* 11 June 1985, 8.

33.    For a succinct statement from a slightly different perspective
       of a similar argument, see Howard J. Wiarda's stimulating es-
       say, *Ethnocentrism in Foreign Policy: Can We Understand the Third
       World?* (Washington, D.C.: American Enterprise Institute,
       1985).

34.    For a superb study of the cultural bases of power and authority
       in Asian societies, combining the approaches of area specialists
       and comparative politics scholars, see Lucian W. Pye, *Asian
       Power and Politics: The Cultural Dimensions of Authority* (Cam-
       bridge, Mass.: Harvard University Press, 1985).

MYRON WEINER

# Political Change: Asia, Africa, and the Middle East

THIS ESSAY REVIEWS the major political changes that have taken place in Asia, Africa, and the Middle East over the past quarter of a century. Enduring characteristics will be emphasized rather than transient phenomena, and major processes of change rather than specific events. Some of the political changes that many scholars expected to occur in the developing countries, but have not, will be noted, as will some not wholly anticipated changes. The object of this essay, as with others in this volume, is to assess not only whether the approaches and theories of political development have enabled us to see, understand, and predict, but also whether our approaches and theories have restricted and inhibited us from seeing, understanding, and predicting political changes.

In order to provide a broad overview I shall often make sweeping generalizations, putting aside the numerous exceptions. I shall focus on five major themes: (1) the persistence of juridical states, even when they lack effectiveness and internal legitimacy; (2) the growth of hegemonic ethnic politics; (3) the demise of pluralistic political institutions and the extension of autocratic rule; (4) the limits of political participation and the creation of political movements, often around religion and ethnicity rather than class; and (5) the ubiquitous involvement of the state in the economy, either to induce market-oriented profit-seeking behavior or to induce rent-seeking behavior. An examination of these themes will lead

33

us to contrast some of the patterns of political change in Asia, Africa, and the Middle East over the past quarter of a century.

## JURIDICAL STATES

The postcolonial states, with their boundaries often arbitrarily set by former rulers, have remained remarkably intact. As juridical entities the newly independent states persist in spite of the civil warfare many of them have experienced. In Africa civil strife has erupted in the Sudan, Rwanda, Zaire, Ethiopia, Zanzibar, Botswana, Chad, Uganda, Nigeria, and Angola; and, in Asia and the Middle East, in Lebanon, Afghanistan, Burma, Malaysia, Sri Lanka, Pakistan, Vietnam, Thailand, Kampuchea, Laos, Indonesia, India, and Iran. But notwithstanding these upheavals, only two of these countries no longer retain the boundaries they had at the time of independence — Pakistan, where Indian military support for the East Bengalis led to the partition of the country, and Malaysia, where a Malay-dominated government chose to expel Chinese-majority Singapore to prevent a threatened Chinese takeover.

Emphasis should be placed on the word "juridical," for though the political boundaries of the new states have not changed, several postcolonial states still remain unable to exercise effective political control over all of their territory.[1] The "government" of Lebanon, to take the most extreme situation, has little authority outside of Beirut. Pakistan describes some of its North-West Frontier Province honestly but euphemistically as "unadministered," — unadministered, that is, by the central government, but "administered" by independent tribes. The Afghan government, even with the aid of over 100,000 Soviet troops, cannot hold sway in all of its territory. The government of Ethiopia has little influence in portions of Eritrea and of its Somali-populated Ogaden region. And after more than the third of a century since independence the government of Burma still cannot exercise sovereignty over the Shan- and Kachin-populated regions in the north and the Karen-populated region in the south.

Other states have been somewhat more effective in establishing jurisdiction in their territories, though not without considerable difficulty. Those that have achieved effective control have often done so largely by committing resources to the development of the military and the police. Nigeria, Indonesia, Sudan, Pakistan (since 1972 in Baluchistan), and India (in its northeast) have successfully suppressed secessionist movements through the use of military force.

A further element in the persistence of juridical states is provided by the "international community," which has almost always opposed the effort of any state to support secessionist movements in another state. While that stand has not always deterred intervention, third-world governments have generally refrained from intervention, if only because few states are not themselves vulnerable to the intervention of others. The Organization of African Unity, ASEAN, and other regional and international organizations support the status quo as far as the boundaries of states are concerned, and almost no governing elites advocate the principle of self-determination of peoples. Even the repression by the Pakistan government of an ethnic group that constituted a majority did not lead third-world countries to support India's intervention on behalf of the Bengalis. Border disputes have occurred (India and China, Ethiopia and Somalia, Pakistan and Afghanistan, Iran and Iraq, etc.), but support by third states for the redrawing of boundaries to accommodate the claims of a stateless group is virtually nonexistent. States are thus given legitimacy in the international arena even when they lack legitimacy among all the groups within their own society.

## ETHNIC HEGEMONIC STATES

Hegemonic rather than accommodative ethnic politics characterize the new states. In country after country, a single ethnic group has taken control over the state and used its powers to exercise control over others. Indeed, among the multiethnic states, the process continues to be one of "nation-destroying," to use Walker Connor's term[2] for the process by which the state attempts to assimilate, absorb, or crush ethnic groups that do not accept the legitimacy of the state within existing boundaries. The earlier hope by some scholars[3] that consociational power sharing among divergent ethnic elites might provide the basis for stable authority — in the sixties Lebanon and Malaysia were often cited as possible models — has been shattered by events. In retrospect there has been far less "nation building" than many analysts had expected or hoped, for the process of state building has rendered many ethnic groups devoid of power and influence.

Ethnic hegemony has been exercised in a variety of ways, from the repression of ethnic and religious minorities to the more benign use of state power to give preferences in education and employment to the dominant ethnic group. In Malaysia, for example, it is the Malays who dominate; in Sri Lanka the Sinhalese; in Mauritania the Arabs; in Pakistan the Punjabis; in Sudan the northern Muslims; in Zanzibar Black Africans; in Burma the Burmans; in Syria the minority Alawites; in Iran the Persians; in Afghanistan the Pashtuns; in Indonesia the Javanese. "Nationalism" in many of these countries is the sentiment toward the national territory expressed by the dominant ethnic group.

Several newly independent governments have even expelled economically successful minorities they considered alien in origin. The deportation of Chinese by the Vietnamese government is the most recent example, but earlier the Burmese and East African governments ejected their Indian trading communities; Indonesia ejected (and killed) many of their Chinese; and Iraq, Syria, Yemen, and the North African states forced their Jewish populations to leave. Though their economies often suffered from the expulsion of trading, entrepreneurial, and professional classes, politically dominant elites have been prepared to pay that price.

Even in democratic India, with its system of accommodative politics at the national level and a federal system that permits power sharing by linguistic groups in the states, a form of hegemonic politics exists at the state level. In many of the states the demographically and politically dominant linguistic group — Assamese in Assam, Maharashtrians in Maharashtra, etc. — has used its control over state governments to give educational and employment preferences to "sons of the soil"; and most recently the Sikhs, unable (even with 60 percent of the state population in the Punjab) to exercise hegemony over the non-Sikh population, have pressed for a more compact (and, by some Sikhs, an independent) state of their own.

The efforts of the Maronite Christians to establish their political hegemony in the distintegrating state of Lebanon demonstrate yet another aspect of this tendency. Indeed, as the Lebanese state itself disintegrated, each of the territorially based ethnic groups sought to establish exclusive political control within its own territory. As a result, Lebanon has become a country of ethnic-dominated feudal-like entities with Druse, Shi'ites, and Maronites each exercising authority within their own territory.

A curious exception to the pattern of territorial exclusivity is provided by the states of the Persian Gulf. While other new states have often expelled aliens, the oil-rich, labor-short Gulf states have recruited an alien labor force to work in the construction industry and in the expanding service sector. Indeed, in most of the Gulf states the non-Arab immigrant workers outnumber the indigenous Arab labor force; moreover, workers are recruited not only for unskilled and manual occupations, but for technical and professional employment as well. To make this immigration politically palatable the Gulf states have incorporated their indigenous middle class into the state apparatus to manage the government bureaucracy and public sector firms and to exercise control over the private sector. Moreover, political activities among the migrants are prohibited, and migrants are restricted from purchasing property, changing employment without permission, or in other ways establishing themselves as a permanent presence. The governing elites thereby seek to ensure that indigenous Arabs exercise political control over the aliens and that the dominant cultural system remains Arabic even as the Arabs share some of their wealth and employment. The Gulf experience thus once again demonstrates the key importance of ethnic political and cultural hegemony in the new states.

## STATE STRUCTURES

Almost everywhere the state structures of postcolonial states have been transformed. Parliaments, competitive parties, free elections, and other pluralistic institutions that third-world countries often inherited from their colonial rulers have largely disappeared, and autocratic rule has become the norm. The handful of exceptions to autocratic rule[4] among the post-colonial states are all former British colonies: Malaysia, India, Sri Lanka, Botswana, Papua New Guinea, Gambia, Mauritius, Fiji, Nauru, and, in the Western Hemisphere, several of the Caribbean island states. In these countries the elites accept the legitimacy of adversarial politics and value competitive political parties, an independent judiciary, a free press, and freedom of assembly. But the British record of successfully leaving behind functioning democratic institutions is by no means universal. But why the British, almost alone among the former colonial rulers, successfully transplanted their institutions to some countries while other imperial powers were less successful is one of the most interesting questions for comparative analysis. Many former British colonies, however, have long since given up the Westminster system — Tanzania, Kenya, Uganda, Pakistan, Bangladesh, Ghana, and, most recently, Nigeria. Nor can one speak with confidence of the future of democratic parliamentary institutions in those countries that are currently democratic. But still it is noteworthy that, among the newly independent countries, only in certain former British colonies does one find competitive democratic politics.[5] None of the former American, Dutch, Belgian, or French colonies has successfully sustained democratic institutions. Indonesia, Zaire, Vietnam, and, until recently, the Philippines have not sustained the democratic political institutions created by their former rulers.

Stable democratic institutions, according to conventional social science analysis, require certain social, cultural, and economic preconditions and an "appropriate" fit between those institutions and society. Social scientists thus often reject the notion that institutions can be "transferred" or "borrowed" and argue that the transfer of alien institutions from one society to another will result in either their total transformation or their rejection. Actually, it is striking that a number of political, administrative, and legal structures have moved successfully across national boundaries and become well institutionalized. The adoption of British and French legal institutions by many of their former colonies is one such example. But clearly the most successful diffusion of institutions (and ideologies) has been among the Communist countries, with North Korea, Vietnam, Mongolia, and China closely adhering to Soviet political institutions and practices and, for much of their history, Soviet economic policies as well. The British institutional transfer was less universal, but then it has been sustained without force.

While the postcolonial states are predominantly autocratic, the institutional structures of these autocracies vary considerably. As Samuel Huntington has argued, the familiar divisions — one-party Communist (and non-Communist), praetorian, bureaucratic authoritarian, monarchical, and theocratic — may be a less useful distinction than whether the institutions are pervasive or not, in the sense of whether they can exercise authority throughout the society. Autocratic regimes are not necessarily strong states capable of raising resources, mobilizing populations, enforcing law, and delivering services. In each of these dimensions many of the African states are quite weak and many Asian and Middle Eastern states are relatively strong.

One of the best measures of the strength or weakness of a state is not the amount of resources potentially under its control but the *extent* of its system of direct taxation, that is, what proportion of its population is reached directly through land and income taxes. A state that taxes widely needs an extensive and reasonably effective administrative system and a base of popular social support, and strong states too can build and maintain these. Weak regimes in need of resources have two options: they can build up their administrations to establish a national system of taxation, or they can seek resources through a variety of other alternatives. For example, countries engaged in primary exports can tax the exports at the port of exit or through the control or ownership of export commodities. Wealthy oil-producing countries are able to extract profitable rents from the resale of oil abroad. Overvalued exchange rates provide another form of indirect taxation; so does any system that requires farmers to sell their produce to a marketing board for resale in urban markets.

Through such mechanisms the weak states of Africa are able to extract resources from society without developing the administrative structure or political institutions of stronger states. The Iranian regime under Reza Shah, though it had a tradition of a strong administration, felt little need to build support since the wealth of the government depended upon oil. Similarly, oil-producing Nigeria, Indonesia, Libya, and the Gulf states and mineral-exporting Zaire are not stronger states as a result of their resources. Indeed, in the absence of a need for administrative efficiency and popular support (and some measure of accountability that such support implies), governing elites of these countries are easily corruptible, and state resources are increasingly diverted to their personal gain.

Foreign aid, it should be noted, is another alternative resource for regimes without a system of direct taxation. Foreign aid may contribute to a country's development (but not if it, too, becomes a source of wealth for a corrupt elite). But aid does not contribute significantly to state building if it becomes an alternative to a national tax system. While a number of Asian countries have strong states capable of effective utilization of foreign aid, that is not so for many African countries. It may very well be that the foreign aid received by many African countries has served as a disincentive to build a national taxation system and hence has further contributed to the persistence of weak states.

Political domination by the military does not, of course, make for a strong state. Indeed, in much of Africa the military itself is a weak institution capable of repression but little else. The military in many African countries is not a disciplined praetorian force, a corporate entity; the armies lack command and discipline, organization, professionalism and esprit de corps. Rather, the military simply provides support for personalized rule and is often no less attached to tribes, kin groups, and factions than are other forces in society; nor should one assume that the military is necessarily committed to building either the state or the economy, for in many African countries the military lives off the state, not for the state.

This combination of a state that does not permeate society and weak military institutions in control of the state may account for the high rate of coups in Africa as one ambitious military leader with a small following readily replaces another.

Many such distinctive features of African politics can best be explained by the existence of personal rule in political systems that lack effective political institutions, Robert Jackson and Carl Rosberg argue in an important study of autocratic regimes in Africa.[6] Some of these distinctive characteristics include political conspiracies to overthrow the rulers, frequent coups,[7] factional and clientalistic politics with highly personalized patron-client relationships, rampant political corruption, frequent purges from the government, the party, and the military of those who are regarded as disloyal, and maneuvering for succession.

In contrast, Asian and Middle Eastern states have a long precolonial history of well-established bureaucratic institutions that were further strengthened by the colonial governments. Contemporary Asian states may be no less autocratic than those of Africa, but they are typically more effective in extracting taxes, delivering services, enforcing law, and mobilizing populations into productive activities.

Asia's stronger states also produce a military that tends to be larger, more professional, and more deeply involved in the economy than the military of most African states. In South Korea, Thailand, Indonesia, and Taiwan, for example, the military has in the main played a positive role in building the economy, in contrast to many of the military-dominated regimes of Africa. In a number of Asian countries, the military directly exercises operational control over portions of the economy. In Indonesia the military manages its own public sector firms (although a very high level of corruption parallels that of the military in many African countries); and in Taiwan, in South Korea, and in the Philippines military personnel exercise direct control over government-run public sector firms. At the same time, the military regimes of East and Southeast Asia have resisted efforts to transfer power to civilian rule and to expand political participation. Thus far, none of the military regimes in Asia has successfully transferred power to civilians, as have the governments of Argentina, Colombia, Venezuela, Greece, Portugal, and Turkey.

We cannot generalize about the tendency of military regimes to divert resources from development to military expenditures. A cursory examination of military sales and purchases in the third world suggests that forms of government do not readily correlate with military expenditures. From 1974 to 1984, 116 third-world countries spent $237 billion; some of the largest acquisitions were by the Middle East monarchies (especially Saudi Arabia and Iran) and by Communist countries (Cuba, China, and Vietnam); India has also obtained substantial amounts of military equipment. Nor can we generalize about the impact that military purchases have had on economic growth. While military expenditures probably slowed the growth of some developing countries, others may have benefited from the transfer of technology, the training of manpower and the stimulus of exports. South Korea and Taiwan, for example, commit substantial resources to arms acquisitions, though both are among the fast-growing economies in the world.

While military regimes have proven to be unstable in Africa, they have been relatively stable in Asia and the Middle East. The widespread involvement of the military in the management of the economy may predispose military personnel to be as concerned with the preservation of a stable government as are members of the business community. Neither Burma, Indonesia, Pakistan, South Korea, nor Taiwan, it should be noted, has been as coup ridden as have African military regimes, and each has an autocratic ruler who has proven relatively adept at retaining power.

Even more surprising has been the stability of the Arab states over the past fifteen to twenty years. The Iranian revolution, the coup and Soviet invasion of Afghanistan, and the terrorist movement and military takeover in Turkey have led observers to overlook the durability of the nearby Arab regimes. Syria and Iraq, both inconstant in the fifties and early sixties, have retained the same rulers for an extended period. So too have the governments of North Africa. Egypt, the assassination of Anwar el-Sadat notwithstanding, has maintained a stable government since the overthrow of the monarchy. And the monarchies of Jordan, Saudi Arabia, and the smaller Gulf states, nervous as they (and outsiders) are, have endured.

Whether the stability of these regimes should be regarded as an indication of institutionalized political development or itself as a transient phenomenon is a matter of considerable uncertainty. The assassination of one's opponents, the use of the military to crush dissident groups, the balancing of one faction against another, the use of one's family members for political purposes (and the willingness to dispose of members of one's own family if it becomes politically necessary), and the use of financial rewards to create loyalty among one's allies may not be the stuff of democratic politics, but as tactics in the hands of skilled practitioners they can and have been successful at enabling Middle East political leaders to govern. For six centuries, it should be recalled, successive Ottoman sultans survived with just such tactics. True enough, some sultans were driven out of office by janissaries, dethroned during a mutiny or killed by janissaries or by members of their own family after relatively short reigns. But while the reigns of some sultans were short-lived, the Ottoman Sultanate as a system endured.[8]

The lack of institutionalized procedures for leadership succession creates considerable uncertainty among the states of the Fertile Crescent and the era of stable governments may well come to an end with the demise of the present leaders, but fundamental changes in the political system are considerably less probable. Instability among the Gulf state monarchies, however, is a different matter. Externally supported antiregime movements from within or direct external interventions are not unlikely developments, and either of these could result in fundamental systemic changes.

However stable the military regimes and monarchies may be in Asia and the Middle East compared with those of Africa, it would be difficult to demonstrate that they have popular legitimacy. Often the strength of particular regimes rests upon the repressive capabilities of the state. Intelligence services and secret police — SAVAK in Iran under the Shah, the Korean Central Intelligence Agency, KHAD in Afghanistan, the secret police in other Communist countries and their equivalents elsewhere — have become more pervasive and terrifyingly effective. While fragile regimes may be particularly predisposed to exercise terror against political dissidents — the behavior of the secret police and military under the Shah of Iran and under Idi Amin in Uganda provides many examples — other regimes that are widely regarded as strong have been no less repressive — China under Mao Tse-tung, for example.

The absence of the use of terror or large-scale repression by no means ensures that a regime is regarded by the population as legitimate. Nonetheless, there is some merit in distinguishing between mildly and ruthlessly repressive regimes. A number of authoritarian regimes in Asia have accumulated a record of being relatively benign in their treatment of the opposition and have even tolerated a considerable degree of dissent — if not at the national level, then at the local and regional levels. Taiwan, for example, permits opposition parties to compete in elections and puts up with dissenting voices from the press to a certain degree. Both the Pakistan and the Bangladesh military regimes have permitted opposition groups to function (though the Pakistan press in reporting meetings of opposition parties refers to them as the "defunct" parties!). Data on the number of political prisoners in the authoritarian states of East and Southeast Asia are hard to come by, and reports of police arrests and torture are, to say the least, hardly unknown. But most observers would regard these states as considerably less repressive than the totalitarian Communist states of Asia or, for that matter, several of the right-wing regimes of Central and South America.

## POLITICAL PARTICIPATION

The authoritarian regimes of Asia, Africa, and the Middle East have sharply limited political participation. Few developing countries permit free competitive elections; most impose restrictions or ban political parties and organizations opposed to the government; only a handful of countries tolerate a free press or public meetings by opponents. Governments, again with few exceptions, have destroyed those institutions intended to facilitate popular political participation in the political process; instead governments have sought to create institutions to mobilize citizens to support the regime, without allowing them to make demands upon the government. Thus, many military regimes have founded political parties — in Indonesia and Bangladesh, for example — as a means of giving the appearance of popular participation and of mobilizing popular support for the regime. Political participation is sometimes permitted at the local level with elections for local councils, but the formation of factions or parties that link groups in one community to those of another is restricted. The Gulf-state monarchies have organized councils — majlis — institutions that enable individual complainants to seek redress from authorities without recourse to political organization. Each of these various institutional mechanisms is intended to allow some limited outlet for demands for participation, provide authoritarian regimes with some ways to deal with local grievances, facilitate popular mobilization by the regime, and give a semblance of legitimacy to an authoritarian government.

The denial of opportunities for popular political participation has, surprisingly, been less a source of political instability than one might have expected. The proposition that modernization would lead to increased demands for political participation that, if repressed and blocked, would lead to large-scale opposition, extremist movements, and revolutionary upheavals has not been proven by events of the last two decades. Indeed, one of the surprising developments in East Asia is that such high levels of modernization have taken place with relatively low levels of mass political participation. Singapore has been politically quiescent and, in the main, so has Taiwan. South Korea has had several popular movements, many of them student led, but they have not seriously weakened military rule. In all three countries, security considerations, the sense of being under seige by larger threatening states, and Confucian patterns of authority[9] may be factors in the strength of autocratic governments and the weakness of popular opposition to them.

The most widespread and, in retrospect, the most successful

popular movements against autocratic regimes in Asia have taken place in Iran under the Shah and in Pakistan under Zulfiqar Ali Bhutto. In both instances the movements proved to be a prelude not to broader political participation but to further militarization and autocratic domination. Similarly, the overthrow of the autocratic regime of South Vietnam by a combination of an internal armed opposition and external military force can hardly be said to have resulted in the creation of an open, participatory political system. The overthrow of the monarchy in Kampuchea resulted in the creation of one of the most authoritarian and brutal regimes ever experienced in Asia. Similarly, the overthrow of the monarchies in Ethiopia, Afghanistan, Iraq, Syria, and Egypt did not lead to the creation of pluralistic participatory political systems. Only in the Philippines has a popular movement against an autocratic regime successfully created a democratic system.

Peasant revolutions, regarded in the fifties and sixties as among the most likely political developments in Asia, have not occurred. Communist-led peasant movements — in northeastern Thailand, in the Malaysian countryside, in the rural areas of Luzon — have largely faltered. Peasants have entered politics in many Asian countries but they have often done so as commercial farmers seeking higher agricultural prices and greater access to seeds, fertilizer, irrigation, pesticides, and credit, not as land-hungry peasants seeking land. One of the paradoxes is that the political influence of peasants on public policies affecting the agrarian sector has been slightest when peasants predominate demographically and the urban centers remain small, while peasants' influence often grows when their numbers have diminished and the urban sector has expanded. Indeed, as we shall discuss later, the inability of the peasantry to influence agricultural policies, most especially among the narrow-based authoritarian regimes in Africa, has enabled regimes to pursue policies that have been harmful to the agrarian sector and inhibited the growth of agricultural productivity.

Nor is there any indication, as Jorge Dominguez notes in his contribution herein, that the urban slums of Africa and Asia, with their large migrant populations from the rural areas, have become centers of radical political activity. The evidence we have suggests that urban squatters have been mobilized to seek the legalization of their squatter settlements, to protect themselves against government bulldozers and to obtain urban amenities; they have not engendered radical political movements.

Some of the most popular widespread political movements during the past decade were not organized around class or, for that matter, economic issues, but centered around religion or ethnicity: the Kurds in Iraq, the Shi'ite clergy in Iran, the Tamils in Sri Lanka, the Sikhs and Assamese in India, the Moros in Mindanao, the Timorese in Timor, the Palestinians in Israel's West Bank, the mujahidin movement in Afghanistan. Certainly the most successful mass political movement was inspired and led by the Shi'ite clergy in Iran. Without military force, and without support from outside, Islamic fundamentalism proved to be the most successful revolutionary movement of the decade. It destroyed the monarchy, undermined the military, and created a wholly new structure for governance.

The expectation that religion would wither away under the pressures of secularism, or that at least it would cease to play a role as a salient political force, has been shattered not only by the events in Iran but by the resurgence of religion in much of the third world in the past decade. A Buddhist revival occurred in several countries of South and Southeast Asia, notably Sri Lanka, Burma, and Vietnam. Christian groups have become an important force opposed to authoritarian regimes in Latin America and in the Philippines. In Israel, religious parties have become more powerful as they have taken an increasingly nationalist turn. But what was unique about the resurgence of Islamic fundamentalism in Iran was its political success, for nowhere else in modern times has the clergy emerged as a political ruling class.

The political triumph of the clergy in Iran suggests that religious groups are likely to continue as a political force in that country irrespective of the political transformations that might occur after the demise of the Ayatollah Khomeini. In some countries, however, religion has served more as an instrument of the state than as a force for popular opposition to the regime. Governments of Islamic countries have used Islamic beliefs as a means of creating an aura of legitimacy for the state. Similarly, East Asian governments have used Confucianism as a means of inculcating obedience, an acceptance of political authority, and discipline in schools, in the workplace, and in politics.

While many unique features of Islam may explain the particular role this religion has played in politics, it is important to note that revivalist movements have emerged in many societies experiencing modernization. One might properly ask whether points occur in the development process when, under the pressure of modernization, there are strong popular urges toward a "return" to indigenous and "authentic" values and toward a rejection of Western intrusion. It should also be noted that the religious revivalist movements represent not simply a *return* to a traditional heritage, but rather the emergence of new ideologies that make use of a reinterpreted "traditional" heritage. The often-made distinction between "tradition" and "traditionalism" is relevant here, the former referring to attachments to one's past, the latter to the new political ideologies that draw upon these attachments.

While the use of religion by governing elites is as characteristic of modern states as it is of developing countries, religious elites in fact rarely take political power, and their influence on the political institutions of most countries is restrained by secular political forces. Religious elites in prewar Japan, among the Buddhist countries of Southeast Asia and within Latin America, for example, play a substantially lesser role than the clergy and their supporters in Muslim countries. It is by no means certain that the Islamic revival, in the sense of clerical domination, is an enduring one, developments in Iran notwithstanding. Nor is the importance yet fully understood of its appeal to young people, very often rural young people who have acquired limited education, who have entered the urban centers for education and work, and for whom religious and ethnic identities are particularly important. It is clear, however, that the Islamic revival, like religious revivals elsewhere, has become an important force in strengthening indigenous cultural identities in opposition to the West, and that it has also created very sharp social and ideological cleavages within the Islamic world.

More generally, it is noteworthy that large-scale popular political movements in Asia and the Middle East have often attracted the most modern, most educated, most developed sectors of society, not the most deprived, lowest-income groups. Politicization often seems greater among the successful, or near successful, than among those who are totally left behind in the development process.

To assess which classes and ethnic groups are most effective at influencing government policies and programs, and which groups are most likely to be disaffected from government, it is particularly useful to understand precisely what stance a government takes toward the economy and, more generally, the role played by the state apparatus in economic development and in the distribution of the benefits of development.

## THE STATE AND THE ECONOMY

The countries of the third world can be divided between those that have experienced a rapid increase in per capita incomes during the past two decades and those that have not. In the main the low-growth countries are also low-income countries, that is, those with per capita incomes of under $400, while the high-growth economies tend to be among the lower-middle-income economies ($400 to $1,700) and most often among the upper-middle-income ($1,700 to $6,000). The per capita incomes of the poorest countries — putting gigantic India and China aside[10] — increased on the average of less than 1 percent per year between 1960 and 1981; many of the African countries — Chad, Zaire, Uganda, Somalia, Madagascar, Niger, Sudan, Ghana, Guinea, Benin, Central African Republic, and Sierra Leone — remained stagnant or actually declined in per capita income. Among the middle-income group of countries the variations in growth rates are considerable. On the average, per capita income in the lower-middle-income countries grew 3.4 percent yearly, the upper-middle-income countries at 4.2 percent. Several of the African countries had low growth rates (Senegal, Liberia, Zambia, Zimbabwe,

TABLE I.2 *Growth Rates in East and Southeast Asia*

| Country | Population, 1981 (millions) | GNP per Capita Average Annual Growth, 1960–80 (%) | Per Capita Income, 1981 ($) |
|---|---|---|---|
| Indonesia | 150.0 | 4.1 | 530 |
| Malaysia | 14.0 | 4.3 | 1,840 |
| Thailand | 48.0 | 4.6 | 770 |
| Republic of Korea | 39.0 | 6.9 | 1,700 |
| Hong Kong | 5.0 | 6.9 | 5,100 |
| Singapore | 2.4 | 7.4 | 5,240 |
| Taiwan (1980) | 18.0 | 9.6 | 2,720 |

Congo) while a handful of countries, all in East and Southeast Asia, had growth rates that were above average (see Table I.2).[11]

Although all of these countries are currently middle income, several were low income until relatively recently. In 1950 South Korea had a per capita income of $146, more or less the same as Nigeria, Kenya, and Egypt in 1950. Taiwan was then slightly ahead of Korea with a per capita income of $224, lagging well behind Brazil ($373), Mexico ($562), and Argentina ($2,720). Thirty-one years later per capita income in South Korea was $1,700, compared with Nigeria's $870, Kenya's $420, and Egypt's $650. Taiwan's per capita income was $2,720 as compared with Brazil's $2,220, Mexico's $2,250, and Argentina's $2,560.[12] No countries of the third world, however, have achieved as high per capita incomes in so short a time as the two high-growth city-states of Singapore (per capita income in 1981 was $5,240) and Hong Kong ($5,100).

## Market-Oriented Policies in Postcolonial States

The four newly industrialized countries of South Korea, Taiwan, Singapore, and Hong Kong have not merely experienced high growth rates, but in a more fundamental sense they have modernized their economies and societies. New technologies have been introduced, adapted, and invented, populations have become more educated and urbanized, media exposure is high, and opportunities for social mobility have been encouraged.[13] Considerable equity has been achieved in terms not only of income distribution, but in the widespread decline in infant mortality, improved longevity, and the near disappearance of illiteracy.[14] The average income per family in the top 20 percent in Taiwan, for example, was fifteen times that of the bottom 20 percent in 1953, but by 1979 the ratio had been reduced to 4.2 times. The literacy rate of Singapore is 83 percent, Hong Kong 90 percent, South Korea 93 percent and Taiwan 89 percent. (In contrast, the literacy rate of China is 69 percent.) No other countries of Asia, Africa, or the Middle East have achieved the level of economic development, equity, or modernization of the countries of East Asia.

Four other countries of Southeast Asia show signs of growing as rapidly as have these four. From 1970 to 1981 Indonesia had a GDP annual growth rate of 7.8 percent, Malaysia 7.8 percent, Thailand 7.2 percent, and even the politically troubled Philippines grew at a surprising 6.2 percent, though a high population growth rate brought its per capita income growth rate down to only 2.8 percent per year, hardly higher than Vietnam's 2.4 percent. "Looking Eastward" — that is, pursuing the economic growth strategies adopted by Japan and by South Korea, Taiwan, Hong Kong, and Singapore — has become the catchword in the ASEAN countries.

Both South Korea and Taiwan initially pursued state-protected import-substitution policies similar to those adopted by the countries of Latin America in the 1960s, but by the end of the decade both countries shifted to export-promotion policies. The decision to promote exports had far-reaching consequences for many aspects of economic policy. Not all the policies pursued by the two countries were alike. Taiwan placed more emphasis on public sector investment than did South Korea; Taiwan provided tax breaks for investors while South Korea made greater use of loans; Taiwan placed its reliance upon loans from private banks, while South Korea made greater use of government banks. But these differences aside, in both countries the state provided incentives to increase savings, investments, and exports. Price policies were adopted to mobilize resources toward spheres of the economy regarded by state bureaucrats as likely to be competitive and profitable, particularly for export. Both countries — following Japan — supported the development of conglomerates of vertically and horizontally integrated industrial groups on the assumption that large combines could best provide entrepreneurship and take greater risks at home and abroad. In both South Korea and Taiwan, industrial policy has often been highly personalized as government officials work closely with individual firms rather than rely exclusively on general policies to nurture particular sectors of the economy. In short, the state has played an active role in the economy primarily to induce market-conforming behavior on the part of both public and private sector firms and to use state resources to promote efficiency, productivity, and profitability.

To what extent this high-growth, state-supported, export-oriented capitalist model depends upon the existence of an authoritarian state is a matter of considerable controversy. However one answers this question, it should be noted that most of the authoritarian states of the third world have not pursued this development strategy, and none has demonstrated a capacity to produce anywhere near comparable levels of either growth or equity. None of the Communist states has done as well, nor have any of the mildly socialist states such as Tanzania or Sri Lanka.

While today Japan can be regarded as a relatively open political system with competitive political parties, during the country's early development, from the turn of the century until the Second World War, an authoritarian government prevailed. Much the same can be said for South Korea, ruled by a military regime; Taiwan and Singapore, both controlled by one-party governments; and Hong Kong, with its British administration. Malaysia can be described as a limited democracy, but Indonesia and Thailand both have military governments, while the Philippines was under martial law administration for many years. In each of these countries the bureaucracy shapes business policy; in Taiwan economic decision-making authority rests in the Executive Yuan; in Korea an Economic Planning Board works closely with the Korean Development Institute, which is manned by professional economists.

In the East Asian states "administrative guidance" is used by the bureaucracy to direct the resources of individual firms; less emphasis is placed on general legal principles, more on the use of discretionary controls by officials. It would be more accurate, though not entirely so, to say that the state controls business than that businesspeople control the state; perhaps one should characterize the relationship between the state and the private sector as a symbiotic one. But the state itself, or more precisely the bureaucracy, is open to people of talent. The regimes of East Asia are committed not to a diffusion of power, but to a diffusion of knowledge and the creation of a social and economic framework that facilitates opportunities for social mobility.

The single most important step taken by both the Taiwanese and South Korean governments for improving income distribution was their land reform program. Beyond that, neither state can be regarded as welfare minded, although as we have noted, both countries have achieved a revolution in income distribution that is greater than any achieved by a Communist or socialist country.

While the level of income equality may be a factor in reducing class conflict, the much-heralded disciplined and politically subdued industrial labor force in East Asia shows signs of restiveness. Although job security is high, industrial wages have been kept down and have generally grown more slowly than productivity. The potential for industrial unrest is high, though restrictions on trade unions have thus far curbed strikes.

Whether an authoritarian framework has been a necessary condition for the pursuit of these economic policies is, as noted earlier, by no means clear. Thus far we have only a few examples of countries seeking to pursue similar policies within a democratic framework — Sri Lanka (since 1977), Jamaica (since 1980), Barbados, and Malaysia — but the record is not yet in on any of these countries. A number of countries have created export-promotion zones — Senegal, for example — in an attempt to duplicate the East Asian successes, but these are often enclaves intended to permit the government to promote exports while at the same time maintaining an import-substitution policy for the rest of the country. Few countries of the third world have been prepared to adopt the far-reaching economic policies adopted by the East Asian and now several of the Southeast Asian states.

It may very well be the case that the kinds of policies adopted by the newly industrialized countries can more easily be adopted by authoritarian than by democratic countries. But none of these cases supports the proposition that the adoption of export-promotion strategies must result in the emergence of restrictive bureaucratic authoritarian states. If anything, the East Asian experience suggests a different causal relationship; each of these states was authoritarian prior to the decision to shift from import-substitution to export-promotion policies.[15]

### Rent-seeking Behavior in Postcolonial States

The governing elites of many of the new states have often been more concerned with using their control over the state to extract resources for their personal use than with adopting policies intended to accelerate growth or improve income distribution to the poor. Many of the policies adopted by regimes in Africa can best be understood in this framework. A number of scholarly analyses of African states have noted that many governments have taken steps to increase state revenues even when the policies were clearly a disincentive for increased productivity. Government-run marketing boards, for example, pay producers prices well below prevailing market prices in order to increase their own earnings. Exchange rates are often overvalued in order to enable well-to-do elites, within the government or closely tied to government, to import at below-market prices at the cost of producers, with the result that rural-urban terms of trade and the balance of payments have worsened.

State controls over prices and markets have enhanced the capacity of governing elites to enrich themselves and to use their control over the economy to provide benefits to allies and deny economic benefits to opponents. The result is a politicized economy where individual economic gain results not from increased productivity and efficiency, but from access to political power — that is, through rent-seeking rather than profit-seeking behavior. The contrast between these states and those of East Asia is not over the question of whether the state plays an active role in the economy, but over precisely what kind of intervention takes place: market-inducing policies intended to increase the productivity, efficiency, and competitiveness of producers, or rent-seeking policies intended to enhance the income of those with access to political power.

Rent-seeking policies are not only inefficient for the economy and a loss for consumers. They also induce cynicism, undermine the legitimacy of the state, erode acceptance of income inequalities, and stimulate antisocial behavior. Income inequalities, based not upon differences in productivity but upon political privilege, grow as the state uses its power to extract resources from one section of society and transfer them to those with political power or access to power. Black markets flourish, thereby distorting relative prices, and official corruption proliferates as producers pay bribes to gain the benefits from state policies. The much-commented-upon high level of corruption in such countries as Zaire and Nigeria can be explained more by the kinds of policies pursued by the government than by the moral character of officials and businesspeople. While it may not always be so clear as to how, if at all, the character of a people shapes a political system, it is clear that the political system and the policies pursued by governments can and do shape the character of a people.

It is also clear that the rent-seeking policies so widely followed by many governments in Africa have had a devastating effect on agricultural productivity. Although low agricultural prices, overvalued exchange rates, and overstaffed and overpaid government marketing boards have benefited government employers and importers, these policies have also created balance-of-payment deficits, eroded foreign exchange reserves, discouraged investment in agriculture and weakened the capacity of producers of coffee, cotton, cashews, sisal, tea, tobacco, cocoa, and other traditional exports to produce for world markets and of food producers to produce for local markets. As a result, per capita agricultural production in

Africa declined by an estimated 1.5 percent per year throughout the 1970s and early 1980s, notwithstanding the growth
of agricultural productivity elsewhere in the third world.[16]
According to the World Bank, the index of food production
per capita for 1982 (1969–71 = 100) was 101 for India, 154
for Sri Lanka, 125 for South Korea, 150 for Malaysia, 124
for the Philippines, and 117 for Indonesia — Asian countries
that provided incentives for agricultural producers — as compared with 88 for Tanzania, 86 for Uganda, 92 for Nigeria,
87 for Zaire, 68 for Mozambique, 82 for Ethiopia, and 77 for
Angola.

While the international recession may have contributed to
worsening the economies of Africa, economic performance
was poor even before the oil crisis. Food production stagnated
in Africa in the sixties and, as just noted, declined in the
seventies. In a number of countries — most notably in Tanzania — the decline in agriculture was associated with the
growth in the size and scope of state bureaucracies and public
sector institutions such as parastatals — publicly owned but
autonomous state institutions with the exclusive right to buy
food grains, to purchase and export crops, and to import.
The parastatals not only maintain a legal monopoly over procurement, but also control processing and the distribution of
inputs to growers. As production declined, exports went
down, food imports increased, and shortages in foreign exchange materialized, affecting the import of raw materials
and spare parts for industry. By the early 1980s the various
international donor agencies — the World Bank, International Development Association (IDA), U.S. Agency for International Development (USAID), etc. — recognized that the
support they had provided the parastatals had had little if
any positive impact, for the policies pursued by the parastatals
had not only damaged the economies, but they had encum-
bered the parastatals as well.

The earlier literature on development tended to assume
that governing elites were committed to economic development objectives, or (sometimes alternatively) that they chose
economic policies that may have been detrimental to growth
but were perceived as necessary for state building or for elite

survival. Today's analysts are more aware of the ways in which governing elites use their domination of the state to extract resources from society for their own benefit or for the benefit of groups who give them support. Thus, the expansion of the state bureaucracy, the growth of public sector institutions, the increasing capacity of the state to extract resources from the population, and the progressive intrusion of the state into the management of the economy may indeed be described as "state-building" activities, but they can also be the means by which governing elites transfer resources from one social class to another. Perhaps this is what Karl Marx had in mind when he spoke of the "Asiatic mode of production" to characterize a political system in which the state plunders society by extracting resources for the private use of the governing classes. There is, of course, nothing exclusively "Asiatic" about such states, for one can find examples throughout the third world, more often in fact in Africa than in contemporary Asia.

**CONCLUSION**

The great surprises of the sixties and seventies in the third world were not the decline of democratic institutions, the rise of autocratic regimes, the continued instabilities of regimes, and the limited effectiveness of states, for these were the mainstays of most scholarly analyses. Many scholars were disappointed with what they witnessed but not surprised.

Many of the surprises pertain more to what was expected but did not occur. Leftist revolutionary upheavals and successful guerrilla movements did not materialize, though they were predicted for Southeast Asia after the fall of Vietnam. No significant peasant uprisings erupted, not to mention peasant revolutions. Massive urban growth and urban crowding notwithstanding, neither the urban poor nor the urban industrial proletariat have turned against their governments. Class politics have not replaced ethnic politics either in Africa or in Southern Asia. Many regimes have been unstable, especially in Africa, but the instabilities can be attributed more often to intra-elite conflicts than to the imbalance between political participation and political institutionalization. Indeed, even the rapid modernization of East Asia has not led to the expected massive growth of demands for popular participation and the expected (and, for some, hoped-for) demise of autocratic governments.

Instead, as we have discussed, there have been three significant trends in Africa, Asia, and the Middle East, each in its own way distinctive to the region, and each in its own way not wholly anticipated.

The first trend, and clearly the one of the greatest historical importance, has been the extraordinary rate of modernization in East Asia and in parts of Southeast Asia. For the first time in this century, another group of non-European countries, excluding Japan, has entered the modern era. South Korea previously had been regarded as one of the poorest, least likely countries to develop; Taiwan's political future seemed uncertain; and the countries of Southeast Asia seemed likely to be infected by the turmoil of Vietnam. But if the degree of their economic development itself was not anticipated, the significant elements in that development were already regarded by scholars as of central importance: the critical role of human capital formation, the importance of the state in providing for political order, the ability of the state in extracting resources and using them effectively for education, health, and the basic infrastructures of development, the effectiveness of government policies in inducing market-oriented behavior, the willingness of government leaders to take the risk of plunging their economies and societies into the international marketplace.[17] On each of these dimensions the newly industrialized countries of East and Southeast Asia acted decisively, and on most of these dimensions there could hardly be a sharper division between them and many of the states of Africa.

As to expectations, much of the political economy literature of the sixties and seventies emphasized the growing gap between rich and poor countries and growing income differences within poor countries, both of which were described as a consequence of what Immanuel Wallerstein[18] called the "modern world system" of capitalism — at the very time when the newly industrialized countries of Asia were entering that modern world system! The neo-Marxist dependency literature, by emphasizing the "place" of countries in the world system as a way of explaining and predicting the economic and political dynamics of countries, underplayed the internal political dynamics and the critical importance of decisions made by political leaders.

The second significant trend has been the entrenchment of personal autocratic rule in many of the African states, without the underpinnings of strong political parties, a professional military, effective bureaucracies or, for that matter, popular support. States have intruded into the economy not with the goal of inducing market-oriented behavior, but of transferring resources from one social class to another, and often from those who pay taxes to those who control the state. Corruption has supplied more than the grease for making the bureaucracy work, the cream for satisfying the personal tastes of top officials or the spoils of patronage for strengthening a political party. Rather, corruption has led to a massive transfer of wealth to those who control the state. The state itself can create social classes — not simply be the product of what Marxists call the "modes of production" — and in turn these social classes can control and exploit the resources of the state for their own benefit. As the state increasingly extracts wealth for society, and as it becomes the till from which political elites extract for their own gain, those who seek to improve their personal well-being turn to politics. In this highly politicized atmosphere, with few alternative nonpolitical means for improving status and income, the struggle for power becomes acute, often violent, and both institutional development and market-oriented growth policies are precluded. In this sense it is appropriate to speak not only of the stagnant economies of much of Africa, but of the stagnant political systems as well.

The growth of Islamic fundamentalism in the Middle East has been the third significant trend, though more broadly this development should be seen in the context of the vitality of religion in the third world: the conversions to Islam in much of Africa, the spread of Christianity in South Korea, the revitalization of Buddhism and Hinduism in South and Southeast Asia and the elevation of Confucian ethics and authority patterns by the secular regimes of East Asia. Little of this was anticipated, and its political importance certainly was under-estimated. In Japan, too, as Winston Davis points out in his essay, Shintoism and magic live side by side with modern secular behavior. But what is striking about the Islamic re-surgence is its rejection of much of what is generally regarded as modern in the twentieth century: secularism, democracy, and even nationalism. In this respect Islam has come to play quite a different role from that of the religions of moderni-zation — Christianity, Judaism, Confucianism, Shintoism, even Buddhism and Hinduism. Each of these religions, in its own way, has been interpreted or reinterpreted so as to induce people to behave in ways conducive to modernization, or to function alongside of, without impeding, modern behavior, yet to provide personal comfort, a sense of continuity with one's past, and a group identity.

Why were scholars so slow in anticipating and explaining many of these developments? Perhaps scholars did not antic-ipate the East Asian developments because they paid too little attention to the values and attitudes that underlay the eco-nomic development strategies chosen by the governing elites. Perhaps scholars did not anticipate the emergence of auto-cratic regimes in Africa because they paid too little attention to the rapacious character of the new governing classes. And perhaps the Islamic fundamentalists were not taken seriously because scholars assumed that while they might play a role in bringing down an unpopular monarchy they were incapable of governing a modern state. Perhaps, more generally, one of the reasons for the overprediction of some phenomena and the underprediction of others has been the tendency of schol-ars — a tendency shared by neoclassical economists, political liberals, and neo-Marxists — to overemphasize the political outcomes of economic changes. What this suggests is that scholars need to give more analytical attention to the social, cultural, and psychological determinants of political behavior by taking more seriously, for example, the independent role of ideologies and values as determinants of elite behavior; the durability and importance of ethnic-linguistic and religious group identities; the place of resentment in both popular and elite behavior; and the popular need for what sociologist Peter

Berger[19] has characterized as a social meaning to accompany the process of modernization.

**NOTES**

1. For a discussion of the limited effectiveness of most of the juridical states of Africa, see Robert H. Jackson and Carl G. Rosberg, "Why Africa's Weak States Persist: The Empirical and the Juridical in Statehood," *World Politics* 35, no. 1 (October 1982):1–24.

2. Walker Connor, "Nation-Building or Nation-Destroying?" *World Politics* 24, no. 3 (April 1972):319–55.

3. The concept of consociational democracy was first put forward by Arend Lijphart in his *Politics of Accommodation: Pluralism and Democracy in the Netherlands,* 2d ed. rev. (Berkeley: University of California Press, 1975), then subsequently applied to developing countries in his *Democracy in Plural Societies: A Comparative Exploration* (New Haven, Conn.: Yale University Press, 1977).

4. On the growth of autocracy in the third world, see Clifford Geertz, "The Judging of Nations: Some Comments on the Assessment of Regimes in the New States," *European Journal of Sociology* 18, no. 2 (1977):245–61.

5. I have developed this argument and compared it with other explanations for the development of democracy in an essay, "Empirical Democratic Theory," in: *Competitive Elections in Developing Countries,* edited by Ergun Ozbudun and Myron Weiner (Durham, N.C.: Duke University Press, forthcoming).

6. Robert H. Jackson and Carl G. Rosberg, *Personal Rule in Black Africa: Prince, Autocrat, Prophet, Tyrant* (Berkeley: University of California Press, 1982).

7. According to one study, there were forty-one military coups in twenty-two African countries between 1958 and 1981. See Jackson and Rosberg, "Why Africa's Weak States Persist," 8.

8. It has been reported that in pre-Mogul India, twenty-nine of the thirty-two rulers over the course of 320 years took power in a bloody conflict, and only fifteen died a natural death. See M. A. Karandikar, *Islam in India's Transition to Modernity* (Westport, Conn.: Greenwood, 1969), 120.

9. For an insightful analysis of the way in which the fear of what he calls "primitive power" leads to a popular acceptance of authoritarianism in East and Southeast Asia, see Lucian W. Pye, *Asian Power and Politics: The Cultural Dimensions of Authority* (Cambridge, Mass.: Harvard University Press, 1985).

10. According to the World Bank, India's per capita growth from 1960 to 1981 was 1.4 percent, China's, 5 percent, but it is difficult to take the figures on China seriously. The World Bank also reports China's per capita income in 1981 as $300, India's as $260. The economist A. K. Sen has pointed out that in 1960, if the 5 percent figure is correct, China's per capita GNP would have been $108, as compared with India's $194. The extrapolated Chinese figure for 1960 is incompatible with any known data. Most estimates for 1960 put China's per capita income at higher than India's per capita income, suggesting that GNP growth rates over the past two decades have been roughly the same, with neither country doing significantly better than other current low-income countries. But it should also be noted that postwar per capita incomes for South Korea and Taiwan were roughly at the same level as those of India and China.

11. All data used here, except for Taiwan, are from the World Bank, *World Development Report 1983* (New York: Oxford University Press, 1983). Data on Taiwan are omitted from all World Bank publications. I have taken the Taiwan data from Shirley W. Y. Kuo, Gustav Ranis, and John C. H. Fei, *The Taiwan Success Story: Rapid Growth with Improved Distribution in the Republic of China, 1952–1979* (Boulder, Colo.: Westview Press, 1981).

12. Had India's GDP grown as rapidly from 1960 to 1980 as South Korea's, it would today stand at $531 billion rather than at $150 billion, surpassing that of the United Kingdom, equal to that of France, and double the present Chinese GDP! India's per capita income would have been $740 (instead of $260), two-and-a-half times that of China. India's standing in the world economy and as a world power would be quite different, especially, to pursue this imaginary projection, if India's share of world trade had grown in Korean-like proportions. (India's current exports are $8.4 billion, as compared with $21.8 billion for South Korea, $21.8 billion for China, $20.9 billion for Hong Kong, and $20.7 billion for Singapore. India's exports are slightly below Hungary's $8.8 billion.)

13. Few neo-Marxists have come to grips with the economic realities of East Asia since they have rejected Marx's own view that capitalism is not an impediment to development, but its condition. For a revisionist view by a Marxist returning to Marx's own formulation, see Bill Warren, "Imperialism and Capitalist Industrialization," *New Left Review* 81 (September–October 1973): 3–44, which provides documentation to demonstrate

that "neo-colonialism" has often been accompanied by high rates of economic growth, that industrialization has become independent in the sense that domestic markets are growing and becoming increasingly diversified, that foreign private capital is coming under the control of third-world governments and that technological dependence has been declining.

14. For example, Taiwan's illiteracy declined from 55 percent in 1946 to 11 percent in 1978; the crude death rate decreased from 9.9 per thousand in 1952 to 4.7 per thousand in 1979; and life expectancy increased from 58.6 years to 70.7 years over the same period. The Gini coefficient in 1953 was 0.56, about the same as in present-day Brazil and Mexico, but by 1964 the coefficient had dropped to 0.33, among the lowest in the world. Much of the improvement can be attributed to Taiwan's effective program of land redistribution and to a rapid increase in agricultural productivity. For details, see Kuo, Ranis, and Fei, *Taiwan Success Story.*

15. The same argument has been put forward by Albert Hirschman in his criticism of O'Donnell's effort to account for the rise of authoritarianism in Brazil as a consequence of its economic policies. Dependency theorists, Hirschman argues, have confused analysis of the economic policy *consequences* of authoritarian regimes with the question of whether there are economic *determinants* of authoritarianism. See Albert O. Hirschman, "The Turn to Authoritarianism in Latin America and the Search for Its Economic Determinants," in *The New Authoritarianism in Latin America*, edited by David Collier (Princeton, N.J.: Princeton University Press, 1979), 61–98.

16. For an analysis of the attitude of African states toward markets and the policies of disincentives they have adopted for agriculture, see Robert H. Bates, *Essays on the Political Economy of Rural Africa* (Cambridge: Cambridge University Press, 1983). Also see D. Gale Johnson and G. Edward Schuh, eds., *The Role of Markets in the World Food Economy* (Boulder, Colo.: Westview Press, 1983).

17. For a development of the argument that Japan's achievement as an economic superpower was made possible through a process of internationalization, see Hiroshi Mannari and Harumi Befu, eds., *The Challenge of Japan's Internationalization: Organization and Culture* (Tokyo: Kodansha International, 1983). I am grateful to Winston Davis for calling this collection of papers, mainly by Japanese scholars, to my attention.

18.  Immanuel Wallerstein, *The Modern World-System: Capitalist Agriculture and the Origins of the European World-Economy in the Sixteenth Century* (New York: Academic Press, 1974).

19.  Peter L. Berger, *Pyramids of Sacrifice: Political Ethics and Social Change* (Garden City, N.J.: Doubleday Anchor Books, 1976).

JORGE I. DOMÍNGUEZ

# Political Change: Central America, South America, and the Caribbean

POLITICAL CHANGES in Central America, South America, and the Caribbean from about 1960 to the mid-1980s show the uniqueness of the region's experience as well as shared concerns with countries in Africa and in Asia.[1] This overview will reflect briefly on the political experiences of these Western Hemisphere countries, making occasional references to the research of other scholars. Necessarily, only major themes can be highlighted, at the cost of failing to attend enough to the particularity of individual country histories. The essay focuses on broad concerns with states, regimes, incumbents, and societies in the Western Hemisphere, with special attention to patterns of political stability and political economy from about 1960 to the mid-1980s.[2]

## STATES

States have endured in Latin America as they have in Africa and Asia, but that has not surprised Latin Americanists. The consolidation of Latin American states began mostly in the last third of the nineteenth century, and it continued through the first quarter of the twentieth century. States did not sub-

For comments on a preliminary presentation I am grateful to Myron Weiner and Samuel Huntington, and to JOSPOD members; and on an earlier draft, to Gilbert Merkx, Kevin Middlebrook, and J. Samuel Valenzuela. Errors, of course, are mine alone.

65

sequently yield to the efforts to create supranational institutions in Latin America that would have modified their own authority over their territory. The Andean Pact, the Central American Common Market, and the Latin American Free Trade Association were moderately successful at stimulating regional trade for some years; Andean Pact states coordinated some policies to promote democratic outcomes in the late 1970s. However, these accomplishments have been modest; most of the more ambitious integration efforts had stalled by the mid-1980s. The most serious effort to create a "grander" state in the Western Hemisphere, the Federation of the West Indies, sought to bring the Caribbean's English-speaking islands toward federated independence. The federation failed because loyalty to each island mattered more than loyalty to a West Indian abstraction. Each island became independent alone, or in very small groups (such as Trinidad-Tobago, St. Kitts-Nevis, and St. Vincent and the Grenadines). This failure is familiar to students of integration efforts in East or West Africa or in the once United Arab Republic between Egypt and Syria. The Caribbean's newly independent states have also endured. The territorial fragmentation of the late colonial period did not continue after independence, despite the existence of secessionist movements in several of the independent small-archipelago states.

The strength of the state, defined by a set of institutions with a claim to a legitimate monopoly of force over a certain territory and an ability to exercise it, increased in these political systems. The state's capability to penetrate the society and the economy has grown in a number of dimensions.

State enterprises have developed in many economic sectors, and state regulation over the private economy has also expanded,[3] as research on corporatism[4] during the past two decades has demonstrated.[5] The state's strength also increased in the realm of international political economy. Contrary to the expectations of some, Latin American states have expropriated large foreign-owned firms in the mineral and oil sectors and regulated remaining foreign-owned firms in other sectors, despite differences in regime types. For example, the foreign-owned copper companies in Chile were expropriated by Salvador Allende's Popular Unity government; their large mines were not returned to the private sector under the authoritarian military regime of General Augusto Pinochet. They have remained state firms.[6] And in an enduring democratic regime, such as that of Venezuela, the expropriation of foreign firms in the oil sector was accomplished through national consensus.[7] State regulation of multinational firms has also become the norm.

Latin American states have also reoriented parts of their economy to promote exports of nontraditional products, including manufactured products. Some of this export-promotion strategy was also brought about by the successful exercise of state pressure on multinational firms. Of course, this new capacity did not secure their complete international autonomy or break their links with international markets. Indeed, state strategies were often designed to induce more vigorous participation in international markets, not to cut off or reduce those ties. What did change, however, was the capacity of Latin American, and some Caribbean, states to act positively in international economic matters. They were no longer just objects of the international political economy.[8]

The state's capacity to repress has also grown. Beginning in the 1960s, many states in Latin America underwent at least one severely authoritarian period, when imprisonment for political reasons, torture, killings, or disappearances became an administrative routine. The pattern of political imprisonment was most severe in Cuba; the pattern of death through disappearances was most severe in Argentina and Chile; and the pattern of mass killings appears to have been most severe, relative to the size of their populations, in El Salvador and Guatemala. By comparison, military rule in Peru (1968–80) was mild, and Brazil after 1964 had the least repressive of the conservative South American authoritarian regimes.[9]

The state's capacity to repress served also to defeat insurgencies of varying significance throughout Central and South America in the 1960s and to defeat comparable efforts in the cities in the 1970s. This capacity was demonstrated by democratic regimes in Venezuela and Colombia as well as by many authoritarian regimes. Revolutionary situations did not arise in northern Central America until the end of the 1970s.[10]

State strength also increased because states acquired the capacity to exert power throughout the national territory up to the boundary; then they often discovered that they did not know where the boundary really was and, if they did, they did not like it. South America's last interstate war had ended in 1942, and no war occurred until 1981, when Peru and Ecuador fought each other for a week. Argentina and the United Kingdom fought in the South Atlantic in 1982. The threat of war in South America, however, had reappeared already in the late 1970s between these states and also between Peru, Chile, and Bolivia, and between Argentina and Chile. The latter two had fully mobilized their armies and put their civilians on war footing in late 1978, to pull back thanks only to the pope's mediation. Interstate violence has been more probable in Central than in South America. A major war broke out between Honduras and El Salvador in 1969. In subsequent years, interstate and revolutionary conflicts have combined to unravel Central American politics.[11]

Increased military expenditures in real terms and the consequent increase in the capacity of the armed forces helped to raise the state's capacity to impose its power throughout the national territory. This was a "painless militarization." Because the economies grew so much, the proportion of gross national product allocated to military expenditures actually fell in several countries even as real military expenditures increased. For example, Brazil's real military expenditures doubled while the military expenditure share of GNP was cut in half from the late 1960s to the late 1970s.[12] Of course, real social opportunity costs were incurred because resources allocated to the military were not committed to achieve other social goals.

Caribbean islands differed. Except for an international accident — a conventional attack by the Cuban Air Force on a Bahamian Coast Guard boat in May 1980 — interstate war was absent from this subregion until the invasion of Grenada in October 1983 by the United States and six other English-speaking Caribbean countries. The lack of military capacity of all Caribbean states other than Cuba has had the effect of making it more difficult for them to attack one another.

Finally, the relative autonomy of the state's institutions and elites with regard to the society has also increased. That is most evident in revolutionary Cuba. Cuban state elites have ruled continuously for over a quarter century, with little rotation of top personnel. Challenges to state authority, at home or from abroad, have been defeated. The state's capacity to control the society is unparalleled in Cuban history, or in the hemisphere in the mid-1980s.[13]

The increase in the state's autonomy could be seen as well in the relative independence of Brazilian or Peruvian military governments from their respective business or labor sectors in the mid- and late 1960s as these governments imposed their preferred changes on the society.[14] Such autonomy was also evident in the Argentine military government of the early 1980s, which continued economic policies that brought about the bankruptcy of many industrial enterprises.[15] The decision of Mexican President José López Portillo to expropriate the nationally owned private banking system in 1982 on his own authority represents a classic case of an individual ruler's autonomy.

The increase of state autonomy is not an unqualified social good. Autonomous state elites can make disastrous mistakes because there is little countervailing power in the society to prevent their political suicide. The development of extreme state autonomy may lead to the loss of touch with the state's social bases. Arguably, that happened to the military government in Argentina in the early 1980s as it had to Anastasio Somoza in Nicaragua in the late 1970s through quite different processes. In such cases, relatively few people in key state positions become committed to implement certain policies, acting so autonomously that they undermine their basis of support. Only very strong rulers can survive near-suicidal state autonomy policies. One was Fidel Castro, who survived the collapse of the Cuban economy and the implementation of unpopular policies of "cultural change" in the late 1960s. Another was Augusto Pinochet, who survived a vigorous effort to redemocratize Chile in the midst of an economic collapse in the early 1980s.

## REGIME TYPES AND PATTERNS OF INCUMBENTS

If states in Latin America became stronger, regimes became weaker, and incumbents weaker still. A regime is a set of norms and rules that further define and support the state at any given moment, shaping how governments are constituted and regulated. The state's continued ability to extract resources from society, or to induce people to do what they would not otherwise do, is a measure of state power. State power has continued to grow, but the regimes that wield it, be they democratic or authoritarian, have been increasingly unstable. They have fallen through coups, elections, or voluntary resignations.

Some regimes have been overthrown by coups. Since 1960, thirteen Latin American countries (all except Cuba, Haiti, Paraguay, Venezuela, Colombia, Costa Rica, and Mexico) have witnessed at least one coup; Nicaragua has witnessed a full-scale revolution. The first three exceptions have had authoritarian regimes of quite different ideological stripes and accomplishments; the next three exceptions have been the only stable competitive civilian regimes (although the degree of competitiveness in Colombia was restricted by a power-sharing agreement between the two major parties that alternated the presidency through 1978); Mexico has an authoritarian civilian regime, much milder than the regimes of the first three countries.[16]

In some Latin American and Caribbean nations, regime changes have been very frequent: Bolivia and Argentina, in particular, and Peru, Ecuador, and Honduras, to a lesser extent. Brazil, Uruguay, and Chile have had only one regime change in this time period. The Dominican Republic entered a period of considerable political stability under civilian competition after the U.S. intervention of the mid-1960s. Voluntary resignations by the armed forces, leading to elections, have been an important avenue for regime change in Argentina, Bolivia, Peru, and Ecuador, and, less decisively, in Panama, Honduras, Guatemala, and El Salvador, at various times.

And, in Haiti, Jean-Claude Duvalier resigned the presidency under U.S. pressure.

The non-Latin Caribbean is quite different. Competitive civilian regimes have been the norm everywhere except for Grenada and Suriname. Some island countries (Barbados, Dominica, Jamaica, and St. Lucia) have had elections as a result of which power has even passed from incumbent to opposition. In contrast to perceptions common in the United States and Western Europe, the Caribbean has differed from the mainland because of its considerable and enduring political stability, either in competitive regimes in the English-speaking Caribbean, as well as the Dominican Republic, or in authoritarian regimes in Haiti (1957–86) and in Cuba.[17]

The pattern in the English-speaking Caribbean is consistent with the more general observation, noted by Myron Weiner herein, that the successor states of the British Empire have been more likely to be governed by stable, competitive civilian regimes than are successor states of other empires — an empirical observation still in search of adequate explanations. Fiji, Sri Lanka, Mauritius, Barbados, and Jamaica, for example, all have the remarkable combination of this British heritage and plantation economies. In the Americas as in Africa and Asia, the successor states of the U.S., French, Dutch, Spanish, and Portuguese empires have been less likely to be governed by stable, competitive civilian regimes.

In those countries in Latin America and the Caribbean where elections are fair and frequent, the most common pattern has been for incumbent parties to be defeated (not unlike what has happened in Western Europe or the United States in recent years). Turnover between incumbent and opposition parties may strengthen the competitive regime though at a cost to particular incumbents; it also makes for more frequent policy changes and for greater difficulty in implementing long-term policies. In presidential elections from the mid-1950s to the mid-1980s except twice, every incumbent party in Costa Rica was defeated; the same has happened in Venezuela since the mid-1960s; it had happened in Chile from the late 1940s until the 1973 military coup; it emerged as the pattern in Uruguay from the mid-1950s to the slow-moving coup in the early 1970s; and it characterizes Colombia in the 1980s (Colombia's presidential alternation before 1978 was mandated by the National Front power-sharing agreement). In the late 1970s and early 1980s, incumbent parties were also defeated in the Dominican Republic, Peru, Ecuador, Barbados, Dominica, St. Lucia, and Jamaica.

One factor promoting the stability of authoritarian rule in several Latin American countries has been the scheduled rotation of power. For example, every Mexican president since Lázaro Cárdenas in 1940 has stepped down at the end of the six-year term.[18] These rotations have brought about important changes in policy and in the inclusion of social groups in the exercise of power. Similarly, the Brazilian political system became more stable after the 1964 coup compared with neighboring authoritarian regimes, thanks in part to the establishment of fixed nonrenewable terms for all presidents.

Indeed, the fixed, nonrenewable presidential term provides for some stability in both authoritarian and competitive Latin American countries. Stable authoritarian regimes such as those of Mexico, Brazil since 1964, and El Salvador from the early 1950s to the late 1970s relied on this procedure; so too have the stronger stable competitive systems of Costa Rica, Venezuela, and Colombia, and so had Chile before 1973. In societies where a suspicion exists that there might be an "authoritarian propensity" among some political leaders — and good historical reasons to think so — reliance on an abstract fidelity to the rules of democratic competition is often insufficient. Stability requires an implicit bargain between the present and the future: you let me rule now, and I guarantee you that I will step down at the appointed time to give you a chance to rule.

This procedure, and the bargain on which it rests, distinguishes Latin America's competitive regimes from those in the English-speaking Caribbean as well as from those in Western Europe, Japan, and the other democratic heirs of the British Empire that permit the immediate reelection of the head of the government. The English-speaking Caribbean's modal political organization is a parliamentary form of government. Latin America's fixed, nonrenewable presidential term also distinguishes its authoritarian regimes from those of Eastern Europe, Africa, and Asia because these do not set fixed, nonrenewable limits for their rulers. Serial authoritarian rule, or electoral rotation, provides one underpinning of often-precarious regime stability in Latin America. This regime-stabilizing procedure, however, has come at the expense of incumbents, whom it has weakened even near the ends of their terms.

*The Bureaucratic Authoritarian Regimes*

The military regimes that emerged since the 1960s in Argentina, Brazil, Chile, and Uruguay were a type, which has been termed bureaucratic authoritarian. Research on bureaucratic authoritarian regimes, defined as a "type of authoritarianism characterized by a self-avowedly technocratic, bureaucratic, non-personalistic approach to policy making and problem solving,"[19] commanded much scholarly attention during the 1970s. Most authors emphasize that bureaucratic authoritarian regimes seek to exclude and demobilize previously mobilized social forces from politics (especially workers and peasants and the political parties that appeal to them) by the use of force whenever necessary. These regimes thus differ from more traditional sultanistic authoritarian regimes and from fascist or Marxist-Leninist mobilizational regimes.

There is debate on whether authoritarian regimes where the military do not play a central role, such as that of Mexico, or where a military regime, such as that of Peru (1968–80), sought both to exclude and to include certain though different lower-class parties and movements, should also be called bureaucratic authoritarian. The narrower definition — which I prefer — highlights important differences between the southern South American "gang of four" and other authoritarian regimes in the hemisphere. It emphasizes their use of state violence against regime enemies, the coalition of military and certain upper-class and middle-class groups, the important role of corporate military rule, and the excluding and demobilizing features of the regime.

The emergence of these regimes as a new political phenomenon was recognized as an important empirical and theoretical step, one pioneered by the preeminent scholar in this subfield, Guillermo O'Donnell. Much fruitful debate was also devoted to a particular set of hypotheses that turned out to be incorrect, though much was learned in the process of reaching that conclusion. Relating certain political regimes and economic structures and policies, O'Donnell argued that bureaucratic authoritarian regimes had emerged in response to a structural economic crisis.[20] Countries had followed an economic development strategy of import substitution. Its earlier phases were relatively easily achieved and were associated with multiclass "populist" regimes and coalitions. With time, as this strategy became more difficult to implement, a structural economic requirement, necessitated a shift toward the deepening of industrialization, namely, the vertical integration of industrial production to include the manufacture not only of finished consumer products but also of the intermediate and capital goods needed to produce a wide array of products. Bureaucratic authoritarian regimes were installed in response, in part, to such a structural economic crisis in order to institute the new deepening strategy.[21] O'Donnell's argument included other factors such as the role of populist parties and the appearance of technocrats to explain the emergence and change of bureaucratic authoritarian regimes. His most novel contribution, however, has been the argument just summarized about economic structure.

After a decade of research by many scholars, that hypothesis has been disconfirmed.[22] There was little industrial deepening in Chile or in Uruguay, or in Argentina in the late 1970s and early 1980s; indeed, some of what occurred in these countries deserves the label of deindustrialization, or "undeepening," or re-agrarianization.[23] The strategies in these countries — as in Brazil in the years immediately following the 1964 coup — relied more on economic austerity policies with distinct social class consequences and on an emphasis on the production and export of primary products (often nontraditional products, such as soybeans in Brazil or forestry products in Chile).[24] Contrary to what O'Donnell had argued, it is difficult to find an "elective affinity" between regime types and certain economic structural conditions and policies in the countries about which O'Donnell intended to generalize, namely, upper-income, developing South American countries (or "newly industrializing countries" in Latin America). Moreover, import-substituting strategies have been followed by a wide variety of regimes, as have export-promotion strategies in recent years. Economic strategies with a strong monetarist content and deindustrializing consequences have been featured in the 1980s not only in bureaucratic authoritarian Chile but also in competitive civilian Peru under President Fernando Belaúnde and Prime Minister Manuel Ulloa. Bureaucratic authoritarianism, in short, did emerge as a new regime type. And it proved just as unstable as other regime types in Argentina, Brazil, and Uruguay, which, by 1985, were again ruled by competitive civilian regimes. Its defining features, causes, and consequences, however, were not systematically well related to economic structures and policies.

### The Paradox of Strong States, Weak Regimes, and Weak Incumbents

States have become stronger while regimes and incumbents have shown greater weakness and instability. This paradox is rooted in a common cause: the link between economic performance and political legitimacy.

The growth of real gross domestic product (GDP) of Latin America and the Caribbean was 211 percent from 1960 to 1980; the growth of real per capita GDP was 89 percent. Real GDP increased for every country in Latin America and the Caribbean from 1960 to 1970, with the possible exception of Cuba; real per capita GDP increased for every country in that decade except for Haiti and Cuba. From 1970 to 1980, every country except Jamaica witnessed real GDP growth, and every country except Jamaica and Nicaragua experienced real per capita GDP growth.[25]

Economic growth funded the growth of the state, including the "painless" growth of military budgets. However, such growth was associated with high rates of inflation, especially in the larger countries. In 1975, ten Latin American countries had double-digit inflation rates; by 1980, sixteen Latin American countries (out of nineteen with price data) and three

English-Caribbean countries (out of four with price data) had double-digit inflation rates. In 1983, a disastrous year for economic performance in the region by any standard, Argentina and Brazil were in their third year of triple-digit inflation; the rate of inflation in Argentina had been accelerating for four consecutive years and in Brazil for five. Bolivia entered triple-digit inflation in 1982 and Peru in 1983. Mexico stayed just under that level in 1982 and 1983. Double-digit inflation remained pervasive among the rest.[26]

Inflation itself has strong redistributive consequences. Its rise is politically troublesome because it sharpens the struggle for control of resources. Survival may be at stake. Inflation introduces a destabilizing element in the more normal means of economic distribution, and may, eventually, require the imposition of harsh and unpopular austerity measures. The ones who come out ahead are those well organized to advance their interests, especially when inflationary periods are sharp, prolonged, and, at times, virtually out of control. If economic growth strengthened the state, inflation weakened the regime and the incumbent.

While good economic growth performance helped regimes and incumbents to generate legitimacy, poor performance served to undermine legitimacy. Good performance assisted the consolidation of competitive civilian regimes in Colombia, Venezuela, the Dominican Republic, and Costa Rica; the long endurance of the authoritarian civilian Mexican regime; and aspects of the consolidation of authoritarianism in Brazil after 1964, Chile in the late 1970s, and Guatemala in the 1970s. Less good performance was associated with the fall of Presidents João Goulart in Brazil in 1964 and Isabel Perón in Argentina in 1976, and also with the withdrawals from power of the military in Peru in 1980 and in Argentina in 1983. A weakening of economic performance in a democratic regime can be handled by voting the incumbents out in the next election; in Latin America, however, such economic malperformance has often led to the overthrow of the regime itself because antiregime forces have been enduringly strong, especially in the armed forces.

Economic growth became the "crutch" to provide regime

legitimacy because other means of legitimation weakened. In every enduring competitive civilian regime, major scandals have increased public skepticism and weakened public allegiance. The rise of the illegal drug economy with political connections in Colombia, the investigations for corruption of Presidents Carlos Andrés Pérez in Venezuela and Rodrigo Carazo in Costa Rica (once they were out of power), and allegations of corruption in the Dominican Republic (ending in the suicide of President Antonio Guzmán) weakened the bases of democratic legitimacy.

The authoritarian regimes have to rely even more on economic growth performance for legitimation because they lack the legitimating contributions of elections and other forms of open competition. Their task may be easier, however, because they require mainly obedience from the society and active support only from a narrow elite. Nonetheless, these regimes, too, have been vulnerable to charges of corruption for personal gain. From Argentina and Chile to Honduras and Guatemala, the personal probity of military officers has been deeply and publicly questioned. The bureaucratic authoritarian regimes of southern South America and the traditional authoritarian regimes of northern Central America have also opened themselves to charges that they grossly and systematically violate human rights. In Mexico, legitimacy was weakened in the early 1980s by the combination of declining economic growth, allegations of corruption against the López Portillo Administration (including the president), and the very limited legitimating contribution of elections whose fairness is often questioned.

Ideological changes have undermined the consensus that might have provided for greater legitimacy. The military's definition of their mission has undergone various changes. In the 1960s, many in the military turned to combat internal subversion; they thought that their obligation to protect the national security required them to be concerned with wider social and economic issues. What Alfred Stepan called the "new professional" military[27] came to occupy roles and affect policies of diverse and extensive importance in economy and society. However, with the intensification of the possibility of conventional interstate conflict in the late 1970s and the experience of some interstate warfare in the early 1980s, some officers sought to return to their more traditional military roles. As a result, greater dispute and less consensus about the proper role of military institutions ensued.

There was also less consensus among businesspeople. While national businesspeople often supported bureaucratic authoritarian coups, they also characteristically opposed some of the policies of these regimes in due course. They suffered the de-industrializing consequences of the policies of such regimes in Argentina and Chile in the 1970s. In Brazil, they opposed the considerable preference for multinational firms in the 1960s, and they opposed the rise of bureaucratized state enterprises in the 1970s and 1980s. In addition, national businesspeople came to support the expropriation of foreign-owned copper in Chile, oil in Venezuela, and sulphur in Mexico. In the manufacturing sector, their relationship to foreign firms and to the state grew more complex. In the larger countries, regardless of regime type, there has been a long-term trend toward greater conflict between national and multinational business firms, and greater support by national businesspeople for policies of state selection and discrimination aimed against foreign firms. Business nationalism thus emerged as a more divisive strategy that also weakened the bases for elite consensus.[28] (A third ideological schism, which occurred within the Roman Catholic church, will be discussed in a later section.)

The erosion of the bases of legitimacy other than economic growth, and the intensification of redistributional struggles as a result of accelerated and persistently high inflation, have weakened regimes and incumbents while continued economic growth strengthened states. Regimes and incumbents were also helped by economic growth while it lasted; regimes were strengthened at a cost to incumbents by the use of procedures such as the fixed-term, nonrenewable presidency. States, regimes, and incumbents were all weakened, however, by the economic depression of the early 1980s, of which the foreign debt problem is but one aspect.

Two concluding empirical observations are in order. First,

scholars mistakenly interpreted the rise of authoritarian regimes in the 1960s and early 1970s as an enduring shift of regime rather than as one more example of a pattern of political instability. The form and intentions of the new authoritarian regimes were different but that did not mean they would endure longer. Douglas Chalmers may have come closest to an early accurate diagnosis. Even in the heyday of bureaucratic authoritarianism, he was skeptical that these regimes would become permanent: "The enduring quality of Latin American politics in this century may not be a particular form of regime, but rather the fact of change . . . in any regime which has only a short history and the prospect of a brief future."[29]

A second observation points to a "herd effect," or waves of regime changes in Latin American countries (of course, with a great many exceptions throughout). Many of the more traditional political systems collapsed around 1930; a generalized democratic opening ensued in the late 1940s, soon interrupted, but later followed by another democratic opening at the end of the 1950s, with an authoritarian wave from the mid-1960s to about 1973. The most recent change away from authoritarian military regimes began in the late 1970s and has yet to run its course. The herd effect may reflect the impact of international relations on internal affairs.

Latin American military leaders communicate with one another; they often know one another personally as a result of common education in international (often U.S.) schools and formally joint military responsibilities.[30] Latin America's Communist parties have often cooperated since the 1920s; non-Communist parties have done so beginning at least as far back as the collaboration among APRA (Peru), Acción Democrática (Venezuela), and Liberación Nacional (Costa Rica) in the 1940s. Joint work today is reflected more formally in international federations of kindred Communist, Social Democratic, or Christian Democratic parties. Parties have helped one another in the periods of democratic transition in the late 1940s and late 1950s and since the late 1970s.

The most important international effects, however, reflect economic circumstances and U.S. policy. The collapse of the world economy in large part explains the herd effect in 1930, and it played an important role in the rather different herd effect in the late 1970s and early 1980s when several military regimes abandoned power during the world economic troubles. Changes in U.S. policy have been associated with most of the changes since the Second World War: democracy's victory in that war, followed by the Cold War alliance with the military, an openness to democratic regimes in the late 1950s, and a concern with insurgent radicalism from the mid-1960s through the early 1970s, which was replaced with a new concern with promoting human rights and democracy.

One should not, however, exaggerate the herd effect. For example, despite prevalent international factors, the events of the first half of the 1980s are difficult to explain. Latin America has suffered the worst economic shock since the Great Depression of the 1930s. The Reagan Administration in the United States entered office in 1981 with a clear rationale for tolerating and working with authoritarian regimes.[31] And yet no competitive civilian regime was overthrown in Latin America between 1980 and 1986 while Bolivia, Honduras, Argentina, Uruguay, Brazil, and, less clearly, Panama, El Salvador, and Guatemala made transitions away from military rule. It may be that the U.S. impact on the larger Latin American countries has continued to decline so that this feature of the herd effect is less influential (a Reagan Administration policy change in 1984 helped the subsequent transitions in El Salvador and Guatemala). It may also be that the armed forces are too reluctant to intervene when economic conditions are so dire.

If regimes and incumbents have, indeed, weakened as economic performance and legitimacy have eroded, if competition for resources has intensified, and if the likelihood of military coups in the first half of the 1980s has lessened as growth fell and inflation rose, the military have become reluctant to rule and as the inability of the United States to shape events in the large countries has become increasingly apparent, then the process in the early 1980s is not a transition "to" democracy. It is a transition "from" the past to an uncertain future for less governable societies.

## POLITICAL REGIMES AND ECONOMIC STRUCTURE
## AND POLICIES

The rejection of the O'Donnell hypotheses concerning the link between certain political regimes and certain economic structures and policies left the field with few useful hypotheses to take their place. Authoritarian regimes do not necessarily have an edge in the promotion of economic growth in Latin America. Consider the changes in per capita GDP in 1980 constant dollars from 1960 to 1980. Authoritarian Brazil led Latin America with an increase of 137 percent. Two non-oil producers with more competitive civilian regimes, however, also did very well. Colombia's growth rate was 92.5 percent, and Costa Rica's was 83.5 percent. Countries governed by military authoritarian regimes for most of those decades grew less: Guatemala grew by 66 percent; Peru, by 36 percent; and Argentina, by 41 percent. Among major oil producers, competitive civilian Venezuela grew by 49 percent while authoritarian civilian Mexico grew by 105 percent. Regimes of various types, therefore, presided over and stimulated considerable real per capita economic growth, but no one type of regime had an advantage or a disadvantage over the rest.[32]

What can be observed across countries can also be observed within them. Argentina's economy performed well under the civilian government of Radical party President Arturo Illia in the mid-1960s as well as under military rule in the late 1970s; Argentina also experienced a disastrous economic downturn under the Perón family's governments (1973–76) and under the military authoritarian governments in the early 1980s. Peru endured very difficult economic circumstances in both the late 1970s and the early 1980s under military and civilian rule, respectively. Over the long run, Brazil has been able to generate growth as well as occasional serious economic crises under both civilian and authoritarian regimes (in the early 1960s and early 1980s).[33]

Moreover, there is in Latin America a lack of association between regime type and level of economic development, apart from the performance of economic growth. Let us focus on level of per capita gross domestic product in 1980 constant dollars.[34] In 1960, Argentina, Chile, Uruguay, and Venezuela were the only four countries with a per capita GDP level above $1,000. Only Venezuela retained a democratic regime during the next twenty-five years. By the mid-1980s, Argentina and Uruguay had regained civilian rule. Other Latin American countries with per capita gross domestic products above $1,000 in the early 1980s were Brazil, Costa Rica, Ecuador, Guatemala, Mexico, Panama, Paraguay, and Peru. A long-standing democratic regime remained in power in Costa Rica, as did a long-standing personalist dictatorship in Paraguay and an equally long-standing "soft" authoritarian regime in Mexico; Brazil was engaged in its slow shift toward civilian rule while Ecuador stayed under civilian rule through the early 1980s; Panama had edged toward more civilian rule with a strong military veto while the impact of Guatemala's military on politics first rose, then ebbed. The politics of the wealthier countries did not show an enduring or common pattern.

Consider the problem from the other end of the income scale: those countries with a per capita GDP below $1,000 in 1980. To be sure, Haiti's sultanistic political system was at the bottom, followed by Bolivia (at this writing under civilian rule, but marked typically by short-lived governments), followed by Honduras under weakly institutionalized civilian rule, then El Salvador in civil war, revolutionary Nicaragua, long-standing civilian rule in Colombia, and a consolidated democracy in the Dominican Republic. The poorer countries show also, therefore, a wide array of regime types, joined by only one characteristic: weak stability, though no weaker than wealthier Argentina.

Ask the question in yet another way: Which were the only stable democracies from 1960 to the mid-1980s and what was their income level? They were remarkably the same throughout the period: Venezuela, at the top of the scale; Costa Rica, at about the median; and Colombia, well below the median.

It is virtually impossible to argue that democracy or authoritarianism in Latin America is consistently associated with a given economic development level if one considers not just a single point in time but a longer time span. What appeared to be a shift toward authoritarianism after 1960 looked like a transition to democracy twenty-five years later. In fact, it may be a transition to neither — it may reflect, instead, the inability of any regime type to endure. Nor are such generalizations more credible in the English-speaking Caribbean, where civilian rule (generally democratic) has prevailed except in Grenada.

Some generalizations are possible, however. Economic stabilization policies are more likely to be implemented effectively under authoritarian than under democratic regimes, as in Argentina, Brazil, Chile, and Uruguay. Some reduction of political competition appears to be associated with the more thoroughly implemented and effective stabilization plans.[35] However, authoritarian regimes do not invariably effect more "prudent" economic management. The propensity to international indebtedness in Latin America in the 1970s was nearly universal: in authoritarian Brazil and Chile as in competitive Venezuela and Costa Rica. Nor can authoritarian regimes provide immunity against runaway inflation. Brazil's authoritarian regime of the 1960s brought inflation down, but the level of inflation rose again steadily through the 1970s and into the 1980s. The same pattern, though with even less success, marked Argentina's authoritarian governments of the late 1970s and early 1980s. The only authoritarian regime that brought down the inflation rate, at great cost, and kept it under control was that of Chile.

Another useful generalization is that strong government efforts toward economic redistribution intended to benefit the lower class exact a heavy toll by reducing the economic growth rate in the medium run.[36] Military reformism in Peru in the 1970s was also associated with an economic growth rate, noted earlier, much lower than that of hardly reformist Colombia.[37] Jamaica's Prime Minister Michael Manley introduced important reforms in his mineral-rich country throughout the 1970s, while Barbados's Prime Minister Tom Adams was a more conservative economic manager in his mineral-poor country. Both countries, however, were hurt by the oil shocks of the decade. Barbados managed a real per capita growth of GDP 11 percent from 1970 to 1980; Jamaica's fell 16 percent during that same decade.[38] Revolutionary Cuba remains the region's best long-term example of the link between strong performance on economic redistribution to benefit the lower classes and poor performance on generating sustained economic growth.[39]

If left-wing reformism is associated with weak economic growth, bureaucratic authoritarianism appears especially vulnerable to a crisis in the international capitalist economy. For example, from 1981 to 1983, real per capita GDP fell by 9.5 percent in Latin America. The better performers were the three countries that had positive growth rates during those years: competitive civilian Dominican Republic; politically opening, mixed civilian-military regime Panama; and revolutionary Cuba. The relatively good performers (though they had negative growth rates) included competitive civilian Colombia and Ecuador, revolutionary Nicaragua, mildly authoritarian Mexico, and the traditional dictatorships of Haiti and Paraguay. However, all the bureaucratic authoritarian regimes were among the worst performers (as were all Central American regimes except Nicaragua). The single worst one-year disaster occurred in Augusto Pinochet's Chile in 1982 with a one-year drop of 15.8 percent.[40] Right-wing regimes have been more likely to seek to increase their country's participation in the international economy (more exports, more foreign direct investment) and simultaneously less likely to adopt protectionist or subsidy policies to shield the population from the swings of the world market.

Revolutionary regimes in Latin America (Cuba, Nicaragua) are not necessarily marked by negative growth rates but by relatively little variation in the size of gross domestic product: they neither grow nor decline much as they redistribute resources. Competitive regimes may have built in more insulation between their economies and the international market. Democratic competition may force them to adopt some protectionist or subsidy policies that shield their societies somewhat from international market swings. The only large economy governed by a civilian regime that experienced a very sharp drop in these years was that of Peru; the Belaúnde-Ulloa Administration was also the only civilian regime to systematically dismantle many protectionist and subsidy policies that had insulated the economy from international market forces in previous years.

In short, there are no discernible differences in the likelihood of economic growth between authoritarian and competitive civilian regimes, although left-wing reformist regimes are likely to grow less but redistribute more. Authoritarian regimes are more likely to implement effective economic stabilization policies, but they are just as likely as competitive civilian regimes to pursue policies that require the eventual imposition of such economic austerity. Right-wing authoritarian regimes appear more vulnerable than either left-wing authoritarian regimes or competitive civilian regimes to severe international market crises. Finally, there is no difference by regime type in the likelihood of pursuing import substitution, industrial deepening, or various export-promotion strategies, nor is there a clear association between regime type and level of economic development in Latin America and the Caribbean. Twenty-five years of scholarly research have ended with a great deal less certainty on these matters than they began.

## SOCIETIES

Research on Latin America during the past quarter century emphasized work on states, regimes, and economic performance, as emphasized in this essay. The societies themselves, however, changed rapidly, in part as a result of economic growth. By 1980, in one measure alone, life expectancy at birth surpassed sixty years throughout South America (except in Peru — fifty-eight years), and it surpassed fifty-three years throughout all Latin America. The median increase in life expectancy at birth from 1960 to 1980 for the twenty Latin American countries was ten years; all but two (Argentina and Uruguay, with life expectancies already over seventy years) increased by at least seven years in that period.[41]

Among political scientists one research topic was addressed infrequently: most continue to write about Latin America as if the societies were ethnically and linguistically homogeneous, with little discussion of the social and political importance of language, color, and race.[42] Most Latin American countries, however, are ethnically heterogeneous; several are linguistically heterogeneous to a substantial extent.[43] According to a venerable hypothesis on comparative politics, processes of social mobilization are expected to strain, perhaps break, the politics of societies that were already heterogeneous while they would consolidate the politics of societies that were already homogeneous along these criteria.[44] Latin American countries, by and large, have not experienced mass-based political movements and parties above the local level that have a predominantly ethnic or linguistic character (with limited exceptions). While this could mean that the hypothesis is incorrect, it is more likely, instead, that Latin American countries have had a culture, a grand tradition, that has institutionalized ethnic subordination, the consolidation of which was helped by social mobilization.[45]

The English- and Dutch-speaking Caribbean, in contrast, resembled the rest of the world more because ethnicity, language, and religion matter enormously for the strength of political parties and movements.[46] The ethnic politics of Guyana, Trinidad-Tobago, or Suriname are comprehensible to a scholar of Africa, Asia, Canada, Belgium, or the Netherlands. Both Guyana and Trinidad-Tobago have been governed by the same ethnic-based political party since independence, although the fairness of Guyana's elections has become increasingly doubtful; both went through a peaceful transition of power upon the death of Eric Williams in Trinidad-Tobago and of Forbes Burnham in Guyana, who had governed uninterruptedly since independence.

The story of Suriname is more tragic. Suriname is a deeply segmented society whose peoples come from the Netherlands and other European countries, Africa, the South Asian subcontinent, and Indonesia, as well as Amerindian descendants. They have different languages, cultural traditions, and religious beliefs. Under Dutch rule, a self-governing system that included some of the Netherlands's provisions for what has been called consociational democracy was tried out with some effectiveness.[47] However, civilian rule lasted but a short time after independence; the country's experience in the 1980s has been marked by rank praetorianism and abuse of power.

In the 1950s, some students of modernization expected

religion to become much less significant as societies became secularized; others disputed this forecast, and they proved closer to the mark. Religion has become more important, not less, in Latin America during the past twenty-five years.[48] The Roman Catholic church, the region's most important, has undergone worldwide changes since the Second Vatican Council, with repercussions in the Americas. Roman Catholicism is now a more clearly articulated global, hemispheric, as well as national religion. Bishops, clergy, and some laity now communicate regularly and exchange experiences. National episcopal hierarchies have become better organized and better staffed: the church, too, became modernized. Christian Democratic parties, with varying ties to Roman Catholicism, came to power in Chile, El Salvador, Guatemala and Venezuela beginning in the 1960s.[49]

Important religious changes have also occurred somewhat independently from ecclesiastical authorities. In some countries, a process of religious reconversion has taken place — that is, nominal Roman Catholics have thought afresh about what it means to be a religious person faithful to some transcendental ideas. They have reaffirmed and strengthened their religious beliefs, unleashing psychological, social, and political energies. Whether within the context of the new "basic Christian communities" or more traditional forms of promoting religious experiences, the new fidelity to ideas concerning the transcendental has stimulated such reconversion, most dramatically in Brazil,[50] Chile,[51] and Nicaragua.[52] In some countries, a part of Roman Catholicism has become a "sect" whose members are deeply committed to the total religious, social, and political experience of being a Christian. Conservative Catholics, organized in the often-powerful societies for Tradition, Family, and Property, have resisted these trends. Religion has thus become more important to the society, at times even in opposition to the state or to the bishops. Modernity, divisiveness, and reconversion are the themes of Latin America's contemporary Roman Catholicism, which have made for the ideological schism that has also weakened regime legitimacy.

Substantial changes have occurred as well in the labor movement, often in response to the rise of authoritarian regimes. At their origin, many Latin American labor movements relied on political connections to gain benefits for labor. Political bargaining would serve the working class. But the emergence of repressive, exclusionary authoritarian regimes made this strategy less fruitful in some countries. The defense of labor rights then took several paths. In less authoritarian or in competitive systems, labor federations proliferated following the weakening of the power of the former top labor federation. This happened in Mexico,[53] Peru,[54] and Colombia.[55] At times, new unions or federations were created by the government to weaken preexisting labor federations. This happened clearly in Peru and, more subtly, in Mexico. Some new unions, however, were fairly independent of governments.

Another path was the greater reliance on collective bargaining. Because the state, especially in authoritarian regimes, could no longer be trusted to be labor's friend, labor unions had to make sure that they confronted the employer, and only the employer, over "bread and butter" issues. Collective bargaining led to strikes that ran less risk of involving the police or the labor ministry, that relied less on violence, but that also relied more on the mutual exhaustion of management and labor by being quite long. It is too soon to tell whether the passing of authoritarian regimes in several countries since the end of the 1970s might mean a return to political bargaining, although it is likely that the arsenal of collective bargaining techniques will remain in use.[56]

While insurgencies were common in most Latin American countries in the 1960s, none won in South America, Mexico, or the Latin Caribbean after the Cuban revolution. A revolutionary government ruled Grenada from 1979 to 1983, until overthrown by U.S. troops aided by six English-speaking Caribbean countries. The Latin American societies most shaken by revolutionary upheavals are those in northern Central America. There, as in the successor states of the Portuguese empire and in white southern Africa, contemporary revolutions have developed where a strong "alien" or "foreign" presence exists. These revolutions emerged from the guts of each society.

The Somoza family's rule in Nicaragua was ended by a national mutiny in which business, labor, the churches, and the guerrilla forces united to topple the regime. Pedro Joaquín Chamorro, a conservative publisher, and Carlos Fonseca Amador, the founder of the Sandinista revolutionary movement, are heroes of the same process that overthrew the continent's most long-lived dynasty. The Somoza family government had centralized, expanded, and made autonomous its power in Nicaragua and stimulated considerable economic growth, especially during the 1960s. These trends, in turn, modernized Nicaragua enough to make revolution — and eventually revolutionary rule — possible.[57]

The revolutionary situations of Guatemala and El Salvador are less clearly defined than that of Nicaragua.[58] However, Guatemala has witnessed a revolutionary war in which, for the first time in this century, indigenous peoples have taken up arms against the state. El Salvador's revolutionary upheaval has entailed thus far more the fragmentation of authority in the most significant social sectors than the agglutination of enough power to ensure one side's victory.[59]

Revolutions, however, are only one, infrequent form of political participation. Political participation in Latin America has become multifaceted and substantial. Patterns of participation in Latin American countries are comparable to those elsewhere in the world, including industrial countries. National political participation has increased in recent years. Elections, when they are held, show very high rates of electoral turnout (much higher than in the United States), with the persisting exception of Colombia. There is extensive involvement in the public life of political parties and in election campaigns, especially in Costa Rica and Venezuela, and in Uruguay and Chile before the 1973 coups. There is also much political activism in small community settings as well as the particularistic contacting of public officials. Moreover, the correlation between political participation and socioeconomic status is not uniform. Upper-class participants tend to predominate in national politics while lower-class participants often predominate in community activism. The opportunities for political participation, therefore, have become considerable under competitive civilian regimes, while they remain certainly more limited but not negligible under authoritarian regimes.[60]

State-directed political participation has been tried in various Latin American countries, but only Cuba has succeeded in implementing thoroughly a wide array of controlled political participatory activities. The Cuban government and the Communist party sponsor mass organizations that are organized territorially (committees for the Defense of the Revolution, by neighborhoods) and functionally (labor unions, the women's federation, the peasants' federation, etc.). These organizations facilitate policy implementation, build support for the regime, and have, over time, also become sources of societal influence on state and party. While the latter trend remains quite modest, it is strongest for the peasants' association. In the mid-1970s, the Cuban government also permitted the expression of complaints in an organized manner at the municipal level over the quality of goods and services, amounting to a government-sponsored policy of citizen contacting. This policy has improved the quality of public services in Cuba. More generally, the changes in Cuban politics in the 1970s amounted to the institutionalization of authoritarian rule, reducing arbitrariness and ensuring a respect for existing laws, but also guaranteeing the supremacy of the leadership of party and government.[61]

Finally, research on the political consequences of migration has laid to rest the view that the very experience of migration would lead to violent participatory explosions by the migrants.[62] On the whole, the experience of migration to the cities satisfied some needs and aspirations of the migrants;[63] their political behavior was at times conservative or at least not politically destabilizing; they often worked with political machines, whether in Mexico City, Lima, or Caracas.

Recent migration has also been strongly international. Refugees have come from Cuba and from the wars in northern Central America, and economic migrants have come from Mexico and the rest of the Caribbean to the United States. International migration also pulled citizens of neighboring countries into Argentina and Venezuela; Guatemalan refugees have streamed into Mexico. One key question for host societies about national and international migrants is the nature of their new political experiences. And one key consequence, in the cases of international migrants from Cuba and from Haiti (1957–86), was the consolidation of the political systems they left behind through the export of the opposition.[64]

## CONCLUSION

By the mid-1980s, Latin America differed from some predictions scholars had made. The economies grew and diversified considerably from 1960 to 1980; the living standards of many have improved; life expectancies have lengthened. The argument that Latin America had been witnessing the "development of underdevelopment" is wrong.[65] However, the argument that "the more well-to-do a nation, the greater the chances that it will sustain democracy" is also insufficient.[66] On a worldwide canvas, there does appear to be a correlation between democracy and very high levels of economic development for market-economy countries. But the relationship is indeterminate for middle-income developing countries such as those of Latin America and East Asia. They are in what Samuel Huntington has called a "zone of choice" about how to organize political regimes: "What is predictable for these countries ... is not the advent of democracy but rather the demise of previously existing political forms."[67]

In short, changes in religion, in labor unions, in peaceful forms of political participation, and in migration patterns changed the politics of these societies the most, while ethnic stratifications remained, as in the past, most resistant to change. And revolution occured only by exception. Most of these changes worked to disperse rather than to concentrate power. Along with weaker regimes and incumbents, these societal changes make more difficult the governing of these countries — except through sustained, and still rare efforts, for those who rule in the name of the people to obtain the consent of the governed.

The level of growth of Latin American economies has not been associated with democracy. It is also remarkable that competitive civilian regimes have endured in the Caribbean, on the basis of political norms that have weathered economic decline in Jamaica and poor economic performance everywhere in the 1970s, and that civilian regimes have returned to some South American countries in the midst of economic crisis in the early 1980s. Democracy survives in Latin America and the Caribbean despite the poor economic performance of that time.

Revolutions have not broken out as often as some hoped and others feared around 1960, but neither have economic reform and the reduction of inequalities made appreciable progress. Latin American states proved to be much less meekly dependent on the U.S. government or on multinational firms than some thought, but they have remained extraordinarily vulnerable to the fate of the international economy. That, of course, makes them just like everybody else, although the form of Latin America's vulnerability in the mid-1980s — high financial debt and economic depression — sets it apart from other regions of the world.

The main story in South America and the English-speaking Caribbean has been fairly straightforward: states and economies have grown while political regimes have behaved as they had before: in stable, competitive civilian fashion in the English-speaking Caribbean and in unstable, weakened fashion in most of South America. This broad pattern, of course, obscures some important individual changes. Stable civilian rule was consolidated in Venezuela and in Colombia in the early 1960s, breaking with the past. Similarly, the establishment of bureaucratic authoritarian regimes in Chile and Uruguay in the early 1970s was a break with earlier civilian traditions, while Paraguay remained under the same ruler throughout and Grenada was under revolutionary rule for four years.

Northern Latin America was less easily characterized. Authoritarian regimes of very different types long ruled in Haiti (until 1986) and Cuba, and continued in Mexico. A stable civilian regime endured in Costa Rica, while Panama and Honduras retained a pattern of unstable politics. The most dramatic changes occurred in Nicaragua, which experienced a successful revolution; El Salvador and Guatemala, which experienced the collapse of the old order without the clear emergence of a new one; and the Dominican Republic, which shifted away from the politics of dictatorship and of chaos toward competitive civilian rule.

Changes of pattern were thus least likely in the English-speaking Caribbean and most likely in Central America and the Latin Caribbean, with South America in the somewhat odd circumstances that it was stable in its instability. Everywhere, however, states sought to govern more, had more resources to do so, and found it more difficult to govern effectively. What many state elites still lacked was wisdom.

In the mid-1980s, the region's future was uncertain not only because the deteriorating economic situation had a disastrous impact, but also because many of the leaders who had structured politics for so long died in a brief interval of years in the late 1970s and early 1980s: Juan Perón and Ricardo Balbín in Argentina, Víctor Raúl Haya de la Torre in Peru, Eduardo Frei in Chile, Omar Torrijos in Panama, Rómulo Betancourt in Venezuela, José María Velasco Ibarra in Ecuador. If these deaths create uncertainty, however, they also make hope possible. The rise to the presidency of Raúl Alfonsín in Argentina or Alan García leading APRA in Peru was made easier by the deaths of long-standing leaders in their countries. Throughout the hemisphere, moreover, the armed forces had lost the political confidence that had propelled them to power two decades earlier. The future was troubling because the dawn of a new era was not yet at hand, but it was hopeful because the leaders and social forces that might hasten it began to appear.

## NOTES

1. South America includes nine Spanish-speaking countries, plus Brazil. Central America includes six mostly Spanish-speaking countries from Panama to Guatemala. The Caribbean includes all the islands, plus Guyana, Suriname, French Guiana, and Belize. Latin America includes Central and South America, plus Mexico, Cuba, Haiti, and the Dominican Republic.

2. For another recent, thorough (though brief) overview, see Gilbert W. Merkx, "Social Structure and Social Change in Twentieth-Century Latin America," in Jan Knippers Black, ed., *Latin*

*America, Its Problems, and Its Promise: A Multidisciplinary Approach* (Boulder, Colo.: Westview Press, 1984), 145–58.

3.  For a discussion of the state's growth in Brazil, see Werner Baer, *The Brazilian Economy: Its Growth and Development* (Columbus, Ohio: Grid Publishing, 1979); Robert T. Daland, *Exploring Brazilian Bureaucracy: Performance and Pathology* (Washington, D.C.: University Press of America, 1981).

4.  Frederick Pike and Thomas Stritch, eds., *The New Corporatism: Social-Political Structures in the Iberian World* (Notre Dame, Ind.: University of Notre Dame, 1974); Howard, J. Wiarda, *Corporatism and National Development in Latin America* (Boulder, Colo.: Westview Press, 1981).

5.  James M. Malloy, ed., *Authoritarianism and Corporatism in Latin America* (Pittsburgh, Penna.: University of Pittsburgh Press, 1977).

6.  Theodore H. Moran, *Multinational Corporations and the Politics of Dependence: Copper in Chile* (Princeton, N.J.: Princeton University Press, 1974).

7.  Franklin Tugwell, *The Politics of Oil in Venezuela* (Stanford, Calif.: Stanford University Press, 1975); Gustavo Coronel, *The Nationalization of the Venezuelan Oil Industry* (Lexington, Mass.: Lexington Books, 1983).

8.  Werner Baer and Malcolm Gillis, eds., *Export Diversification and the New Protectionism: The Experience of Latin America* (Urbana, Ill.: National Bureau of Economic Research and Bureau of Economic and Business Research, University of Illinois, 1981).

9.  Jorge I. Domínguez, "Assessing Human Rights Conditions," in Jorge I. Domínguez et al., *Enhancing Global Human Rights*, (New York: McGraw-Hill, 1979), especially 93–102.

10.  Richard Gott, *Guerrilla Movements in Latin America* (Garden City, N.Y.: Anchor Books, 1972).

11.  For a good analysis and constructive suggestions, see Michael A. Morris and Víctor Millán, eds., *Controlling Latin American Conflicts* (Boulder, Colo.: Westview Press, 1983).

12.  U.S. Arms Control and Disarmament Agency, *World Military Expenditures and Arms Transfers* (Washington, D.C., various years).

13.  Jorge I. Domínguez, *Cuba: Order and Revolution* (Cambridge, Mass.: Harvard University Press, 1978); Jorge I. Domínguez, ed., *Cuba: Internal and International Affairs* (Beverly Hills, Calif.: Sage, 1982).

14.  Alfred Stepan, *The State and Society: Peru in Comparative Per-*

*spective* (Princeton, N.J.: Princeton University Press, 1978); Peter Evans, *Dependent Development: The Alliance of Multinational, State, and Local Capital in Brazil* (Princeton, N.J.: Princeton University Press, 1979).

15.  Alejandro Foxley, *Latin American Experiments in Neoconservative Economics* (Berkeley: University of California Press, 1983).

16.  Abraham F. Lowenthal, ed., *Armies and Politics in Latin America* (New York: Holmes & Meier, 1976).

17.  Virginia R. Domínguez and Jorge I. Domínguez, *The Caribbean: Its Implications for the United States,* Headline Series, no. 253 (New York: Foreign Policy Association, 1981).

18.  Peter H. Smith, *Labyrinths of Power: Political Recruitment in Twentieth-Century Mexico* (Princeton, N.J.: Princeton University Press, 1979).

19.  David Collier, ed., *The New Authoritarianism in Latin America* (Princeton, N.J.: Princeton University Press, 1979), 399; see also 24.

20.  Guillermo A. O'Donnell, *Modernization and Bureaucratic-Authoritarianism: Studies in South American Politics,* Politics of Modernization Series, no. 9 (Berkeley: Institute of International Studies, University of California, 1973).

21.  See also Guillermo O'Donnell, "Reflections on the Pattern of Change in the Bureaucratic-Authoritarian State," *Latin American Research Review* 13, no. 1 (1978):3–38.

22.  The most comprehensive empirical critique has been done by Robert R. Kaufman, "Industrial Change and Authoritarian Rule in Latin America: A Concrete Review of the Bureaucratic-Authoritarian Model," in Collier, *New Authoritarianism,* 165–253.

23.  Two other critiques appear in Collier, *New Authoritarianism*: José Serra, "Three Mistaken Theses Regarding the Connection between Industrialization and Authoritarian Regimes," 99–163, and David Collier, "The Bureaucratic-Authoritarian Model: Synthesis and Priorities for Future Research," 362–97.

24.  For an excellent critique of O'Donnell's arguments about those regimes after their installation, see Karen L. Remmer and Gilbert W. Merkx, "Bureaucratic-Authoritarianism Revisited," *Latin American Research Review* 17, no. 2 (1982):3–40.

25.  Inter-American Development Bank, *Economic and Social Progress in Latin America: Natural Resources, 1983 Report* (Washington, D.C., 1983), 345.

26.  U.N. Economic Commission for Latin America, *Preliminary Ov-*

erview of the Latin American Economy during 1983, E/CEPAL/ G.1279 (New York, 1983), 27.

27. Alfred Stepan, "The New Professionalism of Internal Warfare and Military Role Expansion," in *Authoritarian Brazil: Origins, Policies, and Future*, edited by Alfred Stepan (New Haven, Conn.: Yale University Press, 1973), 47–651.

28. Jorge I. Domínguez, "Business Nationalism: Latin American National Business Attitudes and Behavior toward Multinational Enterprises," in *Economic Issues and Political Conflict: U.S.–Latin American Relations*, edited by Jorge I. Domínguez. (London: Butterworth, 1982), 16–68.

29. Douglas A. Chalmers, "The Politicized State in Latin America," in Malloy, *Authoritarianism and Corporatism*, 23.

30. John Child, *Unequal Alliance: The Inter-American Military System, 1938–1978* (Boulder, Colo.: Westview Press, 1980).

31. Jeane Kirkpatrick, "Dictatorships and Double Standards," *Commentary* 68, no. 5 (November 1979):34–45.

32. Computed from Inter-American Development Bank, *Economic and Social Progress in Latin America, 1983*, 345.

33. For a related discussion, see William Ascher, *Scheming for the Poor: The Politics of Redistribution in Latin America* (Cambridge, Mass.: Harvard University Press, 1984).

34. Inter-American Development Bank, *Economic and Social Progress in Latin America, 1983*, 345.

35. Thomas E. Skidmore, "The Politics of Economic Stabilization in Postwar Latin America," in Malloy, *Authoritarianism and Corporatism*, 149–90.

36. For a general discussion, see Montek Ahluwalia, Nicholas Carter, and Hollis Chenery, *Growth and Poverty in Developing Countries*, Staff Working Paper, no. 309 (Washington, D.C.: World Bank, 1978).

37. Richard C. Webb, *Government Policy and the Distribution of Income in Peru, 1963–1973* (Cambridge, Mass.: Harvard University Press, 1977).

38. Computed from Inter-American Development Bank, *Economic and Social Progress in Latin America, 1983*, 345.

39. Carmelo Mesa-Lago, *The Economy of Socialist Cuba: A Two-Decade Appraisal* (Albuquerque: University of New Mexico Press, 1981).

40. U.N. Economic Commission for Latin America, *Preliminary Overview, 1983*, 25.

41. World Bank, *World Development Report, 1982* (New York: Oxford University Press, 1982), 150–51.

42. Pierre Michel Fontaine, "Research in the Political Economy of Afro-Latin America," *Latin American Research Review* 15, no. 2 (1980):111–41; Leslie B. Rout, Jr., *The African Experience in Spanish America* (London: Cambridge University Press, 1976).

43. For example, on Mexico, see Shirley Brice Heath, *Telling Tongues: Language Policy in Mexico* (New York: Teachers College Press, 1972).

44. Karl W. Deutsch, "Social Mobilization and Political Development," *American Political Science Review* 55, no. 3 (September 1961):493–514.

45. Samuel P. Huntington and Jorge I. Domínguez, "Political Development," in *Handbook of Political Science*, edited by Fred I. Greenstein and Nelson W. Polsby, vol. 3: *Macropolitical Theory* (Reading, Mass.: Addison-Wesley, 1975), 1–114, especially 68–73.

46. M. G. Smith, *The Plural Society in the British West Indies* (Berkeley: University of California Press, 1965).

47. Arend Lijphart, *Democracy in Plural Societies: A Comparative Exploration* (New Haven, Conn.: Yale University Press, 1977), 201–2, 216–22.

48. A seminal work was Ivan Vallier's *Catholicism, Social Control and Modernization in Latin America* (Englewood Cliffs, N.J.: Prentice-Hall, 1970).

49. Daniel Levine, ed., *Churches and Politics in Latin America* (Beverly Hills, Calif.: Sage, 1980); Daniel Levine, *Religion and Politics in Latin America* (Princeton, N.J.: Princeton University Press, 1981).

50. Thomas C. Bruneau, *The Political Transformation of the Brazilian Catholic Church* (Cambridge: Cambridge University Press, 1974); Ralph Della Cava, "Catholicism and Society in Twentieth-Century Brazil," *Latin American Research Review* 11, no. 2 (1976):7–50.

51. Brian Smith, *The Church and Politics in Chile* (Princeton, N.J.: Princeton University Press, 1982).

52. Michael Dodson and Tommie Sue Montgomery, "The Churches in the Nicaraguan Revolution," in *Nicaragua in Revolution*, edited by Thomas W. Walker (New York: Praeger, 1982).

53. Manuel Camacho, "Control sobre el movimiento obrero en México," *Foro internacional* 16, no. 4 (April–June 1976):496–525.

54. Denis Sulmont, "Conflictos laborales y movilización popular:

Perú 1968–1976," *Revista mexicana de sociología* 40, no. 2 (April–June 1978):685–725.

55. Miguel Urrutia, *The Development of the Colombian Labor Movement* (New Haven, Conn.: Yale University Press, 1969).

56. Francisco Zapata, "Las relaciones entre la Junta Militar y los trabajadores chilenos: 1973–1978," *Foro internacional* 20, no. 2 (October–December 1979):191–219; Elizabeth Jelin, "Conflictos laborales en la Argentina, 1973–1976," *Revista mexicana de sociología* 40, no. 2 (April–June 1978):421–57.

57. John A. Booth, *The End and the Beginning: The Nicaraguan Revolution* (Boulder, Colo.: Westview Press, 1982); Walker, *Nicaragua in Revolution.*

58. Donald Castillo Rivas, ed., *Centroamérica: más allá de la crisis* (Mexico: Ediciones SIAP, 1983); Centro de Estudios Internacionales, *Centroamérica en crisis* (Mexico: El Colegio de México, 1980).

59. Enrique Baloyra, *El Salvador in Transition* (Chapel Hill: University of North Carolina Press, 1982); Tommie Sue Montgomery, *Revolution in El Salvador* (Boulder, Colo.: Westview Press, 1982).

60. The best work is in the two-volume study by John A. Booth and Mitchell A. Seligson, *Political Participation in Latin America* (New York: Holmes & Meier). Volume 1 is *Citizen and State* (1978); Volume 2 is *Politics and the Poor* (1979).

61. Domínguez, *Cuba: Order and Revolution;* Domínguez, *Cuba: Internal and International Affairs.*

62. Wayne Cornelius, "The Political Sociology of Cityward Migration in Latin America: Toward Empirical Theory," in *Latin American Urban Research,* vol. 1, edited by Francine F. Rabinowitz and Felicity M. Trueblood (Beverly Hills, Calif.: Sage, 1971).

63. Thomas Merrick and Douglas Graham, *Population and Economic Development in Brazil, 1800 to the Present* (Baltimore, Md.: Johns Hopkins University Press, 1979).

64. Virginia R. Domínguez, *From Neighbor to Stranger: The Dilemma of Caribbean Peoples in the United States* (New Haven, Conn.: Antilles Research Program, Yale University, 1975).

65. André Gunder Frank, *Capitalism and Underdevelopment in Latin America: Historical Studies in Chile and Brazil* (New York: Monthly eview Press, 1967).

66. Seymour Martin Lipset, *Political Man: The Social Bases of Politics* (Garden City, N.Y.: Anchor Books, 1963), 31.

67. Samuel P. Huntington, "Will More Countries Become Democratic?," *Political Science Quarterly* 99, no. 2 (Summer 1984):201.

**PART II**

# Society and Development

JOAN M. NELSON

# Political Participation

NO ONE DOUBTED, in the early 1960s, that the spread of political participation to mass publics was one major aspect of political modernization. Democratic theorists welcomed the prospect. Strikingly, so did many theorists and leaders in decidedly nondemocratic systems. But both groups also harbored grave doubts and questions about the implications of the process. In the twenty years since then, we have learned a good deal about the causes of participation and have discarded some of the more sweeping and naive assumptions about consequences. Perhaps the most striking evolution, however, has been in the progressive — though still incomplete and contested — shift in our basic conception of participation from an older to a newer image.

The older image of political participation reflects the intimate connection between the concept of participation and the concept of democracy. The two ideas have been intertwined at least since Aristotle. The processes by which electoral and other forms of political participation spread in the nations that became the Western industrial democracies have fascinated historians and political scientists for a century and a half. After World War II, the advent of the computer and the refinement of survey research jointly stimulated an explosion of research into the correlates, at the level of individual citizens, of voting and electoral participation. The 1950s were also a tranquil decade, compared with what came both before and after, in terms of political participation in Western democracies. These were the main legacies of theory, research, and recent trends with which scholars in the late 1950s and early 1960s began to approach the study of participation in a much wider array of political systems and stages of development.

Reflecting this legacy, the first image conceives of participation almost entirely in democratic contexts. Participation in other settings is at best suspect and at worst a hoax: the notion of participation outside of democratic settings evokes images of regime-organized parades, demonstrations, and uncontested ceremonial elections in Communist or Nazi systems. True participation is the upward flow of influence that shapes government agendas and determines policies. It is normally orderly, although it can occasionally become unruly. Widespread protest and above all political violence reflect the absence, or the breakdown, of participatory institutions and processes: protest is the antithesis of participation. And participation is good, both for individual citizens and for systems. It is both an inherently desirable goal and a means to other goals; it protects liberty, promotes equality, and encourages stability. This image is of course a caricature, yet its basic premises are obvious in much of the writing on the subject in the 1960s.

The alternative image of participation is much more recent, growing out of efforts to encompass intellectually a wider geographic and temporal range and also to integrate the fact of protest within democratic systems with more conventional participation patterns. In this image, participation is simply the efforts of ordinary people in any type of political system to influence the actions of their rulers, and sometimes to change their rulers. It may focus on agenda and policies, or more modestly on implementation. The extent and pattern of participatory action of course varies in different kinds of systems, but participation is uncoupled from the concept of democracy. Put differently, participation can be logically separated from contestation, as Dahl most clearly pointed out. While in fact one may not find much of the first without some of the second, they are conceptually distinct. The second image also makes no a priori assumptions about the nature of political participation: it may range from civil conversations and orderly voting to riotous rebellion. Finally, the second image is normatively neutral: participation may be good or bad or both, depending on the values that one seeks to maximize and the conditions under which participation occurs.

A major theme in the evolution of scholarly thought and research on participation over the past quarter-century has been the replacement of the first image by the second. But their uneasy coexistence during this time has shaped our research on the topic. The second image was certainly on the scene by 1960: histories and case studies of political dynamics did not draw neat lines between orderly participation and disorderly protest, and discussions of trends in the newly independent countries of Africa and Asia already treated the spread of mass participation as potentially destabilizing. Conversely, the first image is clearly still alive in the mid-1980s, reflected not only in general public discourse but also in more scholarly circles. And the inconsistencies of the two images may still be influencing our choice of questions and our research designs.

**TWENTY YEARS AGO**

Lester Milbrath's volume, first published in 1965, set out to pull together what was then known about political participation, at least at the level of individuals. It is a convenient benchmark for our purposes.[1] Milbrath's formal definition of participation is not very different from the definitions used since and generally accepted now. His topic, he states in his opening page, covers "behavior which affects or is intended to affect the decisional outcomes of governments."[2] As in current definitions, Milbrath focuses on action, treating attitudes and values as possible determinants but not as participation itself. Also as in contemporary definitions, he confines his concept of political participation to behavior and processes involving government, excluding, for example, corporate or church "politics." But his list of concrete types of participation starts with exposure to political stimuli (reading or listening to political news, listening to or engaging in political discussions) and ranges through voting and more active campaign actions to running for and holding political office (these last being activities that current definitions normally exclude). Milbrath then lists protests and demonstrations as additional forms of participation. But, he argues, such forms are "extraordinary rather than normal." They are usually used by minorities "lacking ready access to decision-makers or who feel that the system does not respond to their demands." Moreover, Milbrath notes, protest is difficult to integrate into his conceptual scheme, which posits a heirarchy of activities from least to most demanding.[3] He does not deal further with the topic.

Milbrath's setting aside of dissent and violence reflected a much more general bias in American political science. Gurr commented in 1970 that of all the articles appearing in the *American Political Science Review* from its beginning in 1906 through 1968, only 1 percent "appear from their titles to be concerned with political disorder or violence," and of these half had appeared after 1961.[4] For Milbrath, as for most political scientists at the time, there was a sharp discrepancy between the broad formal definition and the narrow working concept of participation — a discrepacy flowing not from lack of evidence but from the pervasive image of participation as part and parcel of democracy, as good, and (therefore?) as mainly orderly.

The explicit decision Milbrath took to set aside dissent and protest behavior also has characterized much of the comparative and theoretical research on participation since then. Research on dissent, protest, and political violence has not been neglected since the mid-1960s, but it has proceeded on a largely separate track.

## Determinants of Participation

Within the limits of his working concept, Milbrath catalogued virtually all of the determinants of individual political participation that were explored in greater detail in later studies. He offered a comprehensive shopping list, although the scattered sources on which he drew made it difficult for him to weigh different factors or to trace their interrelationships in other than a speculative manner. His discussion emphasized two main sets of determinants of individual involvement in politics: socioeconomic status (SES) and "social centrality." Both sets portrayed participation as fundamentally rational and goal oriented.[5] People who view government policies and programs as relevant to their interests, and further believe that their own actions, as individuals or jointly with others, can influence government decisions, will try to exert such influence (unless they are prevented by structural features of the political system). Higher education, status, and income are more likely to be associated with such perceptions and beliefs: high SES is one path to politics. Social centrality is a second path. People who are long-time residents in a community, are property owners, are members of various organizations, are neither quite young nor quite old, and are not members of minority groups — that is, those who are well integrated into their communities — are more likely to be politically active. Men are more active than women. Contextual factors such as the degree of competition or the crisis atmosphere associated with particular elections can also affect participation independently of the more durable determining factors. The research of the last two decades added few new factors to Milbrath's list. Rather, it focused on understanding better how these various determinants operate and interact in different contexts and with respect to different types of participation.

In addition to the survey research on voting and campaign activity that formed the core of Milbrath's compendium, two other strands of research fed into knowledge of and expectations about political participation in the early and mid-1960s. The first of these additional strands also utilized survey research at the micro or individual level of analysis, but focused on shifts in attitudes, values, and beliefs in countries undergoing rapid social change. Lerner,[6] Almond and Verba,[7] and Inkeles[8] each had somewhat different concerns, but all shared in the implicit concept of political participation as a result of perceived relevance and efficacy. Their surveys were designed to trace the ways in which the spread of communications and education, urbanization, factory experience, and other trends associated with modernization would lead to the ability to envisage changes and improvements, to regard desired goals less fatalistically and more as matters over which the individual himself might have partial control, to empathize with and develop trust toward a circle of people wider than the immediate family or clan, and to conceive more specifically of politics as a realm that was comprehensible and subject to citizen influence. Studies of changes at the level of the individual in developing countries dovetailed with the second strand of research, the broader social mobilization literature. That literature, as is well known, portrayed the spread of education, communications, urbanization, the cash economy, geographic mobility, and voluntary associations, all tending to promote broader participation.

The social mobilization literature also introduced an important additional theme: the interaction among the changing needs of people, the spreading scope and penetration of government activities, and political participation. The erosion of traditional semiautarchic, localized economies, the breakdown or inadequacy of traditional social mechanisms for meeting temporary or long-term welfare needs, and the increasing complexity and interdependence of economic activities all created needs that could be met best, or only, by governmental programs and regulations. Deutsch's well-known 1961 article[9] stressed this autonomous growth of need as the main force behind the spread of governmental activity. Later writing attributed the spread as much to "elite push" — the goals and preferences of ruling elites — as to "societal pull," but in either case the effect was seen to be increased motivation on the part of citizens to try to influence governmental action.

The social mobilization literature also explicitly raised a possibility that the survey-based strands played down or ignored: the prospect that some, or much, of the participation generated by economic and social change might be disorderly or violent. Systematic cross-national studies of the correlates of political violence lay in the future. But plenty of theories were available on the determinants of political violence. Durkheim and others had long pointed toward the disintegrative impact and the potential for anomie and violence they believed to be inherent in industrialization and urbanization. Anthropologists studying village life in Asia, Africa, and Latin

America voiced fears that modernization would erode the tightly integrated, delicately balanced traditional social organizations and relationships. This line of thought saw rapid social and economic changes as inherently disruptive. The mechanisms of potential social and political violence lay in disorientation, anomie, the atomized society. The processes of violence were either largely spontaneous, or mobilized by leaders playing on available masses. An alternative line of analysis grew out of social psychological theories of frustration/aggression and relative deprivation. Violence (as Gurr was to argue in great detail in 1970) was the outcome of intense collective relative deprivation. For those subscribing to this line of thought, the crucial issue was the race between "the revolution of rising expectations" and the capacity of growing economies and changing societies to meet those expectations. Both schools of thought stressed psychological responses to broad processes of social and economic change. More strictly political organizations and institutions and the strategies and tactics of regimes were not entirely overlooked, but certainly were peripheral to the major mechanisms at work. And in this respect there was a curious parallelism with prevailing ideas about determinants of conventional participation.

### Expected Trends in Political Participation

All of the various theories of determinants converged in predicting that political participation would increase in the world's developing areas. The same logic pointed toward increasing participation among less privileged strata and less integrated groups in the United States. Convergence theory also predicted gradual evolution of more participatory patterns in Communist systems.

There was also a broad consensus that participation would be based increasingly on class and sectoral interests, while more parochial ties of family, clan, locality, and ethnic or religious groups would fade in importance. But ideas about the more specific roles of various strata and groups were varied, and often conflicting.

Probably most agreement existed about the growing importance of the burgeoning middle classes in the developing nations. Mobilized in Africa and Asia by recent anticolonial struggles, and empowered and enlarged in Latin America by economic and political trends in the two decades after World War II, the middle classes were viewed as likely to challenge and overwhelm traditional established elite interests.

Industrial labor was also viewed as likely to emerge as a significant political force. This expectation was less an extrapolation of trends already observed (save in the more advanced Latin American nations) than a derivative of our general ideas about modernization, based on interpretations of Western European experience. Urbanization and industrialization would swell the ranks of industrial labor, which could be expected to become increasingly self-conscious as a social and economic class. Whether by themselves, or possibly as a vanguard for less privileged urban strata, industrial workers would play a growing political role.

Paradoxically, the failure of industrialization to keep pace with rapid urban growth was widely regarded as generating a third base for growing participation. The growing urban proletariat or mass that failed to find "modern" jobs, and had to resort to odd jobs and scrounging to survive could be expected to become increasingly embittered, providing tinder for inflammatory politicians. An alternative view arrived at similar conclusions about the volatility of the urban masses via a different route. Extrapolating from Kornhauser's[10] theory of the atomized and alienated society available for mobilization by chiliastic leaders (originally formulated to describe conditions in modern mass society that might pave the way for totalitarian movements), some analysts of Latin American politics in particular suggested that the urban masses of uprooted migrants and impoverished slum dwellers were likely to be attracted to populist leaders and to simplistic and extremist ideologies. In contrast to these theories stressing the disruptive or radical potential of the urban poor, the theories of marginality (in Latin America) and the "culture of poverty" (in North America) took a different tack. The urban poor were viewed as weakly integrated into society, with strong feelings of powerlessness, dependency, and inadequacy. Their horizons, theorists argued, are limited in time and space; they are mistrustful not only of the larger society but also of one another. While these theories were already drawing sharp criticism by the mid-1960s, they certainly led many scholars to expect class-based nonparticipation.

In contrast to the sweeping but conflicting predictions about the role of the urban poor, it is probably fair to describe expectations about peasants as more guarded. The spread of the market economy and of government services and regulation were widely expected to undermine established social, economic, and political arrangements in the countryside, creating the potential for upheaval. This might be particularly true where, as a result of government policy or market forces, economic conditions were deteriorating for significant sections of the peasantry. More generally, the assault of modernization on deeply held values and life styles could be expected to prompt sporadic but intense reactions. On the other hand, the objective obstacles to peasant political organization, such as geographic dispersion and/or dependence in local elites, were well recognized. Conventional wisdom also posited subjective obstacles: the peasant was widely believed to be fatalistic and passive, hence difficult to arouse not only because of his life situation, but also because of his psychology. While the comparatively limited anthropological and sociological literature on the urban poor in developing countries was only beginning to be assimilated into political analyses, the older and larger literature on rural villages and local structure was better known and led some analysts to differentiate conditions under which peasants might play different roles. The varying exploitative and symbiotic ways in which peasants are integrated into larger societies played an important part, for instance, in Barrington Moore's assessment of peasant potential for rebellion.[11]

Ethnic and communal identities, as already noted, were expected to fade as modernization proceeded. The central importance of ethnicity to politics in many of the new states of Africa and Asia was, of course, well recognized. But the consensus of the early 1960s was that such "primordial" identities would be replaced by more "modern" affiliations, including both a sense of national citizenship and a growing consciousness of class and sectoral interests. For many scholars, these expectations grew out of a more fundamental image of "modern society" described in terms of Parsonian pattern variables. Modern societies would be characterized by patterns of status and identity that were achieved rather than ascribed; such societies would operate much less on the basis of affective responses and more on rational judgments and choices. Since (it was assumed) a rational basis of self-interest was associated with class affiliation, whereas ethnic and religious ties were affective and nonrational, the latter would prove increasingly nonfunctional. This conventional wisdom was, of course, challenged. Some scholars clearly anticipated that increasing interaction and competition for economic resources, status, and political power would heighten ethnic conflict and intensify ethnic affiliation. But these were minority voices at the time.

While political scientists in the mid-1960s were certain that political participation would expand dramatically concommitant with modernization, and they had fairly clear expectations with regard to social bases of that participation, they were much less sure what forms the increased participation would take, and therefore what its likely consequences might be. Would political participation mainly take forms consistent with the peaceful adjustment of public policies and priorities and with the gradual evolution of political systems themselves? Or would much participation take disruptive and violent forms — demonstrations, riots, land invasions, small or large rebellions, coup attempts, even revolution? As already noted, most scholars' and observers' speculations on these questions hinged on their assumptions about the links between economic and social change, on the one hand, and political stability, on the other: their adherence to either the relative deprivation or the societal disruption theories. Although their prescriptions for minimizing violence were contradictory, both schools of thought saw widespread protest and instability as highly likely. And while they differed as to the most important causal mechanisms at work, both schools concurred in paying most attention to nonpolitical factors — rates of economic and social change, or cultural and psychological reactions to change.

In contrast, Huntington's 1965 article "Political Development and Political Decay"[12] spotlighted the evolution of political institutions and the values associated with those institutions by the public as the key determinants of orderly or disruptive forms of broadening participation. The pace of institutionalization relative to the rate at which participation expanded would determine whether such participation was compatible with reasonably stable, efficient, and responsive political systems or with less desirable consequences.

By this time also (though more clearly a few years later) a number of scholars were suggesting broad political relationships and mechanisms that might shape the forms, and hence the consequences, of expanding participation in developing countries. Rustow[13] and others emphasized the timing of rapid expansion of participation relative to other aspects of political change, particularly the centralization of state power and the growth of a sense of national integration. Widespread participation that preceded these other two processes, it was suggested, would very likely take destabilizing forms. Other studies focused on the sequence of entry of various groups into the political arena, and particularly the political mobilization of peasants. That sequence, they suggested, shaped the possibilities for alliances and the relative weight of conservative versus more radical forces.

*Consequences*

Most of the strong interest in political participation flows from the presumption that it has important consequences. Speculation about the consequences of expanding participation, twenty years ago, focused heavily on its orderly or violent forms, and therefore its stabilizing or disruptive consequences. But the legacy of broader political theory proposed a wider range of consequences flowing from widespread participation, consequences not only for stability but also for liberty, equality, efficiency, and economic growth. However, different schools predicted quite different consequences. It is worth reviewing the conflicting assumptions briefly since some of them have been the focus of more recent research.

The liberal school of thought expected conventional participation to enhance citizens' sense of control and dignity, hence their commitment to the government and the larger political system. Participation might also constitute a form of civic education, leading to better informed, more realistic, and more tolerant citizen demands. For the society as a whole, participation was first and foremost a bulwark of liberty, a defense against arbitrary or invasive government. Stability would also be enhanced as citizen participation broadened and deepened the sense of legitimacy. Empowering the poorer strata would increase equality. And though efficiency and growth were more peripheral concerns, participation was often viewed as conducive to efficiency in solving public problems and managing public affairs, since it facilitated wider inputs of ideas and information and provided incentives for legislative and executive diligence and honesty. Stability and efficiency jointly would promote growth.

All except the most naive proponents of these ideas held some reservations, most of which were more sharply stated by conservative critics of the liberal assumptions. The critique was based on less optimistic premises about the capacity of most citizens to grasp the complexities of public affairs, to perceive their own longer-term interests, and to compromise in their own interests (much less to sacrifice for the larger social interests). Exposure to other groups' views and to public debate might fail to moderate demands or alter opinions; indeed, involvement might harden positions and intensify conflict. Thus, widespread participation could threaten liberty — of minorities, at least. It might reduce stability by heightening group conflict and by escalating demands, prompting frustration when those demands were not met. While mass participation could lead to temporary gains in equality, bourgeois democracies might be less mindful of the needs of the poor than were elites with strong social consciences. And mass pressures on government might lead to inconsistent policies or to paralysis.

By the mid-1960s, a third school of thought, blending some

of the assumptions of both the liberal and the conservative theories, was becoming influential. The newer school of thought posited (usually not in quite so sharp terms) an "optimum" degree of participation: up to the optimum level, broadened participation could be expected to generate many of the benefits predicted by liberal theory, but the consequences of intense, prolonged, widespread participation were likely to be much less desirable. Thus, Almond and Verba posited a need at the level of individual citizens for a blend of more passive subject and more active citizen orientations. And Milbrath, starting with the observation that participation (in his sense of the term) was often fairly low in the United States and sometimes in some other democracies, argued that moderate amounts of participation were desirable, helping governments to balance the need to be responsive and the need to act consistently and decisively. Indeed, very high and intense levels of participation can only be generated by very strong interest, which implies sharp cleavages that are difficult to bridge. Moreover, high participation itself may hinder the process of developing a consensus.[14]

All of these hypotheses were cast almost entirely in terms of consequences flowing from varying levels of participation. They did not explicitly address the consequences of varying bases (except implicitly in the assessment of effects on equality, where the effects flow from class-based participation). All three sets of hypotheses tacitly assumed that most participation is conventional, that is, legal and within the system. Although strands of conservative theorizing focused on the links between conventional participation and unruly participation, most of the predicted ill effects flowed from system overload, not widespread violence.

Despite the proliferation of theories about consequences of participation, and the intervening variables or conditions that might shape those consequences, as of the mid-1960s little systematic empirical research had been conducted on the topic. But it was becoming clear to even the most casual observers of events in the developing countries that participation, liberty, stability, and equality were not all progressing together. In particular, it was obvious that stability was an elusive goal, whether defined in terms of the durability of regimes or in terms of the absence of civil strife. Political and civil liberties were clearly waning in many of the new states of Africa and Asia. In Brazil and, a bit later, in Argentina the beginnings of what later would be called the emergence of bureaucratic authoritarian states were evident. Huntington's "Political Development and Political Decay" sounded the death knell (at least in scholarly circles) of the optimism of the 1950s. But it remained for the next two decades to try to come to grips with the empirical consequences of mass political participation.

**THE REAL WORLD, 1965–85**

The variety and complexity of trends in political participation over twenty years defy concise summary. But even a crude sketch can suggest some points where the expectations of the mid-1960s were broadly fulfilled and others where they were badly off the mark.

The prevailing impression of broad trends in political participation in Africa and Asia is that participation has declined over the past twenty years, and the same trend applied in Latin America until the very recent resurgence of democracy in several nations. "Departicipation" since the mid-1960s has been particularly clear in sub-Saharan Africa, where mass involvement in politics peaked in the period just before and after independence. The participation-reducing trends of the later 1960s and 1970s in sub-Saharan Africa have been widely documented: attempted (and often fairly successful) centralization of the limited power and authority generated by the system (which did not, of course, produce "strong" governments); the co-opting, repression, or simple atrophy of previously autonomous (though often weak) parties and associations; the bridling of whatever degree of independent journalism had existed; the failure of single parties to gain, or to maintain, broad support; the near ubiquitous pattern of military coups. In Asia, partly similar patterns occurred in Burma, Bangladesh, Indonesia, Pakistan, and (with a lag) in the Philippines and Singapore. And in Latin America, countries with considerable traditions of broad democratic participation, like Chile and Uruguay, and others with significant if episodic experience, like Brazil, Argentina, and Peru, virtually closed off electoral participation and sharply limited other forms.

There were a number of counterexamples, but they comprised a shorter list. In Latin America, perhaps the most striking instance of unexpected democratization has been the Dominican Republic. Colombia and Venezuela had fragile participatory institutions and understandings in place by the mid-1960s, and these have strengthened over the past two decades. Jamaica and Costa Rica maintained their highly participatory systems. In Asia, India and Sri Lanka also maintained open systems, while Thailand and Malaysia continued their semidemocratic arrangements, in each case despite serious challenges. Indeed, Thailand on balance probably broadened the scope for participation. Turkey and Morocco vacillated; Spain, Portugal, and Greece moved decisively toward democratic systems.

Depending on one's definition of participation, two other dramatic changes should be noted: Ethiopia and Iran replaced highly restrictive monarchies with revolutionary systems that demand and achieve broad "participation" in some forms, but bar contestation.

Is the prevailing impression of departicipation valid?[15] And if so, where did the multiple and apparently compelling theories predicting expansion go wrong? The fairly clear replies are that the impression is partly valid (above all in Latin America until recent changes) and partly invalid, and that the theories were not wrong, but only partial.

Take first the nations where the processes of economic and social change and experience with participatory institutions were very limited as of 1960, including most of sub-Saharan Africa. With the exception of a few nations where the urban middle classes were sizable and had been politically involved for some decades, one can argue that departicipation in sub-Saharan Africa was an artifact of artificially inflated levels just before and after independence. Once that simple and compelling issue had been resolved, the effects of low literacy, poor communications, and other aspects of limited modernization reasserted themselves. Trends in Africa, of course, reflected the decisions (often highly constrained) of elites, but also the relative weakness, in global perspective, of mass pressures for participation. Similar arguments might be put forward with respect to Burma, Bangladesh, perhaps Pakistan and Indonesia. In all of these countries, prior to drives for national independence, fairly small urban upper- and middle-class groups, some labor unions, and rural notables (traditional and modern) were in varying degrees participant (depending also on colonial policies and institutions). But in most of them *mass* participation was limited to the last few years of anticolonial movements. Departicipation in these areas could be interpreted in part as reversion to a level more in keeping with broader social and economic forces, in the absence of countervailing historical experience and elite strategies. (Both India and the Philippines, of course, had longer histories of widespread participation; in India "departicipation" has been successfully resisted, and in the Philippines its imposition has been recently reversed.)

In the semi-industrialized nations of Latin America, conversely, the redemocratization of recent years supports the argument that the compression of participation under the bureacratic authoritarian states during the late 1960s and the 1970s was a temporary phase, reflecting elite decisions and strategies and some degree of mass acquiescence in the context of economic crises. But the attitudes, expectations, and values of much of the public were such that the restraints on participation could not be prolonged indefinitely. And those attitudes and expectations result largely from the kinds of forces identified in the theories of the 1960s.

But even if departicipation in Africa and some other countries reflected a reversion to "expected" levels, should not twenty years of social and economic change have produced pressures for and actual increases in participation? They should, and they probably have, but in large part in forms that are hard to observe and harder still to measure. While formal business and labor organizations that functioned before and during the first years after independence were usually repressed or co-opted, a great deal of informal lobbying and manuevering persists. Where the variety and incidence of firms, parastatal corporations, and other organizations have increased (as they have almost everywhere) such informal participation has almost surely increased too. The strength of such lobbying can be gauged in part by the resistance to policy measures urged by international organizations, such as trade liberalization. Both peaceful lobbying and more forceful strikes sprinkle the history of wage policy. Ethnic associations in the cities, lobbying for benefits for their members and particularly for improvements for home districts, have burgeoned with the rising volume of cityward migration; they are more numerous and aggressive under permissive governments, but are also active in many countries where national regimes are far from democratic. In the countryside, especially in those areas where small- and medium-scale producers produce commercial (particularly export) crops, as in parts of Nigeria, Senegal, and Kenya, informal communal lobbying and negotiating with local politicians and officials of national agencies is vigorous and often sophisticated. And in both cities and villages, it is a fair guess that individualistic contacting may well have increased, reflecting the proliferation of government activities into new spheres and regions and the growth in government budgets and in numbers of public employees. Not only the growth of government, but also the substitution of indigenous for colonial officials and growing numbers of somewhat educated people, have probably spurred the frequency of contacting activity.

The point is not to deny the reality and importance of the "departicipation" trends in much of the developing world in the past two decades. Where electoral participation and organized interest groups engaged much of the citizenry in the 1950s and early 1960s, as in a number of Latin American countries, the late 1960s and the 1970s clearly saw a severe contraction. But where such participation had never, or only briefly, involved more than small minorities, the atrophy of these channels and forms may well have been counterbalanced by the spread of other, mainly informal channels and forms. The social mobilization theories were largely right in their predictions of forces generating demands for some form of participation. They were defective in their failure to anticipate the crucial role of elite strategies and choices.

Expectations about political participation were wrong less with respect to overall level than with respect to prevalent bases. Outside of Latin America, class as a basis of participation simply has had limited relevance. The industrial working class has neither acted as a semiautonomous force nor provided the core for effective parties, again with a few exceptions such as Argentina and, less clearly, Chile in the late 1960s and early 1970s. In a few other cases such as miners in Bolivia and Zambia and bauxite workers in Jamaica, a relatively small and highly organized category of workers controls the key export of a nation (which generates not only foreign exchange but also, via export taxes, the main source of government revenues); these workers are therefore in a position to wield considerable political power. But this was hardly the mechanism envisaged by those who expected the emergence of a politically powerful industrial working class. In most countries, industrial workers have remained a much smaller fraction of the urban labor force than was the case in Western Europe at comparable levels of urbanization. Perhaps more important, labor unions have typically been fragmented and ineffective and/or co-opted and restricted.

The urban poor proved neither particularly passive nor particularly radical. They were and are, it is all too true, economically exploited, socially downgraded, and politically neglected. But for the most part they have not constituted a class apart, but are more accurately viewed as closely linked to and interacting with other strata of society; their multiple ties have shaped their attitudes and political behavior. They have participated through patron-client networks (generally of a more limited, contingent, and fluid nature than rural networks), through special-interest associations based on neighborhood or occupation, through ethnic ties where these are salient, and, in countries where parties are active, through parties (which build in turn on all the more limited bases). They have on occasion taken part in violence and looting, as part of broader multiclass protest. But they virtually never have taken part in politics as a self-conscious class.

Peasant support for national revolution in Vietnam, in particular, and peasant protest and violence elsewhere erupted as a dramatic theme in the late 1960s and the 1970s, perhaps (as Bates argues in his essay in this volume) startling and certainly disconfirming those who still subscribed to the "apathetic peasant" image. But as Bates also makes clear, "peasants" are far from homogeneous; diversity in their economic and social circumstances and status generates complex patterns of conflict and alliance, which shift in the course of modernization and in response to government penetration. The broad thrust of government policy in a great many countries has been to milk the countryside to support elites' political and economic goals, but "peasant" responses have been highly diverse. Often they have taken the form of strictly local bargaining, maneuvering, or evasion. In some countries — India and Japan come to mind — middle "peasants" or cultivators have been, on the whole, highly supportive. In still other cases most of the rural population has indeed been largely apathetic, either despite (or in reaction to) efforts to engage them (as in Tanzania) or because they have been largely ignored (as in Zambia).

Urban business interests have emerged (or, in some cases, continued) as a significant political class in parts of Latin America and Asia, though their participation has most often been channelled through informal networks rather than more open and formal processes. In Africa, and in a number of poorer countries elsewhere, patterns of economic development have cut off the rise of an indigenous and autonomous business class. Fledgling businesses are intimately tied to and dependent on the government for survival, or all but the smallest retail and artisan opportunities have largely been preempted by the parastatal sector. As Jackson observed as early as 1973, "The state and its functionaries . . . often constitutes the only national business class."[16] Parastatal officials and managers often constitute a powerful and privileged class able to manipulate government policy in their own interests, not through the techniques envisaged in conventional participation theory but instead by the incorporation of these interests into the government itself. Civil servants and the military have also been widely effective in protecting and advancing their own interests.

In contrast to broad classes, narrower interest groups based on neighborhood, village, or sometimes occupational affiliation turned out to be unexpectedly active in some countries, perhaps precisely because such groups could operate through nonelectoral modes of participation, and could pursue their interests even where elections were closed off, ceremonial, or tightly manipulated. Since neither contacting as a mode of participation nor many forms of communal activity had been part of the mental map of most political scientists in the mid-1960s, they were not prepared for the spate of studies in the late 1960s and the 1970s of efforts by urban squatter neighborhoods to gain legal recognition and basic municipal services. (Such activity, of course, ran counter to expectations about either the apathy or the potentially violent protest behavior of the urban poor.) Ethnic associations were also active lobbyists (mainly on behalf of their home districts) in many African cities.

Patron-client networks turned out to be an unexpectedly important basis for political participation, overlaid upon or working within (and occasionally cross-cutting) other bases of participation. Such networks had long existed, but their relevance to changing political organization and activity was largely overlooked until the flurry of empirical and theoretical discussions on the topic in the early 1970s. It is impossible to say whether such networks became more or less common. But their composition and character probably changed in response to altered opportunities and resources in the postcolonial era.

While class was relatively unimportant in Africa and Asia (and also was declining as a basis for participation in Europe), ethnic and linguistic groups turned out to be far more important for both orderly and violent participation than the theories of the early 1960s predicted. By the late 1960s it was already clear that ethnicity, far from fading, was the most important single factor in the politics of most of the African nations and in much of Asia. More startling was the resurgence of intense ethnic/regional/religious cleavages as central issues in the politics of several more industrialized nations, including not only Canada, Belgium, Ireland, and Spain, where such tensions had long simmered, but also France and England, where the "crises of integration" had been presumed long settled.

Still less did the theories and discussions of the 1960s presage the political role of religious affiliation and old and new forms of religious associations — most dramatically in the Middle East, but also as bases for dissent and opposition in Latin America, Poland, and Korea.

While much of the attention of the 1960s, and almost all of this discussion, has focused on developing nations, two aspects of participation in the advanced industrial nations over the past two decades have challenged our general theories of participation. The less surprising, indeed partly anticipated trend was the growing political importance of issue publics, uniting otherwise diverse individuals sharing intense concern on specific issues. Such issue publics now take a major — sometimes dominant — role in electoral and nonelectoral politics. The almost entirely unexpected change was the emergence of protest and unconventional means of participation, engaging not merely fringe groups, but large fractions of the population.

**WHAT HAVE WE LEARNED?**

Twenty more years of evidence, plus vigorous and varied research, have changed our concept of participation and improved our understanding of its determinants. Consequences are a different story. About all that can be said is that now we know more clearly what we do not know.

In looking back not just at the formal definition of political participation (which has changed little if at all) but at the scope and connotations of the concept as it is actually used by scholars, it is clear that these have broadened greatly. Communal participation and contacting are now squarely within the ambit of most political scientists' concept of participation. There is much less implicit or explicit emphasis on voting and related electoral activity. And various forms of protest and political violence are increasingly conceived not as sharply contrasted or opposed to participation (and a result of the breakdown of participatory processes) but as themselves forms of participation.

Closely linked to this broadened scope is the revised conception of participation as multidimensional rather than unidimensional. Here the contributions of Verba, Nie, Kim, and their associates[17] have been compelling and widely adopted. Using survey data from broadly representative samples in seven nations, they demonstrated that a lengthy list of specific activities can be grouped through factor analysis into four modes of participation: voting, campaign-related activity, communal activity, and individual contacting. Each mode is distinguished by a particular combination of characteristics, including the degree of conflict entailed in the activities, the scope of the outcomes sought, and the amount of influence exerted through communication or pressure. The modes are highly comparable across nations, although the precise activities included in each mode vary slightly; the variations often can be traced to differences in political institutions and processes. The modes cannot be arranged in a hierarchy (like Milbrath's) such that participation in a higher mode implies participation in a lower mode. Instead, many people "specialize" in one mode or another. Different modes are associated with different patterns of determinants (again with substantial uniformities across nations). The broad pattern found by Verba and his associates has been replicated in several independent studies in other nations.

The notion of modes of participation that vary somewhat independently from one another, plus the explicit recognition of nonelectoral modes, have made it easier to divorce the concept of participation from the context of democratic regimes and to open up the study of participation in various kinds of authoritarian systems. The shift to a multidimensional concept coincided with several flurries of research focused on participation in authoritarian systems (such as the studies of interest groups in Communist systems, especially in Eastern Europe, in the early 1970s) or on forms of participation found in both open and authoritarian systems (such as the studies of Latin American neighborhood associations and their interactions with local and national authorities). Thus far, however, despite considerably greater receptivity to the notion that multiple and varied forms of participation exist even in clearly undemocratic systems, and despite a growing body of relevant case studies, there has been little systematic comparative research on participation outside democratic contexts.

*What Have We Learned about Determinants?*

*Determinants of individual participation.* Research on determinants of individual participation has received more systematic attention and achieved clearer results than research on determinants of participation at the level of groups or whole societies. In particular, the Cross-National Program on Comparative Participation of Verba and his associates has given form and structure to Milbrath's shopping list. With respect to conventional participation (that is, excluding not only violence but also protest behavior) we now have quite a clear picture of the relative importance of various major determinants, their commonalities and variation across a fairly varied set of nations, and the different patterns of determinants that are associated with different modes of participation.

Looking first at broad changes in our understanding of major determinants, we find:

• Socioeconomic status does influence individual participation levels in most modes, and in all countries for which we have data. But its impact is a good deal weaker than was assumed in the mid-1960s.[18]

• Organizational affiliations — membership in unions, parties, and other partisan and nonpartisan associations — are considerably more important as determinants of individual participation than the discussions of the mid-1960s implied. By the late 1960s, Nie, Powell, and Prewitt's reanalysis of the Civic Culture[19] data argued that membership in secondary associations affected participation much more uniformly and directly than did socioeconomic status. This theme was refined in Verba, Nie, and Kim's 1978 study of seven nations, which traces the relative importance of organizational affiliation as a determinant of different modes of participation, and in different countries, as well as the interaction among SES, affiliation, and participation.[20]

• Identification with a distinctive social group (ethnic, religious, linguistic, regional) also affects participation. The seven-nation study concludes that where such cleavages are "well-structured" — that is, where political issues are defined at least partly in terms of such social groups, and where parties or other political institutions are linked to them — then individuals who identify with such groups are likely to be politically active. Where social cleavages are not well structured — as in India and the United States, where the major party or parties are "catchall" and blur rather than reflect cleavages — then group identification will have comparatively little independent impact on rates of participation.

• As was well known in the 1960s, women are less participant than men, and later cross-national survey research has confirmed that finding for all countries surveyed and all conventional modes of participation. The gender gap in participation persists, though narrowed, after adjusting for differences in education and organizational membership. Even women with a strong interest in politics tend to participate less than men. Verba and his associates conclude that in many countries women are inhibited by internalized or external social constraints as well as lay differences in education and organizational affiliations.

• The prevailing assumption in the 1960s was that urban residents were likely to be more active politically than rural people (although some theorists argued that the "decline of community" in big cities would depress rates of participation). In the seven-nation study, *rural* residents are slightly more participant, though patterns vary among nations. Closer analysis of different modes suggests that community size has little impact on voting and campaign activity (once data are adjusted for rural versus urban differences in SES profiles and degree of organizational activity), but communal participation is consistently more extensive among rural residents. The "decline of community" theorists therefore seem to be indicated.[21]

A closer look at each mode of participation separately indicates different patterns of determinants. Voting, early identified as the "easiest" of the participatory acts, turns out to be affected only modestly by socioeconomic status, and rather more strongly by patterns of organizational affiliation. In the seven-nation study, in all cases except the United States, organizational affiliation is "both a necessary and a sufficient condition for voting." That is, strong affiliations produce high voting participation regardless of SES, while weak organizational ties are associated with low voting participation regardless of SES.[22] Participation in campaign activity, generally viewed as more demanding than voting, is associated with SES and less with organizational affiliation. In most of the seven nations, institutional or organizational ties seem to be a prerequisite for campaign participation among the "have-nots," though the more privileged strata of the population may take part in campaign activities even without organizational affiliations.[23] For both voting and campaign activity, being female reduces the likelihood of participation. And for both modes of participation, urban versus rural residence per se is not very important, although differences in socioeconomic profiles and in organizational activities may produce sharp contrasts in participation rates in cities versus the countryside.

With respect to communal activities, the seven-nation study found that socioeconomic resources are still more important determinants than is true for voting and campaign activities.[24] Organizational affiliation, on the other hand, plays a weaker role than for either voting or campaign activity.[25] As already noted, communal activity is the one mode in the seven-nation study that is systematically affected by size of community: after adjusting the data for differences in rural and urban socioeconomic levels, rural residents showed a stronger propensity for communal activity in all seven countries surveyed. The difference is greatest in India and Nigeria, the countries where the social contrast between urban and rural environments is sharpest.

There has been much less research on particularistic (or parochial) contacting than on other modes of participation. Verba, seeking to understand what makes people view the government as (1) capable of and (2) likely to provide help with personal and family problems, found those perceptions most clearly related to past experience with government programs and with the availability of alternative sources of aid (mainly from the family), although the links were complex and not always obvious.[26] Zuckerman and West,[27] drawing on data from the seven-nation study, suggest that individuals who have ties with political activists and politicians (as indicated by their involvement in campaign activities) are considerably more likely than those lacking such ties to seek government aid on individual problems. Particularistic contacting is unrelated to socioeconomic status, in contrast to "social contacting" (that is, individual contacting of officials with regard to broader community or national issues).

Survey-based, cross-national research has taught us a great deal about the relative importance of different kinds of determinants for different modes of participation and about consistencies and contrasts among countries. It does not detract from these contributions to note that a good deal remains unexplained regarding differences in individual levels and patterns of participation. Verba and his associates found that socioeconomic resource level, sex, and "social segment" taken jointly showed consistent but moderate statistical associations (in direction and pattern) with various modes of participation in their seven countries. The largest multiple r level (for particular modes, in particular countries) were in the 0.43–0.44 range.[28] Much of the impetus to political action flows from contextual or situational factors that are difficult to capture through this kind of research, and are better reflected in sociological and anthropological descriptions at the level of neighborhoods, villages, and other "micro" settings, and in broader historical/political approaches at the level of groups and nations.

While cross-national survey-based research has modified and elaborated the legacy of the mid-1960s with respect to determinants of individual participation, different lines of research have highlighted a set of considerations that was absent from the logic of the 1960s. Built into the main 1960s model of determinants of individual participation was a partial cost-benefit logic. If people perceive government action as relevant to their interests and believe that they can influence the relevant action, they will participate. This simple form of the model was then elaborated: participatory action entails costs, including both inherent demands on time and energy (which vary from one type of activity to another) and costs imposed by the institutional context, such as registration requirements. The act of participation may also entail inherent benefits or rewards, such as satisfying a sense of civic duty or fulfilling personal desires for excitement, recognition, or fellowship. Such costs and benefits of the action itself enter into the assessment of whether to take political action and, if so, in what form.

What was missing from the main 1960s model but has cropped up in diverse forms in research over the past two decades is the comparison of costs and benefits of political participation with alternative possible means of achieving whatever goals, or solving whatever problems, that participation is intended to address. People considering whether to contact the government for help with particularistic problems are influenced, Verba notes, by whether aid might also be available from the family and by their preferences for family versus government aid. Research on squatter settlements in developing countries suggests that collective self-help can often be a partial substitute for government aid in resolving certain community problems; contextual factors determine which alternative seems more attractive. Olson's *Logic of Collective Action*[29] underlines the free rider's option: if benefits can be achieved through others' efforts without incurring the costs of participation, why participate? Hirschman's *Exit, Voice, and Loyalty*[30] focuses on alternative responses to decline (or, one could say more broadly, dissatisfaction) in "firms, organizations and states." Migration — local, national, or international — is clearly one alternative to political action for many people in declining or otherwise unsatisfactory neighborhoods, for rural peasants, and for persecuted minorities or dissatisfied intellectuals.

The range and relative attractiveness of nonpolitical individual, or group strategies for pursuing goals or solving problems is, of course, extremely variable for different groups, at different times, and with respect to different issues. This category of determinants of the decision to participate (and the choice of methods for participation) does not relate in any systematic way to the kinds of causal factors examined in survey-based, cross-national research (although one could imagine narrower cross-national research designs that focused on differential responses by comparable groups to similar problems, and tried to trace the differences to perceived available options.) Variation in available and attractive nonpolitical strategies is probably one source of the large variance that surveys to date do not explain.

It is worth noting that one category of problems faced by individuals or groups is more likely than any other to evoke some form of political response: problems patently and directly caused by governmental action. Squatters faced with destruction of their neighborhood, market vendors confronted with increased license fees or restrictions on when and where to vend, manufacturers facing sharp cuts in tariff or quota protection, consumers informed of a steep increase in government-controlled food prices, farmers ordered to deliver specified quantities of grain at low fixed prices: in all these situations the government is the clear source of difficulty and there are few options other than some form of peaceful or violent participation (including bribery or other means of gaining an exception to the government decision), compliance, or sometimes exit (from neighborhood or occupation). The theories of the 1960s emphasized the point that as people's needs and desires increased, and as governments attempted a wider range of economic and welfare functions, demands for government benefits would grow. While that is certainly true, in many of the developing countries increased governmental regulation and activity (usually in the name of broader public welfare) have prompted a good deal of participation aimed not at extracting benefits but at avoiding burdens. The observation is important because it points toward elite decisions to expand the scope of government activity, rather than mass pressures for governmental benefits as the impetus for increased participation.

*Determinants of protest and violence.* Parallel with, but largely separate from, the research of the 1970s on determinants of conventional political participation has been a varied set of studies on protest and political violence. During the 1960s, a good deal of effort had gone into gathering and organizing data on protest, instability, and political violence: names that come to mind are the Feierabends, Tanter, Rummel, and Bwy.[31] Simultaneously, Eckstein[32] pioneered attempts to develop more qualitative, integrative frameworks for thinking about protest and violence. Gurr's 1970 study on *Why Men Rebel* built on these efforts and also drew heavily on the work of social psychologists and sociologists concerning frustration/aggression theory and relative deprivation. Like the survey-based research on conventional participation, Gurr put individual psychological mechanisms at the center of his analysis, although much of his discussion was cast in terms of social groups. Political violence, he argued, reflects both utilitarian and normative justifications. Phrased differently, such action reflects a means/ends calculus not unlike that generally assumed to motivate conventional participation, but it also expresses righteous anger. A variety of culturally determined norms affects the normative justification of political violence, including attitudes and expectations about violence in general and the legitimacy of the regime. (Again, there is an analogue in conventional participation theory: the incidence and strength of the sense of civic duty to participate.) Anticipated costs of political violence also enter into the calculus.

Gurr's model of relative deprivation as the psychological wellspring for political violence implies a greater propensity for such action among the less privileged. He specifically suggests that the most intense relative deprivation is generated by discrepancies between economic reality and expectations, rather than shortfalls in security, status, or other values. He also argues that narrow opportunities "increase the impetus to collective violence"[33] But he focuses much less than Milbrath on socioeconomic correlates of participation; of course, he lacked an empirical base of survey research on which to draw.

The absence of survey research on protest activity in the 1960s in part reflected concern about the frankness of responses to questions about actual or potential illegal or violent activities, but it probably also reflected the general tendency not to think about protest and violence as kinds of participation. But the late 1960s had seen a startling surge of aggressive, sometimes violent protest action in the United States and much of Western Europe. Noting that these waves of protest "fitted uneasily into the tentative picture of the political process being sketched out by a generation of empirical researchers," Barnes, Kaase, and their associates[34] set out to study protest not as an isolated category of behavior but as a form of political participation — unconventional, but allied to other forms. In surveys in Austria, West Germany, the Netherlands, the United Kingdom, and the United States, they asked respondents about their views on political activity in general, conventional forms of participation, and a list of seven forms of protest behavior, ranging from signing petitions and taking part in lawful demonstrations through participating in boycotts or rent strikes and blocking traffic, to damaging property or attacking persons. Respondents were asked whether they had in fact engaged in any of these actions. They were also asked whether they would or might do so, or would not consider ever doing so.

The findings were striking in several respects. First, very sizable fractions of the total samples had actually taken part in the least aggressive of the activities or stated that they would do so. Strong majorities in four of the countries had signed or would sign petitions; between 29 and 46 percent in the various countries claimed experience or willingness to take part in lawful demonstrations. The proportions willing to take part in the more extreme forms of protest varied among countries, by age group and by sex, but if respondents over 50 are excluded, the proportions ranged from roughly one in twelve in conservative Austria to almost one in three in the Netherlands.[35] However, those willing to engage in violence to property or persons were few or nil.[36] Age, as already indicated, was strongly related to protest potential, as conventional wisdom assumed. But even among men in their thirties and forties, roughly 15 to 20 percent (37 percent in the Netherlands) scored high on protest potential.[37] And protest, far from being the tool of the poorly educated and less privileged, was fairly clearly associated with higher levels of education and income.[38]

These first-order findings were somewhat modified after categories of participants (and nonparticipants) were developed based on varying combinations of psychological involvement and extent of conventional and unconventional participation. "Activists" — the fairly small category whose members were strongly interested in politics and engaged extensively in both conventional and unconventional activity — tended to be drawn from among the better educated. However, "protestors" — the larger category who were not particularly interested in politics in general and engaged in little conventional activity but were protest prone — tended to be drawn more heavily from the less educated, and, particularly in certain countries, from among women.

Gurr's central hypothesis fares poorly in the Barnes, Kaase, et al. study. Drawing not only on their own data but also on a number of other studies, they first point out that personal levels of dissatisfaction — measured as a gap between aspirations and self-evaluated reality — are largely unrelated to socioeconomic level. More generally, "the utility of social background variables for understanding personal dissatisfaction is severely limited."[39] Those who feel severely deprived (whatever their objective situation) are somewhat more protest-prone than those who feel extremely satisfied.[40] But the relationship is weak, and clearly overshadowed by other factors, including (for these five countries) age, "postmaterialist values," and "strength of ideological conceptualization."

> It is difficult to dismiss entirely the relevance of dissatisfaction to political action. But it is clear that the former lies far back in the causal chain, that the translation process is crucial, and that

other, more proximate influences condition the extent and the form of political action.[41]

The very fact of extensive protest behavior in affluent Europe (and above all in the Netherlands), the values and perceptions that seem most clearly associated with protest potential, and the combined use of conventional and unconventional techniques by those most actively involved in politics, all support the concept of protest as an extension of more conventional participation. Parallel to findings about determinants of conventional participation, the Barnes and Kaase study suggests that mobilizing groups and organizations are more important influences on the volume and nature of participation than more strictly socioeconomic factors.

Barnes and Kaase also stress the importance of the changing "political repertoire." More than a dozen years earlier, the surveys on which the Civic Culture study rested had included questions about attitudes toward protest and violence in three of the same countries. Barnes, Kaase, and their associates compared their data on attitudes toward various protest techniques with the earlier findings and concluded that the repertoire of action regarded as acceptable by large segments of the public had broadened dramatically. "What was extremism in the 1960s is becoming the legitimacy of the 1970s."[42] They speculated that the uses of protest had been pioneered by better-educated activists as an extension of more conventional participation and had filtered more widely into the repertoires of less involved and active citizens.

The studies, of Tilly and his associates during the 1970s[43] focused on precisely those kinds of factors Barnes and Kaase identify as crucial for translating dissatisfaction into political action — the roles of groups and organizations, the constraints and opportunities for conflicting groups created by the broader political context and by their alliances and enmities with other groups and with the government, the changing repertoire of political action. This work has the added interest of a long historical perspective, encompassing much of Western Europe and North America, but above all France, throughout the nineteenth and well into the twentieth centuries. For this essay, perhaps the most salient points emerging from their varied studies are as follows:

- The demonstration of changing political repertoires, with specific forms of protest emerging or falling into disuse as a reflection of changing values, relationships, and technology;
- the inferential evidence of the generally purposive, calculated nature of collective protest, reflecting also constraints on choice of action imposed by groups' internal structure, their relations to other groups, and the opportunities and threats inherent in the broader political context; and
- the evidence that outbreaks of violence, specifically, were often or usually not planned, but resulted from a chain of events that could not have been firmly anticipated — in particular, governmental violence often sparked citizen violence.

The last point finds support in Hibbs's 1973 analysis[44] of aggregate cross-national data, testing various theories about determinants of mass violence. Like earlier analysts of violence, Hibbs distinguished different modes: collective protest (corresponding to Eckstein's "turmoil" and measured by data on riots, antigovernment demonstrations, and political strikes) and internal war (measured by armed insurgent attacks, actual and attempted political assassinations, and numbers of deaths in antistate or antigroup conflicts). His data spanned the twenty years from 1948 through 1967, permitting analysis of lagged as well as short-run relationships. The strongest findings that emerged in his "multiequation model" were the reciprocal short-run links between negative sanctions taken by regimes and both types of political violence, particularly collective protest.[45]

Hibbs also found a series of intriguing indirect links. "Elite electoral accountability" was clearly associated with lower levels of repression, and thereby with reduced mass violence. High "institutionalization" relative to the rate of social mobilization was linked to less resort to repression by elites, hence less political violence (thus supporting Huntington's thesis).[46]

All of these findings, it is interesting to note, point to the dynamics of mass challenge and elite response, or to political institutions, rather than to sources of the initial impulse to protest, as determinants of political violence. Tilly and Hibbs sound themes that Skocpol also emphasizes in her analysis of determinants of revolution: explanations must take into account not only motives and discontents of particular segments of the population and their political capabilities but also regime capabilities, goals, and responses. Explicit in Skocpol and Tilly, and implicit in Hibbs, is recognition of the indeterminant nature of much political violence: protest that starts with particular goals, tactics, and participants may evolve (and spread) quite quickly and in unplanned fashion into other forms directed to different goals, with different participants.

## *What Have We Learned about Social Bases?*

Parallel to the research focused directly on conventional participation and on protest and violence, the past twenty years have seen a rich proliferation of studies on major social groups, particularly peasants and the urban poor.[47] Bates's essay in this volume reviews the shifts in perspective flowing from accumulating evidence regarding the political roles of peasants. Images of the urban poor and research strategies directed to them have also been fundamentally revised in the past two decades. The recognition and study of the "informal sector" have revealed a range of highly differentiated economic activities, some yielding quite respectable incomes, and some associated with a great deal of personal satisfaction, as well as complex economic ties to larger-scale and more "conventional" economic institutions and firms. Anthropological, sociological, and political science micro studies have described a rich array of social ties ranging from small-scale, informal support networks and credit circles to neighborhood associations, moderate or even large-scale ethnic and home-place associations, venders' unions and craft guilds, and patron-client networks, as well as traditional and newer religious groups and associations. Many of these not only link together some among the poor, but also tie them in varying ways to nonpoor individuals and organizations. This radically altered image of "the poor" explains the failed predictions of class-based apathy or class-based radicalism. More information on the varied circumstances and ties of low-income urbanites has also let us understand better their varied patterns of political participation — just as, a decade earlier, we began to appreciate why different peasant groups displayed such varied political behavior.

The explosion of research on ethnic identity and ethnic conflict has also contributed tremendously to our understanding of a major base for political participation and also demonstrated why the expectations of the 1960s proved so faulty. Connor's essay in this volume eloquently underscores the durable psychological and emotional sources of ethnonational identity. Connor places less stress on another point: rather than ethnicity becoming increasingly irrelevant to the practical concerns of daily life, as theories of the early 1960s assumed, in many plural societies ethnicity has become the framework through which much of the population pursues employment, business opportunites, housing, and emergency aid, as well as the ceremonial and ongoing social amenities of life. In other words, ethnic identity is often not only a crucial element of psychology and emotional attachments, but also the major context for survival and progress.

In contrast to the explosion of theory and comparative analysis with respect to ethnicity in the politics of developing countries, comparative and theoretical research on the role of religion and religious groups as vehicles for participation remains in its early stages. In the Middle East, the importance of Islamic sects and of organizations such as the Muslim Brotherhood had been long recognized and extensively studied in the context of particular countries; there has also been some comparative analysis. In other regions, while there are excellent case studies of, for instance, the Hao Hoa and the Cao Dai in Vietnam, or the recent grassroots Catholic community groups in Latin American countries such as Brazil and Chile, there has been little effort to make comparisons and develop broader principles above the level of specific country experience. In this sense the topic is at a stage comparable to studies of ethnicity and politics some years ago. Its importance is recognized and much valuable information is available, but development of broader comparative theory lies in the future.

## What Have We Learned about Consequences?

Efforts to sort out the conflicting theories of the 1960s regarding consequences of participation have largely taken the form of cross-national analysis of aggregate indicators. The value of these studies has been limited by the inherent fuzziness of some of the key concepts, as well as the more mundane but crucial lack of consistent, relevant data. Participation has most often been measured by voting turnouts, sometimes also by indicators of democracy, in either case raising obvious questions of interpretation and relevance.[48] Despite these difficulties, some conclusions emerge. Briefly stated:

- Political participation, at least as usually measured, does not seem to be associated in any systematic way with cross-national differences in equality. The reasons for the lack of association, which are fairly clear, are summarized in the following subsection.
- Voting participation and indices of democracy are weakly associated with slower economic growth. Plenty of reasons have been suggested, but there is little empirical evidence to substantiate conclusions.
- Voting participation does not seem to be associated with instability and political violence. Elite accountability appears to be somewhat associated with lower instability, through the mechanism of less resort to regime repression. The main proposed connection between participation and stability is increased legitimacy, but here we have limited and conflicting evidence.

Each of these points bears further discussion.

*Equality as a consequence of political participation.*    Although several studies in the 1960s and 1970s reported positive connections between democratic regimes or voting turnout and indices of economic equality and social security, the most extensive and careful analysis, by Jackman in 1975,[49] concluded that the apparent links were spurious. And there are several reasons why there might indeed be no systematic connection at this aggregate level of analysis.

First is the crucial question of who participates and how much. Aggregate volume is a poor proxy for incidence. In developmental perspective, more privileged groups usually become politically active earlier than the less privileged. To take only one set of examples, it is quite clear that in much of sub-Saharan Africa, the more politically active urban middle classes have in the past twenty years powerfully biased government policies in their own favor to the detriment of the rural majority. And this has occurred in nations with strikingly different kinds of leadership and ideology (or lack thereof). At the local level, Verba and his associates analyzed data from American communities measuring the extent to which local leaders' judgments of community priorities coincided or diverged from ordinary citizens' judgments. They found that the disparity was greatest not in the communities with least participation, but in those with next-to-lowest levels, where the small number of politically active people exercised a disproportionate influence on leaders' views.[50]

All this suggests a curvilinear relationship between levels of participation and equality, rather like that between levels of economic development and equality. But as Verba and his associates make clear, even where participation becomes very widespread the privileged are still likely to be more active than the poorer strata, in the absence of countervailing organizational and cleavage forces. The bias in favor of higher SES participation applies with considerably greater force and cross-national consistency to forms of conventional participation other than voting. (Since the cross-national aggregate studies fail to capture these other forms of participation, they are biased in favor of links between "participation" — as they measure it — and equality, and the absence of valid statistical associations becomes more striking.) If we consider not only different degrees of activity but also differences in "quality" of participation, the bias in favor of the privileged is reinforced. All forms of participation other than voting can be qualitatively "better" or "worse": that is, well or poorly timed, with clear and feasible or muddy and unrealistic goals, clearly and persuasively presented to those most likely to be able and willing to respond, or misphrased and misdirected. In general, the more privileged are more likely, by virtue of education, information, contacts, and self-confidence, to design their nonvoting participation so that it is effective. And this is still further reinforced by the observation of Verba and his associates that leadership is recruited from and will reflect the characteristics of political activists.[51]

The impact of broadened participation on equality, then, depends crucially on how much, and how effectively, the less privileged strata exercise the opportunity to participate relative to participation by the "haves." The effects also obviously depend on regime responses and the political dynamics set in motion between regimes and participants. Huntington and I summarize two frequent patterns of participation, regime response, and effects on equality (and stability) as "populist" and "technocratic" models; the dynamics inherent in each model often leads to its collapse and replacement by the other.[52]

Kabashima's analysis[53] of the effects of broadened participation in Japan underscores the possibility of other, more constructive patterns. Japan since World War II is one case where all (or at least many) good things have really coincided: broadened political participation, rapid economic growth, and sharply narrowed income inequality. But Kabashima's analysis clarifies the unusual constellation of conditions that made this happy outcome possible.

First, participation in Japan is comparatively income neutral; this is mainly (though not exclusively) a result of higher political participation rates in rural than in urban areas.[54] High rural participation reflects local social and political organization. Japanese villages are usually cohesive. When the earlier role of local notables was undermined by amalgamation of administrative units in the 1950s and 1960s, both agricultural cooperatives and the Koenkai took on the role of relating local social networks to broader political processes.[55] National political organization also perpetuates rural bias: rural areas are overrepresented, and "most electoral districts in

Japan's lower house retain a small but critical agricultural component."[56]

Second, the government has responded handsomely to pressure and support from rural areas. Japan has consistently directed roughly 11 percent of its (rapidly expanding) national expenditures to the agricultural sector, mainly in the form of generous price supports and subsidies for agricultural inputs. Not only is this proportion far higher than in other advanced nations, but during the same period the absolute number of farm households declined dramatically,[57] while farmers as a fraction of the total labor force shrank from more than a third to a twelfth.[58] The resulting substantial redistribution of income in favor of farm households was greatly facilitated, of course, by Japan's spectacular economic growth and by its buoyant tax system. These benefits, in turn, generated sustained rural political support for the Liberal Democratic party, contributing to governmental continuity and stability. And stability, Kabashima suggests, facilitated economic growth.

What is striking about this "benign circle" is that it diverges at almost every point from structure and trends in many of today's developing nations. Even in those nations (including immense China and India) where some features are roughly similar, other key elements are absent. But Japan's experience does highlight issues that need to be addressed, particularly where elites favor expanded participation. The participatory patterns in Japan were rural biased. Under what conditions and how can the urban bias in the incidence of participation in most developing countries be shifted in favor of rural sectors? More broadly, under what conditions is broadened participation likely to encourage growth? Stability?

*Political participation and growth.* The sporadic attempts to relate participation (or, more commonly, democracy) to economic growth have not arrived at either consistent or strong conclusions. The two most recent such studies of which I am aware are those by Marsh[59] and Weede.[60] Both concur in finding a weak negative relation between indices of competitive democracy and rates of economic growth in developing nations, using controls for initial levels of development and for some other factors.[61] Both emphasize that the relationships are weak: Weede argues that "the negative impact of democracy on growth is too small to be of either statistical or political importance,"[62] and Marsh calls for closer specification of the mechanisms by which different regime types affect economic growth.

There is no lack of theories about possible mechanisms producing such results. Three oft-proposed contenders are the following:

• High participation (or, more often suggested, democracy) will slow growth by biasing the allocation of resources in the public sector and (via tax and other policies) in the private sector in favor of consumption and to the detriment of investment.

• High participation (or democracy) will decrease the efficiency of decision making, leading to inconsistent and vacillating policies or to paralysis.

• High participation will be associated with high instability, which will slow growth.

Remarkably little comparative analysis has taken place testing the first two propositions. No one familiar with the political economy of almost any country can doubt that the incidence of participation (including those forms that are not usually measured) affects government decisions and implementation regarding taxes, government expenditures, and economic policies. Cross-national research has been conducted on aspects of these relationships, including the effects of participation and regime type on social security coverage and expenditures and on certain types of welfare expenditures, as well as on the policy effects in Western European democracies of governments dominated by social democratic parties. But these are very partial approaches to the broad proposition that systematic relationships exist between patterns of participation (not merely volume, but also incidence) and government economic policies. The broad proposition, however, is highly plausible.

The second proposed mechanism — the "inefficiency hypothesis" — to my knowledge is wholly untested.[63] Clearly, however, democratic regimes have no monopoly on internally inconsistent policies, policies that vacillate over time, or policy paralysis. Two factors other than the amount or kind of political participation clearly shape "policy efficiency": the security and internal cohesiveness of the regime, and the balance of pressures placed on the regime. Sharp factional or ideological disputes within regime circles or among fairly narrow participatory groups can paralyze a regime as effectively as can highly mobilized and conflicting mass groups.

Weede points to a set of conditions under which both mechanisms of the "misallocation of resources" and "inefficient policies" may be particularly sensitive to regime type or to the volume of participation. While regime type in his general sample had only a weak relationship to economic growth rates, in those countries where "the state strongly interferes with the economy" (as measured by government revenues in excess of 20 percent of gross domestic product), political democracy had strongly negative effects on rates of economic growth. Weede stresses that these findings survive controls for level of development and include a sample of both advanced and developing nations in roughly equal proportions. Of course, a wealth of specific mechanisms might link together relatively high participation, extensive government intervention into the economy, and reduced economic growth rates. These ought to be specified if the theme is pursued further. A variety of indicators of different types and degrees of intervention might also be used to explore the hypothesis.

The third hypothesized mechanism linking regime type or participation to slow growth does so via instability. Evidence on relations between political participation and instability is briefly surveyed as a separate set of consequences in the next subsection. But even the apparently obvious connection between instability and slow growth may be less clear than we assume. Hibbs concluded on the basis of the aggregate evidence available to him in 1973 that there was little systematic relationship between mass political violence, including turmoil, internal war, and various measures of economic growth.[64] One cannot help feeling that the aggregate measures must be failing to capture effects well known to observers closer to the reality of individual cases. Perhaps a threshold effect of political violence on economic growth operates: above that threshold, there are snowballing effects of reluctance to invest or even to disinvest, interruptions of production and of transport and marketing mechanisms (private or public) affecting both the domestic economy and trade, reduced government revenues, and increased expenditures on internal security. If such a threshold were verified, the core question would still remain: do high levels of (conventional) participation have any systematic relationship to such a threshold?

*Political participation and stability.*    Any attempt to discuss the consequences of political participation for stability confronts the problem of overlapping concepts. Dissent and protest are clearly modes of participation, and the freedom to engage in at least nonviolent forms of protest, hence the potential for such action, probably increases regimes' responsiveness to more conventional forms. But dissent and protest, particularly when violence is entailed, are also an integral part of most images (and quantitative indices) of instability.

Taylor and Jodice in the 1983 edition of the *World Handbook of Political and Social Indicators* directly raise the question of how to "better conceptualize stability" so as not merely to equate it with the absence of violence or to confound it with repression. They raise and reject a few possibilities but do not arrive at any clear formulation.[65] A glance at their tables on types of protest, however, is instructive. What is striking about those nations ranking among the top six or eight in numbers of reported incidents of various types is the heterogeneity of regime types.[66]

Theories based on older images of participation, of course, avoided this problem. Liberal theory, as sketched earlier, hypothesized that broad (conventional) participation would enhance stability mainly via strengthened commitment and legitimacy. Conservative theory worried more that mass participation would heighten conflict among groups and would generate frustrated expectations, thereby promoting instability and violence. Hibbs's analysis of aggregate cross-national data supports neither hypothesis, but points toward a third. Hibbs found that neither election turnout nor elite accountability, singly or jointly, had any direct effect on political violence in the 108 nations in his universe (nor in a ninety-nine-nation subsample that omitted Communist nations). But accountable elites were more reluctant to resort to repression. Since repression often escalates violence, regime moderation was associated with less political violence.

Both the liberal, optimistic theory (that participation strengthens legitimacy) and the conservative, pessimistic theory (that participation is likely to generate frustration and instability) hinge crucially on the responses of regimes. Therefore, perhaps it is not surprising that attempts to find relationships independent of data on regime responses fail. Other kinds of research on participation do provide some clues, for instance, regarding the effects of participation by low-income urban citizens on their perceptions of regimes and the political system. Put most simply, the various studies suggest that individuals learn what the system teaches them. In Lima, for instance, residents in poor neighborhoods where participation has brought benefits are more likely to feel efficacious and somewhat more likely to have positive feelings about the national political system. Where efforts to influence the authorities failed, the lessons obviously are different. In a squatter settlement in Madras, according to one study, the lesson learned was that "any formal obstacle can be circumvented if one has the right patron or the right amount of money."[67] In short, for those who do not value participation as an inherent good, the government's response, not the act of participation itself, is crucial.

But some strata and groups in many countries, and much of the citizenry in some countries, have come to value participation as a goal in itself. It is virtually always one among a number of goals among which there are trade-offs, and therefore a regime that denies participation rights but provides or seems likely to provide other benefits may not be illegitimate. But in such countries, restricting participation eventually reduces legitimacy, as evidenced recently in the Philippines, Brazil, and Chile.

What of the alternative theories asserting that participation is likely to increase instability? The findings of Verba and his associates lend support to the hypothesis that widespread participation may intensify group conflicts and contribute to instability via that route. They note that perhaps the strongest factor boosting participation above levels that might be "expected" in a group or a nation, on the basis of socioeconomic characteristics, is "well-structured cleavages" — precisely the kind likely to both reflect and perpetuate intense conflict. Experience in many ethnically divided nations certainly fits this pattern.

The second pessimistic premise — that participation may generate, or intensify, demands the regime cannot meet, thereby prompting frustration and instability — receives some support from different quarters. Barnes and Kaase, Tilly, and their respective associates argue that unconventional participation is an extension or escalation of conventional participation. The very novelty of unconventional forms of participation — that is, the absence of well-understood rules and boundaries, plus the intensity of the demands that prompt such participation — increases the odds of violence by the regime, the participants, or both. Thus, high levels of conventional participation may indeed provide the context in which protest and potential violence may thrive.

Huntington's formula offers a partial solution: where institutional development keeps pace with mounting pressures for participation, so that these are channeled and "tamed," increased participation need not spill over into violent forms. But the institutions themselves must be not only adequate or appropriate in some objective senses, but also legitimate, valued among much of the population. And — unless I am mistaken — our theories tell us remarkably little about how institutions and procedures (as distinct from regimes) come to be widely viewed as legitimate. Revolutions are perhaps the most discussed context for legitimation, though the institutionalization of the revolution is, of course, a process full of pitfalls. Coups in time of widely recognized national crisis accord a regime temporary and contingent legitimacy, and some political generals have successfully built institutions to capitalize on and provide more durability to that legitimacy. But most have not tried, or have tried but failed. We have given least systematic attention to the cases of more piecemeal construction of new arrangements, or conversion of older ones, so as to provide more varied and broadened channels for participation concomitant with growing pressure to participate — as in one or two of the few remaining modernizing monarchies (Morocco? Thailand?) or in a few of the more stable of the African nations (Senegal?), and perhaps most clearly in some Latin American nations like Venezuela and Colombia. How, and under what conditions, do such partial or gradual changes in institutions and procedures come to be accepted and valued as legitimate?

If it is true, as I believe, that we know a good deal more about determinants of participation than about its consequences, it is interesting to ask why. Surely there is no lack of interest in the consequences of mass participation, both among scholars and among political practitioners.

To some degree the contrast may be an illusion. More precisely, it may be a result of our having settled, up to now, for somewhat narrow working definitions of participation. We know most about the determinants of voting, campaign activity, and communal action. But these are only part of a wider array of forms, about which we know much less (and that are intrinsically more difficult to study). When we turn to consequences, we are interested in broad concepts like "equality" and "stability." While we are somewhat fuzzy on precisely what we mean, we are usually not willing to settle for partial indicators such as, say, social security coverage and benefits as a proxy for equality. But perhaps we should "settle" for such partial indicators, not as proxies for the broader consequences that concern us, but as variable *components* of those consequences. If we knew more about the links between various kinds and degrees of participation, on the one hand, and a rather long list of equality-promoting stategies and measures, on the other (for instance, social security, land reform, reduced urban bias in investment patterns and pricing policies, wage policies, promotion of labor-intensive industries), we would be in a much better position to discuss the impact of participation on equality, in a variety of real-world contexts. Similar arguments hold for growth and for stability. We might learn more by disaggregating broad sets of consequences and examining more specific links than by pursuing highly aggregate relationships that abstract from the crucial mechanisms, interactions, and contexts of reality.

Our understanding of consequences would also benefit from more systematic attention to time horizons. Rulers' perspectives on participation, understandably enough, are usually very short term. Analysts like Moore or Bendix focus on long-term relationships. The mechanisms assumed to link participation to various consequences vary in their implications about time horizons. For instance, the proposition that participation intensifies group conflict suggests a short lead time, while the proposition that participation enhances legitimacy and hence stability probably implies a longer lag. But efforts to think about the consequences of participation have often not been very explicit about the time horizons involved, and part of the confusion about consequences may flow from this failure.

Furthermore, the general failure to think hard about the consequences of protest and political violence other than in the specific context of revolution may contribute to our lagging knowledge of consequences. The ill effects of political violence are obvious, even when violence is used for causes that many would value highly. But as far as I know, the roles and results of limited violence have not been examined systematically. There is a widely repeated proposition, for instance, that major redistributive shifts in social and economic policies do not occur without violence or the threat thereof. In 1963, Hirschman's *Journeys toward Progress* sketched some of the ways in which limited violence contributed to social and economic reform. To my knowledge not many have followed his lead. Or perhaps it is simply that the literature on consequences of protest and violence has not been integrated into the "participation" stream. If this is the case, it is probably another casualty of the persistent "first image" of participation. Research on effects of protest and violence may also have been inhibited by the fear that one cannot study the topic without being misconstrued as an advocate of violence. Whatever the reasons for scholarly neglect in the past, since protest and violence are demonstrably forms of political participation, a fresh and thoughtful appraisal of their consequences must be part of future efforts to improve our knowledge of the effects of participation in general.

### SOME PRIORITIES FOR THE FUTURE

The altered working concept of participation resulting from the experience and research of the past two decades removes some intellectual blinders and permits us to work toward a better understanding of participation outside of clearly democratic contexts. The arguments for such a priority are clear. Most of the world's regimes are not democratic, most of the world's people do not live under democratic regimes, and the democratic ranks are not likely to swell greatly in the foreseeable future.[68] But in all save the most efficient and repressive of authoritarian regimes, many forms and channels of participation exist. Moreover, the forces identified by the theories of the 1960s will continue to generate pressures for broadened participation.

If we are to study participation outside of clearly democratic contexts, we need to look again, more carefully and critically, at the widely accepted conceptual distinction between autonomous and mobilized participation. In general, activities such as "expressing [orchestated] support for the government, marching in [regime-organized] parades, working hard in developmental projects, participating in youth groups organized by the government, or voting in ceremonial elections" have been regarded as bogus participation.[69] McCloskey in 1968 noted that totalitarian regimes valued manipulated "participation," but he excluded from his definition of participation actions not "designed to allow the masses to wield influence over policy or the selection of rulers."[70] Weiner in 1971 excluded actions that were involuntary or did not entail choice.[71]

And more recently, LaPalombara[72] has argued vehemently against widening the concept of participation to include topics such as the role of interest groups in Communist systems.

What is at issue is not the fact of profound contrasts in extent, forms, and functions of participation in democratic versus strong authoritarian systems, but the utility, and even the feasibility, of drawing a sharp distinction between autonomous and mobilized participation. As with many conceptual distinctions, what is clear at the extremes is blurred in the middle — and in this case the middle is very broad indeed. Clearly we are dealing not with dichotomies but with continuas with respect to degrees of voluntary involvement versus regime-instigated activity, and with respect to the extent of real choice among policies and rulers. In a world of ever more pervasive and complex interpenetration of public and private sectors, it is often difficult to determine whether an organization or a group of people should be viewed as autonomous or government controlled. Even in the "Western democracies" (including Japan, Australia, and New Zealand), the lines blur between purely autonomous participation by specific interest groups and co-opted collaboration by such groups with governments. More precisely, in many countries there is a spectrum of ties with government, ranging from organizations that are clearly regime instruments to groups and associations that are strictly independent of and perhaps ardently opposed to the regime. How are we to classify the activities vis à vis government policies and composition on the part of the many groups and associations in between these extremes? The decision is particularly difficult when those actions support the regime, and yet obviously not all support (even in repressive systems) is mobilized and manipulated.

The point is still more relevant if one takes a dynamic rather than a static viewpoint. Organizations and activities originally established or encouraged by a regime as channels for mobilized support — say, unions, youth associations, peasant syndicates, neighborhood committees — may evolve in unexpected directions, and become foci for (usually limited, but real) pressure on rulers. That is particularly possible in weak authoritarian systems. Conversely, originally autonomous associations may become co-opted and manipulated by regimes. In principle, all associations and organizations are potentially two-way streets: communication, pressure, and influence may flow up or down, in varying proportions, and those proportions may change over time. In a world consisting largely of political systems that are neither clearly competitive democracies nor highly and efficiently repressive authoritarian regimes, one can argue forcefully that clean boundaries between autonomous and mobilized participation are illusory. If we want to understand how and in what degree people try to influence their governments — that is, the extent and nature of participation — we need to look not only at clearly autonomous organizations and processes, but at a wide range of behavior and structures that are linked in various ways to the regime itself.

The research agenda ought to include not only fuller and more systematic information on channels, forms, and issues of participation outside of democratic contexts, but also the consequences of such participation. We should be giving particular attention to effects of various kinds and patterns of participation, in various contexts, for the legitimacy of the institutions immediately involved and also of the overarching regimes. This is particularly challenging since the notion of participation as a, or the, main source of legitimacy in the modern world has spread far beyond democratic contexts. Of course, there is much cynicism in the lip service many authoritarian regimes accord to participation, and there is calculating manipulation in the institutions they establish to permit and channel limited participation. But in many cases there is more than cynicism and manipulation. There is at least a tentative belief (and sometimes the conviction) that some forms and channels of participation are indeed good for the larger system, not merely as ploys for maintaining control but to serve other and broader goals. Many nondemocratic regimes seek to "transform the attitudes and behavior of their citizens" in the interests of national integration, international security, economic viability and growth, or social reform. They need and seek to mobilize active rather than passive support.[73] They probably hope to do so without generating demands, but are likely to find that is not possible; they must then calculate the trade-offs. Even where participatory experiments backfire — as seems to have happened, for instance, with respect to referenda on social issues put by Qaddafi to local congresses in Libya in February 1984 — one can speculate that some consequences linger on both for regime strategy and for attitudes among some of the public.[74]

If we are to look more seriously at participation in non-democratic contexts, we should examine not only those instances where regimes have tried to mobilize and channel mass participation (Ayub Khan's Basic Democracies; the Peruvian generals' SINAMOS) but also at a range of more specific, narrow-gauged institutions and arrangements that permit particular groups to exercise some influence on issues of importance to them. For instance, in 1983 Zambia set up a Price and Incomes Commission as part of a broader set of reforms freeing most prices from previous extensive controls. The commission includes representatives of the powerful labor unions as well as of business and the government. It is possible that the new system will give labor a sense of some influence on matters of key concern through a channel other than crippling strike action. The arrangement may also, of course, exercise a mild co-opting influence, somewhat moderating wage demands. Will labor come to accept the process as legitimate? Why or why not? We might learn a good deal from systematic comparisons of similar mechanisms in a number of countries, and from comparisons of their effects on participation by organized labor. Other kinds of arrangements may provide channels for other kinds of interest groups. And the evolution of such channels, both formal and informal, may be as or more important for the broadening of participation in many nations in the next few decades as the creation of new parties or elaborate systems of local and district councils and committees — precisely because the more focused, narrower-gauge institutions pose less of a threat to insecure regimes.

The particular illustration of the Zambian Price and Incomes Commission points toward a different, though overlapping, issue that has thus far received little attention (except perhaps obliquely in the literature on "corporatism"). The core notion of political participation envisages a process in which private citizens confront or interact with agents of the state. Implicit in the image is a large citizenry vis à vis a comparatively small, clearly delineated state. In the real world, not only has the scale of government grown immensely, but quasi-public organizations and institutions have proliferated tremendously, and private associations have increasingly been penetrated by government (via regulation and assistance or, in more invasive systems, control and finance). Private citizens and groups have also penetrated into government agencies and programs through a varied array of advisory and consultative commissions and councils. How does such mutual (though not necessarily balanced) interpenetration affect our understanding of the nature and processes of participation? While the question applies to both developing and advanced nations and across most regime types, it may be particularly relevant in advanced industrial societies, given the widespread malaise and tension between desires for high levels of security, welfare, and regulation of others' actions, on the one hand, and desires for less invasive and more accessible, controllable government, on the other.

In sum, the working concept of political participation has been transformed in the past twenty years. A rather parochial and naively optimistic image has been largely replaced by a much broader, normatively neutral concept applicable in a far wider range of systems and circumstances. Moreover, the world has not stood still while theory changed. Evolving institutions and informal arrangements even in the long-established democracies call into question some of our old ways of thinking about participation. And some of the most basic questions about the consequences of participation remain unresolved. The new working concept of participation, the changing real world, and the unanswered questions jointly offer a challenging agenda for future research.

**NOTES**

1. For the purposes of this essay, I focus on the 1965 edition and do not consider the 1977 revision, done jointly with M. L. Goel.

See Lester W. Milbrath, *Political Participation: How and Why Do People Get Involved in Politics?* (Chicago: Rand McNally, 1965).

2. Milbrath, *Political Participation*, 1.

3. Ibid., 27.

4. Ted Robert Gurr, *Why Men Rebel* (Princeton, N.J.: Princeton University Press, 1970), 6–7.

5. The introduction to Milbrath's *Political Participation* notes that participation may be instrumental or expressive, and that many acts combine both types of motives, but Milbrath makes little further reference to expressive participation except to assert that little is known about it (88).

6. Daniel Lerner, *The Passing of Traditional Society: Modernizing the Middle East* (Glencoe, Ill.: Free Press, 1958).

7. Gabriel A. Almond and Sidney Verba, *The Civic Culture: Political Attitudes and Democracy in Five Nations* (Princeton, N.J.: Princeton University Press, 1963).

8. Alex Inkeles, "Participant Citizenship in Six Developing Countries," *American Political Science Review* 63, no. 4 (December 1969):1120–41.

9. Karl W. Deutsch, "Social Mobilization and Political Development," *American Political Science Review* 55, no. 3 (September 1961):493–515.

10. William Kornhauser, *The Politics of Mass Society* (New York: Free Press, 1959).

11. Barrington Moore, Jr., *Social Origins of Dictatorship and Democracy: Lord and Peasant in the Making of the Modern World* (Boston: Beacon Press, 1966).

12. Samuel P. Huntington, "Political Development and Political Decay," *World Politics* 17, no. 3 (April 1965):386–430.

13. Dankwart A. Rustow, *A World of Nations: Problems of Political Modernization* (Washington, D.C.: Brookings Institution, 1967).

14. Milbrath, *Political Participation*, 143–47.

15. There are generally no available indicators for assessing trends in participation over time, across a variety of systems. Voting turnout is available but clearly inappropriate, except within the subset of competitive democracies. And there are very few data on the various other modes of conventional or peaceful participation, including campaign activity where that is meaningful, and the globally relevant (though highly disparate) lobbying and communal actions to attempt to influence governmental policies and programs. Individual contacting, of course, is still less available. The most recent *World Handbook*

*of Political and Social Indicators,* by Charles Lewis Taylor and David A. Jodice (3d ed.; New Haven, Conn.: Yale University Press, 1983) includes data spanning almost three decades (from 1948 to 1977) on five different types of protests activity plus "regime support demonstrations" (see Vol. 2, *Political Protest and Social Change*).

16. R. H. Jackson, "Political Stratification in Tropical Africa," *Canadian Journal of African Studies* 7, no. 3 (1973):381–400.

17. Sidney Verba, Norman H. Nie, and Jae-On Kim, *The Modes of Democratic Participation: A Cross-National Comparison*, Sage Professional Papers in Comparative Politics 2, no. 01–013 (Beverly Hills, Calif.: Sage, 1971); Sidney Verba, Norman Nie, and Jae-On Kim, *Participation and Political Equality: A Seven-Nation Comparison* (Cambridge: Cambridge University Press, 1978).

18. Milbrath and others lacked data, in the mid-1960s, to assess weights of various determinants, but they did place socioeconomic status at the center of their semi-explicit model. They would probably have been startled had some prophet told them that the Cross-National Program, more than a decade later, would find the correlation between "socio-economic resource level" and an overall index of participation for Austria and Japan a weak 0.12 (though the correlation ranged up to 0.35–0.36 for India, the United States, and Yugoslavia).

19. Norman H. Nie, G. Bingham Powell, Jr., and Kenneth Prewitt, "Social Structure and Political Participation," pts. 1 and 2, *American Political Science Review* 63, no. 2 (June 1969) and no. 3 (September 1969).

20. In the Netherlands, people lacking organizational affiliations tend to be politically inactive regardless of their socioeconomic status, while those with affiliations tend to be active, again regardless of SES. In Austria and Japan, the unaffiliated are "locked out" (that is, even high SES individuals are nonparticipants if they are unaffiliated), while the affiliated participate in varying degrees depending on their SES. And in the United States and India, organizational affiliation and SES are additive: those with such ties are more active than people at similar SES levels who are unaffiliated, but the unaffiliated also participate in varying degrees according to their SES level.

21. The extensive literature on squatter-settlement participation suggests that where certain community conditions are fulfilled and where community problems that can be solved only or mainly through government action are viewed as high priority

by neighborhood residents, urban squatters may take an active role in communal participation. This suggests that one of the mechanisms reducing communal participation among urbanites more generally may be shifts in the nature of their political agenda, such that issues amenable to solution through communal participation tend to rank lower on individuals' priority lists—a mechanism somewhat different from that suggested by the "decline of community" theory.

22. Verba, Nie, and Kim, *Participation and Political Equality*, 120.
23. Ibid., 120–21.
24. Ibid., Table 4.5, 75.
25. Ibid., 130.
26. Sidney Verba, "The Parochial and the Polity," in *The Citizen and Politics: A Comparative Perspective*, edited by Sidney Verba and Lucian W. Pye (Stamford, Conn.: Greylock, 1978), 3–28.
27. Alan S. Zuckerman and Darrell M. West, "Knocking on Government's Door: Citizen Contact in Comparative Perspective," paper prepared for delivery at the 1984 Annual Meeting of the American Political Science Association.
28. Verba, Nie, and Kim, *Participation and Political Equality*, 287.
29. Mancur Olson, *The Logic of Collective Action: Public Goods and the Theory of Groups* (Cambridge, Mass.: Harvard University Press, 1965).
30. Albert O. Hirschman, *Exit, Voice, and Loyalty* (Cambridge, Mass.: Harvard University, Press 1970).
31. Ivo K. Feierabend and Rosalind L. Feierabend, "Aggressive Behaviors within Politics, 1948–1962: A Cross-National Study," *Journal of Conflict Resolution* 10, no. 3 (September 1966):249–71; Raymond Tanter, "Dimensions of Conflict Behavior within Nations, 1955–60: Turmoil and Internal War," *Peace Research Society Papers* 3 (1965):159–84; Rudolph J. Rummel, "Dimensions of Conflict Behavior within and between Nations," in *General Systems*, Yearbook of the Society for General Systems Research, Vol. 8, 1–50 (Ann Arbor, Mich.: Society for General Systems Research, 1963); D. P. Bwy, "Political Instability in Latin America: The Cross-Cultural Test of a Causal Model," *Latin American Research Papers* 3, no. 2 (Spring 1968):17–66.
32. Harry Eckstein, "Rational Choice Perspectives on Modes of Participation: Longitudinal Data across Regime Types in the Third World," paper prepared for delivery at the 1984 Annual Meeting of the American Political Science Association.
33. Gurr, *Why Men Rebel*, 71, 74.

34. Samuel H. Barnes and Max Kaase et al., *Political Action: Mass Participation in Five Western Democracies* (Beverly Hills, Calif.: Sage, 1979).

35. Estimated from Barnes and Kaase, *Political Action*, Table 4.2, 108.

36. Ibid., Table TA.3, 548.

37. Ibid., Table 4.2, 108.

38. Ibid., 130.

39. Ibid., 388.

40. Ibid., 390.

41. Ibid., 396.

42. Ibid., 135.

43. Charles Tilly, *From Mobilization to Revolution* (Reading, Mass.: Addison-Wesley, 1978).

44. Douglas A. Hibbs, Jr., *Mass Political Violence: A Cross-National Causal Analysis* (New York: Wiley, 1973).

45. Ibid., 180–85.

46. Ibid., 196–97.

47. In view of the expectations of the early 1960s that industrial workers would become increasingly important political actors, it is curious that there has been rather little empirical research on this group — certainly much less than on peasants and the urban poor.

48. In fairness, some of these studies were intended to test the effects of regime type, not of participation; they have been seized upon by later analysts concerned with participation specifically.

49. Robert W. Jackman, *Politics and Social Equality: A Comparative Analysis* (New York: Wiley, 1975).

50. Norman H. Nie and Sidney Verba, "Political Participation," in *Handbook of Political Science*, vol. 3: *Nongovernmental Politics*, edited by Fred I. Greenstein and Nelson W. Polsby (Reading, Mass.: Addison-Wesley, 1975).

51. Verba, Nie, and Kim, *Participation and Political Equality*, 296–307.

52. Samuel P. Huntington and Joan M. Nelson, *No Easy Choice: Political Participation in Developing Countries* (Cambridge, Mass.: Harvard University Press, 1976).

53. Ikuo Kabashima, "Supportive Participation with Economic Growth: The Case of Japan," *World Politics* 36, no. 3 (April 1984):309–38.

54. Ibid., 318.

55. The Koenkai are constituency-wide individual support groups organized by conservative politicians, which are "the principal means for mobilizing rural voters and distributing governmental benefits" (Kabashima, "Supportive Participation," 334).

56. Kabashima, "Supportive Participation," 334.

57. Ibid., 327.

58. World Bank, *World Development Report* (Washington, D.C.: The World Bank, 1984), Table 21, 259.

59. Robert M. Marsh, "Does Democracy Hinder Economic Development in the Latecomer Developing Nations?," *Comparative Social Research* 2 (1979):215–48.

60. Erich Weede, "The Impact of Democracy on Economic Growth: Some Evidence from Cross-National Analysis," *Kyklos* 36 (1983):21–39.

61. Marsh, "Does Democracy Hinder Economic Development?," 244; Weede, "The Impact of Democracy on Economic Growth," 35.

62. Weede, "The Impact of Democracy on Economic Growth," 35.

63. Olson offers evidence for a special version of this hypothesis, which is in one sense narrower (since it focuses on long-established systems and the growth of rigid, powerful interest groups in such systems) and in another sense broader (since it postulates social as well as governmental stagnation and paralysis). See Mancur Olson, *The Rise and Decline of Nations: Economic Growth, Stagflation, and Social Rigidities* (New Haven, Conn.: Yale University Press, 1982).

64. Hibbs, *Mass Political Violence*, 37–40.

65. Taylor and Jodice, *Political Protest and Government Change*, 18.

66. There is also a "large nation effect." India, the Soviet Union, and the United States regularly rank among the highest, although smaller nations like Czechoslovakia and Syria also appear. Probably more important, but difficult to pinpoint, is a "selective press coverage effect."

67. Quoted in *Access to Power: Politics and the Urban Poor in Developing Nations*, by Joan M. Nelson (Princeton, N.J.: Princeton University Press, 1979), 307; see also references cited 305–7.

68. Samuel P. Huntington, "Will More Countries Become Democratic?," *Political Science Quarterly* 99, no. 2 (Summer 1984):193–218.

69. Verba, Nie, and Kim, *Participation and Political Equality*, 47.

70. Herbert McCloskey, "Political Participation," in *International Encyclopedia of the Social Sciences*, vol. 12 (New York: Macmillan and Free Press, 1968), 252–65.

71. Myron Weiner, "Political Participation: Crises of the Political Process," in *Crises and Sequences in Political Development,* by Leonard Binder et al. (Princeton, N.J.: Princeton University Press, 1971), 164–65.

72. Joseph LaPalombara, "Political Participation As an Analytical Concept in Comparative Politics," in Verba and Pye, *Citizen and Politics,* 167–94.

73. Weiner, "Political Participation," 197.

74. *Washington Post,* 4 October 1984, A22–A23.

**ROBERT H. BATES**

# Agrarian Politics

POLITICAL DEVELOPMENT became a recognized field in political science in the late 1950s. Shortly thereafter, the study of agrarian politics emerged as an active and contentious subfield in development studies. The political behavior of rural populations, rural radicalism in particular, violated the expectations generated by the dominant theories in development studies. And the rise of rural studies produced a major shift in theoretical perspectives. As a result, political development became a subfield of political economy. Peasant rebellions overthrew not only governments but also intellectual traditions.

## THE PASSIVE SECTOR

Reviewing the standard works of the early development literature discloses a characteristic treatment of agrarian populations. Early theorizing was marked by an awkward combination of both static and dynamic elements. The statics took the form of ideal types: traditional and modern components of society were defined in terms of a distinctive combination of traits coexisting at particular moments in time. The dynamics were captured in the combination of such constructs: development was held to involve a passage from one ideal type to another. Within this form of analysis, the agrarian sector was consigned to the "traditional" category. The dynamic forces that induced development originated within the "modern" sector, and rural society was held to be the recipient of the forces of change. It was what was modernized as part of the development process.

Early work in developmental politics was dominated by such "typological theorizing." Talcott Parsons, for example, derived from his critical review of the classic sociologists — Weber, Durkheim, Toennies, and others — his list of "pattern variables," which generated a dichotomous categorization of human societies. One type was affective, diffuse, particularistic, and collectivity oriented; the other was affectively neutral, specific, universalistic, and self-oriented. Rural societies belonged to the first category; urban and industrial societies belonged to the second. Clearly, the modernization of any society required it to move from the first category to the second.[1]

The polarities outlined by Parsons found their parallel in the work of others. Despite early cautions against such usage, the "traditional-modern" dichotomy was echoed in virtually every major work in the field.[2] Even more clearly, the habits of thought established by typological theorizing implicitly located the dynamic growth points of development in the urban and industrial sectors.

Two of the earliest contributions to the study of developmental politics, the works of Daniel Lerner and Karl Deutsch,[3] serve to illustrate these contentions. In his seminal study Lerner classified people as modern the more they held political opinions and were capable of "empathy," i.e., of conceiving themselves in positions other than those that they occupied in their day-to-day lives. Lerner moved from static classification to dynamic analysis through the time-honored legerdemain of promoting correlation to causation: he established that the more modern were those who possessed literacy, enjoyed access to the mass media, and dwelt in urban areas, and he located the cause of the transition to modernity in the growth of education, the media, and towns. The passage of traditional society thus became the parable of the grocer and the chief. The preliterate, isolated village was the locus of tradition, and development began with the establishment of roads and a bus route to the city, the growth of education, and the intrusion of the urban-based mass media. Modernization took place when rural society was penetrated by forces arising from without.

Deutsch's work paralleled closely that of Lerner. While reluctant to posit such psychological qualities as empathy as central to the development process, Deutsch nonetheless concurred in affirming that the growth of literacy and education were central. Deutsch amplified as well Lerner's conviction that modernization involved a movement away from rural life. He pointed to the growth of industrial employment and urbanization as characteristic features of the social mobilization of underdeveloped societies.

Lerner and Deutsch possessed a common research objective: to discover the origins of mass politics. For Lerner, empathy was important because it facilitated the holding of political opinions and therefore provided the basis for participant politics; for Deutsch, social mobilization was critical because it represented a prelude to involvement in nationalist movements. These early milestones in development studies therefore helped to structure a characteristic image of the political role of the rural areas. Modernization involved a movement away from rural society, a society that was politically inert: it was unmobilized, its people lacked political sophistication, and they were incapable of and unwilling to take the political initiative and thereby shape their own political future or that of their societies. Rural dwelling was equated with political apathy.

It is therefore understandable why early researchers, in studying the transformation from traditional to modern societies, tended to shy away from study of village dwellers and to focus instead on the "modernizing" sectors. They concentrated on the formation of urban elites and the resultant growth of nationalist politics.[4] They studied bureaucrats, administrators, and planners.[5] They investigated the behavior of businesspeople and entrepreneurs[6] and those in command of the mass media.[7] Their inattention to rural populations is striking but unsurprising, given the habits of thought of the time.

Of course, the rural sector was not entirely ignored. But where it was addressed, it was treated in characteristic form.

Illustrative is the work of Everett Rogers, which represents a major attempt by those within this early tradition to analyze the rural areas.[8] The majority of peasant producers, according to Rogers, belonged to the "traditional sector" of developing societies. While hard working, perforce, they were illiterate and tradition bound. They tended to be apathetic and, left to their own devices, unresponsive to new ideas. What led to the transformation of traditional agriculture was the introduction of new technologies from the outside. Farmers who were more literate and better educated, and who were tied to the modern sector through their participation in social and media networks radiating from the city, would adopt the new technologies and diffuse them through the rest of rural society.

Rogers's work was widely read by students of political development — in part, I should think, because it worked so closely within the intellectual framework that they themselves employed. It combined the static and dynamic elements of typological reasoning. The rural sector clearly was cast as the embodiment of tradition. The majority of its members were held to be passive. And the transformation to modernity was to be initiated from without.

Backward, apathetic, passive: the agrarian segment was portrayed as socially and economically inert.

**THE ACTIVE SOCIETY**

In the late 1960s and early 1970s, the intellectual orthodoxy in development studies was overthrown. And a central reason was the widespread recognition that it had failed to analyze correctly the nature of agrarian politics in developing societies.

As underscored traumatically by Vietnam, quite obviously agrarian societies were not passive and inert. Revolutionaries could tap and direct powerful political forces within rural societies and thereby shape the pace and direction of historical change. Rarely has any social theory been confronted with so convincing an array of discordant facts. And with the challenge to the manner in which it analyzed the rural areas, modernization theory was itself attacked and largely supplanted as a form of social thought.

However, while I will stress the new sources of theory, it should be recognized that many scholars continued to operate within the conventional paradigm. Some located the origins of political violence in the "breakdown" of traditional societies under the disruptive impact of modernizing forces.[9] Others explained it in terms of the growth of expectations engendered by rising incomes, the spread of urban life styles, and the whetting of consumer appetites.[10] Still others stressed the formation of new interest groups and the rise of new social forces that were created by the process of social change and that sought to claim political power in efforts to advance their own interests and political agendas.[11] By promoting social disintegration, the multiplication of wants, and the mobilization of new interests, modernization, it was recognized, could lead to political violence.

In its attempts to deal with the fact of political revolution in backward societies, the dominant tradition introduced two further amendments. One was a renewed emphasis on the significance of political organization, which marked much of the literature on insurgency. Revolutionary parties, it was held, capitalize on the political opportunities created by the modernization process. Through the creation of local "cells" and front organizations, and through the propagation of political ideologies, insurgent political organizations offer socially and psychologically meaningful forms of membership and participation; they thereby offer a substitute for the loss of primary community experienced with the breakdown of tradition. The parties also offer opportunities for upward mobility; possibilities for advancement are attractive in societies characterized by frustrated desires for progress. While focused about a disciplined core of true believers, insurrectionary parties also cast an inclusive net of ancillary political organizations in an effort to incorporate and channel the political energies of newly emergent political interests. Revolutionary and destabilizing political organizations, it would appear, were designed to take advantage of the politically explosive features of the modernization process.[12]

The focus on violence thus brought a renewed emphasis on the study of agrarian change. In the analysis of agrarian politics, political scientists turned to other intellectual traditions and to a host of works on agrarian societies that most had hitherto ignored. One of the literatures from which they drew was the work of anthropologists.[13] Another was composed of studies of land tenure and land reform.[14] The third was made up of research into rural development, much of which was carried out by persons affiliated with international aid programs.[15] And a fourth encompassed the rich and voluminous literatures on preindustrial Europe and the agrarian societies of Asia, India, Southeast Asia, and Latin America. In pursuit of ways to analyze the politics of agrarian societies, political scientists synthesized these materials from new perspectives.

## INTERNATIONAL POLITICAL ECONOMY

In attempting to deal with the power of peasant revolutions, scholars could not succeed by merely tinkering with the tradition. Peasant revolution largely discredited the established orthodoxy. In search of a new intellectual framework, scholars turned to political economy. One branch focused on the international level; the other on the domestic.

Those who adopted an international perspective argued that peasant revolutions derived from the structure of the world economy. The growth of capitalism in the developed world resulted from the exploitation of the periphery and, in particular, of the backward economies that produced raw materials and agricultural commodities. Through Prebisch-like mechanisms of declining terms of trade through Emmanuel-like mechanisms of embodied labor power, or through the agency of the multinational corporation, resources flowed from the periphery to the center.[16] The backwardness of the periphery thus stood as the necessary corollary of the development of the center. In a sense, then, the underdeveloped areas — the producers of agricultural and raw materials — assumed the position of an exploited international stratum. From their structural location in the world economy derived their revolutionary potential.[17]

This line of analysis found its origins in debates among Marxists in the early twentieth century. One debate concerned the revolutionary potential of the eastern portions of Europe. Another represented an attempt to comprehend the political behavior of the working class in World War I, and, in particular, to understand its tendency to behave as if it possessed an identity of interests with domestic capitalist classes. Both debates represented attempts to understand the dynamics of imperialism. And an important inference drawn from both was that the major conflicts of interest characterizing mature capitalist economies were inter- as opposed to intranational, with capitalist accumulation leading to the relative prosperity of all segments of the "mature" economies at the expense of the more backward.[18] In the second half of the century, these early writings were revived by Paul Baran and Paul Sweezy and even later by Immanuel Wallerstein and Andre Gunder Frank.[19] In various guises, they took the form of a major alternative to — and challenge to — the modernization school of development.

This literature helped to explain why political violence should take place in the underdeveloped areas. This approach also helped to explain to Marxists why revolution should take place in preindustrial societies. Under the impact of this literature, moreover, the study of underdevelopment became the study of the perpetuation of agrarianism. The transition from agriculture became the hallmark of development.

This approach, however, exhibited several critical deficiencies. A key weakness was the tendency to lump all the major segments of an underdeveloped country into broad and undifferentiated categories: those segments that operated on behalf of the extractive world economy and those segments that were exploited and therefore underdeveloped. Such a broad dichotomization represented little by way of an advance of the crude categorizations of the modernization theorists. Moreover, this dichotomization failed to highlight the conflicts of interest existing within the underdeveloped societies themselves; it therefore offered little insight into the *intra*national sources of underdevelopment. In this regard, it is important to recognize that the origins of this tradition lay in tactical debates; they lay in part in the efforts of revolutionaries to promote cross-class alliances within developing nations and thereby to lay the foundations for the overthrow of the imperialist powers. The theory of capitalist underdevelopment thus represented a tactically motivated species of nationalism, based upon populist assumptions of a uniformity of interests of persons in third-world societies. As many Marxists were quick to note, it therefore made more sense as a political doctrine that legitimated the formation of interclass alliances than as a method of class analysis.[20]

The failure to differentiate among domestic segments of the developing economies and to recognize conflicts of interest among them led to a third major flaw: the failure to comprehend the dynamics of the transition from agrarianism. This failure imposed as well limitations on the ability to adequately comprehend the origins of rural protest. In particular, the manufacturing and industrial sectors — the sectors whose rise to ascendancy stands as the hallmark of the development process — seek to extract resources — labor, capital, and raw materials — from the rural sector. And with the growth of domestic economies, important conflicts of interest break out within the rural segment itself. The populist assumption of uniform interests within the developing economies obscured the significance of these internal dynamics. It therefore provided little by way of an understanding of the set of grievances that impelled rural dwellers to political action in response to the development process.

**DOMESTIC POLITICAL ECONOMY**

A second current in the literature approached the study of agrarian politics from the point of view of the domestic, as opposed to international, political economy. This strand, too, implicitly defined development as a movement from a rural and agrarian to an urban and industrial society. But it located the sources of political conflict within the developing world. Many of these it attributed to struggles occasioned by the development process itself, and, in particular, by efforts to secure the redistribution of resources from the rural to the urban areas — resources with which to effect "the great transformation."

Two major schools of thought dominate the "intranational" tradition. One is based upon conventional development economics and will be labeled the theory of structural change; the second is based upon Marxian economics and is called the theory of primitive accumulation. Both antedate the international tradition of the political economy of development as well as the field of political development itself. While the intellectual and political explosions of the late 1960s drove development specialists to theories of imperialism, more recent efforts to analyze the role of agriculture in the development process have returned to these two schools — schools of political economy that locate the political dynamics of development within the domestic economy.

Both versions concur in the basis definition of development: development is defined as the growth of the (per capita) gross domestic product. Both also concur in their perception of the implication for the rural sector. A necessary condition for growth, they contend, is the decline in the proportion of the national product originating from agriculture. Notationally, their basic argument can be summarized as

$$\frac{d\,GDP}{dt} > 0 \rightarrow \frac{d\,Ag./GDP}{dt} < 0,$$

where GDP represents the value of the gross domestic product, Ag. represents the value of agricultural production, and t stands for time.

Within "conventional" development economics, the work of such noted scholars as Simon Kuznets, Walt Rostow, W. Arthur Lewis, and Hollis Chenery pointed to the structural transformation of the origins of the gross domestic product as the most meaningful regularity marking the growth of national economies and the rise over time of per capita incomes.[21] In the spirit of these works, many scholars studied the domestic origins of development by examining the ways in which agriculture released resources — labor, capital, and raw materials — to the growing off-farm sectors of the economy.[22]

From this perspective, the study of agrarian politics becomes the study of three major themes. The first and most pervasive is the struggle over the terms of trade between the rural and urban areas. Politics centers on the contest for control over the extent to which rural resources are rewarded as they contribute to the growth of the nonfarm sector. And the study of agrarian politics therefore focuses on such diverse events as the "scissors crisis" in the Soviet Union, the McKinley tariff and "parity" in the United States, and the corn laws in England.[23] From this point of view, the study of agrarian politics also becomes the study of the politics of rural decline. It becomes a study of the way in which what was once the core of the economy is displaced and marginalized as part of the development process. In some instances, the process entails the vanquishing of a stubborn and resistant rural sector; collectivization in the Soviet Union is a case in point. In others, it is marked by efforts to co-opt or to compensate the elites of the declining rural sector: land rights are exchanged for securities and financial instruments, in the case of Japan; tariffs on rye for tariffs on iron, as in Prussia; or elite positions in the feudal political economy for elite positions in the industrializing state bureaucracy — a trend that has been related to the rise of militaristic patterns of state-led industrialization in several developing nations.[24] Lastly, the structural transformation interpretation of the development process leads to the study of conflicts within the rural areas themselves, as the more efficient farmers displace their less efficient brethren, who then abandon the declining rural sector and assume the role of urban immigrants or industrial proletarians.

The Marxian alternative to the structural transformation approach is the theory of primitive accumulation. While those who view development as a structural transformation tend to stress that development leads to an expansion of economic opportunities and therefore to gains for all, the Marxian approach stresses that there are winners and losers in the development process and that development is fundamentally based on forceful expropriation. Rapidly sketched out by Marx in his analysis of British industrialization, the theory of primitive accumulation locates the origins of industrial capitalism in agriculture. The rise of dynamic, large-scale farming leads to the separation of the mass of the rural population from the means of production. And it is through the development of wage labor that the owners of capital are able to secure access to surplus value and thereby achieve the power to accumulate and thus generate economic growth.[25]

With the movement to radical political economics in the 1960s and 1970s, there was a major revival of interest in Marx's thesis. This revival helped to establish several major themes in the study of agrarian politics. One of the most prominent was the thesis of immiserization: economic growth was based upon the forceful deracination of the peasantry and their involuntary entry into the burgeoning industrial centers. This theme has long echoed through the history of British industrialization;[26] it was revived in the 1960s in the justly famous work of E. P. Thompson;[27] and while it is strongly and persuasively challenged in the works of R. M. Hartwell, J. D. Chambers, and the Cambridge demographic historians, it retains the status of orthodoxy in development studies.[28] A second and closely related conviction derived from Marx's analysis: that industrialization required not just the bidding of resources from agriculture to more productive (and thus more highly rewarded) uses in the industrial sector — as the structural transformation thesis would have it — but rather their forceful expropriation from agriculture. Coercion, not exchange, provides the motor of economic growth. Such a conviction underlay not only Marx's historical vision of the origins of capitalism but also the theory of primitive socialist accumulation as propounded in the industrialization debates in the Soviet Union.[29] More surprising, this view has dominated much of Western development economics as well, with many practitioners advocating the "squeezing" of agriculture as a means of securing rapid growth.[30] While strongly challenged by empirical investigations of the history of British industrialization,[31] the presumption that the resources for development should and could be forcefully extracted from the rural sector remains a basic assumption in the development field. Lastly, the revival of the theory of primitive accumulation fixed a third major theme in development studies: the theme of rural class struggle. According to this interpretation, the origins of the working class lay in the fight for control over land, the primary means of rural production. Whether in the form of the "mir-eating" Kulak or his putative counterpart, the prosperous Tanzanian peasant, in the triumph of capitalist agriculture in Britain and corporate agriculture in the United States, or in the rise of cash-cropping plantations and export enclaves throughout the third world, the commercialization of agriculture was seen as promoting the ascendancy of a dominant agrarian class and the concomitant expropriation of the mass of rural producers.

Both the structural transformation and the primitive accumulation theories of the role of agriculture in economic development are heavily "macro" in orientation: they analyze the transformation of whole economies. Before turning to the "micro" literature, it is interesting to note the ways in which these macro traditions stand as commentaries upon alternative approaches to the study of development. For both traditions, the origins of development lie in the rural sector. For the structural transformation school, it is the progressive rightward drift of the agricultural supply function that sets in motion the "Mills Marshall treadmill" and leads to the sustained flow of resources from the agrarian to the industrial sector. For the primitive accumulation school, the origins of development lie in capitalist agriculture and the efforts of commercially minded owners of rural property to expand and so compete in the marketplace. In contrast to the modernization school, both forms of political economy thus insist that development does not originate from the orchestrated intervention of the modern sector into the backward agrarian segments of society. Rather it is the rural sector that furnishes the impetus to the development process.

These literatures also stand as a criticism of the dependency school. The primary determinants of development do not lie in the international economy, they hold; rather, agrarian economies possess the potential for self-transformation. What is to be studied, then, is not market relations between the domestic and international economy, but rather the relations between industry and agriculture and between class segments within the rural sector itself. It is striking that Lenin in his criticism of the Narodniks overtly advanced this thesis in his *The Development of Capitalism in Russia*. But, at least in the 1970s, most scholars took their direction from his study of imperialism and its emphasis on the external determinants of economic growth.[32]

## PEASANT STUDIES

As both literatures evolved, a significant dissident group emerged. Its members belonged to what I shall call the "peasant studies" school. This school differed from the structural transformation and primitive accumulation schools in several major respects. It was more micro in orientation; its practitioners focused on small-scale peasant societies. Both the structural transformation and primitive accumulation schools were heavily "economist"; the fundamental dynamics of agrarian society were supplied by economic forces. The dissidents were far less convinced of the preeminence of economic forces; they stressed instead the significance of social institutions and cultural values. The peasant studies school also sought to answer the basic question that motivated the original turn to agrarian politics: What were the origins of political violence in developing countries? But the answer it supplied was that the origins of violence lay in the rejection by peasant communities of the economic forces unleashed upon them by the growth of capitalism.

The "peasant studies" approach to the study of agrarian politics drew upon two major strands of social thought. One was the work of Karl Polanyi, who saw agrarian societies as precapitalist and based upon notions of social reciprocity.[33] Another was Marx's notion of the natural economy, in which value was determined by use rather than exchange and in which "commoditization," particularly of labor, had not arisen.[34] Both approaches rejected market economics on methodological and ethical grounds. Agrarian societies were organized on principles other than economic exchange, it was held, and allocations within them were determined by factors other than supply and demand and the resultant formation of prices. Rather, resources were distributed in accordance with social values and in conformity with normatively pre-scribed patterns of social organization. Moreover, the insti-tutional arrangements of rural societies were able to secure social states that were ethically preferable to those sustained by markets. Among the most important of these values was equity and, in particular, equality of access to endowments with which to secure survival. Whereas in market economies one could starve for want of the ability to purchase commod-ities, in peasant societies, community membership guaranteed to everyone access to the resources with which to survive. In this fundamental sense, the peasant societies were more moral; they constituted a normatively superior alternative to the market.[35]

From this perspective, the origins of political violence were clear. Peasant movements constituted an anticapitalist reac-tion to the growth of markets. And the basic sense of outrage that these movements expressed was based upon the peasants' refusal to relegate the fate of the disadvantaged to the im-personal operations of the market.

For some, the anticapitalist themes of peasant rebellions represented a reactionary appeal. Certainly this was the clas-sically Marxist point of view, which saw the peasantry as posing the economic danger of perpetuating a precapitalist and un-productive mode of production and the political danger of providing a political base for those reactionary forces that wished to use the political weight of the countryside to oppose the industrializing forces of the urban centers.[36] It is also the point of view of such contemporary scholars as Goran Hyden, who sees peasant-based economies as possessing the capacity to elude the market and to undermine the state and thereby forestall the transfer of resources necessary to secure devel-opment.[37] For others, however, the anticapitalist mentality of the peasantry was progressive. The moral themes of peasant rebellions offered foundations for the establishment of a post-capitalist, rather than precapitalist, social order. In the spirit of the Narodniks, they saw the social and cultural principles of the countryside as adumbrating a just social order. For these scholars, the peasantry stood as a revolutionary force.[38]

The ambiguity that arises in the micro literature concerning the role of the peasantry in development extends beyond assessments of its ethical and political tendencies to assessments of its economic performance. Some see the economic properties of peasant production as a threat to economic development. One reason offered is that peasants control their own means of production and do not depend upon markets; in particular, it is held, they do not buy or sell labor power. As a result, they engage in self-exploitation and so transfer little surplus to other sectors. Some also contend that the peasant farm, unlike the capitalist farm, is a unit of consumption as well as production. Because peasants produce only to consume, they will produce less as agricultural prices rise; they therefore cannot be relied upon to supply the market. Moreover, because they expend whatever resources are required to sustain the family household, they drive up the price of land to levels beyond what considerations of commercial advantage require; from a purely economic point of view, rural resources are therefore allocated inefficiently, as market-oriented as opposed to consumption-oriented producers are unable to compete for land.[39]

From a different point of view, however, the very features that are seen by some as posing a danger are interpreted by others as a blessing. For the noneconomic orientation of the peasantry, these others contend, can be manipulated by the nonfarm sector to turn the terms of trade of agriculture to their advantage. For example, the "backward bending" supply response of peasants can be manipulated to secure more abundant supplies of farm products at lower prices. And the peasantry's capacity for self-exploitation means that industrializers can "starve" the peasant sector of inputs, relying upon the peasantry to substitute increased levels of labor power in an effort to sustain their households in an adverse economic environment. The "noncapitalist" features of peasant production can thus be exploited by the nonfarm sector to secure rural production more cheaply, in terms of both product prices and off-farm inputs. While viewed by those who do micro studies as precapitalist and anti-industrial, the peasantry can nonetheless be exploited to secure the growth of capitalism.[40]

The tendency of the literature of the 1960s and 1970s, then, was to view development in terms of the growth of industrialization. Within that framework, clearly, the rural sector occupied an anomalous position. For some, the peasantry posed a political danger; for others, it was the harbinger of a just political future. For most, it was a preindustrial fragment — a residue of tradition. To some, it therefore posed a threat to capitalism; to others, it posed an opportunity. To paraphrase the title of one of the classics of the literature, the peasantry was an ambiguous class.[41]

It has been convenient thus far to discuss the micro literature in the context of the broader themes that arise in political economy — themes relating to "the rise of capitalism" and thus to the "peasant question." The risk of such a presentational strategy, however, is that we may overlook the more purely sociological portions.

From the sociological perspective there is no "peasant." At best there is a wide variety of peasants and, more properly, there is a wide variety of rural types, of which the peasant is but one. The peasant is contrasted with the tribesman, who in turn is contrasted with the hunter and gatherer;[42] the point at which a rural dweller becomes a peasant remains hotly contested.[43] Moreover, within any given rural society, it is the variety of sizes and types of rural dwellers that receives attention. Some own small farms; others, large ones. Some possess capital; others do not. Some borrow; others lend. Some sell labor; others hire it. Some have access to off-farm incomes; others do not. Some work as traders or artisans; others, solely as farmers.

Persons within the sociological tradition stress such variation in part because their research agenda is dominated by the need to account for the permanence and stability of contrasting forms of human behavior; thus, too, their preoccupation with socialization, an issue of little interest to political economists. But they also underscore the variety of forms of rural society in an effort to employ empirical materials to challenge the power of social theories. If the relevant measure of explanatory power is the percentage of variation explained, then what the sociologists are pointing to is the magnitude of the variation that must be accounted for. This tactic provokes modesty and stands as a challenge to any approach to the study of rural society.

The sociological tradition not only challenges the tendency to oversimplify, as when referring to all rural dwellers as peasants, it also challenges the tendency to invoke methodological individualism, as by employing the household as the relevant unit of analysis. It does this by insisting that rural households do not stand alone; rather, they are embedded within broader social institutions. Moreover, it is these social structures that stand between the rural dwellers and the outside world, and that therefore should be analyzed when studying the incorporation of rural societies into market systems and the state.

Some sociologists focus on kinship systems and lineages.[44] Others concentrate on village systems.[45] Still others look at castes and/or tribes.[46] Others focus on ethnic groups.[47] And others study systems of rural stratification and patron-client relations.[48] Moreover, sociologists have developed full literatures devoted to examining the way in which each of these social institutions has reacted to incorporation into the larger systems of market and political relations. The "African literature," for example, contains an enormous range of materials concerning the incorporation, or lack of it, of tribal groups and ethnic communities.[49] M. N. Srinivas and others have looked at the way in which castes use "modern" sources of wealth and power to pursue "traditional" objectives of upward mobility.[50] Scott, Wolf, Migdal, Popkin, and others have examined the interaction of "closed villages" with the external market and the intrusive nation-state.[51] These examples could easily be multiplied and expanded.

The sociological literature thus rejects any premise of uniformity in rural social forms. It attacks the premise of methodological individualism, even at the level of the rural household. And it stresses the importance of larger social institutions and underscores their vitality and significance, particularly at the point at which rural societies are being incorporated into national and international political economies.

**FUTURE RESEARCH**

Perhaps the most fundamental weakness in the literatures concerning the political economy of development arises from the basic theme that the several schools hold in common: the presumption that development requires the transition from an agrarian to an industrial society. At the outset, however, and solely for purposes of argument, I leave this assumption unchallenged. For, historically, development has involved such a transition. Accepting this premise, two topics, both drawn from history, claim positions on the research agenda.

If development has entailed a movement away from agrarianism, then there is a crying need for comparative analysis. How have different societies undergone this transition? Why have they differed in the speed with which the transition has been made? Why in some cases was the transition violent while in others it was peaceful? How was the transition politically managed: who took the lead in initiating it, who opposed it, and who brought the process to fruition? Barrington Moore, Theda Skocpol, Robert Brenner, and others have shown the value of such comparative analysis.[52] The work of these contemporaries provokes renewed respect for the work of the classical economists and the nineteenth-century social theorists who took as their subject the impact of industrialization and the division of labor upon Western society. Comparative history — and specifically the comparative history of the transition from agrarianism — thus becomes a prime candidate for scholarly research, given this perspective on the field.[53]

A second item on the research agenda would also draw upon history. Many of the development policies adopted by contemporary governments are chosen because "everyone knows" they were the way in which development was secured in an earlier era. I am convinced that many of these lessons have been inferred wrongly and that contemporary development strategists may be the victims of poor history. One of the major contributions that historians can make is to reexamine these lessons. Does rapid development require the growth of large, capital-intensive farms? Many policy makers and intellectuals believe that history shows this to be true. But is the record so clear? Most certainly not.[54] Does rapid development in fact require that peasants be driven off the land? Was the capital for industrialization in fact accumulated from the countryside? Historical research suggests that these beliefs are not valid; standard assumptions about the development process should therefore be revised.[55] Are peasants easily enticed into debt and their lands seized by acquisitive money lenders? Is share tenancy a form of exploitation and one that leads to economic stagnation? These "lessons of history," largely drawn from British experiences in the Indian subcontinent, are also controversial.[56] Clearly, a critical reevaluation of historical encounters with the peasantry is in order. As what has been learned from the past informs policy choices in the present, such a reexamination of the historical record would be of the greatest significance.

The study of these topics is relevant insofar as development, historically, has entailed the economic and political marginalization of agriculture. Scholars commonly assume this marginalization to be necessary for development. But this conviction transforms history into teleology; the direction of change in the past is taken to signify an end state toward which all societies must converge — an end state that is labeled development. Apart from questionable logic, this presumption runs afoul of the problem of feasibility: given the sectorial composition of such developing countries as China, India, or Kenya, for example, the rates of industrial growth required to transform them from rural societies would be so massive as to be virtually unattainable. As a defining property of development, this transformation may therefore be insufficiently general to be of relevance to many third-world nations. A clear implication is that the politics of agriculture in these nations must have origins other than these transformational dynamics.

*Topics in Rural Studies*

A rapid transition from agrarianism may well be infeasible. Since the size and relative magnitude of the rural sector will endure for the foreseeable future in most third-world nations, the political issues that have been studied by those who believe in the relevance of the "great transformation" should continue to be studied as a part of the analysis of agrarian politics. They do not in fact become less significant simply because the prospects of industrialization are dimmed.

The fights between sectors endure: wage earners want cheap food and industrialists want low-priced raw materials, whereas agricultural producers would like higher prices for their products. Within agricultural industries, producers, consumers, and processors compete in efforts to capture a privileged share of the profits. Producers of different sizes compete for dominance in the rural sector. Conflicts center on access to land, the level of rents, and the structure of rural property rights. They center on access to labor, the level of wages, and the form of its organization. They center on access to farm inputs: water, traction power, credit, and off-farm inputs such as chemicals, fertilizers, and public services. Precisely insofar as the rural sector remains ascendant, this mix of issues constitutes a major portion of the stuff of politics in the developing areas. Given their prominence on the political agenda, the study of these issues should be prominent on the research agenda as well.

In addition, just because scholars question the feasibility of the transition to industrialization does not mean that others share their reservations. In particular, there exists a "development coalition" — of industrialists, urban wage earners, bureaucrats, and intellectuals — in many of the developing countries who see the future prosperity of their nations tied to their ability to secure rapid industrialization and who are committed to elicit, if necessary, the transfer of resources from agriculture with which to secure this transformation. In many countries, these interests dominate policy making: they set agricultural prices, they staff and manage marketing agencies, and they administer the public bureaucracies that structure the economic and political environment of rural producers. They systematically intervene in the policy process so as to pursue development, by which they tend to mean undergoing the same structural transformation that took place with the growth of the major industrial powers. The organization of this development coalition, its intervention in the policy process, and the links it maintains and mobilizes in the international development community — these are subjects that must be researched.

Many of the nations of the third world contain populations that are overwhelmingly rural in composition. Their economies are agrarian. For the foreseeable future, these societies are likely to remain that way. And precisely for these reasons, it is sensible and important to approach the study of the political economy of third-world nations by analyzing the politics of agricultural policy making.[57] This subject deserves pride of place in the research agenda.

## Approach to the Subject

In the study of these topics, what intellectual framework should be applied? One of the most striking recent innovations in the study of agrarian politics was advanced by Samuel L. Popkin: the application to this field of the theory of rational choice.[58] In choosing a form of political economy, I would draw upon this foundation. Moreover, I would be guided by the properties of the subject we are seeking to analyze.

Consideration of these properties quickly leads to a rejection of two major forms of political economy: conventional microeconomics and standard radical approaches. The study of agrarian politics reveals the limited relevance of voluntary exchange: economic coercion is a fact of everyday life. The study of rural communities reveals as well the significance of institutions other than markets. And the study of agricultural policy making demonstrates that consideration of objectives other than economic efficiency drives the selection of policies and forms of policy intervention. Clearly, then, conventional economics provides a weak foundation for the study of agrarian political economy. Radical political economy does little better. Consideration of the fate of the peasantry demonstrates that effective class action is problematic. And the analysis of public policy reveals that a theory of politics cannot rest on the presumption of historical materialism; political intervention as frequently retards the growth of productive forces as it promotes it. In the absence of either motive force, then, political action is difficult to analyze from a Marxian point of view.

A useful place to turn is to the literature on collective choice.[59] Based upon the application of rational choice analysis to nonmarket institutions, this form of political economy offers useful insights at both the macro and the micro levels. Indeed, a major problem with present day approaches to the study of rural societies is that the micro literature stands apart from and in partial opposition to the micro literature; and, as has been shown, the source of this dissent is largely methodological. A major attraction of the collective choice approach is that it promises to reintegrate the two within a common methodological framework.

*"Macro" Level Topics*

The collective choice approach provides a variety of tools for analyzing the political process of resource allocation in poor societies, both within the rural sector and between the rural and other sectors.

*The study of pressure groups.*    Clearly a major factor influencing the allocation of resources in agrarian societies is the interplay of organized interests. While farmers constitute the majority of the citizens of the developing nations, their interests are frequently defeated in the struggle for control of the state. The outcome that one would expect to result from the impact of political majorities is, in fact, repeatedly overborne by the impact of organized minorities.[60] Because the collective choice approach offers insight into the relative ability of interests to organize and so influence the allocational behavior of governments,[61] it therefore promises to make a significant contribution to our understanding of the intersectoral patterns of economic bias characteristic of the developing nations. By the same token, it would appear to offer an alternative theoretical basis for explaining the rise of industry and the marginalization of agriculture — one grounded on micro foundations rather than on the simplistic projection forward of trends observed in the past histories of the industrial nations of the world.

*Political competition.*   The collective choice literature can also provide important insights into political competition since its practitioners have analyzed the incentives created for the formation of public policies by politicians' searches for the support of political majorities.[62] Popular impressions notwithstanding, the electoral mechanism is in fact frequently employed in third-world nations to mediate claims for high office. The developing nations are largely agrarian in composition, and farmers therefore constitute electoral majorities. What is the impact of this configuration of votes? Are there, for example, "electoral cycles" in such things as credit programs, pricing policies, and agricultural subsidies? Insofar as the electoral mechanism is in fact abandoned, does this make a difference? Does the disenfranchisement of rural majorities matter? Do, for example, countries adopt different agricultural policies when they shift to military rule? When elections do remain in place, but take place outside the framework of party competition, what is the effect? Since one-party systems are common, one challenge is to develop the tools with which to represent the effect of electoral competition within single-party systems. Another is to analyze the consequences for public policy of the quest for majority support *within* the ruling party.

*The study of public agencies.*   Precisely because the set of issues surrounding the development of agriculture has been so intensely politicized, government intervention and control is a commonplace feature of the rural economies of third-world nations. Bureaucracies span and regulate many of the markets of relevance to farmers: the markets for the commodities they sell, the inputs they employ, and goods they purchase for consumption purposes. The collective choice approach attempts to analyze the ways in which allocational decisions are taken in nonmarket environments, i.e., in settings in which bureaucratic or political institutions regulate the allocational process. In the literature, there are attempts to understand how those seeking to maximize their incomes would manipulate such bureaucracies;[63] how public officials who seek noneconomic objectives (such as political support) would manage them;[64] and how the bureaucrats themselves shape the behavior of public agencies.[65] Where the public sector is so deeply involved in the allocation of economic resources, it is extremely important that analysts turn to this literature in attempts to understand the political origins of economic choices.

### *"Micro" Level Concerns*

One criticism of the micro literature is based on the allegation of economic reductionism; as argued most vividly by Karl Polanyi, George Dalton, and others, allocational decisions in small-scale societies are often made outside of markets, and the application of the laws of supply and demand with the resultant formation of prices is often of little use in studying social decisions.[66] A second criticism is aimed at the premise of methodological individualism; the sociological tradition denies the relevance of the individual as the unit of analysis and instead stresses the significance of social institutions. What is striking is the degree to which the collective choice school concurs in these criticisms. By focusing on the way in which nonmarket institutions aggregate preferences into collective social outcomes, it approaches the study of human behavior in a manner that these critics of market economies should find congenial. It therefore holds forth the prospect of reintegrating the micro and macro materials on rural societies in developing nations.

Not only does the collective choice school co-opt key elements in these positions, it also offers new tools for the study of social institutions. Employing the assumption of rational behavior, scholars can ask: In the context of a given institutional environment, how are people likely to behave? An example of such analysis is Dennis Chinn's work on communal institutions in rural China; Louis Putterman's examination of village decision making in Tanzania stands as another.[67] Richard Posner's analysis of the economic role of kinship in "traditional" societies and my own examination of the political role of kinship among the Nuer represent other attempts, as do the numerous studies of sharecropping and tenancy.[68]

Viewing institutions as means for securing desired ends gives rise to new questions — questions that should also promote a convergence between sociology and political economy. While sociologists tend to describe the social institutions prevailing in particular locales and to portray their variety across different societies, the collective choice theorist is driven to ask: Why, in this situation, does this institution reign instead of any of these others? And under what circumstances will a given institution be replaced by another? The issue being raised is thus one of institutional adoption and change. In my own work, for example, I have examined hypotheses about why kingships and chieftaincies replaced kinship systems in Africa; Margaret Levi, Aristide Zolberg, Douglass North and Robert Thomas, David Friedman, and others have raised similar questions for preindustrial Europe.[69] Samuel Popkin, Ammar Siamwalla, and others have examined the circumstances under which markets will be replaced by hierarchies, such as bureaucracies or patron-client relations, in agrarian settings.[70] Insofar as sociologists and collective choice analysts come to work together, this type of investigation is bound to a more prominent place in the research agenda in development studies.

Some institutional changes, we have learned, represent the results of coercion: collective property, village dwelling, and communal forms of government, for example, may represent mechanisms put in place by states seeking to extract resources from rural populations. They represent, in effect, instruments of taxation.[71] But the use of rational choice theory also suggests that many of these institutions may have evolved in a Darwinian manner: being more efficient, they may have outcompeted and displaced alternative institutional forms. This interpretation is, of course, in keeping with historical materialism and its neoclassical alternative: the new institutional economics.[72] But it is also apparent that some of these institutions have been consciously innovated. In the manner of a social contract, they may have been put in place in an effort at constitutional design and so have been supplied in an attempt to give institutional underpinning to more desirable social states.[73] The study and characterization of such institutional transformations should also be featured on the research agenda.

## CONCLUSION

This essay has reviewed the study of agrarian politics in development studies. It has argued that the major impact of the study of agrarian politics has been to transform the study of political development into the study of political economy. The essay has expressed dissatisfaction with the dominant forms of political economy applied to the study of rural societies, however, and has advocated the use of an alternative approach: that of collective choice. While this alternative does not require the strong assumption of "aggregate transformation," it nonetheless offers significant insights into the forms of political struggle characteristic of rural societies. It also offers the promise of bridging the macro and micro traditions in the study of agrarian politics and of reintegrating the two within a common framework.

The political power of the peasantry moved rural societies from the periphery to the center of development studies. The power of the study of agrarian societies to stimulate new ways of analyzing the politics of the developing areas may well keep them there.

## NOTES

1. Talcott Parsons, *The Social System* (New York: Free Press, 1964). See also Talcott Parsons and Neil J. Smelser, *Economy and Society* (New York: Free Press, 1965); Lucian W. Pye and Sidney Verba, eds., *Political Culture and Political Development* (Princeton, N.J.: Princeton University Press, 1965); and Fred W. Riggs, *Administration in Developing Countries* (Boston: Houghton Mifflin, 1964).

2. See the criticisms offered in Alfred Diamant, "Is There a Non-Western Political Process?," *Journal of Politics* 21 (1959):123–27, and Joseph R. Gusfield, "Tradition and Modernity: Mis-

placed Polarities in the Study of Social Change," *American Journal of Sociology* 72 (January 1967):351–62.

3.  Daniel Lerner, *The Passing of Traditional Society: Modernizing the Middle East* (Glencoe, Ill.: Free Press, 1958); Karl Deutsch, *Nationalism and Social Communication* (Cambridge, Mass.: M.I.T. Press, 1953), and "Social Mobilization and Political Development," *American Political Science Review* 55, no. 3 (September 1961):493–514.

4.  Thomas Hodgkin, *Nationalism in Colonial Africa* (New York: New York University Press, 1957), and Immanuel Wallerstein, *Africa: The Politics of Independence* (New York: Vintage Books, 1961).

5.  See such diverse contributions as Joseph LaPalombara, ed., *Bureaucracy and Political Development* (Princeton, N.J.: Princeton University Press, 1963); Warren F. Ilchman and Norman T. Uphoff, *The Political Economy of Change* (Berkeley: University of California Press, 1969); Benjamin Higgens, *Economic Development* (New York: Norton, 1959); and Everett E. Hagen, ed., *Planning Economic Development* (Homewood, Ill.: Richard D. Irwin, 1963).

6.  David C. McClelland, *The Achieving Society* (Princeton, N.J.: D. Van Nostrand Company, 1961), and Everett E. Hagen, *On the Theory of Social Change* (Homewood, Ill.: Dorsey Press, 1962).

7.  See the contributions in Lucian W. Pye, ed., *Communications and Political Development* (Princeton, N.J.: Princeton University Press, 1963).

8.  Everett M. Rogers, *Diffusion of Innovations* (New York: Free Press of Glencoe, 1962). Extremely interesting too are the rejoinders to this work contained in Clifton R. Wharton, ed., *Subsistence Agriculture and Economic Development* (Chicago: Aldine Press, 1968), and to the "diffusion" of innovations approach in general contained in such works as Zvi Griliches, "Hybrid Corn: An Exploration in the Economics of Technical Change," *Econometrica* 25 (October 1957):501–22.

9.  The spirit of these works is captured in such books as O. Mannoni, *Prospero and Caliban: The Psychology of Colonization* (New York: Praeger, 1956); Colin Turnbull, *The Lonely African* (New York: Simon & Schuster, 1962); and Louis S. B. Leakey, *Mau Mau and the Kikuyu* (London: Methuen, 1952). Structural theories of disruption were advanced in the study of urbanization and ably debated in such studies as Joan M. Nelson, *Migrants, Urban Poverty and Instability in Developing Nations* (Cambridge,

Mass.: Center for International Affairs, Harvard University, 1969), and Wayne A. Cornelius, *Politics and the Migrant Poor in Mexico City* (Stanford, Calif.: Stanford University Press, 1975).

10. "Gap" theories were advanced by James C. Davies, "Toward a Theory of Revolution," *American Sociological Review* 6 (February 1962):5–19, and, in a slightly different guise, by Ted Robert Gurr, *Why Men Rebel* (Princeton, N.J.: Princeton University Press, 1970).

11. See such diverse works as Anthony Oberschall, *Social Conflict and Social Movements* (Englewood Cliffs, N.J.: Prentice-Hall, 1973); Mancur Olson, Jr., "Rapid Growth as a Destabilizing Force," *Journal of Economic History* 23, no. 4 (December 1963):529–52; and Samuel P. Huntington, *Political Order in Changing Societies* (New Haven, Conn.: Yale University Press, 1968).

12. See such works as Lucian W. Pye, *Guerilla Communism in Malaysia: Its Social and Political Meaning* (Princeton, N.J.: Princeton University Press, 1956); Paul Berman, *Revolutionary Organization: Institution-Building within the People's Liberation Armed Forces* (Lexington, Mass.: Lexington Books, 1974); and also Huntington, *Political Order*. There is, of course, a deep debt to be paid to Leon Trotsky, *The Russian Revolution* (Garden City, N.Y.: Doubleday Anchor Books, 1959), and Philip Selznik, *The Organizational Weapon: A Study of Bolshevik Strategy and Tactics* (Santa Monica, Calif.: Rand Corporation, 1952).

13. Perhaps the best example of the use of this literature is Joel S. Migdal, *Peasants, Politics and Revolution* (Princeton, N.J.: Princeton University Press, 1974). See also Eric R. Wolf, *Peasant Wars of the Twentieth Century* (New York: Harper Torchbooks, 1969).

14. See, for example, David Lehman, ed., *Peasants, Landlords and Governments: Agrarian Reform in the Third World* (New York: Holmes & Meier, 1974); Ernest Feder, *The Rape of the Peasantry: Latin America's Land Holding Systems* (Garden City, N.Y.: Anchor Books, 1971); and Rodolfo Stavenhagen, *Social Classes in Agrarian Change* (Garden City, N.Y.: Anchor Books, 1975).

15. See, for example, Donald R. Mickelwait, Charles F. Sweet, and Elliott R. Morss, *New Directions in Development* (Boulder, Colo.: Westview Press, 1979).

16. See, for example, Raoul Prebisch, "Commercial Policy in the Underdeveloped Countries," *American Economic Review* 49 (May 1959):251–73; Arghiri Emmanuel, *Unequal Exchange: A Study*

*of the Imperialism of Trade* (New York: Monthly Review Press, 1972); and Stephen Herbert Hymer, *The Multinational Corporation: A Radical Approach* (Cambridge: Cambridge University Press, 1979).

17. This is a vast literature, slighted by so cursory a summary. For useful introductions to it, see the general overviews contained in Ian Roxborough, *Theories of Underdevelopment* (Atlantic Highlands, N.J.: Humanities Press, 1979), and the special issue of *International Organization* 34 no. 4 (Autumn 1980). See also the critical treatment offered in Alain de Janvry, *The Agrarian Question and Reformism in Latin America* (Baltimore, Md.: Johns Hopkins University Press, 1981), and Bill Warren, *Imperialism: Pioneer of Capitalism* (London: New Left Books, 1980).

18. Thoughtful overviews of the historical origins of the dependency literature are offered in de Janvry, *Agrarian Question,* and especially in Gabriel Palma, "Dependency: A Formal Theory of Underdevelopment or a Methodology for the Analysis of Concrete Situations of Underdevelopment," *World Development* 6 (1978):881–924.

19. Paul A. Baran, *The Political Economy of Growth* (New York: Modern Reader Paperbacks, 1957); Paul M. Sweezy, *Theory of Capitalist Development* (New York: Oxford University Press, 1942); Immanuel Wallerstein, *The Modern World System* (New York: Academic Press, 1974); Andre Gunder Frank, *Capitalism and Underdevelopment in Latin America: Historical Studies in Chile and Brazil* (New York: Monthly Review Press, 1967).

20. Excellent critiques were offered by Bill Warren, "Imperialism and Capitalist Industrialization," *New Left Review* 81 (September–October 1973):3–45; Robert Brenner, "The Origins of Capitalist Development: A Critique of Neo-Smithian Marxism," *New Left Review* 104 (1977):25–92; Fernando Henrique Cardoso, "Associated-Dependent Development: Theoretical and Practical Implications," in *Authoritarian Brazil,* edited by Alfred Stepan (New Haven, Conn.: Yale University Press, 1973), 142–76; and Ernesto Laclau, "Feudalism and Capitalism in Latin America," *New Left Review* 67 (May–June 1971):19–38. See also Andre Gunder Frank, "Dependence Is Dead, Long Live Dependence and the Class Struggle: An Answer to Critics," *World Development* 5 (1977):355–70.

21. See, for example, Simon Kuznets, *Economic Growth of Nations: Total Output and Production Structure* (Cambridge, Mass.: Harvard University Press, 1971); W. W. Rostow, *The Process of Eco-*

*nomic Growth* (New York: Norton, 1952); W. Arthur Lewis, *Theory of Economic Growth* (New York: Harper & Row, 1970); and Hollis Chenery, *Structural Change and Development Policy* (New York: Oxford University Press, 1979).

22. Perhaps the classic article in the genre is Bruce F. Johnston and John W. Mellor, "The Role of Agriculture in Economic Development," *American Economic Review* 51 (1961):566–93. But see also the tradition of "two-sector" growth models in the development economics literature, some of the best of which have been anthologized in Joseph E. Stiglitz and Hirofumi Uzawa, *Readings in the Modern Theory of Economics Growth* (Cambridge, Mass.: M.I.T. Press, 1969).

23. See the discussion in Maurice Dobb, *Soviet Economic Development since 1917* (New York: International Publishers, 1948); Frank W. Taussig, *The Tariff History of the United States* (New York: Putnam, 1931); Walter W. Wilcox, Willard W. Cochrane, and Robert W. Herdt, *Economics of American Agriculture* (Englewood Cliffs, N.J.: Prentice-Hall, 1960); Phyllis Deane and W. A. Cole, *British Economic Growth, 1688–1959* (Cambridge: Cambridge University Press, 1962); and J. H. Clapham, *An Economic History of Modern Britain,* 3 vols. (Cambridge: Cambridge University Press, 1950–52).

24. See, for example, William W. Lockwood, *The Economic Development of Japan* (Princeton, N.J.: Princeton University Press, 1954); Alexander Gerschenkron, *Bread and Democracy in Germany* (Berkeley: University of California Press, 1943); Barrington Moore, Jr., *Social Origins of Dictatorship and Democracy: Lord and Peasant in the Making of the Modern World* (Boston: Beacon Press, 1966); and Ellen Kay Trimberger, "A Theory of Elite Revolutions," *Studies in Comparative International Development* 7, no. 3 (Fall 1972):191–207.

25. Karl Marx, "The So-Called Primitive Accumulation," pt. 4 of *Capital* (New York: Charles A. Kerr, 1906).

26. See, for example, J. L. Hammond and Barbara Hammond, *The Bleak Age* (New York: Penguin Books, 1934), and *The Village Labourer, 1760–1832* (1913; New York: Harper Torchbooks, 1970).

27. E. P. Thompson, *The Making of the English Working Class* (New York: Vintage Books, 1963).

28. See, for example, R. M. Hartwell, *The Industrial Revolution and Economic Growth* (London: Methuen, 1971); J. D. Chambers, "Enclosure and Labour Supply in the Industrial Revolution,"

and other articles in *Agriculture and Economic Growth in England, 1650–1815*, edited by E. L. Jones (London: Methuen, 1967); and E. A. Wrigley and R. S. Scofield, *The Population History of England, 1541–1871: A Reconstruction* (Cambridge, Mass.: Harvard University Press, 1981).

29. See, for example, E. Preobrazhenskiv, *The New Economics*, translated by Brian Pearce (Oxford: Clarendon Press, 1966), and Alexander Erlich, *The Soviet Industrialization Debate, 1924–1928* (Cambridge, Mass.: Harvard University Press, 1960).

30. The most famous attack on this tradition is T. W. Schultz, *Transforming Traditional Agriculture* (New York: Arno Press, 1976).

31. See the contributions in Francois Crouzet, *Capital Formation in the Industrial Revolution* (London: Methuen, 1972). See also D. N. McCloskey, "The Industrial Revolution 1780–1860: A Survey," in *The Economic History of Britain Since 1700*, edited by Roderick Floud and Donald McCloskey, vol. 1 (Cambridge: Cambridge University Press, 1981).

32. The relevant comparison is between V. J. Lenin, *Imperialism: The Highest Stage of Capitalism* (New York: International Publishers, 1939), and *The Development of Capitalism in Russia* (Moscow: Progress Publishers, 1956).

33. See, for example, Karl Polanyi, *The Great Transformation* (Boston: Beacon Press, 1957).

34. The basic writings on this subject have been collected into Karl Marx and Frederik Engels, *Pre-Capitalist Socio-Economic Formations: A Collection* (London: Lawrence & Wishart, 1979).

35. This point of view is championed most fervently, perhaps, in the writings of George Dalton. See, for example, his contributions in George Dalton, ed., *Tribal and Peasant Economies* (Garden City, N.Y.: Natural History Press, 1967). It has been applied to politics by Eric R. Wolf in his *Peasant Wars of the Twentieth Century*, by Joel S. Migdal in *Peasants, Politics and Revolution*, and, perhaps most notably, by James C. Scott in *The Moral Economy of the Peasant: Rebellion and Subsistence in Southeast Asia* (New Haven, Conn.: Yale University Press, 1976). This perspective on the peasant issue has been forcefully and, to my mind, successfully attacked by Samuel L. Popkin in his *The Rational Peasant: The Political Economy of Rural Society in Vietnam* (Berkeley: University of California Press, 1979).

36. See the discussion, for example, in David Mitrany, *Marx against the Peasant* (New York: Collier Books, 1961).

37. Goran Hyden, *Beyond Ujamaa in Tanzania: Underdevelopment and an Uncaptured Peasantry* (Berkeley: University of California Press, 1980).

38. A beautifully presented argument exhibiting this point of view is James C. Scott's paper "Protest and Profanation: Agrarian Revolt and the Little Tradition," *Theory and Society*, pts. 1, 2, 4 (1977):1–38, 211–46.

39. The basic argument is presented by A. V. Chyanov, *The Theory of Peasant Economy*, edited by D. Thorner, B. Kerbley, and R. E. F. Smith (Homewood, Ill.: Richard D. Irwin, 1966).

40. Both sides of the debate are presented ably in Gavin Williams, "The World Bank and the Peasant Problem," in *Rural Development in Tropical Africa*, edited by Judith Heyer, Pepe Roberts, and Gavin Williams (New York: St. Martin's Press, 1981).

41. Teodor Shanin, *The Awkward Class* (Oxford: Clarendon Press, 1972).

42. Eric R. Wolf, *Peasants* (Englewood Cliffs, N.J.: Prentice-Hall, 1966), and Marshall Sahlins, *Stone Age Economics* (Chicago: Aldine Press, 1972).

43. L. A. Fallers, "Are African Cultivators To Be Called 'Peasants'?," in *Economic Development and Social Change*, edited by George Dalton (Garden City, N.Y.: Natural History Press): 169–77.

44. This theme pervades the African literature. For an early classic, see A. R. Radcliffe-Brown and Daryll Forde, eds., *African Systems of Kinship and Marriage* (London: Oxford University Press, 1950). See also Jack Goody, ed., *The Character of Kinship* (London: Cambridge University Press, 1973).

45. The classic contribution is Eric Wolf, "Closed Corporate Peasant Communities in Mesoamerica and Central Java," *Southwestern Journal of Anthropology* 13 (1957):1–18. See also Migdal, *Peasants, Politics and Revolution;* Scott, *Moral Economy of the Peasant;* and Popkin, *Rational Peasant.*

46. See, for example, Lewis Dumont, *Homo Hierarchicus: The Caste System and Its Implications* (Chicago: University of Chicago Press, 1970). One of the early classics on tribes is Meyer Fortes and Edward E. Evans-Pritchard, eds., *African Political Systems* (London: Oxford University Press, 1940).

47. See, for example, the contributions in Victor A. Olorunsula, ed., *The Politics of Cultural Sub-Nationalism in Africa* (Garden City, N.Y.: Anchor Books, 1972).

48. See the contributions in Steffen W. Schmidt, et al., *Friends,*

*Followers and Factions: A Reader in Political Clientelism* (Berkeley: University of California Press, 1977).

49.  Donald Rothchild and Victor A. Olorunsula, eds., *State versus Ethnic Claims: African Policy Dilemmas* (Boulder, Colo.: Westview Press, 1983).

50.  M. N. Srinivas, "A Note on Sanskritization and Westernization," *Far Eastern Quarterly* 15 (November 1955–August 1956):492–96.

51.  Scott, *Moral Economy of the Peasant;* Wolf, *Peasant Wars;* Migdal, *Peasants, Politics and Revolution;* Popkin, *Rational Peasant.*

52.  Moore, *Social Origins;* Theda Skocpol, *States and Social Revolutions: A Comparative Analysis of France, Russia, and China* (Cambridge: Cambridge University Press, 1979); and Robert Brenner, "Agrarian Class Structure and Economic Development in Pre-Industrial Europe," *Past and Present* 70 (February 1976):30–75, and "The Agrarian Roots of European Capitalism," *Past and Present* 97 (November 1982):16–113.

53.  See also such works as Peter Alexis Gourevitch, "International Trade, Domestic Coalitions, and Liberty: Comparative Responses to the Crisis of 1873–1896," *Journal of Interdisciplinary History* 8, no. 2 (Autumn 1977):281–313, and "The Reemergence of 'Peripheral Nationalisms,'" *Comparative Studies in Society and History* 21 (1979):303–22; Trimberger, "Theory of Elite Revolutions"; Michael Hechter and William Brustein, "Regional Modes of Production and Patterns of State Formation in Western Europe," *American Journal of Sociology* 85 (1980):1081–94.

54.  Contrast, by example, the divergent — but equally rapid — patterns of agricultural development documented in Yujiro Hayami and Vernon Ruttan, *Agricultural Development: An International Perspective* (Baltimore, Md.: Johns Hopkins University Press, 1971).

55.  See the sources in notes 27, 28, and 31.

56.  See, for example, Steven N. S. Cheung, *The Theory of Share Tenancy: With Special Application to Asian Agriculture and the First Phase of Taiwan Land Refarm* (Chicago: University of Chicago Press, 1969), and the outpouring of articles published in response to this work (e.g., David M. G. Newbery, "The Choice of Rental Contract in Peasant Agriculture," in *Agriculture in Development Theory,* edited by Lloyd G. Reynolds, (New Haven, Conn.: Yale University Press, 1975).

57.  Specimen contributions would include Willis L. Peterson, "In-

ternational Farm Prices and the Social Cost of Cheap Food Prices," *American Journal of Agricultural Economics* 61 (1979):12–21; Malcolm Bale and Ernst Lutz, "Price Distortion and Their Effects: An International Comparison," World Bank Staff Working Paper, no. 359, 1979; Ian Little, Tibor Scitovsky, and Maurice Scott, *Industry and Trade in Some Developing Countries* (London: Oxford University Press, 1970); Guillermo O'Donnell, "State and Alliances in Argentina, 1956–1976," *Journal of Development Studies* 15 (October 1978):3–33; Robert H. Bates, *Markets and States in Tropical Africa: The Political Basis of Agricultural Policies* (Berkeley: University of California Press, 1981).

58.   Popkin, *Rational Peasant.* See also Robert H. Bates, *Rural Responses to Industrialization: A Study of Village Zambia* (New Haven, Conn.: Yale University Press, 1976).

59.   I distinguish the collective from the public choice literature on the grounds that the latter remains more closely tied to conventional economics. This is revealed, for example, in the tendency of public choice theorists to regard politics as a form of "social cost" and (which leads to the same result) gains from trade as being costless to organize. Economically efficient outcomes remain the basic reference point for most investigations. Collective choice differs in that it tends to engage in positive analysis; it examines the choices that will be made by rational agents in nonmarket institutions. Normative considerations — e.g., departures from efficient outcomes — tend to represent a secondary concern.

60.   See, for example, Bates, *Markets and States.*

61.   The classic text is Mancur Olson, *The Logic of Collective Action: Public Goods and the Theory of Groups* (Cambridge, Mass.: Harvard University Press, 1971); see also Brian Barry and Russell Harden, *Rational Man and Irrational Society?* (Beverly Hills, Calif.: Sage, 1982).

62.   The basic texts on this literature are Anthony Downs, *An Economic Theory of Democracy* (New York: Harper & Row, 1957), and William H. Riker and Peter C. Odeshook, *An Introduction to Positive Political Theory* (Englewood Cliffs, N.J.: Prentice-Hall, 1973). An extremely interesting application of this reasoning to nonelectoral settings is James DeNardo, *Power in Numbers: The Political Strategy of Protest and Rebellion* (Princeton: Princeton University Press, 1985). See also the literature on the effect of partisan forces on economic policy. A good introduction is Gary C. Jacobson and Samuel Kernell, *Strategy and Choice in Congres-*

*sional Elections* (New Haven, Conn.: Yale University Press, 1981), and a good critical overview is offered in James E. Alt and K. Alec Chrystal, *Political Economics* (Berkeley: University of California Press, 1983).

63. See, for example, George Stigler, "The Theory of Economic Regulation," *Bell Journal of Economics and Management Science* 3 (1971):211–40.

64. Morris Fiorina and Roger Noll, "Voters, Legislators and Bureaucrats," *Journal of Political Economy* 9 (1978):239–54; Barry R. Weingast, Kenneth A. Shepsle, and Christopher Johnsen, "The Political Economy of Benefits and Costs," *Journal of Political Economy* 89 (1981):642–64; Mathew D. McCubbins and Thomas Schwartz, "Congressional Oversight Overlooked: Police Patrols versus Fire Alarms," *American Journal of Political Science* 28, no. 1 (February 1984):165–79.

65. W. A. Niskanen, *Bureaucracy and Representative Government* (Chicago: Aldine-Atherton, 1971). See also Gary Miller and Terry M. Moe, "Bureaucrats, Legislators, and the Size of Government," *American Political Science Review* 77 (June 1983):297–322, and Albert Breton and Ronald Wintrobe, *The Logic of Bureaucratic Conduct* (Cambridge: Cambridge University Press, 1982).

66. Karl Polanyi, *Trade and Market in Early Empires* (New York: Free Press, 1957); George Dalton, ed., *Tribal and Peasant Economies* (Garden City, N.Y.: Natural History Press, 1967).

67. Dennis L. Chinn, "Team Cohesion and Collective Labor Supply in Chinese Agriculture," *Journal of Comparative Economics* 3 (1979):375–94; Louis Putterman, "Is Democratic Collective Agriculture Possible? Theoretical Considerations and Evidence from Tanzania," *Journal of Development Studies* (forthcoming).

68. See Chapter 1 of Robert H. Bates, *Essays, On the Political Economy of Rural Africa* (Cambridge: Cambridge University Press, 1983) and Richard Posner, "A Theory of Primitive Society," *Journal of Law and Economics* 23 (1980):1–53. The most comprehensive review of the sharecropping literature is contained in the forthcoming revised edition of Hayami and Ruttan, *Agricultural Development*.

69. Chapter 2 of Bates, *Essays;* Margaret Levi, "The Predatory Theory of Rule," *Politics and Society* 10 (1981):431–66; Aristide Zolberg, "Strategic Interactions and the Formation of Modern States: France and England," *International Social Science Journal* 32 (1980):687–716; Douglass C. North and Robert Paul

Thomas, *The Rise of the Western World* (Cambridge: Cambridge University Press, 1973); and David Friedman, "A Theory of the Size and Shape of Nations," *Journal of Political Economy* 85 (1977):59–77.

70. Samuel L. Popkin, "Public Choice and Rural Development," in *Public Choice and Rural Development*, edited by Clifford Russell and Norman Nicholson (Washington, D.C.: Resources for the Future, 1981); Ammar Siamwalla, "An Economic Theory of Patron-Client Relations," paper prepared for Thai-European Seminar on Social Change in Contemporary China, April 1980. See also Oliver Williamson, "The Modern Corporation: Origin, Evolution, Attributes, *Journal of Economic Literature* 19 (December 1981):1537–68.

71. See, for example, Philip Hoffman, "Social History and Taxes: The Case of Early Modern France," California Social Science Working Paper, no. 495, October 1983; Katherine Norberg, "The Amoral Economy of Echallon: An Eighteenth-Century Community from the Perspective of Its Seigneurial Court," paper presented to the California Institute of Technology/ Weingart Conference, 6 May 1983; and Robert H. Bates, "Some Conventional Orthodoxies in the Study of Agrarian Change," California Institute of Technology Social Science Working Paper, no. 458, December 1983.

72. Interesting examples of this form of reasoning are offered not only by Marxist historians (see G. A. Cohen, *Karl Marx's Theory of History* (Princeton, N.J.: Princeton University Press, 1978) and the new institutional economics (for example, North and Thomas, *Rise of the Western World*), but also in such interesting works as Posner, "Theory of Primitive Society," and Robert Axelrod, "The Emergence of Cooperation among Egoists," *American Political Science Review* 75 (June 1981):306–18.

73. This is the point of view advanced by such anthropologists as Elizabeth Colson. See Elizabeth Colson, *Tradition and Contract* (Chicago: Aldine Press, 1974).

**WALKER CONNOR**

# Ethnonationalism

## LOOKING BACKWARD

It risks triteness to note that during the past two decades ethnonationalism has been an extremely consequential force throughout the first, second, and third worlds. Even the more casual observers of the world scene are now cognizant that Belgium, France, Spain, and the United Kingdom are not ethnically homogeneous states and that the loyalty of Flemings, Corsicans, Basques, and Welshmen to their respective states cannot be accepted as a given. Although less publicized, ethnic unrest within China, Rumania, the Soviet Union, and Vietnam (to name but a few of the afflicted Marxist-Leninist states) is a matter of record. Awareness of the significance of ethnic heterogeneity within the states of the third world has reached the point where even newspaper accounts of coups, elections, and guerrilla struggles often contain references to the ethnic dimensions that are involved.

Few indeed are the scholars who can claim either to have anticipated this global upsurge in ethnonationalism or to have recognized its early manifestations. With respect to the first world, there was a tendency to perceive the states as nation-states, rather than as multinational states, and, in any event, to presume that World War II had convinced the peoples of Western Europe that nationalism was too dangerous and outmoded a focus for the modern age. A supranational, supra-state identity as European was described as the wave of the future. With regard to the second world, it was broadly held that a highly effective power apparatus and the indoctrination of the masses in Marxist-Leninist ideology had made the issue of ethnonationalism either superfluous or anachronistic. In effect, scholars accepted the official position of Marxist-Leninist governments that the application of Leninist national policy had solved "the national question," leading the masses to embrace proletarian internationalism. In third-world scholarship also, ethnic heterogeneity tended to be ignored or to be cavalierly dismissed as an ephemeral phenomenon. The catchphrase of political development theory at the time was "nation-building," but its devotees offered few if any suggestions as to how a single national consciousness was to be forged among disparate ethnic elements.

How could this wide discrepancy between theory and reality be explained? More than a decade ago, this writer suggested twelve overlapping and reinforcing reasons:[1]

1. *Confusing interutilization of the key terms.* Major result: a tendency to equate nationalism with loyalty to the state (patriotism) and therefore to presurmise that the state would win out in any test of loyalties.

2. *A misunderstanding of the nature of ethnic nationalism resulting in a tendency to underrate its emotional power.* Major result: a perception of ethnically inspired dissonance as predicated upon language, religion, customs, economic inequality, or some other tangible phenomenon, and, *propter hoc,* a failure thus to probe and appreciate the true nature and power of ethnic feelings.

3. *An unwarranted exaggeration of the influence of materialism upon human affairs.* Major result: the implicit or explicit presumption that the wellsprings of ethnic discord are economic and that an ethnic minority can be placated if its living standard is improving, both in real terms and relative to other segments of the state's population.

4. *Unquestioned acceptance of the assumption that greater contacts among groups lead to greater awareness of what groups have in common, rather than of what makes them distinct.* Major result: the optimistic belief that increased ties between groups are both symptomatic and productive of harmonious relations (as reflected, for example, in transaction-flow theory).

5.  *Improper analogizing from the experience of the United States.* Major result: a presumption that the history of acculturation and assimilation within an immigrant society would be apt to be repeated in multinational states.

6.  *Improper analogizing from the fact that improvements in communications and transportation help to dissolve regional identities to the conclusion that the same process will occur in situations involving two or more ethnonational peoples.* Major result: a presumption that the waning of significance of regional identities in an ethnically homogeneous state, such as Germany, has precedent for multinational states.

7.  *The assumption that assimilation is a one-directional process.* Major result: any evidence of a move toward acculturation / assimilation is viewed as an irreversible gain and is a basis for optimistic forecasts.

8.  *Interpretation of the absence of ethnic strife as evidence of the presence of a single nation.* Major result: a tranquil period in the relations among two or more ethnonational groups causes scholars to assume that the society is ethnically homogeneous, or a multiethnic "national liberation movement" is perceived as monoethnic.

9.  *Improper regard for the factor of chronological time and intervening events when analogizing from assimilationist experience prior to the "Age of Nationalism."* Major result: examples of assimilation prior to the nineteenth century are employed as evidence that ethnic identity is a thoroughly fluid phenomenon.

10. *Improper regard for durative time by failing to consider that attempts to telescope "assimilationist time," by increasing the frequency and scope of contacts, may produce a negative response.* Major result: conviction that assimilation lends itself readily to social engineering.

11. *Confusing symptoms with causes.* Major result: explanations for political decay focus upon interim steps, such as the weakening of "mass parties," rather than upon the root cause of ethnic rivalry.

12. *The predisposition of the analyst.* Major result: a tendency to perceive trends deemed desirable as actually occurring.

The list is certainly not exhaustive, and at least five additional reasons suggest themselves:

13. *The mistaken belief that the states of Western Europe were fully integrated nation-states.* A number of leading theorists of political development explicitly maintained that the experiences of the states of Western Europe would be followed by those of the third world in the course of their development. Thus, Western Europe was held up as an exemplar of something it was not, as proof that nation-states would develop in the third world.

14. *A tendency to apply conventional scholarly approaches to the third world.* A great deal of early third world scholarship reflected the first world training of the analysts. Avenues of research, long applied to first-world societies, were transferred to third-world states. Thus, a number of third-world studies explored political party structures and voting patterns in state assemblies, without appreciating that political parties were often viewed at the grass-roots level as the continuation of ethnic rivalry by other means.

15. *Too-exclusive concentration upon the state.* Much of the early third-world scholarship reflected only the view from the capital, to the exclusion of the view from the ethnic homelands.

16. *Too-exclusive concentration on the dominant group in the case of societies with a Staatvolk, such as Burma or Thailand.* One indication of this tendency can be found in purportedly state-wide political culture studies that make no reference to the political cultures of ethnic minorities, even when the latter account for a substantial percentage of the population.

17. *The tendency of many scholars to favor explanations based on class.*[2] Ethnic nationalism poses a severe paradox to such scholars since it posits that the vertical compartments that divide humanity into Englishmen, Germans, Ibos, Malays, and the like constitute more potent foci of identity and loyalty than do the horizontal compartments known as classes.

Whatever the reason(s), the "nation-building" school failed to give proper heed to what, in most states, was *a* if not *the* major obstacle to political development. Today, just as two decades ago, ethnic nationalism poses the most serious threat to political stability in a host of states as geographically dispersed as Belgium, Burma, Ethiopia, Guyana, Malaysia, Nigeria, the Soviet Union, Sri Lanka, Yugoslavia, and Zimbabwe. Given, then, the failure of the political development theorists to reflect proper concern for the problems posed by ethnic heterogeneity, it is disturbing to find no reference to this glaring weakness in Gabriel Almond's retrospective essay on the political development literature and its critics, which appears in this volume. Indeed, although numerous authors have drawn attention over the years to this remarkable slighting of the ethnic factor in the "national-building" literature, the criticism has gone unanswered by those commonly identified with the fathering of political development theory.

## MORE RECENT DEVELOPMENTS

Scholarly indifference to problems arising from ethnic heterogeneity evaporated rapidly in the face of increasing numbers of ethnonational movements. By the mid-1970s, the study of ethnic heterogeneity and its consequences had become a growth industry. Literally thousands of articles focused principally on ethnonationalism have appeared in English-language journals in the last decade. Scores of monographs and collections have been dedicated to the same topic, as have an impressive number of doctoral dissertations. Conferences and round tables on ethnicity have become commonplace, and panels on the subject have become regular parts of the programs at annual meetings of professional organizations. A number of new journals — such as the *Canadian Review of Studies in Nationalism* and *Ethnic and Racial Studies* — further attest to the intensified interest in ethnicity.

That this huge body of knowledge has contributed magnificently to our knowledge of specific peoples, their interethnic attitudes and behavior, their leaders, and their aspirations is beyond dispute. But it must also be acknowledged that all of this scholarly activity has not produced an approximation of a coherent statement. There is a marked lack of consensus concerning how ethnic heterogeneity can be best accommodated, or, indeed, even whether it can be accommodated noncoercively. And, in turn, these disagreements reflect a lack of consensus concerning the phenomenon that is supposedly the common focus of all these studies. In some cases, research, conducted under umbrella terms such as cultural pluralism, has in fact grouped several categories of identity (e.g., religious, linguistic, regional, and ethnonational) as though they were one or, at least, as though they exerted the same impact upon behavior. Others, influenced by the common misuse of the word ethnicity within the context of U.S. society, have used this rubric when investigating nearly any type of minority found in a state (despite the fact that ethnicity was derived from the Greek word *ethnos,* connoting a group characterized by common descent). The analytical utility of such blanket categories is open to serious question. Minimally, such broad categories sidestep raising the key question as to which of several group identities is apt to prove most potent in any test of loyalties.

Still other scholars, while focusing on ethnonationalism, have described it in terms of some other "ism." Having already misassigned nationalism to loyalty to the state, they have perforce enlisted some other term to describe loyalty to one's ethnonational group. Primordialism(s), tribalism, regionalism, communalism, parochialism, and subnationalism are among the more-often-encountered alternatives. Each of these terms already had a meaning not associated with nationalism, a fact further contributing to the terminological confusion impeding the study of ethnonationalism. (Communalism, for example, which refers within Western Europe to autonomy for local governments and within the Asian subcontinent to confessional identity, has appeared in the titles of books and articles in reference to ethnonationalism in Africa and Southeast Asia.) Moreover, individually each of these terms exerts its uniquely baneful effect upon the perceptions of both the author and the reader. And collectively, this varied vocabulary risks the impression that what is misdescribed as regionalism within one country, tribalism within another, and communalism within a third are different phenomena — when in fact it is ethnonationalism that in each case is the focus of the study. Imprecise vocabulary is both a symptom of and a contributor to a great deal of the haziness surrounding the study of ethnonationalism. As noted elsewhere:

> In this Alice-in-Wonderland world in which nation usually means state, in which nation-state usually means multination state, in which nationalism usually means loyalty to the state, and in which ethnicity, primordialism, pluralism, tribalism, regionalism, communalism, parochialism and sub-nationalism usually mean loyalty to the nation, it should come as no surprise that the nature of nationalism remains essentially unprobed.[3]

Indeed, very few scholars have directly addressed the matter of the nature of the ethnonational bond. A common empirical approach of those who did so during the first half of this century was to ask the question: "What makes a nation?" Among the scholarly giants who raised this question were Carlton Hayes and Hans Kohn. They addressed themselves to what was necessary or unnecessary for a nation to exist. The typical response was a common language, a common religion, a common territory, and the like. Stalin's 1913 definition of a nation, which still exerts a massive influence upon Marxist-Leninist scholarship, was very much in this tradition:

> A nation is a historically evolved, stable community of people, formed on the basis of a common language, territory, economic life, and psychological make-up manifested in a common culture.[4]

This approach still has its devotees, most notably Louis Snyder. Certainly it has the merit of emphasizing the wisdom of employing a broadly comparative framework when studying ethnonationalism. On the other hand, comparative analyses establish that no set of tangible characteristics is essential to the maintenance of national consciousness. Moreover, this particular approach would appear to fall into the earlier-mentioned trap of mistaking the tangible symptoms of a nation for its essence. As the late Rupert Emerson cogently reminded us in a few prefatory words before launching an investigation of the elements that most commonly accompany national consciousness:

The simplest statement that can be made about a nation is that it is a body of people who feel that they are a nation; and it may be that when all the fine-spun analysis is concluded this will be the ultimate statement as well. To advance beyond it, it is necessary to attempt to take the nation apart and to isolate for separate examination the forces and elements which appear to have been the most influential in bringing about the sense of common identity which lies at its roots, the sense of the existence of a singularly important national "we" which is distinguished from all others who make up an alien "they." This is necessarily an overly mechanical process, for nationalism, like other profound emotions such as love and hate, is more than the sum of the parts which are susceptible of cold and rational analysis.[5]

As noted, very few of the present generation of scholars have attempted a serious probe of the nature of the ethnonational bond forcing the curious to infer their conceptualization of it from their comments concerning the causes of the solutions to ethnonational restlessness. When employing this yardstick, it appears that many authors have scant respect for the psychological and emotional hold that ethnonational identity has upon the group. To some, ethnonational identity seems little more than an epiphenomenon that becomes active as a result of relative economic deprivation and that will dissipate with greater egalitarianism. Others reduce it to the level of a pressure group that mobilizes in order to compete for scarce resources. A variation on the pressure group concept places greater emphasis on the role of elites; rather than a somewhat spontaneous mass response to competition, the stirring of national consciousness is seen as a ploy utilized by aspiring elites in order to enhance their own status. Finally, in the hands of many adherents of the "internal colonialism" model, entire ethnonational groups are equated with a socioeconomic class, and ethnonational consciousness becomes equated with class consciousness.

All of these approaches could be criticized as a continuing tendency of scholars to harbor what we termed earlier "an unwarranted exaggeration of the influence of materialism upon human affairs." They could also be criticized as examples of a tendency to misapply theoretic approaches (such as pressure group theory, elite theory, and dependency theory). They can all be criticized empirically. (The most well-known propagator of the internal colonial thesis, Michael Hechter, recently recanted his support for that thesis, citing as cause its limited explanatory power.)[6] But they can be faulted chiefly for their failure to reflect the emotional depth of ethnonational identity and the mass sacrifices that have been made in its name. Explanations of behavior in terms of pressure groups, elite ambitions, and rational choice theory hint not at all at the passions that motivate Kurdish, Tamil, and Tigre guerrillas or Basque, Corsican, Irish, and Palestinian terrorists. Nor at the passions leading to the massacre of Bengalis by Assamese or Punjabi by Sikhs. In short, these explanations are a poor guide to ethnonationally inspired behavior.

Among those scholars who demonstrate a more profound regard for the psychological and emotional dimensions of ethnonational identity, there is a small but growing nucleus who now explicitly describe the ethnonational group as a kinship group. Among them are Joshua Fishman,[7] Donald Horowitz,[8] Charles Keyes,[9] Kian Kwan and Tomotshu Shibutani,[10] Anthony Smith,[11] and Pierre van den Berghe.[12] Interestingly, despite the fact that this formulation of the nation runs counter to classical Marxism, the Soviet Union's most influential academician in the study of national consciousness, Yu. Bromley, also acknowledges the role of kinship in nation formation.[13]

Recognizing the sense of common kinship that permeates the ethnonational bond clears a number of hurdles. First, it qualitatively distinguishes national consciousness from non-kinship identities (such as those based on religion or class) with which it has too often been grouped. Secondly, an intuitive sense of kindredness or extended family would explain why nations are endowed with a very special psychological dimension — an emotional dimension — not enjoyed by essentially functional or juridical groupings, such as socioeconomic classes or states.

Unlike scholars, political leaders have long been sensitized to this sense of common ancestry and have blatantly appealed to it as a means of mobilizing the masses. Consider Bismarck's famous exhortation to the German people, over the heads of their individual state leaders, to unite in a single state: "Germans, think with your blood!" Or consider the proclamation that was transmitted throughout fascist Italy in 1938:

> The root of differences among peoples and nations is to be found in differences of race. If Italians differ from Frenchmen, Germans, Turks, Greeks, etc., this is not just because they possess a different language and a different history, but because their racial development is different.... *A pure "Italian race" is already in existence.* This pronouncement [rests] on the very pure blood tie that unites present-day Italians.... This ancient purity of blood is the Italian nation's greatest title of nobility.[14]

Or listen to Mao Tse-tung in the same year describe the Chinese Communists as "part of the great Chinese nation, flesh of its flesh and blood of its blood...."[15] Or read the current program of the Rumanian Communist party that describes the party's principal function as defending the national interest of "our people," a nation said to have been "born out of the fusion of the Dacians [an ancient people] with the Romans."[16] An article written in Hungary in 1982 criticizes a Rumanian publication for promoting "an ethnocratic state" predicated upon "the unity of the 'pure-blooded race' in which there is no room for the *strain,* the outsider."[17] Within Africa, Yoruba and Fang leaders have stressed a legend of common origin, as have Malay leaders within Malaysia.

It might well be asked why scholars have been so slow to discover what the masses have felt and what political leaders have recognized. There are several possible answers, including (1) the intellectual's discomfort with the nonrational (note: *not* irrational), and (2) the search for quantifiable and therefore tangible explanations. But another factor has been the propensity to ignore the vital distinction between fact and perceptions of fact. Several of the studies of the last generation to which we alluded did raise the issue of common ancestry as one of the possible criteria of nationhood. However, the authors then denied the relevance of such a consideration by noting that most national groups could be shown to be the

variegated offspring of a number of peoples. But this conclusion ignored the old saw that it is not *what is*, but *what people
believe is* that has behavioral consequences. And a subconscious
belief in the group's separate origin and evolution is an essential ingredient of ethnonational psychology. A nation is a
group of people characterized by a myth of common descent.
Moreover, regardless of its roots, a nation must remain an
essentially endogamous group in order to maintain its myth.

As noted, there are grounds for optimism in that a small
core of influential scholars has come to recognize the myth
of common ancestry as the defining characteristic of the nation. It may well be, therefore, that effective probing of the
subjective dimensions of the national bond will occur during
the next decade. Fishman has certainly begun excavating in
this area, and in a recent book *(Ethnic Groups In Conflict)* Donald Horowitz indicates one avenue of possibly fruitful research, suggesting how several studies borrowed from
experimental psychology (and dealing with both individual
and group behavior) may lead to a better understanding of
ethnonationalism. And Pierre van den Berghe now maintains
that the literature on sociobiology has much to offer the student of ethnic identity.

Two other possibly productive areas of research for the
probing of the emotional/psychological dimension of ethnonationalism come to mind. The poet, as an adept expressor
of deep-felt passions, is apt to be a far better guide here than
the social scientist has proven to be. National poetry has hardly
been touched upon on a worldwide comparative basis. Quite
aside from aesthetics, it would obviously be of great value to
learn what feelings and images have been most commonly
invoked by recognized national poets, without regard to geography, level of their people's development, etc.

Still another potentially fruitful source when probing the
nature of ethnonationalism consists of the speeches of national
leaders and the pamphlets, programs, and other documents
of ethnonationalist organizations. Too often these speeches
and documents have been passed off as useless propaganda
in which the authors do not really believe. But nationalism is
a mass phenomenon, and the degree to which the leaders are

true believers does not affect its reality. The question is not the sincerity of the propagandist, but the nature of the mass instinct to which the propagandist appeals. Napoleon was unquestionably more a manipulator of than a believer in nationalism, but his armies were certainly filled with soldiers fired up by nationalism. Speeches and programs should therefore be scanned from the viewpoint of comparative content. With what frequency do certain words and images appear? What referents are used to trigger the psychological response?

In any case, it is certain that very few scholars will attempt to probe the nature of nationalism. As in the past, most authors who touch on ethnonationalism will be dealing with its manifestation in one or another society and/or policies aimed at its containment. However, their general treatment of the subject and their assessment of policies will necessarily reflect their unarticulated perception of the nature of ethnonationalism, and it is to be hoped that the literature will increasingly embody that deeper respect for the emotional and psychological depths of ethnonationalism that we have noted in the works of a small but growing number of influential writers.

### A COMMENT ON COMPARABILITY

Before we turn to the issue of accommodating ethnonationalism, a few words on comparability are in order. The leading scholars on nationalism have agreed that a broad comparative approach is essential. As Hans Kohn has noted:

> A study of nationalism must follow a comparative method; it cannot remain confined to one of its manifestations; only the comparison of the different nationalisms all over the earth will enable the student to see what they have in common and what is peculiar to each, and thus allow a just evaluation.[18]

While few would disagree with this advice, the comparative approach has hardly proven to be a magic key to understanding. Comparative works have often disappointed, leaving the reader more struck by the dissimilarities among societies than by their commonalities. In other cases, too-facile analogies have resulted in highly questionable conclusions. Given the absence of perfect analogies, the comparative approach to

TABLE II.1  *Comparability Categories*

*States*

Nation-states
Multinational states
   1. unihomeland
   2. multihomeland
   3. nonhomeland
Immigrant states
Mestizo states

*Peoples*

Prenations/potential nations
Nations
Offshoot nations
Diasporas (migrants and refugees)
Members of immigrant societies

ethnonationalism will remain an imperfect analytical tool, but it could be honed by developing categories of peoples and states that analogies should respect. That is to say, it should be possible to place most peoples and states in compartments that promise a measure of suitability to intracompartmental analogies, while concurrently flashing a warning signal to those who are comparing peoples or states from two or more compartments. Table II.1 represents an exploratory effort to develop categories that would help to avoid some of the more fallacious analogies that have marred the study of ethnonationalism.

Space does not permit more than a passing glance at these categories, but let us begin with the classification of states. Nation-states are those relatively rare situations, characterized by an extremely homogeneous population, where a nation has its own state. Iceland, Japan, Norway, and post–World-War-II Poland are illustrations.

Multinational states are easily the most common. However, an important consideration is whether the state consists of a single homeland, two or more homelands, or no homeland. As made evident by ethnographic atlases, most of the populated world is broken down into ethnonational homelands, regions whose name reflects a special claim upon the territory by a people — Baluchistan, Nagaland, Scotland, Ukraine, and Zululand are but a tiny sampling. The notion of the homeland is intimately associated with the myth of an ancestrally related people. The feeling that this place is indeed *home* to the extended family endows it with a reverential dimension apparent in such universal terms as the fatherland, the motherland, and, not least, the *home*land. Members of a homeland people believe that they possess a primary and exclusive title to the homeland. Outsiders may be tolerated or even encouraged as sojourners (*guest*workers, for example), but the demand that the sojourners *go home* can be raised at any time and may be aimed at compatriots as well as at foreigners. A series of quite extensive studies conducted within the Soviet Union confirms patterns of behavior and attitudes observed in other parts of the world. Whether people are living within or away from their homeland greatly influences, inter alia, their willingness to adopt a statewide language (other than their own), their willingness to marry outside of the group, the choice of ethnonational identity on the part of progeny of mixed marriages, and attitudes toward other ethnonational peoples. Those living within the homeland manifest greater animosity toward other groups and greater resistance to acculturation and assimilation. But the most consequential aspect of homeland psychology has been the hostility engendered by an intrusion of "the native land" by nonnatives. Examples of this phenomenon abound in the first world (Euskadi [Basqueland] and Corsica), the second world (Lithuania, Uighuristan [China], and Slovenia), and the third world (Assam, Baluchistan, Bangsamoro [the Philippines], and Kurdistan).

A *unihomeland, multinational state* is one in which the ethnic diversity is due to immigration. The homeland people consider the entire state to be their historic homeland, although their ancestors may themselves have migrated to the region (e.g., Malaysian Malays and Sri Lankan Sinhalese). Even if in a minority (e.g., the Fijians), a homeland people will feel that as "sons of the soil" they and their culture merit a privileged position relative to the interlopers. The current great increase in global migration may be enlarging this classification of states. Guestworkers who have become "staygrants" may be transforming former nation-states, such as the German Federal Republic and Sweden, into unihomeland, multinational states.

Multihomeland, multinational states, which represent the largest category, vary tremendously in the number of homelands they contain. While some consist of essentially two homelands (Czechoslovakia), some contain more than one hundred (Nigeria). The Soviet Union is one of the more complex states in this category. There, the political system extends various levels of administrative recognition to fifty-three homelands, in many of which Russians now predominate numerically.

Nonhomeland, multinational states are those whose population (1) is overwhelmingly the product of migration and (2) consists of at least two significant groups, each of which is vitally aware of its ethnic difference from the other(s) and is determined to maintain that distinctiveness. The greater Caribbean offers a number of examples, including Guyana, Suriname, and Trinidad-Tobago.

Immigrant states are also nonhomeland states, but with a highly variegated population in terms of ancestry. The officially endorsed archetype — the American in the case of the United States — is not ethnically defined, that is, it is ethnically neutral. Such states are characterized by a good deal of acculturation and assimilation. A relatively few people living in small homelands (e.g., the existence of Amerindian and Eskimo homelands within the United States) do not disqualify a state from the immigrant category.

Mestizo states are limited to Latin America and are characterized by a population in which those of joint European-Amerindian ancestry are dominant (not necessarily numerically so, as in the case of Bolivia). These states have traditionally posed severe problems of classification and analysis to students of ethnonationalism. If the ethnonational image propagated by their governments approximated the self-perceptions of the masses, these states could be treated comparatively as nation-states. This image posits a new breed or race (*La Raza Cosmica*) that has evolved from the melding of the European and the Amerindian. And from this basically undifferentiated whole there has supposedly evolved a nation that is coterminous with the state — that is, a Guatemalan, Mexican, or Peruvian nation. Reality is something else, however. Very significant numbers of Amerindian peoples have clearly not surrendered their diverse ancestral identities and are manifesting increasing hostility to mestizo domination. Antimestizo sentiment is already a key ingredient of guerrilla struggles being waged in Guatemala, Nicaragua, and Peru, and threatens to become so within Bolivia and Ecuador, among others. Amerindian peoples are currently pushing for greater autonomy within Panama. The point, then, is that while the mestizo states merit a separate category for analytical purposes, they more resemble multinational states than nation-states.

Turning now from states to peoples, the first category is prenational or potential nations. There still exist large numbers of people for whom national identity lies in the future. For such people, meaningful identity is still limited to locale, clan, tribe, and the like. It is quite impossible to say what percentage of a people must achieve national consciousness before the group merits treatment as a nation. But it is not enough that a substantial group of intellectuals maintains the existence of nationhood. Indeed, the Arab case reminds us of the danger of placing too great emphasis upon the views of elites in general and intellectuals in particular. The Arabs were among the very earliest non-European peoples to produce an elite that was imbued with national consciousness and dedicated to its development among the masses. And yet, after more than a half-century of such efforts, Arab nationalism remains anomalistically weak. The national literati may therefore be a poor guide to the actual level of national consciousness. But while it may therefore be difficult to say with precision at what point a group becomes transformed from prenation into nation, it is essential to keep in mind the distinction between the two. Examples of a change of identity on the part of the former should not be used to document an alleged ephemerality or situational nature on the part of the second.

We have earlier discussed the essence of nations. They are the largest human grouping characterized by a myth of common ancestry. The historical accuracy of the myth is irrelevant.

Offshoot nations are formed when an important segment

of a nation has been geographically separated from the parent group for a period of time sufficient for it to develop a strong sense of separate consciousness. Members retain an awareness that they derive from the parent stock, but they believe that the characteristics they have in common are less significant than those that make them unique. Examples include the Afrikaaners, the Formosan Han-jen, and the Quebecois.

Diasporas are people living outside of their homeland who have not assimilated to the host's identity.

Members of immigrant societies are those whose primary sense of loyalty is not to the ethnonation(s) of their ancestors, but to the immigrant society.

The preceding classification is at best a very rudimentary scheme for avoiding some of the more obviously fallacious analogies. It could be refined to several levels. Homeland-dwelling people, for example, could be subcategorized according to whether the homeland is essentially coterminous with the state (Sweden), comprises only part of the state (Wales), is divided among states in which the group is dominant (Arabdom), is divided into states in which the group is dominant in one and nondominant in the other (any number of so-called irredentist situations), or is divided into states in which the group is never dominant (Kurds). These and a myriad of other refinements would certainly mitigate the shortcomings of the analogical approach.

It is also evident that some states would not neatly fit the preceding schema. Canada is both part immigrant state (outside of Quebec) and part multinational homeland state. This, however, should not pose any severe problem, so long as the two are treated as separate entities for comparative purposes. "Anglo Canada" has analytical value for immigrant states, as does Quebec for the study of homeland peoples. In any cases, the point is that a greater regard for "comparability compartments" would greatly assist the comparative study of ethnic heterogeneity.

## THE ACCOMMODATION OF HETEROGENEITY

Questions of accommodating ethnonational heterogeneity within a single state revolve about two loyalties — loyalty to the nation and loyalty to the state — and the relative strength of the two. The great number of bloody separatist movements that have occurred in the past two decades within the first, second, and third worlds bear ample testimony that when the two loyalties are seen as being in irreconcilable conflict, loyalty to the state loses out. But the two need not be so perceived. To people with their own nation-state or to those people who are so dominant within a multinational state as to perceive the state as essentially their nation's state (e.g., the English, the Han Chinese, the Thais), the two loyalties become an indistinguishable, reinforcing blur. It is in the perceptions of national minorities that the two loyalties are most apt to vie.

Over the last decade, scholarship has made some important strides in probing the attitudes of minorities toward the state, although much more remains to be done. A number of sophisticated analyses have made good use of attitudinal data to bring us beyond the stage of simply hypothesizing about the two loyalties.[19] It should be noted, however, that the literature is based overwhelmingly, although not exclusively, on first-world states and on homeland peoples.

The following findings emerge from these studies:

1.   Members of ethnonational minorities manifest substantially less affection toward the state than do members of the dominant group.

2.   Minorities of the same state can differ significantly in this regard.

3.   For most persons, however, the matter is not perceived in either/or terms. Affective ties to the state coexist with ethnonational consciousness.

4.   In most cases in which a separatist movement is active, large numbers, usually a majority of the involved group, do not favor secession.

5.   In some cases, the percentage represented by pro-secessionists has remained relatively constant; in other cases it has evidenced profound trends.

6.   Regardless of their attitude toward secession, a preponderant number do favor major alterations in the political system that would result in greater autonomy.

7.   Where separatist parties are allowed to contest elections, their vote is not an adequate index to separatist sentiment.

8.   In all cases for which there are attitudinal data, members of ethnonational groups overwhelmingly reject the use of violence carried out in the name of the national group.

9.   However, a large percentage, including many who do not favor separation, empathize with those engaged in violence and place the blame for the violence upon others.

10.   Separatists draw their support from all social strata and age groups.

11.   Disproportionate support, however, comes from those under thirty-five years of age, with above-average education and income.

12.   Professional people are disproportionately represented.

13.   Lack of support is particularly pronounced among those over fifty-five years of age.

Many of the preceding points probably appear trivial or trite. Given the numerous powers of the state for politically socializing its population, it is hardly surprising that affective ties to the state exist. However, it would be particularly dangerous to take this finding — predicted principally upon first-world states — and apply it wholesale to a third-world environment. For one thing, most third-world states are too young to have developed the sense of institutional and symbolic legitimacy that is a central aspect of state loyalty. And the older states (such as Afghanistan, Ethiopia, Iran, Liberia, and Thailand), given the historic absence of the principal means for inculcating this sense of legitimacy (e.g., a public school system), are not true exceptions. To take perhaps an extreme case, it would be foolhardy to presume that the Kachins, Karens, and Shans harbor any noteworthy level of goodwill toward the Burman state.

The finding that most members of national minorities are

prepared to settle for something less than separation probably has more universal application. The still-revolutionary idea popularly termed national self-determination holds that any people, simply because it considers itself to be a separate people, has the right, *if it so desires*, to create its own state. However, it would appear to be the rule that a majority of members of a homeland people are prepared to settle for autonomy for the homeland. Even when demands are made for actual separation, third-world elites are usually as fragmented as those in the first world — between those who maintain this stance and those who announce their willingness to settle for autonomy. (The Pakistani Baluch, the Iraqi Kurds, the Moros, and the Sikhs are major current illustrations.) Moreover, a number of groups, although having engaged in violent struggle for the stated aim of independence, have subsequently entered into a peaceful relationship with the state authorities on the basis of a grant of autonomy. In the typical pattern, these periods of peace disintegrate in a flurry of charges and countercharges over whether the government's promises of autonomy have been honored. Underlying these failures at accommodation have usually been differing views concerning the content of autonomy.

Although often treated by scholars, state authorities, and ethnonational elites as alternatives, independence and autonomy are hardly that. Autonomy is an amorphous concept, capable of covering a multitude of visions extending from very limited local options to complete control over everything other than foreign policy. It can therefore incorporate all situations between total subordination to the center and total independence. Both autonomy and independence are therefore terms that tend to obscure important shadings in the attitudes that members of a group can be expected to hold concerning goals.

It should not be surprising that ethnonational peoples should blur the distinction between independence and autonomy. Ethnonational concerns, by their very nature, are more obsessed with a vision of freedom from domination by nonmembers than with a vision of freedom to conduct foreign relations with states. They are the reaction to international, not interstate, relations. The average Basque or Fleming, just as the average Kurd or Naga, does not appear to be influenced by a prospect of a seat at the United Nations or an embassy in Moscow. Indeed, in the case of most third-world peoples, meaningful autonomy would represent a return toward either the loose system of feudatory allegiances they knew under Afghani, Chinese, Ethiopian, or Persian empires or to the indirect rule that they knew under colonialism, both of which had more effectively muted ethnonational concerns than have their successor political systems. In short, ethnocracy does not presuppose state independence. It does presuppose meaningful autonomy.

The finding concerning popular sympathy for those who carry out violence in the name of the national group also has momentous implications for the political stability of states, for it explains how guerrilla struggles have been maintained for years in the face of overwhelming odds. It undergirded the wisdom of Guiseppi Mazzini's statement of more than a century and a half ago: "Insurrection — by means of guerrilla bands — is the true method of warfare for all nations desirous of emancipating themselves from a foreign yoke." In the case of wars of (ethno) national liberation, the numbers actually engaged in guerrilla struggle may be quite small, but those who fight in the name of the nation's liberation can expect that degree of sympathy that, as Mao Tse-tung, Truong Chinh, and others have noted, is indispensable to the conduct of a successful guerrilla struggle. And this is why a number of leaders of guerrilla struggles, whose own goals have had nothing to do with minority rights, have gained the necessary local support by promising independence or autonomy to ethnonational groups. Such promises played significant roles in the assumption of power by the Chinese Communist party, the Viet Minh, and the Pathet Lao, and it is today a key element in the propaganda of revolutionary movements in Latin America. In Africa also, the numerous guerrilla struggles cannot be understood without reference to ethnic maps and aspirations.

While the thirteen findings outlined above attest to the formidable threat that ethnic heterogeneity poses to political stability, they also contain much to encourage those in search of formulae for accommodating such diversity. The fact that most members of most ethnic minorities are prepared to settle for something less than complete independence means that such formulae are not sheer whimsy. The likelihood of arriving at a mutually agreeable formula is another matter, however. A successful formula will require a significant measure of decentralization of authority, and governments, by nature, are ill-disposed toward the relinquishing of power. However, governments may come to recognize that a measure of devolution would actually increase their authority over otherwise rebellious national groups. Few students of Spanish politics prior to 1975 imagined that the highly centralized, authoritarian system of Franco would be followed by a government prepared to grant substantial autonomy to the country's non-Castillian peoples. Belgium, Canada, and Panama are other states that have recently diluted support for separatist movements by adopting power-sharing formulae. Most governments, however, have not been prepared to grant the degree of autonomy necessary to avoid the resort to separatism. But the tendency for ethnonational groups to aspire to greater autonomy, while being prepared to settle for something short of full independence, does underline the fact that a solution to ethnic heterogeneity must ultimately be found in the political sphere and not in the economic one. Myron Weiner's advice therefore appears sound:

> In exploring the factors at work in the development of national integration and political legitimacy it is important that we pay particular attention to political variables, and resist the tendency to rely upon economic, social or psychological explanations for political facts. If we use psychological variables to explain psychological behaviors, and social facts to explain social facts, so ought we first turn to one set of political facts to explain another.[20]

## BY WAY OF SUMMARY

The literature on ethnonational heterogeneity has undergone a quantum leap in the last decade. Our knowledge of specific peoples and problems has grown enormously as a result. This outpouring, however, has not resulted in a broad consensus concerning either the nature of ethnonationalism or means to its accommodation, although there are grounds for optimism that substantive progress will be made during the next decade.

My own admonitions for ensuring this progress are five in number:

1. Greater attention must be paid to avoiding imprecise and confusing terminology.[21]

2. Greater appreciation for the psychological /emotional depth of ethnonational identity must be reflected in the literature.

3. Greater refinements are necessary with regard to classifying peoples and political systems for comparative purposes.

4. Greater appreciation that ethnonational demands are at bottom political rather than economic in nature should be reflected in proposals for accommodating ethnic heterogeneity.[22]

5. It should always be remembered that ethnonationalism is a mass phenomenon, and keeping this in mind should counteract the tendency to overemphasize the role of elites as its impresarios.[23]

**NOTES**

1. For a lengthier discussion and illustrations of each of these items, see Walker Connor, "Nation-Building or Nation-Destroying?," *World Politics* 24, no. 3 (April 1972): 319–55.

2. I am indebted to Myron Weiner for drawing attention to this omission from my list.

3. Walker Connor, "A Nation Is a Nation, Is a State, Is an Ethnic Group, Is a . . . ," *Ethnic and Racial Studies*, no. 4 (October 1978): 396.

4. Joseph Stalin, *Marxism and the National Question* (Moscow: Foreign Languages Publishing House, 1950), 16.

5. Rupert Emerson, *From Empire to Nation: The Rise to Self-Assertion of Asian and African Peoples* (Cambridge, Mass.: Harvard University Press, 1960), 102.

6. Michael Hechter, Debra Friedman, and Malka Appelbaum, "A Theory of Ethnic Collective Action," *International Migration Review* 16, no. 2 (Summer 1982): 412–34. The article stresses rational choice as a means of overcoming the explanatory shortcomings of group stratification.

7. Joshua Fishman, *The Rise and Fall of the Ethnic Revival in the USA* (The Hague: Mouton, 1985).

8. Donald Horowitz, *Ethnic Groups in Conflict* (Berkeley: University of California Press, 1985).

9. Charles F. Keyes, "Towards a New Formulation of the Concept of Ethnic Group," *Ethnicity* 3, no. 3 (September 1976): 202-13.

10. Kian Kwan and Tomotshu Shibutani, *Ethnic Stratification: A Comparative Approach* (New York: Macmillan, 1965), 47.

11. Anthony D. Smith, *The Ethnic Revival* (Cambridge: Cambridge University Press, 1981).

12. Pierre van den Berghe, "Race and Ethnicity: A Sociobiological Perspective," *Ethnic and Racial Studies* 1, no. 4 (October 1978): 401–11.

13. Yu. Bromley,"Ethnography and Ethnic Processes," *Problems on the Contemporary World*, no. 73 (Moscow: USSR Academy of Sciences, 1978).

14. "Manifesto of the Racist Scientists ( July 14, 1938)," reprinted in *Mediterranean Fascism: 1919–1945*, edited by Charles F. Delzell, (New York: Harper & Row, 1971), 174–75.

15. *Selected Works of Mao Tse-Tung* (Peking: Foreign Languages Press, 1975), vol. 2, 209.

16. *Programme of the Romanian Communist Party for the Building of the Multilaterally Developed Socialist Society and Romania's Advance toward Communism* (Bucharest: Meridiane, 1975).

17. Gyorgy Szaraz, "On a Curious Book," *Joint Publications Research Service* 82763 (3 January, 1983).

18. Hans Kohn, *The Idea of Nationalism: A Study in Its Origins and Background* (New York: Macmillan, 1944), ix–x.

19. Particularly noteworthy has been the work of Maurice Pinard on Canada and Robert Clark on Spain.

20. Myron Weiner, "Matching Peoples, Territories and States: Post-Ottoman Irredentism in the Balkans and in the Middle East," in *Governing Peoples and Territories*, edited by Daniel Elazar (Philadelphia: Institute for the Study of Human Issues, 1982), 131.

21. Note, for example, in the final essay of this volume, Almond's use of "the nation-state" to describe all states and his use of "nations" to describe the states of the Middle East, Africa, and

Asia. The continuing misuse of these key terms certainly reflects and may very well help to explain Almond's failure to
confront the problems that ethnic heterogeneity poses for political development.

22. For a more detailed discussion, see Walker Connor, "Eco- or
Ethno-Nationalism?" *Ethnic and Racial Studies* 7, no. 3 (July
1984): 342-359.

23. As set forth by a scholar more than forty years ago: A history
of national consciousness should not, like a history of philosophy, simply describe the thought of a limited number of em-
inent men without regard to the extent of their following. As
in the histories of religions, we need to know what response
the masses have given to different doctrines. Walter Sulzbach,
*National Consciousness* (Washington, D.C.: American Council on
Public Affairs, 1943), 14.

**WINSTON DAVIS**

# Religion and Development: Weber and the East Asian Experience

VISITORS TO JAPAN often return home deeply impressed by the sedulous discipline, drive, and energy of the Japanese people. So well does the psychology of the Japanese meet the demands of industrial society that one wonders whether some benevolent, invisible hand has not at last made the perfect match between economics and the human psyche. (Perhaps this was the same hand that made the Japanese short, their homes cramped, and their cities crowded.) Industry is clearly omnipresent in Japan — perhaps even omnipotent. Whether the individual Japanese is arranging a wedding or a funeral, renting an apartment, or planning a vacation, the *kaisha* (firm) is always there. The Japanese seem to live not only in a "*kaisha*-economy" and a "*kaisha*-society," but also in a "*kaisha*-culture." The industry that engulfs their lives seems to be a "total institution," the likes of which Westerners encounter only in prisons and mental institutions.

If our travelers had time to "bone up" on Japanese history before they took off, they would also be impressed by the congruence between the country's religious faiths and the *kaisha*-culture of the present. Zen Buddhism seems to sanctify the secular activities of everyday life, including industry. Shinto lends to that activity a feeling of national identity, optimism, and plain good luck. Confucianism encourages the kind of close social bonds one encounters on all sides. Had our travelers gone back as far as the seventh century in their

221

research, they might have come upon a Confucian document attributed to Prince Shōtoku called the Seventeen Article Constitution. The document — which is actually a sermon to the bureaucracy and not a constitution at all — seems to foreshadow many of the practices and values of today's *kaisha*-culture: its stress on harmony, hierarchy, authority, and decorous or ritualistic behavior. It calls for social consensus: "Decisions on important matters should not be made by one person alone. They should be discussed with many." It sanctifies social conformism: "Let us follow the multitude and act like them" (de Bary 1958, vol. 1, 51, 50).

Unfortunately, the professional student of Asian society cannot return home with the same confidence in his first impressions. Like more casual visitors, he sees many parallels between the modal personality of the Japanese, their values, and daily activities. He also senses that probably all of these things are, somehow or other, congruent with Japan's religious traditions. But do such parallels or patterns unlock the "mystery" of this Asian society? Do they really explain its awesome economic success? Or is the sociocultural *Gestalt* we perceive just one more thing we need to explain? Unlike the tourist, the academic is duty-bound to go home and turn his hunches and intuitions into *defensible hypotheses*.

### PREVIEW

In the following pages, I shall describe two alternative ways of looking at religion and development: Weber's (which I characterize as a theory of hurdles and motivations) and my own (a theory of barricades and assaults). Next, I shall discuss the difficulties entailed by the Weberian approach by examining the claim that Confucianism prevented the rise of capitalism in China but caused it to flourish in Japan. Then I turn to the folk tradition in Japan to see whether or not it gave birth to a genuine work ethic. Finally, I shall point out some of the social costs brought about by the work ethic (and the work ideology) in Japan. In some concluding afterthoughts, I try to persuade myself that there is some merit in this essay and drop some hints as to how defter hands might proceed in the future.

## WEBER'S THEORY OF HURDLES AND MOTIVATIONS

Having been asked to address the problem of the overall relationship between religion and the development of the Far East, I found that my natural instinct was to turn first of all to the comparative studies of Max Weber. In his research on non-Western societies, Weber was interested primarily in demonstrating the uniqueness of the *Entwicklungsformen* of "the specific and peculiar rationalism of Western culture" (Weber 1958a, 26). While he himself did not apply this term to whole societies (Bendix and Roth 1980, 114), his work quite naturally raised a much broader set of issues that subsequent researchers and theorists would treat as "development" or "modernization." Therefore, what I am about to call Weberian may, *sensu stricto*, better be labeled Weberesque.

Weber treated development — or what *we* call development — as though it were an extended obstacle course stretching between traditional and modern societies. He saw this course as one laid out between the authentic human nature of simple societies (the starting line) and the deformed human nature of modern, capitalist society (the finish). In this race, runners (i.e., developing nations) who succeed in surmounting all of the hurdles of the course are rewarded with the trophies of modern civilization — but are also cursed with its "rationality." Because he thought the asceticism of early capitalist society was unnatural (Weber 1958a, 61–62) and (from a human point of view) irrational (1958a, 70; passim), Weber was convinced that these hurdles could be overcome only if the runners were initially motivated by something equally irrational, i.e., by something that would stimulate them to give up, subdue, or deform their own human nature. Only an inhumane, irrational drive would suffice as a motivation for achieving this inhumane, irrational goal. One could therefore say that Weber's investigation into the origins of capitalism was a kind of sociology of pain. What interested him was the question of why *any* society would want to cultivate a spirit of asceticism, i.e., the voluntary suffering that is "the exact opposite of the joy of living" (1958a, 41). Not convinced that the material rewards at the end of the race were sufficient to get the race started, he looked for some other motivating power — for a "mighty enthusiasm" (Weber 1951, 248) or some secret, horrible anxiety like the Puritan's concern for his soul's salvation — that would send society racing pell-mell up the via dolorosa of rational development. While this metaphor may be a bit melodramatic, one comes away from a careful reading of Weber wondering, with his heavy-handed critic, Herbert Marcuse, "Does he by any chance mean to say: And this you call 'reason'?" (1969, 226).

Weber viewed the process of development in terms of three sets of hurdles. The first set consists of the basic characteristics of the capitalist system itself: its rationality, asceticism (at least in early capitalism), continuity (in production and markets), and (formally) free labor markets. The second set of hurdles relates not to the economic system itself, but to its social environment. Developing nations must also establish institutions that will enable their economies to function under (formally) peaceful conditions. They must replace patrimonialism and the kinship base of the economy with rational administrative organizations and legal institutions. They must separate places of business and residence, corporate and private property. Finally, Weber put before the developing nations a third set of hurdles, those of motivation or *Geist*. Developers must also achieve the spiritual ethos Weber associated with the origins of Western capitalism: the duty to work in one's "calling" (the so-called work ethic), the rejection of magic, and the cultivation of an existential tension between the world as it is and the ethical demands of a transcendent deity.

In regard to the last set of hurdles, the comparativist will naturally wonder whether it is reasonable to put before non-Western nations spiritual hurdles that come from a different race track, i.e., "the specific and peculiar" ethos of an entirely different civilization. In the Author's Introduction to *The Protestant Ethic and the Spirit of Capitalism*, Weber repeatedly states that what he is interested in is the fact that only in the West does one find cultural and economic phenomena "having *universal* significance and value" (Weber 1958a, 13). He makes clear that he is *not* saying that Protestantism is the *only* religion that can produce a rational economy (1958a, 91) — a disclaimer he seems to forget repeatedly in his comparative studies.

The rise of capitalism in various parts of the non-Protestant world after Weber's death — especially in the Far East — suggests that history has moved the third set of hurdles from the path of the developing nations. Or has it? Some have tried to salvage Weber's scheme by searching for, and allegedly finding, equivalents or analogues to the Protestant ethic in Japan, Korea, Singapore, Nigeria, and other rapidly developing parts of the world. They have argued, or assumed, that if non-Western nations are not going to surmount the West's own spiritual hurdles, they must at least clear spiritual ones similar to those already cleared by the West. Presumably, other religions and gods can provide a motivation similar to the Puritans' *Angst* over election. Those who have taken this line — I shall call them "the Weberians," though this is merely my own "ideal type" — continue to look at development more or less from Weber's own point of view. While most do not share Weber's own approach-avoidance complex toward the spirit and achievements of capitalism, they continue to look at development as a quasi-evolutionary process of hurdles and motivations. Like their great culture hero (and most of the intellectuals of the eighteenth and nineteenth centuries), many Weberians continue to believe that the rationalization of society necessarily entails the secularization of religion and the decline of magic. Again like Weber, they are concerned primarily about the *Geist* produced by society's elite "culture-bearers" (1958a, 30) and religious virtuosi. And finally, they seem to believe that because this *Geist* takes root in "the central value system" of society (Bellah 1957, 25; passim), it applies univocally, or at least mutatis mutandis, to investors, entrepreneurs, inventors, merchants, consumers, and workers alike.

What then was the impact of religion on economic development? This question, perhaps like all questions of ultimate historical causation, seems to defy ordinary proof in terms of verifiability or falsifiability. My own reaction to the Weber thesis can be summed up briefly in the following "six principles of moderate skepticism":

1. It is impossible to determine the truth-value of the claims that:
   a. religion has had no impact on development.
   b. religion has had an impact of a certain given magnitude.
2. Given what we know about the overall strength of the social and economic variable involved, it is unlikely that religion has always been a necessary or crucial factor in development.
3. The difficulty of separating ex post facto legitimations of economic success from the actual motives behind rational economic behavior often makes the historical study of religion's putative ex ante role in economic life a thankless task.
4. Since religion sometimes provides clues for understanding the contours (if not always the causes) of development, the study of the role of religion in development *may* be of considerable importance.
5. Those who would investigate this problem should look at three questions:
   a. How has religion motivated economic change?
   b. How has religion failed to obstruct change?
   c. How has religion promoted a quiescent acceptance of the social costs imposed by development?

In my later discussion, I shall refer to (5a) as the question of religion's "positive enablement" of development. This is the question that interests Weber and the Weberians most. Unfortunately, this is not all there is to the problem of religion and development. A complete accounting would also include issues raised by questions (5b) and (5c), questions that deal with religion's "negative enablement" of economic change:

6. It is possible that religions that inculcate a this-worldly asceticism have had some impact on development. Perhaps this "Weberian minimalism" can be put more realistically by translating it into negative terms: insofar as strict morality and zealousness in one's "calling" would be boons to any economy, it is unlikely that ascetic religions — assuming they neither encourage hoarding nor discourage investing — do development any harm.

It seems to me that Weberian studies are least convincing when they focus their attention exclusively on question (5a), and when they assume a priori that religion is the source of some "central value system," which, in turn, influences all segments of society with an equal force, or in the same way. Exclusive emphasis on "value systems" is, of course, un-Weberian. In his comparative studies, Weber was deeply interested in the material factors of production, if only so that he could argue, counterfactually, that had the right *Geist* been present, such-and-such a country could have developed a rational economy. Nevertheless, his stress on *Geist* often led him to underestimate the contradictions in "the central value system" and the multiplicity of motivations called for by market societies. Rather than one *Geist,* I see the possible emergence of several different "spirits" in the rise of capitalism. First, buyers and vendors must cultivate the spirit of "credit-worthiness" (Weber 1958b, 315-22) in order to reduce the "cost of information" (Posner 1981) concerning their own reliability. Second, entrepreneurs stand in need of a *Geist* that will promote risk taking.[1] Third, investors need a spirit that will inspire delayed gratification. Fourth, management needs a disciplinary *Geist* to impose on workers. Finally, while workers require no special *Geist* to inspire their involuntary suffering, by adhering to the *Geist* of management they are sometimes able to work their way up in the world. This, we shall see, is especially important in the Far East.

Another general problem with Weber's approach is his treatment of secularization. If modern society is composed of different "spirits," we need not assume that each one will be secularized in the same way. In fact, some "spirits" may not be secularized at all. Now and then, some may even undergo "resanctification" — e.g., the Moral Majority's recent legitimization of the spirit of the American booboisie (if I may use Mencken's apt expression). Secularization entails two very different concepts: *Entgötterung* (the decline of religion) and *die Entzauberung der Welt* (the removal of magic from the world). Weber's general scheme of secularization can be logically reduced to a minimal pattern consisting of three historical (or quasi-evolutionary) moments:

1.   Society turns its attention from other-worldly religious pursuits to this world and invests this world with new positive

significance. It then begins to explore the world with magic, reason, and common sense,

2.   Society frees itself from the archaic "garden of magic" and desanctifies the world so that it can manipulate it in a matter-of-fact way. This transformation is most radical, its results most dramatic, when it takes place as a response to a transcendental ethical imperative.

3.   Finally, as a result of the growing wealth and hedonism of successful development, religion itself begins to decline. The work ethic loses its religious foundation; this-worldly motivations, rewards, and constraints take the place of the "mighty enthusiasm" that formerly drove people to work in their callings.

Here, the first moment roughly corresponds to Weber's concept of this-worldliness; the second, to intellectualization, rationalization, and the decline of magic and magical religions; the third step is equivalent to the "routinization" of the work ethic and the decline of religious zeal in general. Once we reach the third moment of secularization, we encounter one of the primary "cultural contradictions of capitalism." At this point society seems to encounter one of the "perennial gales of creative destruction" that Schumpeter attributed to capitalism itself (1962, 84). The new economy creates, in effect, "a critical frame of mind which, after having destroyed the moral authority of so many other institutions, in the end turns against its own" (1962, 143; see also Weisskopft, 1971, 37–115).

The problem with this view of secularization is twofold. First, although "Weber clearly stated that disenchantment is only a growing *possibility* in modern society, he also regarded it as part of the *fate* of Western civilization" (Davis 1980a, 299). Curiously enough, he never seems to have seen the contradiction between this dogmatic view of secularization as fate and his condescending recognition that "the masses in need are *always* out for emergency aid through magic and saviors..." (Weber 1952, 223, my emphasis). Perhaps it was the logical architecture of his own thought that led him to the conclusion that secularization is the fate of modern society.

That is, since rationalization has power *(Macht)* and domination *(Herrschaft)* at its disposal — rather than vice versa, as in Marx — its power to remove the hurdles of magic and traditional religion is a foregone conclusion. Ultimately, a rational society *must* cast out its gods, ghosts, priests, and shamans.

Weber seems to stress the fateful character of secularization for still another reason. He not only believed that the secularization of the world was a necessary precondition for, and by-product of, the rationalization of society. He also believed that there was an irreconcilable contradiction between the traditional teachings of religion and the competitive spirit of the market society:

> The market community as such is the most impersonal relationship of practical life into which humans can enter with one another.... Where the market is allowed to follow its own autonomous tendencies, its participants do not look toward the persons of each other but only toward the commodity; there are no obligations of brotherliness or reverence, and none of those spontaneous human relations that are sustained by personal unions.... The "free" market ... is an abomination to every system of fraternal ethics (1968, vol. 2, 636–37).

Clearly, then, society must disabuse itself of its traditional religious morality before it can develop a rational economy. Again, the conclusion seems to follow: once development begins, the decline of religion and magic is inevitable.

Against this view, I would argue that the introjection of the romantic notion of fate into social science is a dangerous business (see Berger 1967, 86). I have also argued, on empirical grounds, that the "secularization process" does not always take place the way Weber says it should (Davis 1980a, 1980b). Keith Thomas has demonstrated in magnificent detail that in the seventeenth century the English did rid themselves of magic, even before scientific cures for their ills and anxieties were available (1971, 656–68). From this he concludes, with Weber, that "it was the abandonment of magic which made possible the upsurge of technology, not the other way round." (1971, 657). But should we treat this finding as a necessary condition for development everywhere? I think not. I would argue that the secularization of religion and the decline of magic are "possible, not necessarily unilinear [in their trajectories] and therefore reversible" (Davis 1980b, 264). In the long run, more important than the "decline" of religion and magic are their internal transformation and pragmatic accommodation with the "spirits" of capitalism, science, and technology.

## HURDLES OR BARRICADES?

The obstacles in the way of development can simply be knocked over and dragged off the race course. This is the way the Kemalists took care of Islamic law *(shari'ah)* in Turkey and the way the Puritans disposed of Catholic magic. This is also the way Stalinists and Maoists have dealt with religion per se. This model of secularization looks at religion primarily from the point of view of aggressive modernizers and developers. But this is not the only way to look at the situation. One can also approach it from the standpoint of traditional societies seeking to protect themselves from the disruptive advance of economic values that are "an abomination to every system of fraternal ethics." What these societies fear is not progress but the social turbulence and moral turpitude caused by unrestrained trade and commerce. Because of their nearly static economies, these societies look upon growth as though it were a zero-sum game. St. Jerome put it nicely: "It is not without reason that the Gospel calls the riches of this earth 'unjust riches,' for they have no other source than the injustice of men, *and no one can possess them except by the loss and the ruin of others*" (cited in Viner 1978, 36; my emphasis).

As an alternative to Weber's hurdles cum motivations (which looks at development from the developers' point of view), let us look at the relationships between the economy, religion, and society from the point of view of "traditionalism." One could describe the situation from this vantage point by drawing three concentric rings: an inner one representing the economy and its values (e.g., achievement and universalism); an outer one, society, its existing values, status, and power relations; finally, the middle one standing for the "immunological barrier" that traditional societies erect against the

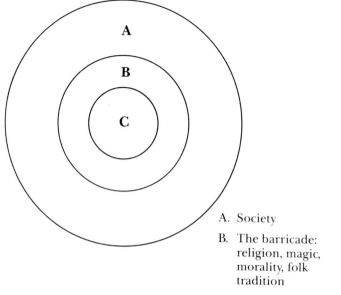

A. Society

B. The barricade: religion, magic, morality, folk tradition

C. Economy (embedded)

FIGURE II.1 *Traditional Society*

economy, or rather against the pestilence they intuitively sense would be released by an unrestricted market (see Figure II.1). Within this barrier we must place taboos, magic, traditional religion, morality, law, philosophy, and the folk tradition in general.[2]

Our new model, or metaphor, can incorporate Weber's notion of traditionalism by treating its various elements (e.g., kinship, patrimonialism, substantive justice, religion, and magic) as *defensive* institutions. Polanyi describes the defensive role of religion, and the "embeddedness" of economies in traditional society, in this way:

> Obscure as the beginnings of local markets are, this much can be asserted: that from the start this institution was surrounded by a number of safeguards designed to protect the prevailing economic organization of society from interference on the part

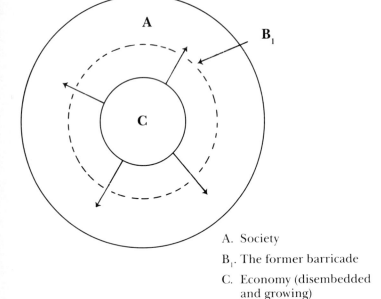

A.  Society

B₁. The former barricade

C.  Economy (disembedded and growing)

Figure II.2 *Development and Secularization*

of market practices. The peace of the market was secured at the price of rituals and ceremonies which restricted its scope while ensuring its ability to function within the given narrow limits (1944, 61–62).

From the point of view of our barricades model, economic development takes place not just when an "enemy" (i.e., a modernizer or developer) scales the ramparts and invades the citadel of society, but when the barriers themselves grow old and weak, and finally begin to crumble, or when their defenders lose heart and surrender. Figure II.2 represents the relationship between development and secularization from this point of view. Here, the porousness of the religious barricades (represented by a dotted line) has allowed the economy and its values to expand and penetrate the domain of society itself.

Without denying that secularization can proceed along the lines suggested by Weber and the Weberians (though not compelled to do so by "fate"), our barricades metaphor seems to encourage us to look at secularization from a different perspective — from *behind* the ramparts, i.e., from the point of view of traditional religion and society. It bids us pay greater heed to the ways in which the old defenses against the forces of Mammon grow weak, allowing society itself to be filled with that *amor sceleratus habendi* against which the preachers of old so ardently inveighed. Secularization of this sort — i.e., an internal secularization involving the complete "transvaluation of all values — has been brilliantly discussed by Marx (1964), Tawney (1980), Simmel (1978), Strauss (1953), Macpherson (1962), Bellah (1975), and many others.

This viewpoint also helps to correct what would otherwise be a very one-sided interpretation of the role of religion in the development of European society. A rational economy came into being not only because "hot Protestants" filled the market with the "zeal of the Lord," but because lukewarm Christians offered so little resistance to exploitation. In England, as nearly everywhere, development spelled misery for those unfortunate enough to be caught beneath the "pyramids of sacrifice" (Berger 1976) imposed by the developers — e.g., enclosures, engrossing, rack rents, poorhouses, and sweatshops. In the face of these moral outrages, the Church had virtually nothing to say. "The old medieval doctrines were quietly dropped and Churchmen came to assume that economic affairs operated according to their own independent principles, and that riches and poverty were part of the divine plan. There was genuine solicitude for the poor, particularly for their spiritual welfare, and there was condemnation for some of the more extreme cruelties of the system — *but the system itself was unchallenged*" (Welsby 1970, 19, my emphasis). As Tawney put it, the Church was out of her element in the new age of "impersonal finance, world markets, and a capitalist organization of industry. . . . " The practical ineffectiveness of her doctrines "prepared the way for their theoretical abandonment. They were abandoned because, on the whole, they deserved to be abandoned. The social teachings of the Church had ceased to count, because the Church itself had ceased to think." (Tawney 1980, 188). In the end the social message of the Church "was neglected, because it had become negligible." (1980, 189). The point not to be missed, however, is that the obtuseness and indifference of institutional religion played into the hands of the developers. A church that does not think also does not protest or get in the way. If it turns out (as many believe) that Weber was simply wrong about the positive role played by Protestantism in the development of capitalism, investigations into religion's "negative enablement" of the new economies may prove to be of greater moment than Weber's fixation on the activism of his Puritan saints. This, I would say, is the significance of Liston Pope's study of religion and the textile industry in Gaston County, North Carolina (1942; see also Darle, Knudsen, and Shriver 1976). Later, I shall argue that religion played a similar collaborative role in the development of modern Japan.

## CONFUCIANISM AND DEVELOPMENT

We turn now to the development of East Asia. Two books (Hofheinz and Calder 1982; Morishima 1982) have recently appeared arguing that Confucianism played a major role in the development of this area. Hofheinz and Calder, capitalizing on the panic and envy stirred up by Ezra Vogel's *Japan As Number One* (Vogel 1979), have pointed out the remarkable difference in real per capita growth between the "post-Confucian" states of the Far East and the Hindu, Buddhist, and Islamic states of South and Southeast Asia. In addition to statist and corporatist factors, the authors discern behind the region's success the impact of Confucian values and discipline. "Loyalty lies at the heart of what we call the 'Eastasia Edge' " (Hofheinz and Calder 1982, viii). Throughout "Eastasia" one encounters nationalism, an emphasis on education (even in premodern times), single-party rule (de facto in Japan since 1955), mutual aid rather than public welfare (even in the People's Republic of China), respect for government and bureaucracy, and a "tradition of agriculturally-based family and lineage organization within centralized state systems." (1982, 43). Behind all of this stands the nonlegal moralism of Con-

TABLE II.2 *How Eastasia Outpaces Its Neighbors: Real per Capita Growth in Asia, 1960–78*

| Eastasia | Real Per Capita Growth Rate (%) |
|---|---|
| Republic of Korea | 9.9 |
| Hong Kong | 9.0 |
| Republic of China | 6.2 |
| Singapore | 6.0 |
| Japan | 6.0 |
| Democratic People's Republic of Korea | 5.4 |
| China | 4.9 |
| *Other Asia* | |
| Pakistan | 4.8 |
| Thailand | 4.1 |
| Malaysia | 3.4 |
| Sri Lanka | 3.4 |
| Indonesia | 3.1 |
| Philippines | 2.9 |
| India | 1.5 |
| Vietnam | 0.6 |
| Nepal | 0.5 |
| Laos | 0.4 |
| Burma | −0.1 |
| Kampuchea | −0.8 |

Hofheinz and Calder 1982, p. 6, citing Donald Wise, ed., *Asia Yearbook 1980* (Hong Kong: Far Eastern Economic Review, 1980) 6.

fucianism itself.[3] "Confucian benevolence" accounts for the weak labor unions (1982, 110) and even the high rate of personal savings in the whole region: "Confucian philosophy, with its stress on proper behavior and respect for one's position in life, hailed prudence and frugality, demanded sacrifice for future enjoyment, and condemned parents who failed to provide for their offspring" (1982, 121). Although the authors credit Confucianism with so much of the success of the Far East, they make no attempt to account for the different rates of development within the region in terms of religion (see Table II.2).

Michio Morishima, however, rushes in where Hofheinz and Calder fear to tread. The difference between Japan's success and China's slow development can be attributed to the different kind of Confucianism that developed in Japan: a Confucianism that replaced the benevolence, humanism, individualism, and literary interests of the Chinese bureaucracy with the loyalty, nationalism, social collectivism, and technological interests of the Japanese samurai. Furthermore, because of the influence of the samurai on Confucianism, the Japanese failed to absorb the West's liberalism, internationalism, and individualism when they imported its science, industry, and technology. *"Because of its ideology* [i.e., Confucianism] Japan's economy is very different from the free enterprise system of the West" (Morishima 1982, 201; my emphasis).

Confucianism also explains the dual structure of Japan's modern economy, i.e., the split between its large industries with their systems of permanent employment and seniority advancement, on the one hand, and the small to middle-size companies in which employment depends on a free market in labor, on the other. Morishima maintains that the ex-samurai who founded and originally managed the larger firms imparted to industry their own Confucian sense of loyalty. For this reason, large-scale industry in Japan today depends on "loyalty markets" for its recruitment (i.e., on employees who "loyally" surrender mobility for a permanent position). But the spirit of the smaller firms, founded and manned (or womaned) by people originating among the three lower classes of Tokugawa society (peasants, artisans, and merchants), is based not on loyalty but on pure profit maximization (or "materialism," as Morishima puts it). Recruitment in these firms takes place in what he calls "mercenary" labor markets, i.e., free labor markets that guarantee no one employment and in which no one makes long-term commitments to his company.

Morishima concludes his book with a self-conscious attempt to update Weber by explaining the basic differences in the development of Europe, China, and Japan in religious terms. He first divides religion into three social or political types. Type 1 legitimates the status quo and is therefore the religion of the ruling classes. Type 2 is a religion for the ruled, i.e.,

TABLE II.3. *Summary of Morishima's Position*

| Type | Function | Class Involved | Historical Example |
|------|----------|----------------|--------------------|
| 1 | Legitimation of status quo | The ruling elite | Confucianism and Imperial Shinto |
| 2 | "For the Individual" and critical of status quo | The ruled | Puritanism |
| 3 | "For the individual" but passive and apolitical | The ruled | Taoism and Folk Shinto |

for the individual subjects (or citizens) of a country. As a religion "for individuals," such a faith, in its more rational forms, is sometimes highly critical of the status quo. It may even legitimate a new political order in which those who are now ruled become rulers. Type 3 religions are also religions "for the individual." Compared with the second type, however, religions of this sort are less rational and more mystical, inclining the believer to a life of reclusion and passivity. Morishima associates the first type with Confucianism and Imperial Shinto, the second with Puritanism, and the third with Taoism or Shinto. These types are summarized in Table II.3.

Morishima seems to be arguing (more strongly than Weber) that it is primarily a country's ideology, culture, or religion that determines its social, political, and economic organization. For him, ethos is not merely a necessary condition of development; it is its primum mobile. Such, at least, is the explanation he gives for the differences between (1) Japan and China, (2) Japan and the West, and (3) larger and smaller industry in Japan.

Morishima goes on to make other bold comparisons. Lacking any rational religious tradition (i.e., Type 2 religion), the Chinese had to import their "rationality" artificially from the West, i.e., in Marxism (1982, 199). In the West, religion itself gave rise to the Puritans' rational spirit (as well as to internationalism, liberalism, and individualism). Like China, Japan had virtually no Type 2 religions. Type 1 religion, the Confucianism of the samurai (and the Shinto of the imperial household), supported the status quo. Type 3, the Shinto of the common folk, inclined the Japanese masses to an ethos of passive obedience. In the end, the masses were saved from a life of passivity by their own biological (?) or ethnic (?) atheism: "the Japanese, though ethical, is non-religious *by nature.*" Since "most contemporary Japanese are atheistic and irreligious" (1982, 43; my emphasis), they are basically "materialistic."[4] This materialism of the masses, combined with the nationalism of the ruling class, makes for a potent, and potentially suicidal, cultural mix.[5]

Morishima's book is difficult to evaluate since it is written in the genre of Japan theory (Nihon Bunkaron), a narcissistic "literary" movement the Japanese are currently engaged in to discover the uniqueness of their own country. A sublimated form of nationalism, Japan theory tends to exaggerate the role of culture in order to account for Japan's essence — and success. Nevertheless, of all of Japan's religious traditions, one would think that Confucianism would be the most likely to inspire this-worldly, rational, economic activity. Even the Sino-Japanese word "economics" *(keizai)* comes from a Confucian expression — *keikoku saimin,* i.e., "rule the country and help the people." Joseph J. Spengler (1980, 51) maintains that "Confucianism introduced and sustained a spirit of laissez faire in Chinese social thought." To prove his point, he quotes the Confucian historian Ch'ien Ssu-ma (145–c. 90 B.C.):

> Each man has only to be left to utilize his own abilities and exert his strength to obtain what he wishes. Thus, when a commodity is very cheap, it invites a rise in price; when it is very expensive, it invites a reduction. When each person works away at his own occupation and delights in his own business then, like water flowing downward, goods will naturally flow forth ceaselessly day and night without having been summoned, and the people will produce commodities without having been asked. Does this not tally with reason? Is it not a natural result? (1980, 58.)

Whether this was laissez-faire economics in the modern sense, however, is dubious. Considering its historical provenance, it might better be thought of as a recipe for a primitive or feudalistic kind of physiocracy. Confucius himself seems to have been opposed to competition for profit. The "economics" of *The Great Learning* aims not at growth but simply at having enough to live on: "There is a great principle for the production of wealth. If there are many producers and few consumers, and if people who produce wealth do so quickly and those who spend it do so slowly, then wealth will always be sufficient" (Chan 1963, 94). To have turned this truism into an economics of development would have taxed even Japanese ingenuity.

There are many points that could be raised against Morishima's book. It betrays a superficial acquaintance with the secular and religious history of Japan. Like most Japan theory, it fails to deal with horizontal social relations, the role of individual self-interest, competition, disloyalty, and conflict. On the basis of Morishima's loyalty theory, how would one account for the rejection of "administrative guidance" by some Japanese industries, or the difficulty Japanese groups have in arriving at a "consensus" on so many issues? If ethos counts for so much, how much weight should we put on the contributions of the banking system, tariffs, government and industry planning, wages and bonuses — factors that other authorities believe have been so important in the development of Japan? As I implied in the second of my "six principles of moderate skepticism," I find utterly incredible explanations of development that stress culture or ethos at the expense of such nitty-gritty factors.

Morishima's main argument about the Confucian influence on Japan assumes the Japanese revalorized the Confucian virtue of loyalty. In China loyalty had meant faithfulness to one's own conscience. In Japan it came to mean an unswerving devotion to one's lord, boss, or company. John Hall, however, questions the significance of this difference. "The actual impact of these two Confucian concepts [loyalty and filial piety] should not be overstressed. There is reason to believe that the conduct referred to as *chū* and *kō* represented no change from the old patterns of samurai behavior — i.e., that Japanese values were read into the Chinese Neo-Confucian texts." (Hall 1959, 294). What was important for the samurai was the "return of benefits" (*hōon*), obligation (*giri*), status (*bungen*), and honor *(na)* (1959, 294–95). If so, the samurai must have lived in a world in which duties and obligations rested upon reciprocal exchange relationships. Thus, even in the Tokugawa period, pure (i.e., unstimulated and unrewarded) loyalty must have been a rare virtue indeed. Loyalty was always situated in a network of incentives, rewards, and constraints. The values of the samurai, like those of the lower classes, were based on an ethos of "hierarchical complementarity" (Dumont 1982) in which service was exchanged for patronage. This was an important aspect of Confucianism from the very beginning. As one of Confucius's disciples put it: "Our Master's teaching is simply this: loyalty *and reciprocity*" (*Analects* 4, 15; my emphasis). Here, Morishima's culture-based theory of Japan's success gets him into trouble. If the loyalty of large-scale *kaisha* workers today is rewarded with high wages (and it is), is it not possible to argue that loyalty can be created, or even bought in the same way? Morishima is being far too idealistic when he explains Japan's dual economy in terms of the impact of Confucian loyalty on the upper strata of industry and the influence of "materialism" on the lower ones. When we look at loyalty as an exchange relationship, his distinction between "loyalty" labor markets and "mercenary" ones — at least as an absolute, cultural distinction — seems to break down. Furthermore, if loyalty and permanent employment were simply parts of industry's cultural inheritance, why were they not present when Japanese industries were first created?[6] And finally, if loyalty was a Japanese absolute, how does one explain the change of masters that occurred so dramatically in 1868 and 1945 — and, indeed, throughout Japanese history?

What is ultimately wrong with Morishima's analysis is not his "idealism" but his lack of a comprehensive or balanced perspective. I have stated elsewhere that "to argue that the Japanese sense of loyalty is an illusion — because only institutional arrangements 'count' — is as misguided as to say that in the West because 'honesty pays' — that is, because it has its own material rewards — there is no such thing as honesty. This radical dichotomizing of culture and institutions, morality and rewards, is a methodological bias that is apt to blind us to the real dynamics and sensibilities at work in Japanese society..." (Davis 1983, 144).

From the standpoint of the history of scholarship, the most surprising thing about Morishima's thesis is its obvious clash with Max Weber's own opinions — not that Weber is the final authority on the development of the Far East! Weber, after all, had dogmatically proclaimed that "a people among whom a stratum of the character of the samurai played the decisive role could not attain a rational economic ethic of their own..." (1958c, 275) — words that, in retrospect, look both pompous and silly.[7]

As for China, Weber was convinced that "from a purely economic point of view, a genuine bourgeois, industrial capitalism *might have* developed...." (1951, 100; my emphasis). What ultimately prevented development was the failure of the Chinese to create the right kind of *Geist*. Although the Chinese were legendary for their capacity for labor, work disipline in the impersonal, capitalist sense was beyond them (1951, 95). Individuals were protected from exploitation and economic disaster by their families, i.e., by groups whose primary identity was established by the rites of ancestor worship. Because it was thought that the kinship group (Weber: sib) had received its land from sacred ancestors, land could not easily be sold — a fact that put severe restrictions on the development of commercial agriculture (which presupposes the ready alienation or "commodification" of land). Weber therefore seems to be arguing that the failure of the Chinese to develop free markets in labor and land was directly or indirectly the result of the worship of ancestral spirits by the sib. Furthermore, because the rural sib was regarded as the individual's true home, a genuine urban spirit did not develop in the cities (1951, 90).[8] Since Chinese cities were merely outposts of the central government, they afforded no free space in which social experiments or economic innovation could take place. Like the countryside, the city was forever under the watchful and suspicious eye of a patrimonial state that was always ready to interfere in the economy — either for its own gain or in the name of "substantive justice" (i.e., distributive justice in the classical sense). For this reason, the social and economic organizations that did develop (e.g., guilds, communal workshops, and clubs) were organized defensively to protect the "individual against the danger of proletarization and capitalist subjection" (1951, 97). Because of the moralistic, antilegal influence of Confucianism, the state failed to produce the kind of rational administration and law necessary for a capitalist system.[9] "Patrimonialism, being ethically oriented, always sought substantive justice rather than formal law" (1951, 102).[10] Like the moralism of Confucianism itself, Chinese law (which Weber calls " 'Solomonic' Cadi-[*qadi*] justice") was aimed at contests between persons, not at the impersonal litigation between abstract organizations (e.g., corporations) or situations (1951, 149). Because of the weak sense of transcendence in Chinese religion, there was naturally little or no tension between sacred (or "natural") law and positive law. Since, for Weber, there is no social change without such tension, religion again seems to have been the major impediment to China's development of a rational economy. Ultimately, it proved to be the insuperable hurdle.

Although Confucianism developed along rational, utilitarian lines, it failed to generate the "mighty enthusiasm" (1951, 248) that alone can initiate the transition to modernity. The life-style of the Confucian bureaucrat was, itself, antithetical to the spirit of capitalism. Scholarship imbued his position with a magical, traditional authority. His education (like the humanism of Catholic Europe described elsewhere by Weber (1958, 38), was innocent of mathematics, natural science, and geography. His philosophy was an undialectical, or categorical, species of thought. His rationalism was a "rationalism of order" incapable of initiating profound social or economic change.[11] Study consisted of the "assimilation of existing ideas" and texts (Weber 1951, 163). Academic specialization was discouraged because the superior man *(chün-tzu)* regarded himself a generalist. In contrast to the Puritan, who regarded himself a "tool" to do God's work on earth, the Confucian literatus thought of himself as a "personality" to be cultivated, as an end in himself.

Here we get to the crux of Weber's analysis. Unlike the

Puritan, who tried to transform and master the world, the Confucian sought merely to accommodate himself to it:

> The Confucian desired "salvation" only from the barbaric lack of education. As the reward of virtue he expected only long life, health, and wealth in this world and beyond death the retention of his good name...all tension between the imperatives of a supra-mundane God and a creatural world, all orientation toward a goal in the beyond, and all conception of radical evil were absent (1951, 228).

In spite of his disclaimer, cited previously (Weber 1958a, 91), Weber believed that this tension was possible *only* in a society where the religious ideal was established by "an absolutely super-creatural, supra-mundane, personal creator and ruler of the world" (1951, 187). From this, it seemed to follow logically, and not just as a matter of fact, that China had not "developed" because the Chinese had developed no "ethical prophecy" stong enough to challenge traditional ways of life.[12] Because of its lack of ethical transcendence, Confucianism failed to overcome the magical manipulation of the world — a failure that the ethical prophet took as an affront to divine majesty. Because Confucianism regarded mankind as essentially good, it was untroubled by the sinfulness of a "fallen humanity." Nothing more radical than a solid, classical education was needed to make the world as good as it ever was, or could be. No mediating priesthood was necessary, no "cure of souls," no "church discipline" (1951, 225).

From his comparative point of view, Weber believed that the Chinese had failed to develop a capitalist economy because they had failed to harken to the God of Deutero-Isaiah and the Puritans. Only He can generate the kind of motivation, tension, and anxiety needed to "goose" society over the hurdles on the road leading to a rational economy. Put in a more formal way, the problem with Confucianism *as a religion* was that its deity was too rational, too immanental, and too impersonal to make the kind of ethical demands people need to hear if they are to break out of their traditional bonds. Its problem *as ethics* was that it was too personalistic, or particularistic, to break the hold of kinship on the individual. In short, Confucianism gave the Chinese no reason to espouse the unnatural, voluntary suffering (i.e., *innerweltliche Askese*) that early capitalism allegedly depended upon. "Alien to the Confucian was the peculiar confinement and repression of natural impulse which was brought about by strictly volitional and ethical rationalization and ingrained in the Puritan" (1951, 244).

While some scholars quickly perceived the ethnocentrism of Weber's comparative studies, the subsequent development of capitalism in the non-Christian Far East should make it obvious to all. Whether Weber was "right" about Chinese Confucianism, I cannot say. But, then, who can? Did the Confucian bureaucrat fail to become a modernizer because he was a Confucian or because he was a bureaucrat (i.e., because of the way his offices and opportunities were structured)? I have invoked Weber's name here for two reasons: (1) by comparing him with Morishima, to indicate the kind of contradictions one often encounters when the cultural analysis of development is reduced to a *Gedankenexperiment* that merely posits correlations ("elective affinities") without investigating actual historical connections, and (2) by assuming he was right about Chinese Confucianism, to stress how *different* Japanese Confucianism would have to have been to give rise to a rational economy.

One could argue in Morishima's defense that the concern the samurai of the Meiji period (1868–1911) had for the safety of their country was a motivation equivalent to the anxiety of the Puritans over their election, and that it was the "mighty enthusiasm" or the irrational goad to rational activity that Weber was looking for. Undoubtedly, this concern was an important factor behind the decision by the Meiji government to establish industries with state funds. But, again, we must ask the question we asked about the Chinese literati: did the samurai play a role in the development of industry because they were Confucians or because they were warriors? Did lower-ranking samurai take positions in these new companies because of their ethic or because, after the disestablishment of their caste, they found themselves out of work? Questions of this sort make moderate skepticism seem a generous attitude.

Truth may not always reveal herself as the golden mean, but it seems to me that Weber and Morishima have gone astray by espousing extreme positions. Weber clearly erred when he failed to see the moral "tension" implicit in the Confucian concepts of the Tao, T'ien, and "the golden age." As Confucius himself put it, "If the Way *(Tao)* prevailed in the world, I should not be trying to alter things" *(Analects* 18, 6 in de Bary, 1960, 22). Throughout its long history, Confucianism repeatedly lent itself to critical social analysis and political action. Its emphasis on "the investigation of things" inspired a spirit of curiosity and inquiry. But to regard this attitude as "science and technology" (as Morishima does) is, again, to exaggerate. While Confucianism gave rise to "practical studies" ( *jitsugaku)* in Japan, *jitsugaku* itself satisfied only the protoscientific curiosity of the amateur collector. It fused, and confused, ethical and natural knowledge so that, for example, Tojo Nakae (1608–1648) could say that the stars themselves stay in place thanks to human virtue. Only in the Meiji period, under the impact of Western science, would Japanese scientists learn to differentiate between the principles ( Japanese: *ri;* Chinese: *li)* of nature and those of morality (Craig 1965, 133–60).

It is possible that Confucianism (in its diffuse form) has had something to do with the diligence, sincerity, and frugality of "post-Confucian" East Asia — or, at least, with the articulation of these virtues. It is possible that the Confucian examination system paved the way for the development of the meritocracies and "diploma societies" of the present. It is not impossible that the moral tutelage of the Confucians prepared the Far East for the "preceptoral systems" that later would guide its economies — from the "massive unilateral persuasion" of the People's Republic of China to the "administrative guidance" of capitalist Japan (Lindblom 1977, 13).[13] It is also possible that the kind of consensual system of decision making and responsibility sharing one finds in Japan today had its origin (at least in part) in the kind of "discussions" commended by the Confucianism of the Seventeen Article Constitution (see the beginning of this essay). I think it is likely that the spirit of cooperative, ethical reciprocity one finds in Japanese industrial paternalism goes back to the moralism of Confucius. (I also think that this "spirit" is largely an ex post facto beautification of industrial relations. While resonating in a positive way with popular tradition, I do not think it was "the cause" of the industrialization of Japan and the Far East.) In all of these cases, all that one can say is that these propositions are possible, not impossible, probable, or likely. In most cases, I find no way to evaluate Morishima's claims at all. For example, how can we know whether it was Confucianism that caused Japanese workers to accept the limited horizontal mobility of their tier-one labor markets, or exploitation by "capitalists and the labor aristocracy" (Morishima 1982, 200)? How can one know whether it was Confucianism — and not Shinto or the indigenous social system — that accounted for the tendency for the Japanese *kaisha* to evolve into a "complete society in itself " (1982, 120)? How can one say with any certainty that Confucianism, and not Buddhism, caused the (alleged) lack of competition between individuals in Japanese industry (1982, 115) or the rare phenomenon of groups competing only to show their loyalty to the firm? In short, how can one identify and control the relevant historical variables?

## DEVELOPMENT AND POPULAR RELIGION: THE JAPANESE CASE

Confucianism is not the only religion to claim responsibility for the "work ethic" of the Far East. Buddhism too vies for the honor. Japan's Shingon (esoteric) Buddhist sect claims that the internalization of its doctrines by the Japanese "may well be one of the underlying reasons for the Japanese devotion to work." *(The East* 11, no. 3 (April 1975, 28).[14] In the Meiji period, entrepreneurs like Kanbara Meizen claimed their entire lives had been spent in the single-minded pursuit of Buddhist truth (Marshall 1967, 35). Even today, the president of Tōkyō Denki Kagakukō-gyo Company, one of the most successful companies in Japan, argues that Buddhism has made his firm both humane and productive: "Making a profit is important, of course, but it is not the ultimate goal. Character building is much more important. At TDK we attach great importance to discovering the meaning of work. As far as valuing relationships goes, it seems to me, Japan is second to none. And at the bottom of this lies Buddhism" *(The Japan Times,* 7 December 1981, 8).[15]

Whether we are looking at Confucianism, Buddhism, or a mixture of the two, there are obvious pitfalls in beginning our search for an Asian work ethic in the obiter dicta of pious entrepreneurs or the sacred texts of the founders of the great traditions. Unfortunately, this is where Weber and most of his followers have begun. This ultimately encourages a purely textual and elitist ("top-down") approach to the problem. In the following sections, I shall turn from the venerable spokesmen for religion and industry and look at some of the leaders of the folk tradition. Because the Japanese government has always exhorted peasants and other workers to be diligent and frugal, we cannot say that the work ethic springing from the popular tradition is absolutely free and spontaneous. But, because these virtues benefited households and government alike, such values cannot be lightly dismissed as mere "false consciousness" planted in the popular mind from above.

Perhaps it will help us understand the development of the popular work ethic if we temporarily replace Weber's hurdles, runners, and motivations with the imagery suggested earlier of barricades and an advancing army of developers. Unlike hurdles, barricades and ramparts must be peopled. This means that we must rewrite our development scenario and people it with *two* sets of actors. In addition to our advancing army (the former runners), we must now write parts for the defenders of the ancient bastions of faith, magic, tradition, and good works. We must be careful to attribute to our new actors the same capabilities we ascribe to the advancing troups. They must be able to think for themselves and maneuver in their own defense and self-interest. We must endow them with the ability to dodge, huddle, feint, fall back, regroup, conspire, collaborate, betray, compromise, and even surrender to the foe. If European history provides any clues, we would expect the battlements defended by the churches of new commercial wealth to fall to the forces of Mammon first, those guarded by old wealth to fall next (after the benefits of peaceful surrender had become apparent; those associated with the churches of no wealth at all (the religions of the oppressed) would hold out longest. Much depends on the material interests of the spiritual leadership — interests that usually differ considerably from those of the laity. Religions of the oppressed led by clergy intellectually or materially beholden to new wealth may be among the first to give in.

We must add two final scenes to our skit. In the first, we must tell the story of the failure of the defenders of the faith to obstruct social and economic development. We must relate how they retreated, compromised, and grew silent or indifferent to the breakdown of traditional communities and social values. We can add a dash of pathos by relating how they turned their backs to the social inequities appearing in their own midst. In our final scene, we shall see how our erstwhile defenders became passive or even active collaborators with the foe, how they grew as proud of development as the developers themselves, and how their rhetoric and strategies were co-opted by the victors and made part of the master plan of development itself.

**THE NEXT-TO-THE-LAST SCENE: NEGATIVE ENABLEMENTS**

First, we must tell the rather paradoxical story of religion's negative contribution to the positive growth of the modern economy. For lack of space, I shall merely summarize the plot as it unfolded in Japan.

Although the Tokugawa period (1603-1868) was formerly thought to be a time of economic stagnation, research by Andō Seiichi and other historians has shown that the country was actually undergoing remarkable structural changes during this time. When the period began, no one could have predicted what lay ahead. In nearly every way, the cards of fate seemed to be stacked against the small island country. It had few natural resources. Government policies did nothing to foster growth and much to hinder it. The regime had cut off external trade out of fear that some domains might profit too much from it. Domestic trade was in the hands of a hereditary merchant caste that stood at the low end of the Confucian social scale. Commerce did not seem to be the way to upward mobility. There was even this common saying: "The offspring of a toad is a toad; the offspring of a merchant is a merchant" (Sheldon 1973; 140). Tolls and poor land transportation limited trade, while sea transport was thought to be too hazardous for most purposes. As in China, peasants were reluctant to sell land they had received from their sacred ancestors. The economy of most villages was "embedded" in the fictive kinship of extended households. Many crafts and markets were cornered by monopolistic guilds *(za)*. In western Japan, households that monopolized economic and political affairs sought to dignify their secular authority by controlling religious guilds *(miya-za)* as well.

In the nineteenth century, when Japan finally opened her ports to the world, she already had many advantages third-world countries today would envy. Literacy was widespread. The prolonged practice of double cropping had created an economic surplus that, in turn, gave rise to a widespread money economy. The hereditary servants and kinship base of agriculture of the early Tokugawa period gradually had given way to the labor of a landless, rural proletariat. Increasingly, a family's welfare was determined as much by distant markets as by its own shrewdness and hard work.[16] The social and moral bonds that previously tied patrons and workers together were shattered and replaced by impersonal relations between landlords and tenant farmers. Employment became a matter of "relations entered into for the convenience of the moment, so that instead of being the guide lines of a way of life, they were episodes that passed and were quickly forgotten" (Smith 1966; 148). Thus, even before Meiji, the economy was becoming "disembedded." Or, to put the same thing in the language of development studies, the commercialization of agriculture and the development of urban trade during the latter half of the Tokugawa period constituted a "gestation period" that enabled the economy to "take off" during the reign of the Meiji emperor.[17]

As development (or disembedding) proceeded, up-and-coming families began to demand their just share of power and prestige. Hereditary village offices were opened to election. Guilds were disbanded, reestablished, and then destroyed through de facto competition. For many families, the costs of this disembedding were high. Under the reactionary slogan "revere grain, despise money" *(kikoku senken)*, some demanded the new money economy be curtailed or abolished. But conservative limits were built into social protest during most of the Tokugawa period. Peasant uprisings were common enough, but they were rebellions, not revolutions. The vast majority aimed at temporary relief and not at permanent structural changes. There was even a ritual aspect to rebellion. Religious upheavals such as the mass pilgrimages to the Ise shrines had clear overtones of social protest. But they had an even clearer "gentling" effect on the populace (Davis 1983–84). When rising families protested the control of the Shinto parish by the old families in their villages, they sought only to be included in the cult, not to abolish the religious status system itself (Davis 1976b, 1978). In the most rapidly developing parts of the country, these protests resulted in the religious enfranchisement of more and more families. These expanding enclosures of the population around the shrine amounted to the development of an active "participant citizenry" (Inkeles and Smith 1974) in the religious microcosm of village Japan.

Since the beginning of recorded history, Japanese religions have largely been under the control of national and local authorities. In Shinto, secular and religious leadership was often identical. Buddhism was muzzled as soon as it was brought from Korea to Japan and was made the religious monopoly of an elite that hoped to keep its magical powers to itself. Even after Buddhism became a popular religion, sect leaders continued to vie for official patronage — which inevitably brought about state control. During the Tokugawa period, Buddhism was used directly by the government to control the masses. The religion proved to be as pliant in the hands of the autocratic Meiji developers as it had been under the bureaucratic feudalism of the Tokugawa regime. More concerned about the suffering and illusions of the individual than about the misery and injustice of society, Buddhism was not a faith that "made waves." Unlike Islam, it sought to impose no sacred law upon society that ultimately could obstruct change. Its concept of karma was reduced to a mere *façon de parler* that never — well, hardly ever — was used to justify sloth or fatalism. Today, most Buddhist priests limit their services to funerals and the routine performance of ancestral rites. Since most no longer preach the dharma, few Japanese seriously confront the somber words the Buddha spoke against attachment to the things of this world. Although traditional Buddhism explicitly forbade certain occupations as hindrances to "right livelihood,"[18] Japanese Buddhism today puts no restrictions on a person's occupation. Because Buddhism passively accepts the "spirit of the times" *(jisei)*, it has quietly gone along with economic and military development. While Theravada Buddhism in Southeast Asia may have helped to prevent the social fragmentation of rural areas (Spiro 1982, 471), Buddhism has done nothing to prevent the rapid overdevelopment of the Japanese countryside. One of the reasons for the weakness of Buddhism and Shinto today is that these religions have not been able to keep pace with demographic change.

Shinto was just as obliging. Because it had no universal prelates to enforce its claims, Shinto readily gave in to the demands of the developers. If a festival interfered with new work schedules, it was postponed, curtailed, or simply dropped from the calendar. Ancient taboos limiting intercourse with outsiders were prudently overlooked or forgotten. (See Davis 1980b for further examples.) The emperor himself, the high priest of Shinto, was equally compliant. Accustomed for centuries to reign without ruling, he presided over meetings of the Japanese cabinet like the *deus otiosus* of primitive religion. One of the leaders of the Meiji period even complained that, unlike the West, Japan had no "spiritual axis." The imperial system was therefore the very opposite of Weber's "sultanism," i.e., the extreme form of patrimonialism which so often stood in the way of development. It could even be argued that the emperor's greatest, unsung virtue was his *failure* to obstruct "progress." In this way, the emperor, and the equally inarticulate cult of State Shinto over which he presided, became the silent accomplices of military and industrial development.

To understand the real influence of religion on the development of Japan we must look at it as it actually functions in daily life, i.e., as a comprehensive, tolerant syncretistic system composed of various elements. Although Weber maintained that toleration had nothing to do with the origins of capitalism, earlier observers, such as Sir Josiah Child in the seventeenth century, noted that "toleration in different Opinions in matters of religion" did contribute to prosperity. Charles Leslie even complained that "toleration is a sacrificing of God to Mammon" (Viner 1978, 163, 169). In the West, political stability traditionally rested on religious uniformity — "one Lord, one faith, one baptism." In Japan, just the opposite was the case. Political order was predicated on mutual toleration and a recognition of the practical value of multiple religious affiliations. In general, the only religions to cause any problems were those that insisted on their own "single practice" — e.g., the True Pure Land, Hokke, and Fuju-Fuse sects of Buddhism; Christianity; and some of the New Religions such as Soka Gakkai. One could argue that this kind of toleration was another way in which religion failed to get in the way of development. (One has only to compare the declining GNPs of countries torn apart by religious or sectarian strife to see my point.) Toleration (the religious face of pragmatism) and flexibility (the secular side of toleration) have undoubtedly enhanced the stability of Japan's rapidly developing society. They have also enabled the Japanese to borrow (at minimal psychological cost) from the science, technology, and cultures of the rest of the industrial world. As important as the spirit of toleration has been, it would be impossible to measure its total impact and folly to regard it as a major or necessary factor in development. As Weber noted, all of Asia "was, and remains, in principle, the land of the free competition of religions, 'tolerant' somewhat in the sense of late antiquity" (1958c, 329).

If religions can be made to give up their absolute, exclusive claims to truth, they can be induced to give up less important doctrines too. Syncretism itself may therefore have had a secularizing impact on religion. A "logic of relative contrasts" (Itō 1973, 3–30), inspired in part by religious syncretism, has inclined the Japanese to make sensible accommodations with the demands of secular life. But in the end, it was urbanization and not toleration or syncretism that made the greatest contribution to the secularization of Japanese religion.

The secularizing impact of urbanization is nothing new. Hakuin, in the eighteenth century, wrote:

> Some time ago I felt a strong desire to go and see what the great city of Yedo [Tokyo], so prosperous and large, looks like. Oh, what a great city it is. It is indeed a great and flourishing city, but it is forsaking the Three ancient forms of the Buddha's teaching (1963, 149).

A secular, this-worldly spirit was often noticed among the merchants of Tokugawa Japan. In the will of a certain Shōshitsu Shimai, a merchant of Hakata (died 1615), we read,

> It is unnecessary to pray for a happy future when one is already in one's fifties.... It is even more unbecoming to spend days and nights at a temple on the pretext of praying for a happy future, abandoning one's family and boasting of worshipping at a temple (Nakamura 1964; 368–69).

The secular attitude of some Confucian scholars went still further. Yamagata Bantō minced no words: "In this world there are no gods, Buddhas, or ghosts, nor are there strange or miraculous things" (Craig 1965, 136). Surveys have shown that, while during the Pacific War 72 percent of the Japanese population claimed to believe in the kami and the Buddha, by 1973 religious belief had dropped to 25 percent (Davis 1980b; 266–67). While these figures need to be qualified and interpreted very carefully, they do seem to indicate that Japan's remarkable postwar reindustrialization has been accompanied by a widespread secularization of *explicit* religious belief. Although no statistics seem to exist describing the social distribution of disbelief, a secular attitude seems to be more prevalent in the educated elite than among the lower classes. This too has done development no harm.

Paradoxically, the postwar period also saw a boom in New Religions — huge mass movements founded by charismatic (or shamanistic) leaders who whipped up new confections in the old pantries of Shinto, Buddhism, Christianity, and Confucianism. These new gospels stressed ancestor worship, pre-war ethnocentrism (now symbolically disguised), and traditional social values. In most cases, their real emphasis was on magical techniques designed to ward off disease, poverty, and bad luck. Curiously enough, these movements did not "take off" during the immediate postwar years, when misery was at its highest pitch. Although several New Religions had existed since the nineteenth century in the more rapidly developing parts of the country, their period of most rapid growth coincided roughly with the "takeoff" of postwar industry itself (roughly, 1950–65). Members were often recruited from among those segments of the population not protected by large industries or labor unions. (The voting habits of the faithful suggest that many were drawn from the country's Tory proletariat (Davis 1980a, 261–71).) One can postulate that religions of this sort not only help believers cope with a fallen world, they also enable them to accept the unequal burdens of a rapidly developing one. However, the fact that the New Religions reached a steady state (and did not simply disappear) once Japan's economic growth reached a self-sustaining level indicates that their staying power has also had something to do with their ability to speak to the human condition as such — at least to the human condition in its Japanese manifestation.

From the beginning of the Meiji period, Japan's development imposed a devastating burden on the common people — a fact Japanologists, social scientists, and Atari Democrats bewitched by the Japan As Number One-ism of the 1980s tend to forget. (See Hane 1982.) Many of the oppressed turned to the New Religions for miracles and magic. Founders of these movements condemned grasping merchants, selfish landlords, and the authorities themselves. They warned vaguely about a "renewal of the world" and the coming of a "Future Buddha" who would set everything aright. In 1838, in the midst of the turbulence of the Tempō period, Naka-yama Miki founded a sect called Tenri-kyō, a movement that later became one of Japan's largest New Religions. Like other founders, Miki had her own vision of "world renewal." She bluntly criticized the leaders of the Meiji regime ("the High Mountains"):

> Til now they've said 'it's a High Mountain'
>> But down in the valleys everything is withering.
> The authorities in this world do as they will.
>> Don't they know the sorrow of God?
> Know this: henceforth the power of God will
>> Rival that of the authorities!
> Up to now the authorities have done as they would,
>> Boasting, "we are High Mountains."
> Trees which grow on the High Mountains
>> And those at the bottom of the valley are the same.
> Harken unto me! Whether on top of the High Mountain
>> Or in the valley below — all are God's children.
> Every day God's heart is impatient to show us our freedom (*jūyo-jizai*).

For these and other impolitic remarks, Miki was repeatedly arrested and harrassed by the "High Mountains."

Another prophetess to suffer a similar fate was the colorful and irrepressible Kitamura Sayo (1900–67), who founded the "Dancing Religion" (properly, Tenshō-Kōtai-Jingū-Kyō) in the last years of the Pacific War. On 6 August 1945, a pious follower rushed to the Kitamuras' house to tell the foundress that an atomic bomb had been dropped on Hiroshima. There she found Sayo eating a bowl of rice gruel. "Calm down and keep quiet," Sayo growled. "The atomic bomb is now eating rice gruel right here."

A few days later Sayo had a revelation that she had become "the only Daughter of the Absolute God of the Universe." Her ministry consisted largely of an unending stream of vitriolic attacks on people she called "maggot beggars" (social climbers, or "developers"), "beggar officials" (petty functionaries who lived off bribes), and "traitor beggars" (militarists responsible for Japan's defeat) (Tenshō-Kōtai-Jingū-Kyō 1954, 55, 20). Even the emperor was not spared a tongue lashing. All of these "maggots," Sato said, are still enslaved in a "meaningless, useless, profane civilization" (1954, 154).

After the war, Mrs. God (Ogamisama), as she was called by

her followers, was arrested for refusing to pay her rice taxes. According to the district attorney's own statement:

> The defendant claims that the world of today consists of nothing but egoistic "traitor beggars." She believes the farmers should not till their fields to feed such beggars, and therefore, she issued instructions for them not to submit to the government even one ounce of rice until the people realize their heavenly calling and are ready to render their services for the establishment of God's Kingdom on earth (1954, 108).

At the trial, Mrs. God stood up "and sang out the following sermon in Her loudest voice":

> Do not worry about position, honor, and fortune
>     But discard them, together with your egoism.
> God has already descended and has taken over
>     The maggot's world into His hands and rules it,
> At this time of the human-world's downfall.
> You beggars of the defeated world, open your eyes —
>     Wake up before it is too late (1954, 115).

After her death, Mrs. God's followers summarized her attitude toward Japan's new economy and values in the following words:

> With all the technology and scientific advancements, many jobs have been eliminated. People tend only to think of themselves. Competition is keen and unsavory practices have developed. People scheme to deceive, cheat, rob, and steal; and humans are pawns for industrial, religious, and political intrigues. In the world of competition, people live in uneasiness and labor suffers, because they are merely used for production. They live for the material things of life but do not improve themselves spiritually. The more they acquire the more they want, so they are never satisfied or happy (Tenshō-Kōtai-Jingū-Kyō 1970, 134).

The Dancing Religion's own solution to these problems was, first of all, that, with "Ogamisma as the central figure of life" (1970, 136), people should devote themselves selflessly and thankfully to the work karma has bestowed upon them. They must curb their appetites and not resent the good fortune of others:

Ogamisama says that in the degenerated beggar's world, if you do not get rid of your selfishness you will never be saved. Since we are human beings, we possess the instincts of self-preservation. We must have certain things in order to exist but we must not want in excess of our needs. Be thankful and satisfied with what you have and live a clean life. If you have what you need, do not be extravagant and if you do not have all you need, do not complain (1970, 135).

These examples of social protest from the underground world of popular religion should not mislead us into thinking that the New Religions were a covert form of social or political activism. They were not. Mrs. God probably spoke for most of the New Religions when, in an interview, she exclaimed: "Political parties are entirely useless . . . I will dissolve the Diets one after another and will confiscate all the belongings of the maggot beggars" (Tenshō-Kōtai-Jingū-Kyō 1954, 153). Her final solution to the problem of society and industry was a religious one.

Miki and Sayo were extreme cases — charismatic women whose disgust for the "High Mountains" and "maggots" could not be repressed. In general, the social protest of the New Religions took safer, more symbolic, or even cryptic forms. Preachers said just enough about the evils of our "meaningless, useless, profane civilization" to establish rapport with those forced to look upon development from the bottom up. Kawate Bunjirō (1814–83), founder of the Konkō sect, condemned the "progress and development" of his day when he said, "They talk about the world 'opening up'; I say it's falling apart!" Again, Itó Rokurobei (1829–94) of the Fuji sect openly lamented, "Enlightenment [i.e., the Meiji word for overall "development"] is the downfall of mankind." Usually, the messiahs of the New Religions touched on social problems only as examples of a more fundamental religious plight: the impending end of the world, possession by evil spirits, rampant egoism, manifestations of bad karma, and so on. By "touching on" social issues in this way, the preacher could keep silent about the "negative externalities" of development while seeming to make a great deal of racket about them. By reducing social problems to instances of otherworldly or demonic predicaments, the founders and preachers of the New Religions were able to keep a safe, if noisy, silence on problems of the greatest social importance. Whatever his diagnosis might be, the preacher's remedy was always a religious or magical nostrum: an amulet, a spell, or a ritual that would take care of everything. Whether in peace or in war, New Religions of this sort — for all their fuss — seldom got in the way of development.[19]

I have argued elsewhere that, contrary to Weber's notion that development rests upon the "disenchantment of the world," magic and miracles are entirely compatible with the "rationality" of industrial society (Davis 1980a, 298–302). Although magic was "sober and rational" when it first appeared, Weber was convinced that the "highly anti-rational world of universal magic" among the religions of Asia could never give rise to "rational, inner-worldly life conduct" (Weber 1968, vol. 1, 424; 1958c, 336). For some reason, it never seems to have occurred to him that workers could be faithful to their industrial "callings" by tending their "gardens of magic" on weekends or on their days off. Because of his preoccupation with the *origin* of capitalism, he gave no attention to the question of whether magic could adapt itself to the rational temper of a modern economy *once that economy was in place*. It seems to me that as long as magic is situational (i.e., as long as it can retreat under inappropriate circumstances) and functional (i.e., subordinate to the controlling rationality of the "better sort of people"), it poses no serious threat to modern institutions. In fact, one might argue that modern economics and politics have become quite dependent on the magician's legerdemain. Like "apotropaic Buddhism" in Southeast Asia, Japanese magic has become "the religion of a rising and prosperous bourgeoisie" (Spiro 1982, 465) — and proletariat. If so, I would argue against Weber that magic, magical religions, and development are not antithetical at all. On the contrary, wherever we look, the magician and the general, the shaman and the developer, the preacher and the industrialist all seem to be following the same drummer, marching to the same beat.

## THE FINAL SCENE: POSITIVE ENABLEMENTS

The idea that preachers, shamans, and magicians indirectly contribute to development by keeping their mouths shut (or vacuously open) rests on an argument ex silentio more easily sensed than proven. This does not mean that religion's passive acceptance of development is unimportant. On the contrary, it is as vital to development as the positive enablements I am about to discuss. To put the relationship between the two in the terms of theology: the negative is to the positive enablement what a nihil obstat is to an imprimatur. One facilitates the process by not objecting; the other, by giving the "go-ahead" and blessing.

Throughout the premodern world, religion and magic were used to enhance the productivity of contained or embedded economies. "What the common man looks for in religion is not metaphysics, but a kind of spiritual, or thaumaturgical, pragmatism. He wants his cow to calve, his wife to bear, the drought to end, the plague to pass him by..." Davis (1980a, 84). In all of the countries of the Far East, religion provided ritual techniques to promote the fertility of fields and wives and to bring merchants and artisans good luck. Each occupation had a festival day for its own guardian deity. Even other-worldly faiths like Buddhism developed their own this-worldly magic and work ethics.

The religious work ethic one finds in Asian countries just before the modern period is, typically, a mixture of magic and common sense, a striving for achievement, and a genuine concern for the well-being of kith and kin. None of the Japanese figures usually mentioned in this context — e.g., Ishida Baigan (Bellah 1957), Suzuki Shōsan (Nakamura 1956; 1964, passim; 1967, vol. 2, 46–61), or Ninomiya Sontoku (Naramoto 1971) — could conceive of a "work ethic" that would encourage a moral disembedding of the economy. All of them sought merely to motivate people to work and achieve as much as they could in the context of the feudal society in which they lived. All presupposed, and sought to reinforce, the social and kinship restraints of traditional Confucian society. As popular as they were, Ishida, Suzuki, and Ninomiya do not stand directly in the folk tradition itself. Was there a work ethic at this still lower level of society?

A good example of the work ethic of the folk (and the mixture of traditional and modern elements in it) is found in the Fuji sect. Originating in the ascetic and shamanistic practices associated with Mount Fuji, this sect was popular among the merchants and artisans of Edo (Tokyo) and among the peasants of the surrounding Kantō plain. The sect developed its own "work ethic," which is said to have influenced Ninomiya Sontoku himself. Among the virtues it extolled were benevolence, self-restraint, frugality, and diligence. Preachers of the sect stressed the importance of developing strong farming and fishing villages, hygiene, and agricultural technology. They urged members to be active in community projects such as the building of roads and bridges. One should labor, they said, not merely to enrich oneself, but in order to support one's family and indigent neighbors. The Fuji sect attacked various magical practices, even those traditionally practiced by the sect itself. Its attitude toward women was also relatively "modern." Itō Jikigyōmiroku (1671–1733), the sect's messiah, declared that women are not polluted by their menstrual period (regarded by Shinto as a source of "red pollution"). On the contrary, if a woman "did not harm, poison, or bewitch her husband" — and as long as she did her housework and followed the traditional Rule of the Three Obediences,[20] — she was a man's equal. "Both male and female are human beings."

In addition to these "progressive" doctrines, the Fuji sect also believed in a fuzzy kind of eschatology called "world renewal" *(yonaori)*, "the shake up" *( furikawari)*, or "the renovation" *(on-aratame)* of the world. The Eschaton was believed to have started when the "male and female ropes" of the god Sengen Daibosatsu were joined together on 15 June 1688 at Shakamuni's Crevice in Maitreya's Fushita Heaven (equal to Mount Fuji itself). This esoteric event ushered in the age of Maitreya's rule *(Miroku no yo)*. One of the early leaders of the movement, Gatsugyō Sōju, called upon the emperor himself to inaugurate the world of Maitreya![21]

If the Fuji sect is at all typical of the kind of religion that had the greatest appeal to the common folk — and I think it was — it is evident that the religious "work ethic" of early modern Japan was steeped in other-worldly expectations and in the values of familyism, community, and political authoritarianism.[22] The individual was expected to follow the line of work of his or her ancestors. He or she was to work for a world that would be richer and more secure, but that would have the same basic structures. In short, *it was an ethic for a society with an embedded economy.* Since it justified diligence without generating any unnatural or "mighty enthusiasm" for it, I would hesitate to call the Fuji sect's work ethic the analogue of the Puritan's (alleged) work ethic. Nor do I find any evidence in the writings of other Japanese moralists for any purely religious, irrational goad to rational labor.

The same must be said of the social teachings of the New Religions of the twentieth century. Many, perhaps most, continue to preach "a feudalistic morality in the context of a capitalist economy" (Davis 1975, parts 4–6, 32). When not blatantly feudalistic, the morality taught by the postwar New Religions is usually rich in the ascetic, nationalistic, and authoritarian values of Japan's wartime "civil religion." Mrs. God, for example, taught that "occupation and religion are both wheels of the same cart" (Tenshō-Kōtai-Jingū-Kyō 1970, 143). While in jail, she wrote a letter to her son with the following practical advice:

> The beans in the fields should be picked while they are green because this will save lots of labor and besides, if you don't pick them while green, the stems cannot be used for fertilizer. Next, do not waste but be as frugal as possible and appreciate what you have. This is one of the most important fundamentals of religious practice (Tenshō-Kōtai-Jingū-Kyō 1954, 113).

Like other Japanese moralists, she taught that the way out of economic strife is to accept the karmic determination of economic and social position. "Each person should remind himself of his responsibilities to God and his employer and make certain he renders his best efforts to both" (Tenshō-Kōtai-Jingū-Kyō 1970, 142). Employers, on the other hand, must treat their workers as human beings. While outsiders may treat these words as pious platitudes, the faithful believe that "by this, Ogamisama taught us how to rise above the economic system" (1970, 136).

Throughout the modern period, the traditional morality of hard work, achievement, and social concern has been modified and reworked countless times, both in secular and in sacred ways. In its most effective form, it has been co-opted and woven into the civil religion and theology that took shape and dominated Japanese life between 1868 and 1945.[23] Confucianism itself encouraged ambition to hide behind the folding Oriental fans of benevolence and patriotism. During the Tokugawa period, Confucian schools aimed at producing men who would be useful to their fiefs. Later on, the same ambition was legitimated in the name of Japanese nationalism.[24] The nouveaux riches in Japan justified its wealth in the name of family and nation, much as early English entrepreneurs dedicated the fruits of their labor to the "glory of God and the improvement of man's estate." As Fukuzawa Yukichi (1836–1901) tartly remarked, even the samurai of the Tokugawa period, for all of their high talk about loyalty and selflessness, were but "gilded, pseudo-*chün-tzu*" (Dore 1965b, 129, n. 46) seeking their own private gain.

During the Meiji period, businessmen sought to justify their activities in terms of Confucianism, nationalism, and the Way of the Warrior *(bushidō)*. In the end, however, the business elite failed to "formulate a persuasive rationale for capitalism" (Marshall 1967, 117). Throughout the 1920s and 1930s, the traditional Confucian "barricades" held, and businessmen were excoriated for their selfishness and profit mongering. This ideological failure helped to polarize social criticism at the extremes: between conservative ultranationalists, on the one side, and radical Marxists, on the other. Each group had its own organic vision of society. The Western ideals of economic individualism, liberalism, and parliamentary democracy were finally squeezed out and replaced by militarism and fascism pure and simple (see Scalapino 1953, 272). The mixture of civil religion and business ideology proved to be far less successful in the end than the mixture of civil religion and the work ethic itself. If it is true that religion often influences the economy through the medium of politics (Finn 1983, 55, 135, 202), Japan's civil religion *may* have had more to do with implementing the popular work ethic than any other symbolic factor.[25] In spite of its failures in the prewar period, "business ideology" (Marshall 1967, 4) and "superordinate goals" (Pascale and Athos 1981, 177–206) continue to be used by Japanese industry to legitimate itself and to motivate its work force. These values are transmitted or instilled in workers (from the "top down") through various initiation rites, training sessions, and "spiritual education" *(seishin kyōiku)* weekends (Davis 1975, 302–9; Rohlen 1974, 34-61).

Finally, the work ethic is propagated in the Japan theory that has appeared during the last two decades (see the preceding discussion under Confucian Development). This literature, which ranges from the erudite to the most banal, seems to perform many of the functions once assumed by civil religion itself. It seeks to create a sense of national identity; it defends the country against foreign criticism (often by stressing the uniqueness of the Japanese "national character"); and it promotes the policy of "building the country through technology" *(gijutsu rikkoku),* just as the old civil religion promoted the policy of "rich country and strong army" ( *fukoku kyōhei).* While the writing of the Japan theorists may be descriptive, analytical, or even entertaining, the authors' final purpose seems to be normative. "By telling the reader who the Japanese are, they are, indirectly, telling the Japanese who they *ought* to be and how they *ought* to behave" (Davis 1984, 216). To be Japanese, a person must work hard, be loyal and sincere, and so on.

Time and space do not allow us to go into the details of the various manifestations of the work ethic. In all cases, work is made part of an inclusive reticulation of such values as harmony, unity, consensus, loyalty, sincerity, and altruistic service to the individual's family, company, and nation. As such, the work ethic has been imposed on workers both from below (by popular religious leaders, "moral entrepreneurs" (Plath 1969, 181), and even by the workers themselves) and from above (by government, industry, and the official ideology). (For this reason, it is helpful to distinguish between a work *ethic* [the former] and a work *ideology* [the latter].) In part, these values are what the Japanese call *tatemae:* principles averred in public. They are part of the rituals of the office, shop, and factory. The worker subscribes to them the way he or she participates in morning calisthenics — sometimes with gusto, sometimes with lethargy — but always by going through the motions. Allegiance to the rhetoric and values of a firm may be thought of as the expressive side of the socioeconomic exchange of service for patronage that lies beneath the individual's overall relationship with his or her company. According to a Japanese proverb, everyone should "wrap him or herself in something long." Usually this means everyone should find him or herself a patron. But by extension, it could just as well refer to the company uniform and the long, invisible cloak of values and etiquette that goes with it. Many find the moral bonds with their company deeply satisfying. Many Japanese are convinced that wrapping themselves in these virtues is the sure way to success. For these reasons, the ideals of loyalty and service have become inextricably intertwined with material rewards, the quest for higher status, and the affirmation of family and national identity.

## DENOUEMENT: EMBEDDING SOCIETY

Today, not much remains of the barricades that once defended traditional Asian society against development. Victorious developers have built their own castles where the ramparts once stood. Above the former citadel now rise the towering spires of Tokyo, Osaka, Seoul, Singapore, and the other dazzling emporia of East Asia. Were we to update Figures II.1 and II.2 and make them correspond to the situation today, we would have to transpose "A" and "C" to show that society is now virtually sequestered or "embedded" in the economy. Today, it is industry that asks to be made safe from society and *its* claims, i.e., the social welfare and justice that, like quasi-religious superstitions, continue to remind us of our tribal past (Hayek, 1976, 66). The new barricades protecting the economy are manned by secular preachers of the gospel of wealth, Reaganomics, administrative reform, and Japan theory. Standing beside them, however, are the evangelists

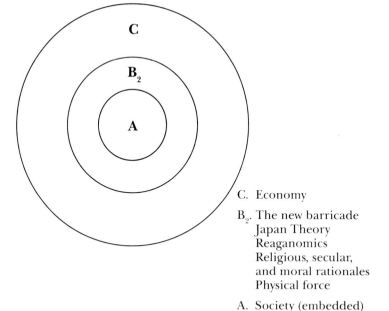

C. Economy

B₂. The new barricade
Japan Theory
Reaganomics
Religious, secular,
and moral rationales
Physical force

A. Society (embedded)

Figure II.3. *Post-Confucian Industrial Society*

shamans, magicians, and high priests of both traditional and New Religions who now bless the very institutions they once cursed.

The relationship between society, religion, morality, and the economy emerging in some of the countries of the Far East today can be represented by Figure II.3. Notice that the barrier protecting the economy in Figure II.3 (B₂) — now a solid line — is being rebuilt and restored to its pristine condition. Here, the organic model of *society* (e.g., the ethic of "hierarchical complementarity") that once fended off the disequilibrating forces of the economy has been turned into an organic model of *industry*.

Figure II.3 represents only an exaggerated ideal type of a society still in the process of "development." Some will regard it as a figment of the imagination, or perhaps a nightmare.

Others will defend it as one of the most successful experiments in postmodernity. Perhaps its closest approximation is modern Japan. In other parts of the Far East, military distatorships dominate society ("A") and industry ("C") alike. In Japan, however, a struggle continues between the forces of society and the all-but-dominant economy. The willingness of so many Japanese to put up with the claims of industry (at the expense of their own "entitlements") has a great deal to do with their own improved financial condition. The economy has paid off handsomely.

Part of this payoff has been ideological and moral. It is deeply gratifying to belong to a large, powerful, and successful organization that seems to "care." The "universal and mutual distrust" that Weber saw in the traditional economies of Asia (1951, 237) ironically reappears with a vengeance once the "rational depersonalizing of business" (1951, 85) has been pushed to its logical conclusion: quick layoffs for quick profits, the flight of capital, and so on. Once business reaches the point where stability is as important as immediate profits, the ruthless ("universalistic") disregard for workers becomes counterproductive. Under these circumstances, the image of the company or bank as a concerned, benevolent family — backed up in some cases by promises of permanent employment and other emoluments — can be a powerful de-alienating force in the business world. Realizing this, industrialists in Japan, Korea, and Singapore have created paternalistic systems that zero in on the psychological needs and cultural identities of their workers. In effect, they have simply co-opted the symbols and values of the traditional households and villages they were actually destroying.

The costs of embedding society in industrial state capitalism have been described by Hane (1982) in moving detail. I shall therefore touch on only two contemporary problems, education and industrial discipline.

No better example of the triumph of economic goals and values could be given than contemporary Japanese education. The costs of development, initially borne by women and peasants, now rest most heavily on school-age children. Over the years, the Japanese have developed an examination-based meritocracy to supply industry with the kind of "human capital" it needs. It aims at, and succeeds in producing, workers who are docile, group oriented, and broadly but not deeply educated — or better — who are *socialized* in the technical and functional rationality of industry itself. To realize the bureaucrats' dream of making the twenty-first century the "century of Japan," the Japanese have, in effect, chained their own children to the walls of Weber's "iron cage." Some children spend as much time at their desks at school and in *juku* (after-school tutoring or "cram" schools) as English children did at their workbenches in the early nineteenth century. This system of "education" is probably the main cause of one of the country's most serious problems, violence in the home and at school.[26] On college campuses, educators and psychologists worry about students who have become "moratorium men" unable to commit themselves to *any* social or industrial institutions (Okonogi 1978; Okonogi 1979).[27] Although the college campuses are quiet at present, it is probably only a matter of time before the violence of Japanese middle schools becomes a problem in higher education.

The ideological and religious defenders of the new industrial order are, of course, backed by physical force. This time the defenders literally "mean business." Industries, armed with their own patrols and spies, brook no opposition. Shortly after the Pacific War, Japanese industry deliberately set out to destroy the militant labor unions. Today, workers who are dissatisfied with the company union are harrassed and sometimes even beaten. Those who take sick leave are sometimes "visited" by company police to see how sick they really are. At Toyota, rebellious union members circulate an underground newspaper similar to the *samizdat* publications of the U.S.S.R. Union elections are supervised by the labor aristocracy (generally a clone of management itself ); voting is sometimes conducted in public view (Kamata 1983, Woronoff 1983). Restrictions on horizontal mobility, a system of seniority pay, and other practices severely limit the freedom of the working force. In other parts of the Far East, the working population is kept in line by the general mobilization of society against foreign enemies. Since the same troops are used against internal dissenters as well, their *real* purpose is open to question. I bring up these unsavory facts to make the simple point that industrial discipline in the Far East depends on much more than a "work ethic."

Our examination of the religious and cultural barricades between society and the economy finally brings us back to our starting point, Max Weber's own sociology of pain. Looking at Japanese young people today, one wonders how they can endure such a massive repression. To be sure, the primordial togetherness of after-hours drinking and cavorting provides workers with some relief from the demands of the office or factory — far more than singing the company song! But in the end, the Japanese will probably contain dissent and make the next century their own by falling back on some kind of nationalism. Once again Japan seems to need a widely accepted and officially endorsed civil religion that will legitimate the country's postwar success and provide a theodicy for the suffering it has caused. Both Japan theory and the New Religions seem to be groping in this direction.[28]

### AFTERTHOUGHTS

As I look over the pages I have just written, I marvel at how easy it was to forget my initial skepticism concerning the feasibility of this project. Nearly every positive statement in the two final "scenes" should be scrupulously qualified by additional "possibly's" and "perhap's." Caveat lector!

Figures II.1, II.2, and II.3 are not intended as a simple, unilinear model of development per se. Rather, they symbolize one way in which the religious rationales sanctifying society and the economy have changed, or have become "secularized." While not denying the possibility that religion may sometimes have a positive, stimulating effect on social change and economic development, I have emphasized the importance of its functional or legitimating role, and the ways in which that role itself has changed in order to accommodate development. While there is evidence of a work ethic among the working classes, this ethic achieved national significance only after it was rationalized and propagated as a part of civil theology and the business ideology and in the new national image making of Japan theory. Whether or not there is such a thing as a "central value system," there clearly is a *resonance* here between the work ethic of the common people and the work ideology of the cultured and industrial elites. That resonance is not natural or accidental; it was planned.

Weber and the Weberians have generally approached the problem of religion and development by analyzing the religion and values established before the onset of industrialization, and by postulating a correlation (or "elective affinity") between them and subsequent historical events. Bellah (1957), for example, has tried to understand the development of twentieth-century Japan by looking at religion and values of the preceding Tokugawa period. Cultural studies of this sort, while suggestive, leave one with the suspicion that their authors are trapped in a post hoc ergo propter hoc argument that says, in effect, that because modern Asian industry developed (or in Weber's own case: did *not* develop) after religious value systems were in place, it developed (Weber: did *not* develop) because of them. Unless the connections between values and development can be made explicit there seems to be no way to turn Weberian speculation into defensible, testable, or falsifiable hypotheses. I would suggest that more attention be paid to the religious attitudes which appear while development is taking place. For example, one can learn far more about the religious background of American capitalism by reading the sermons of Bishop William Lawrence of Massachusetts, Henry Ward Beecher, or Russell H. Conwell than by pouring over Richard Baxter's *Christian Directory*. And, I dare say, one can learn more about the subject from Liston Pope than from Max Weber himself. Perhaps a good example to follow would be research on a parallel problem: the role of religion in colonialism. While missionary zeal paved the way for colonial adventures in some parts of the world, most missionaries simply *followed* the imperialist into the field and collaborated with him.

Weberians have often treated religion as a crucial but unchanging variable in the maelstrom of social and economic change. Here I think we should return to Weber's own interest in the (internal) transformation of the religions that are (externally) affecting development. We must also be aware of similar changes in values in general, e.g., how they are turned into rhetoric, and how rhetoric, in turn, gives rise to new values. Also, we should periodically remind ourselves that values do not generally act on their own, but rather as part of a "team" of factors including physical rewards, constraints, etc.

Before any meaningful work can be done on the problem of religion and development, we must subject the concept of secularization to a thoroughgoing review. We need to recognize the importance of the "disenchantment" of certain strategic elements of society and the economy; but we must be very suspicious of, and finally reject, a priori theories that postulate the *Entzauberung* of the whole damn' *Welt*. For the same reason, the decline of religion itself can no longer be taken for granted as a necessary concomitant of some "universal process of modernization." In no case should we allow theory to blind us to the subtle ways in which very "primitive" kinds of religion and magic continue to coexist and collaborate with the institutions of modern society. The recrudescence and revalorization of religious emotions, ideas, and symbols seem to take place in *all* periods of history. We must pay more attention to the *aggiornamento* of magic and religion, and not focus our efforts exclusively on the tension between them and development. On this point, Weber and other theorists bewitched by the Enlightenment's idle myths of "science and progress" have badly misled both the sociology of religion and the study of development.

**NOTES**

1. Perhaps this is what George Gilder was getting at in the theological passages of *Wealth and Poverty* (1981), where he invokes the spirit of the pagan gods Tyche and Fortuna: "Chance is the foundation of change and the vessel of the divine." Chance or predestination (he assumes they are the same) "taps the underlying and transcendent order of the universe." (See Davis 1982, 11–12.)

2. By religion, in this case, I mean the use of sacred symbols, rewards, and punishments to restrict traditional greed and im-

personal market values. Western examples range from the attack on urbanization and commercialism by the Biblical prophets to the teachings of the medieval Church on usury. By magic, I refer to cases such as the proverbial "pauper's curse" that serve to limit exploitation and the accumulation of capital. By traditional religion, law, morality, and philosophy, I mean those formal and informal teachings that make market values subordinate to social ones (e.g., the medieval dictum: *homo mercator vix aut numquam potest Deo placere*). By taboos, I mean the implicit prohibition against certain classes engaging in commerce, against the extension of the seasons or hours of trade, etc. By the folk tradition, I have in mind the countless tales of poetic justice in which the greedy get their comeuppance and the generous their just reward. The idea that markets and self-interest might encourage "habits of regularity, temperance, moderation, foresight, self-command" (de Tocqueville) was unheard of in most traditional societies (and continues to be looked upon with no little skepticism even today). Most traditional societies probably shared Durkheim's view that economic activity is a centrifugal force, religion a countervailing, centripetal one (1915, 245-55). Thus, it is significant that almost no one has seriously argued that any of the world's historic religions led *directly* to the growth of capitalism. All of the positions examined in this essay posit some kind of mutation occurring in religion before it becomes a force in development: Christianity must turn into Calvinism, Buddhism must assume its Mahayana form, and Confucianism must be Japanized. The defensive function of the social teachings and practices of traditional religion seems indisputable.

3.  That Confucianism is not merely a morality but a form of moralism is of great importance when we consider its putative impact on development. I take moralism to be morality based on the fallacy of composition. Moralism reduces complex social problems to the simpler level of individual conduct so that social conditions can be improved only by converting all (or most) of the individual members of society to the good life. Moralism assumes that the problems of society are simply the quantitative aggregation of individual moral issues. It recognizes no *qualitative* change in moral issues as one moves from individuals to complex organizations. Because it believes social ills can be remedied only by the cultivation of the individual, moralism often counsels long suffering and endurance in the face of

injustice and exploitation. Under the right circumstances, moralism can easily become a "negative enablement" of development.

4. Morishima always seems to assume that atheists are, by definition, materialists.

5. In general, Morishima seems to be more critical of Japan and her Confucian tradition than are other Japan theorists. But typical of Japan theory, he explains the country's economic nationalism (and the dangers lurking behind it) in purely *cultural* terms.

6. This point is often raised against Abegglen (1958), too.

7. Weber's skepticism about the economic potential of the samurai goes back to his conviction that a military caste is "particularly unreceptive to the rationalistic belief in an ethically concerned, yet impartial, wise and kindly providence" (Weber 1968, vol. 1, 431).

8. Kamishima Jirō (1971, 40–89) has argued that Japanese cities also failed to develop a distinctive urban spirit. But this obviously did not hinder their industrialization.

9. Because Weber was not very concerned with the "negative enablements" that encourage a passive acceptance of the "negative externalities" of growth, he misjudged the real contributions of moralism to development. See note 3.

10. In passages such as the ones just summarized, Weber's own analysis lends itself very well to the barricades model suggested above. (See also Weber 1968, vol. 1, 435.)

11. See Schwartz (1975) for a similar view.

12. C. K. Yang (1967, chap. 9), however, argues that some of China's secret societies had leaders who could be called emissary or ethical prophets.

13. Nearly all of the proposals for the reform of the Japanese economy put forward during the Tokugawa period called for strong government policies and intervention.

14. Weber, however, thought that the Shingon sect was full of "magical sorcery" (1958c, 277).

15. The sentiments expressed by the owners and managers of textile mills in Pope's study of Gastonia, North Carolina, are of a similar sort. For example: "We make American citizens, and run cotton mills to pay the expenses" (1942, 16).

16. The secularization of the traditional moral economy is not begun by the marketplace itself, but by networks of markets transcending the local catchment of exchange. Local markets, based

on face-to-face relations, dominated by many dealers (but few middlemen), and controlled by local authorities, can be reconciled with even the most antichrematistic morality. It is external trade *(Fernhandel)* that poses the problem of economic morality in its most serious and threatening form. External trade transcends the moral jurisdiction of the princes and prelates in control of the local economy. In external markets, parasitical middlemen seem to multiply wantonly. Traders make fortunes by investing their money, but nothing of themselves or their own skills. In fact, the great merchants of external trade often bring to the market no skill at all, save the ability to manipulate filthy lucre itself. Finally, the development of external trade meant that the fortunes of entire families (if not generations) could rise and fall through no one's virtue or vice. In the new market system moral "inputs" therefore seemed to have nothing to do with material "outputs." In short, society was faced with an anomic force of its own making that, when aroused, could rage like an implacable storm. This ultimately gave rise to the idea that markets are nonmoral because, like weather itself, they are part of Nature. (See Braudel 1977, 47–63.)

17. In sharp contrast, "gestation" in China would last until the "take off" of the economy under the postwar Communist regime (Fairbank, Eckstein, and Yang 1971, 156-57).

18. Trade in weapons, poison, alcohol, slaves, taking part in the caravan trade (i.e., external trade), or being a butcher or tanner were commonly prohibited.

19. Prophets like Taniguchi Masaharu of the House of Growth (Seichō no Ie), who stood in the forefront of ultranationalism and military development during the war, did a sudden about-face in 1945 and presented themselves as harbingers of international peace and industrial progress. The ambiguity of the theology of these groups and their disregard of common logic (the "morality of thought") gave them a flexibility that enabled them to go along with "development" of all sorts.

20. The Rule of the Three Obediences was that a woman should obey her parents, her husband, and, after her husband's death, her own children.

21. The social teachings of folk religion often combine egalitarian dreams with an absolute respect for authority. For example, Deguchi Nao (1836–1918), foundress of the Ōmoto sect, proclaimed that someday the "World shall be equal all over" (Ōm-

oto 1974, 8). But she also taught that "everyone should be obedient to [him] whom he should obey" (1974, 70).

22.  The Fuji sect was banned in 1849 when it called for government reforms. Under the influence of a samurai by the name of Shibata Shōgyō (1809–90), a related movement called the Practice sect appeared that gave greater emphasis to nationalism and loyalty to the emperor. Shibata and his followers regarded Mount Fuji as the palladium of the nation and the "brain of the planet." After the Meiji period, this sect became closely aligned with State Shinto. The Maruyama sect, a branch supported by middle-and lower-level peasants in Kanagawa, Shizuoka, and Nagano, became actively involved in protests against the Sino-Japanese war. This antiwar activity came to a halt after the death of its founder, Itō Rokurobei. After this, the sect was absorbed by the growing spirit of nationalism and emperor worship. The Fuji sect is, therefore, a good example of the way in which popular religious movements (even eschatological ones) were co-opted by the imperial system of the Meiji state. It also illustrates the close connection between the traditional "work ethic" and nationalism.

23.  "By 'civil religion' I mean a systematic network of moods, values, thoughts, rituals, and symbols that establishes the meaning of nationhood within an overarching hierarchy of significance. While civil religions are the precipitates of traditional religious communities, they transcend specific religious communities and dogmas. The symbols and suasions of the civil religion must speak to 'all sorts and conditions of men.' 'Civil theology," on the other hand, is the articulation of civil religion by the elite. One could say that civil religion — a reticulation of implicit sentiments — is 'thought in.' Civil theology is 'thought out' " (Davis 1976a, 6, n. 3).

24.  Nationalism has always been both a motivation and an ex post facto justification for engaging in economic activity. Some scholars have been inclined to accept it "phenomenologically" as a genuine motivation. See, for example, Marshall (1967, 4), Hirschmeier (1964, 162–75), Moore (1961), and Marris (1964). Others, like Yamamura (1968, 144–58) have regarded it as a mask for self-interest. Given the complexities of the human heart, both sides are probably right.

25.  Unlike Robert Bellah (1970, 168–186), I have never been able to locate the normative center of a civil religion save that established by political authority. In contrast to Bellah, I regard

the perverse elasticity of a civil religion one of its defining characteristics.

26. The opposite of the American problem of child abuse, in Japan it is the children who are the "aggressors," bludgeoning parents to death in their sleep, attacking their teachers at school, and so on.

27. This syndrome is closely related to the appearance of the radically polymorphous, secular ego that Lifton (1969, 37–63) calls Protean Man, a phenomenon not unparalleled in the West. See, for example, Robert Musil's novel *The Man without Qualities* (1930–42; London: Picador, 1979, 3 vols.).

28. For example, one of the New Religions proclaims that in the twenty-first century the world will once again be ruled by the Japanese emperor ( just as it was when the world was young). In the meantime, all misfortune is ascribed to evil spirits. When the "Civilization of the Kingdom of God" is finally revealed, the humble folk who have joined the sect to cast out evil spirits will be made members of the emperor's new ruling elite (see Davis, 1980a, passim).

## REFERENCES

Abegglen, James C. 1958. *The Japanese Factory: Aspects of Its Social Organization*. Glencoe, Ill.: Free Press.

Bellah, Robert N. 1957. *Tokugawa Religion*. Boston: Beacon Press.

Bellah, Robert N. 1970. *Beyond Belief: Essays on Religion in a Post-Traditional World*. New York: Harper & Row.

Bellah, Robert N. 1975. *The Broken Covenant: American Civil Religion in Time of Trial*. New York: Crossroad.

Bendix, Reinhard, and Guenther Roth. 1980. *Scholarship and Partisanship: Essays on Max Weber*. Berkeley: University of California Press.

Berger, Peter L. 1967. *The Sacred Canopy*. Garden City, N.Y.: Doubleday.

Berger, Peter L. 1976. *Pyramids of Sacrifice: Ethics and Social Change*. New York: Doubleday Anchor.

Braudel, Fernand. 1977. *Afterthoughts on Material Civilization and Capitalism*. Baltimore, Md.: Johns Hopkins University Press.

Chan, Wing-Tsit. 1963. *A Source Book in Chinese Philosophy*. Princeton, N.J.: Princeton University Press.

Craig, Albert. 1965. "Science and Confucianism in Tokugawa Japan." In *Changing Japanese Attitudes toward Modernization,* edited by Marius B. Jansen. Princeton, N.J.: Princeton University Press. 133–60.

Darle, John R., Dean D. Knudsen, Donald W. Shriver, Jr. 1976. *Spindles and Spires: A Re-Study of Religion and Social Change in Gastonia.* Atlanta: John Knox Press.

Davis, Winston. 1975. "Ittoen: The Myths and Rituals of Liminality." Pts. 1–3, 4–6. *History of Religions Journal* 14, no. 4 (May): 282–331; 15, no. 1 (August): 1–33.

Davis, Winston. 1976a. "The Civil Theology of Inoue Tetsujirō." *Japanese Journal of Religious Studies* 3, no. 1 (March): 5–40.

Davis, Winston. 1976b. "Parish Guilds and Political Culture in Village Japan." *Journal of Asian Studies* 36, no. 1 (November): 25–36.

Davis, Winston. 1978. "The *Miyaza* and the Fisherman: Ritual Status in Coastal Villages of Wakayama Prefecture." *Asian Folklore Studies* 36, no. 2: 1–29.

Davis, Winston. 1980a. *Dojo: Magic and Exorcism in Modern Japan.* Stanford, Calif.: Stanford University Press.

Davis, Winston. 1980b. "The Secularization of Japanese Religion: Measuring the Myth and the Reality." In *Transitions and Transformation in the History of Religions: Essays in Honor of Joseph M. Kitagawa,* edited by Frank E. Reynolds and Theodore M. Ludwig, Leiden: E. J. Brill. 261–85.

Davis, Winston. 1982. "The Gospel According to Gilder." *Christianity and Crisis* 42, no. 1 (1 February): 11–12.

Davis, Winston. 1983. "Japanese Religious Affiliations: Motives and Obligations." *Sociological Analysis* 44, no. 2 (Summer): 131–46.

Davis, Winston. 1983–84. "Pilgrimage and World Renewal: A Study of Religion and Social Values in Tokugawa Japan." Pts. 1, 2. *History of Religions Journal* 23, no. 2 (November 1983): 97–116; 23, no. 3 (February 1984): 197–221.

Davis, Winston. 1984. "The Hollow Onion: The Secularization of Japanese Civil Religion." In *The Challenge of Japan's Internationalization: Organization and Culture,* edited by Hiroshi Mannari and Harumi Befu. Tokyo: Kodansha. 212–31.

de Bary, William Theodore, et al., eds. 1958. *Sources of Japanese Tradition.* New York: Columbia University Press.

de Bary, William Theodore. 1960. *Sources of Chinese Tradition.* Vol. 1. New York: Columbia University Press.

Dore, R. P. 1965a. *Education in Tokugawa Japan.* Berkeley: University of California Press.

Dore, R. P. 1965b. "The Legacy of Tokugawa Education." In *Changing Japanese Attitudes toward Modernization,* edited by Marius B. Jansen, Princeton, N.J.: Princeton University Press. 99–131.

Dumont, Louis. 1982. "A Modified View of Our Origins: The Christian Beginnings of Modern Individualism." *Religion* 12: 1–27.

Durkheim, Emile. [1915] 1965. *The Elementary Forms of the Religious Life.* Translated by Joseph Ward Swain. New York: Free Press.

Fairbank, John K., Alexander Eckstein, and L. S. Yang. 1971. "Economic Change in Early Modern China: An Analytic Framework." In *Modern China: An Interpretive Anthology,* edited by Joseph R. Levenson. New York: Macmillan. 155–86.

Finn, James, ed. 1983. *Global Economics and Religion.* New Brunswick, N.J.: Transaction Books.

Gilder, George. 1981. *Wealth and Poverty.* New York: Basic Books.

Hakuin Zenji. 1963. *The Embossed Tea Kettle: Orate Gama and Other Works of Hakuin Zenji.* London: George Allen & Unwin.

Hall, John Whitney. 1959. "The Confucian Teacher in Tokugawa Japan." In *Confucianism in Action,* edited by David S. Nivison and Arthur F. Wright. Stanford, Calif.: Stanford University Press. 268–301.

Hane, Mikaso. 1982. *Peasants, Rebels and Outcastes.* New York: Pantheon.

Hayek, Friedrich A. 1976. *Law, Legislation and Liberty.* Vol. 2, *The Mirage of Social Justice.* Chicago: University of Chicago Press.

Hirschmeier, Johannes. 1964. *The Origins of Entrepreneurship in Meiji Japan.* Cambridge, Mass.: Harvard University Press.

Hofheinz, Roy, Jr., and Kent E. Calder. 1982. *The Eastasia Edge.* New York: Basic Books.

Inkeles, Alex, and David Horton Smith. 1974. *Becoming Modern: Individual Change in Six Developing Countries.* Cambridge, Mass.: Harvard University Press.

Itō Mikiharu. 1973. "Nihon bunka no kōzōteki rikai o mezashite." *Kikan jinruigaku* 4: 3–30.

Kamata, Satoshi. 1983. *Japan in the Passing Lane: An Insider's Account of Life in a Japanese Auto Factory.* Translated and edited by Tatsuru Akimoto. New York: Pantheon.

Kamishima Jirō. 1971. *Kindai Nihon no seishin kōzō*. Tokyo: Iwanami Shoten.

Lifton, Robert Jay. 1969. *Boundaries: Psychological Man in Revolution*. New York: Vintage.

Lindblom, Charles E. 1977. *Politics and Markets: The World's Political-Economic System*. New York: Basic Books.

Macpherson, Crawford Brough. 1962. *The Political Theory of Possessive Individualism: Hobbes to Locke*. Oxford: Oxford University Press.

Marcuse, Herbert. 1969. *Negations: Essays in Critical Theory*, Translated by Jeremy J. Shapiro. Boston: Beacon Press.

Marris, Robin. 1964. *The Economic Theory of "Managerial" Capitalism*. New York: Free Press.

Marshall, Byron K. 1967. *Capitalism and Nationalism in Prewar Japan: The Ideology of the Business Elite, 1868–1941*. Stanford, Calif.: Stanford University Press.

Marx, Karl. 1964. *Economic and Philosophic Manuscripts of 1844*. New York: International Publishers.

Morishima, Michio. 1982. *Why Has Japan "Succeeded"?: Western Technology and the Japanese Ethos*. Cambridge: Cambridge University Press.

Moore, Wilbert E. 1961. "The Social Framework of Economic Development." In *Tradition, Values, and Socio-Economic Development*. Edited by Ralph Braibanti and Joseph J. Spengler. Durham, N.C. Duke University Press, 57–82.

Nakamura, Hajime. 1956. "The Vitality of Religion in Asia." In *Cultural Freedom in Asia*. Edited by Herbert Passin. Rutland, Vt.: Charles E. Tuttle. 53–66.

Nakamura, Hajime. 1964. *Ways of Thinking of Eastern Peoples*. Honolulu: University Press of Hawaii.

Nakamura, Hajime. 1967. *A History of the Development of Japanese Thought*. Vol. 2, A.D. 592–1868. Tokyo: Kokusai Bunka Shinkokai.

Naramoto Tatsuya. 1971. *Ninomiya Sontoku*. Tokyo: Iwanami Shoten.

Okonogi Keigo. 1978. *Moratoriamu ningen no jidai*. Tokyo: Chuokōronsha.

Okonogi Keigo. 1979. *Moratoriamu ningen no shinri kōzō*. Tokyo: Chuokōronsha.

Oomoto. 1974. *Ofudesaki: The Holy Scriptures of Oomoto*. Kameoka, Japan: Oomoto.

Pascale, Richard Tanner, and Anthony G. Athos. 1981. *The Art of Japanese Management*. New York: Simon & Schuster.

Plath, David. 1969. *Sensei and His People: The Building of a Japanese Commune*. Berkeley: University of California Press.

Polanyi, Karl. 1944. *The Great Transformation*. Boston: Beacon Press.

Pope, Liston. 1942. *Millhands and Preachers: A Study of Gastonia*. New Haven, Conn.: Yale University Press.

Posner, Richard A. 1981. *The Economics of Justice*. Cambridge, Mass.: Harvard University Press.

Rohlen, Thomas P. 1974. *For Harmony and Strength: Japanese White-Collar Organization in Anthropological Perspective*. Berkeley: University of California Press.

Scalapino, Robert A. 1953. *Democracy and the Party Movement in Prewar Japan: The Failure of the First Attempt*. Berkeley: University of California Press.

Schumpeter, Joseph A. 1962. *Capitalism, Socialism and Democracy*. New York: Harper & Row.

Schwartz, Benjamin I. 1975. "Transcendence in Ancient China." *Daedalus* 104, no. 2 (Spring): 57–68.

Sheldon, Charles David. 1973. *The Rise of the Merchant Class in Tokugawa Japan, 1600–1868*. New York: Russell & Russell.

Simmel, Georg. 1978. *The Philosophy of Money*. Boston: Routledge & Kegan Paul.

Smith, Thomas C. 1966. *The Agrarian Origins of Modern Japan*. New York: Atheneum.

Spengler, Joseph J. 1980. *Origins of Economic Thought and Justice*. Carbondale, Ill.: Southern Illinois University Press.

Spiro, Melford E. 1982. *Buddhism and Society: A Great Tradition and Its Burmese Vicissitudes*, 2d ed. Berkeley: University of California Press.

Strauss, Leo. 1953. *Natural Right and History*. Chicago: University of Chicago Press.

Tawney, R. H. 1980. *Religion and the Rise of Capitalism*. Harmondsworth: Penguin Books.

Tenshō-Kōtai-Jingū-Kyō. 1954. *The Prophet of Tabuse*. Tabuse, Japan: Nakamoto.

Tenshō-Kōtai-Jingū-Kyō. 1970. *Divine Manifestation*. Tabuse, Japan: Nakamoto.

Thomas, Keith. 1971. *Religion and the Decline of Magic.* New York: Scribner.

Viner, Jacob. 1978. *Religious Thought and Economic Society: Four Chapters of an Unfinished Work.* Edited by Jacques Melitz and Donald Winch. Durham, N.C.: Duke University Press.

Vogel, Ezra F. 1979. *Japan As Number One.* Tokyo: Charles E. Tuttle.

Weber, Max. 1951. *The Religion of China: Confucianism and Taoism.* Translated and edited by Hans H. Gerth. New York: Free Press.

Weber, Max. 1952. *Ancient Judaism.* Translated and edited by Hans H. Gerth and Don Martindale. New York: Free Press.

Weber, Max. 1958a. *The Protestant Ethic and the Spirit of Capitalism.* Translated by Talcott Parsons. New York: Scribner.

Weber, Max. 1958b. *From Max Weber: Essays in Sociology.* Translated and edited by H. H. Gerth and C. Wright Mills. New York: Oxford University Press.

Weber, Max. 1958c. *The Religion of India: The Sociology of Hinduism and Buddhism.* Translated and edited by Hans H. Gerth and Don Martindale. New York: Free Press.

Weber, Max. 1968. In *Economy and Society: An Outline of Interpretive Sociology.* Edited by Guenther Roth and Claus Wittlich, vol. 1 and 2, 635–40. New York: Bedminster Press.

Weisskopft, Walter A. 1971. *Alienation and Economics.* New York: Dell.

Welsby, Paul A., ed. 1970. *Sermons and Society: An Anglican Anthology.* Middlesex: Penguin Books.

Woronoff, Jon. 1983. *Japan's Wasted Workers.* Totowa, N.J.: Allanheld, Osmun.

Yamamura, Kozo. 1968. "A Re-examination of Entrepreneurship in Meiji Japan (1868–1912)." *Economic History Review* 2d Ser. 21 (April): 144–58.

Yang, C. K. 1967. *Religion in Chinese Society.* Berkeley: University of California Press.

ALI BANUAZIZI

# Social-Psychological Approaches to Political Development

## INTRODUCTION

In much of the thinking about political development and social change, one can distinguish between two different, occasionally complementary, but often opposing perspectives. The first views the problem of underdevelopment and the processes of change in primarily social-structural terms, focusing on the role of historical, economic, and social factors in the analysis of the causes and characteristics of underdevelopment and the requisite conditions for change. The second approach, pursued by a much smaller number of scholars, places more emphasis on cultural values, beliefs, and psychological orientations as prerequisites or concomitants of social change, and as such indispensable to its understanding. While some proponents of the latter approach would go so far as to view cultural and psychological attributes as the primary determinants of development, most would argue merely for the inclusion of such "subjective" factors as part of any general analysis of development.

For a brief period, in the heyday of the modernization theory in the mid-1960s, the two approaches seemed to be in fair harmony and to some extent even to reinforce each other. Thus, the processes of industrialization, urbanization, secularization, social mobilization, mass communication, and the like, regarded as the hallmarks of modernization at the societal level, were thought to be accompanied by such characteristics at the individual level as empathy, personal efficacy, mental flexibility, rational planning, a greater propensity for social and political participation. It was believed, furthermore, that changes at both the social-structural and psychological levels in the developing societies would proceed along an evolutionary path similar to the one traversed by the Western nations in the course of their modernization some century and a half earlier. And finally, tying the social-structural and the psychological spheres of change together was the end-state of "modernity," as represented in the institutional patterns of contemporary Western societies and the social character and values of their peoples.

This apparent harmony between the two perspectives, however, began to break down as the modernization paradigm itself came under increasing critical scrutiny. The criticism was directed against some of the central premises of the theory: its somewhat simplistic counterposing of the ideal-types of "tradition" and "modernity" as polar opposites in the processes of development; its explanation of the patterns of development in contemporary non-Western societies in terms of concepts stemming from the relatively unique European historical experience; and its gradualist and unidirectional conception of social change.[1] Other criticisms, deriving from the tradition of political economy, faulted the emphasis of the theory on the nation-state as the unit of analysis and its neglect of the larger international context of development. The current underdeveloped state of the third world, it was asserted, is the product of a long process of world-capitalist development, involving inherently unequal and exploitative relations of exchange between the politically dominant (capitalist) centers and their less developed peripheries. And thus, it was argued, development and underdevelopment should be viewed not as two sets of separate *conditions*, but rather as two related and integral parts of the same historical *process*.[2]

While the social-structural aspects of the modernization paradigm were the main targets of criticism, it was the theory's occasional use of cultural and psychological concepts that was subjected to vehement derision. The following remarks by a prominent critic of the paradigm exemplify both the substance and the tone of such attacks:

> No doubt Africa had never invented the wheel, no doubt Asian religions were fatalist, no doubt Islam preached submission, no doubt Latins combined racial miscegenation with a lack of entrepreneurial thrift; but it could now be asserted confidently that these failings were not biological, merely cultural. And if, like the Japanese, the underdeveloped were clever enough to invent an indigenous version of Calvinism, or if they could be induced to change the content of their children's readers (the children first being taught to read, of course), or if transistors were placed in remote villages, or if farsighted elites mobilized benighted masses with the aid of altruistic outsiders, or if..., then the underdeveloped too would cross the river Jordan and come into a land flowing with milk and honey. This was the hope offered up by the modernization theorists.
>
> It was unquestionably a worthy parable for the times. It would be easy to show how this parable was manipulated by the masters of the world. Let us recognize nonetheless that it served to spur devoted and well-intentioned scholarship and liberal social action. But the time has come to put away childish things, and look reality in its face.[3]

Such criticisms had a significant and enduring impact on subsequent writings and research in the field. Along with the greater stress on the international, economic, and political aspects of development, interest in the study of psychological and cultural aspects of the topic ebbed substantially. This shift of emphasis was welcomed particularly by those who feared that concern with the role of cultural values and psychological predispositions often leads to an obfuscation of the more tangible and critical economic and political conditions.

A number of recent trends and phenomena, however, seem to underscore the potentially significant role that cultural and social-psychological factors can play in the processes of development. These events include the rise of religious-revivalist movements in many parts of the non-Western world; the collapse of a major "modernizing" regime in Iran and the triumph of a "traditionalist" revolution whose militant ideology continues to have a strong appeal to millions in the

Islamic world from Morocco to Indonesia; the persistence of ethnic and other primordial sentiments — rather than broad economic interests — as bases of collective identity and political action; and, in a different sense and context, the remarkable economic achievements of several East Asian countries with cultural values and orientations that, to say the least, cannot be viewed as unrelated to their extraordinary economic success. While structural explanations of one sort or another could no doubt be advanced for each of these phenomena, such explanations will be inadequate and limited as long as they fail to incorporate the subjective dimensions of economic and political change.

My goal in this essay is to review critically the intellectual background and some of the underlying premises of the postwar studies of the social-psychological aspects of development in non-Western societies. Inasmuch as the concepts of modernity and tradition have been at the center of the debate about the psychological and cultural dimensions of political change and development, they will serve as the major substantive foci of the essay.

## THE INTELLECTUAL BACKGROUND AND SOME EXAMPLES OF PSYCHOLOGICALLY ORIENTED STUDIES OF DEVELOPMENT

The study of the psychological dimensions of national development and social change in non-Western societies has a relatively short history. Its origins may be found in the confluence during the years immediately after the Second World War of three major intellectual trends and pragmatic concerns in the social sciences. The first of these was the "culture-and-personality" school, which, beginning in the mid-1930s and continuing for nearly two decades, represented a distinct and influential approach to the study of the individual in relation to his or her sociocultural milieu. Guided by the psychoanalytic theory, a number of anthropologists, psychiatrists, sociologists, and others sought to link personality dynamics to cultural configurations and change in mostly non-Western, pre-industrial ("primitive") societies. Central to the conceptual scheme of these scholars was the notion that commonly shared childhood experiences in any society generate a "basic" or "modal" personality structure, which, in turn, helps to shape and functionally integrate the society's cultural institutions such as religion, folklore, rituals, etc.[4]

Later, during World War II and in the years immediately following, some proponents of the culture-and-personality approach, in a series of "national character" studies, applied their concepts and methods to the analysis of the infinitely more complex modern nations. Here again the goal was to identify and analyze the dominant psychological attributes, belief systems, and motives of the members of different national societies and, as much as possible, to explain such characteristics with reference to their members' common sociocultural background and childhood experiences. In spite of their considerable popular appeal, however, these national character studies did not fare so well in academic circles. Their occasional insights were more than outweighed by their often superficial and journalistic tone and exaggerated claims about the potential value of a (diluted) psychoanalytic approach to resolving international understanding and conflict.[5]

By the early 1950s, the entire culture-and-personality approach, including its national-character variant, came under severe criticism and, at least as a scholarly pursuit, suffered a rapid demise. Nevertheless, the leitmotif of the approach — the notion that members of an entire society can be characterized in terms of a single, or at most a few, personality type(s) whose analysis can shed light on their sociocultural and political institutions — continued to influence the thinking behind many future attempts to link individual behavior to its sociopolitical context, particularly in studies of non-Western societies.

The second influence came from within the mainstream of postwar American academic psychology. While the study of group phenomena and social change had held a special appeal for the pioneers of social psychology in the formative phase of the discipline around the turn of the century, this interest became gradually eclipsed by an increasing focus on the dynamics of *individual* behavior in interpersonal and social relations. Even in their studies of collective behavior and extrapersonal social processes, social psychologists relied mainly on the same individual-level constructs and mechanisms that were used in explaining individual behavior.[6] Furthermore, mainly because of methodological reasons, the concept of attitude gained enormous popularity in the field to a point where it became "the most distinctive and indispensable concept in contemporary [mid-twentieth century] American social psychology."[7] Whether in the realm of race relations, housing, voting, international conflict, or pacifism, the typical social-psychological study of the 1940s and early 1950s outside the laboratory focused primarily on individual attitudes and the extent to which they could be modified as a function of interpersonal, situational, or institutional factors. The underlying assumption (and still a matter of considerable controversy in the field) was that attitudes provide the most efficient and reliable clues to understanding social action at both individual and collective levels. In view of this orientation, it is not surprising that the initial contributions of social psychologists to the study of comparative politics and development consisted mainly of quantitative surveys of public opinion, attitudes, and values as clues to understanding the political process.

The third and perhaps the strongest impetus for the study of the subjective aspects of development came from the pragmatic concerns of policy makers and development specialists in the early postwar period. Mindful of the limitations of the institutional approaches, some development theorists turned to cultural anthropology and psychology for insights into the "people side" of sociopolitical development. And, as has often been the case when explanations for the "root causes" of a social problem are sought in its victims, it did not take very long before the analysts discovered that many of the causes of underdevelopment lay in the values, world views, character traits, and cultural traditions of the developing nations themselves. Such views of culture and character as "obstacles to development" were incorporated gradually into the "development ideology" of the 1950s and continued for some years.[8]

The three trends just discussed, then, provided the intellectual backdrop for the new genre of psychologically oriented research on the developing countries that began in in the late

1950s. Depending on whether they treated psychological factors as *preconditions* (independent variables), *concomitants* (intervening variables), or *consequences* (dependent variables), of socioeconomic and political change, the studies under discussion can be grouped into three relatively distinct categories.[9] Examples of the first approach are David McClelland's research on achievement orientation as an independent driving force in economic growth, Lucian Pye's analysis of the Burmese "sense of insecurity" and identity crisis as these relate to the difficulties of that country in building a modern nation-state, and Everett Hagen's emphasis on the role of "innovational" personality as the dynamic cause of economic development.[10]

Daniel Lerner's now classic study of modernization in the Middle East is a good illustration of the third approach.[11] Lerner identified "empathy" (the ability to mentally place oneself in others' roles and to imagine what life is like outside one's own restrictive surround) as the crucial psychological trait enabling newly mobile ("transitional") individuals to adapt themselves more efficiently to the changing circumstances of a modernizing society. The proponents of this approach maintain that the initial thrust toward development comes from changes in the opportunity structure or in other socioeconomic institutions, but that psychological factors then play a key mediating role between the initial macrosocial changes and the subsequent reorientations in the social behavior of individuals that are necessary for political development and sustained economic growth. Ultimately, therefore, the successful functioning of a modern society and its political institutions depends on individuals with the appropriate psychological orientations who can respond effectively to the newly created opportunities and demands of their changing environment.

Surprisingly few studies have taken the third approach, i.e., the treatment of psychosocial qualities as direct consequences of change at the social-structural level. Such a view would be especially compatible with a behaviorist orientation, emphasizing the primacy of institutional arrangements over psychological dispositions in effecting social change. Although it has been advocated from time to time,[12] this approach does not seem to have generated much interest among researchers in this field.

The new generation of studies was distinguished from its precursors in several respects. In the first place, these studies focused on somewhat narrower and more manageable objectives. For example, the earlier concern with such diffuse and unwieldy categories as national character and culture gave way to more limited questions about the relationship between relatively specific personality traits or values and particular developmental processes or outcomes. Second, in explaining individual behavior in economic and political realms, the new studies shifted their emphasis gradually from a "culturalist" mode of explanation (with a focus on shared values and belief systems) to a "structuralist" mode (with emphasis on socio-economic determinants of behavior).[13] Third, the newer studies tended to be more empirically oriented, relying on systematic gathering of data in the field rather than on the impressionistic, "culture-at-a-distance" methods that predominated in the earlier literature.

The research on individual modernity, to which I shall turn in the following section, treats psychological variables as concomitants of socioeconomic and political development. It represents what is generally regarded as the most successful attempt to apply the methods and concepts of social psychology to the study of social and political development.

*Psychological modernity*   Psychological modernity, as the term has come to be used in the literature of modernization, can best be thought of as a "bridge concept" that links processes of change at the individual and societal levels. It refers to a set of individual dispositions (attitudes, values, cognitive styles, personality traits, etc.), which result from such experiences as urban residence, schooling, contact with mass media, and employment in modern enterprises, and which in turn lead to behaviors that are conducive to a society's economic and political development. Given this mediating function, the merits of the concept should be judged not only on the basis of its plausibility and coherence as a psychological construct, but also in terms of its empirical linkages to its purported social-structural and experiential antecedents, on the one hand, and its behavioral and sociopolitical consequences, on the other.

Compared with similar notions in the development literature for linking individual and societal levels of analysis, the concept of psychological modernity offers several distinct advantages. In the first place, it is relatively free from the many ethnocentric biases that characterized earlier writings on the subject. By focusing on the impact of social-structural forces on individuals *within* the same society, it avoids invidious and facile explanations of differences in political and economic development *between* societies in terms of their ethnic, religious, or vaguely specified national-cultural characteristics. Second, "modernizing" influences are not assumed to be limited to those of early socialization, but include the impact of various social institutions within which the individual functions well beyond childhood and early adolescence. Third, since individual modernity is conceptualized as a continuous variable rather than a distinct personality type, it is analyzed in terms of its relative level in an individual or a group rather than its mere presence or absence. And, finally, the successful development of scales for measuring modernity has made it possible to estimate and compare, in relatively precise terms, the effects of social background and various experiential factors on a person's or group's level of modernity.

Among the empirical investigations of psychological modernity undertaken since the late 1950s, undoubtedly the research program of Alex Inkeles and his associates on the social and cultural aspects of modernization stands out as the most extensive, systematic, and methodologically rigorous treatment of the concept and its ramifications.[14] Studies by others, when not superseded by Inkeles's work, have been generally much more limited in their scope, geographic coverage, and sample size.[15] Accordingly, the following review of the empirical research in this area will focus primarily on the work of Inkeles and his associates, with contributions of others introduced only when warranted on substantive or critical grounds.

In their attempt to define the contents of individual modernity, Inkeles and his principal associate, David Smith, "worked back" from an ideal-typical model of an urban, industrial society to psychological attributes that such a society would require of its members if they are to function effectively in their various social roles. Taking the industrial factory to be "the epitome of the institutional pattern of modern civilization,"[16] Inkeles and Smith reasoned that extended factory employment inculcates in workers such qualities as planning and time scheduling, personal efficacy, openness to new experience, and respect for science and technology. Similarly, by examining other domains of modern social life, they identified additional psychosocial qualities that modern societies demand of their members. Included in their final list of some two dozen or so themes of modernity were also certain other, individual-level consequences of modernization, including some potentially adverse ones such as anomie and alienation, which had been suggested in the literature by others.

From their list of modern psychosocial attributes, Inkeles and Smith developed a series of subscales for measuring modernity in various life spheres. After extensive pretesting in the field, they whittled the pool of potential items into a 159-item composite scale of Overall Modernity (the OM scale). The scale's first extensive use was in the authors' massive study of individual modernity conducted in the early 1960s. It was administered to a sample of over 5,500 men between the ages of eighteen and thirty-two in six developing countries — Argentina, Chile, East Pakistan (now Bangladesh), India, Israel (focusing on the "Oriental" Jews), and Nigeria. The "modern man,"[17] as he emerged from this massive mound of data, could be characterized in terms of a set of distinctive qualities (a "syndrome of modernity") that were relatively consistent across the six societies under study. The central elements of this psychosocial syndrome have been summarized by Inkeles as follows:

(1) Openness to new experience, both with people and with new ways of doing things such as attempting to control births; (2) the assertion of increasing independence from the authority of traditional figures, such as parents and priests, and a shift of

allegiance to leaders of government, public affairs, trade unions, cooperatives, and the like; (3) belief in the efficacy of science and medicine, and a general abandonment of passivity and fatalism in the face of life's difficulties; and (4) ambition for oneself and one's children to achieve high occupational and educational goals. Men who manifest these characteristics (5) like people to be on time and show an interest in carefully planning their affairs in advance. It is also part of this syndrome (6) to show strong interest and take an active part in civic and community affairs and local politics; and (7) to strive energetically to keep up with the news and within this effort to prefer news of national and international import over items dealing with sports, religion, or purely local affairs.[18]

In evaluating the Overall Modernity scale, on which the preceding profile of the modern man is based, at least three types of criteria may be applied. The first concerns the scale's reliability, i.e., the degree to which it provides a stable and consistent measure, over time and space, of the construct of psychological modernity. With reported test-retest reliability coefficients ranging from 0.75 to 0.87 in the six countries, the OM scale clearly meets the accepted reliability standards in behavioral research.[19]

The second criterion relates to the internal consistency of the scale, i.e., the degree to which its constituent elements comprise a cohesive constellation or syndrome of modern beliefs, values, and orientations. To evaluate this property of their scale empirically, Inkeles and Smith relied on a factor analytic procedure. They found that the same combination of values, attitudes, and behaviors coalesced around a common factor in all six societies, and, more significantly, that these were essentially the same set of personal qualities by which they had defined individual modernity at the theoretical level. This finding led the authors to what must be regarded as the most cogent — and in some ways startling — conclusion in their entire study:

It [the empirical finding that the same set of qualities defines individual modernity in different cultures] argues for the actual psychic unity of mankind in a structural sense, and the potential psychic unity of mankind in the factual sense. In speaking of the unity of mankind in terms of psychic structure, we mean that the nature of the human personality, its inner "rules" of organization, is evidently basically similar everywhere. That is, the association of the elements or components of personality do not — and we think in substantial degree *cannot* — vary randomly, or even relatively freely.... So far as the future is concerned, moreover, we believe that this structural unity provides the essential basis for the greater factual psychic unity of mankind. Such a factual unity, not merely of structure but of *content*, can be attained insofar as the forces which tend to shape men in syndromes such as that defining the modern men become more widely and uniformly diffused throughout the world.[20]

While Inkeles and Smith felt justified, on the basis of this finding, to combine the various subdimensions of modernity into a single global score of Overall Modernity, other investigators, using the same or similar scales of modernity, have found the evidence in support of a unidimensional modernity construct to be much less compelling. Thus, for example, a study that tested the unidimensionality of five widely used scales of psychological modernity concluded that neither a single factor nor a limited number of common factors could adequately account for the score variances of the modernity scales:

> "Modernism," if useful at all in describing the attitudes and values of the present sample, must be viewed as encompassing a collection of attitudes and activities which do not respond in parallel fashion to influences which may be considered modernizing.[21]

The third criterion for evaluating the OM scale is its "predictive validity," i.e., the extent to which it can reliably identify individuals who would also be regarded as "modern" on the basis of other independent criteria. In the absence of an independent set of criteria by which a person's level of modernity could be judged, Inkeles and Smith settled on a somewhat less rigorous method of external validation. This involved the selection, in each of the six societies under study, of statistically controlled comparisons among several "criterion groups," which, based on their known social background characteristics, were expected to differ in their levels of modernity. The four principal groups chosen for these comparisons were (in ascending order of their presumed modernity): (1) peasants living in traditional rural communities, (2) urban nonindustrial workers, (3) recent migrants from the rural areas who had not yet been integrated into industrial work, and (4) former rural dwellers with three or more years of experience in an urban factory.

As the authors had predicted, individuals with greater exposure to such modernizing experiences as formal education, mass media consumption, and work in an urban industrial factory did in fact score significantly higher on the OM scale than those without such exposure. More specifically, among the men "fully exposed to the institutions which our theory designated as modernizing, some 76 percent scored as modern, whereas among those least under the influence of such institutions only about 2 percent achieved modern scores on our scales."[22]

Reasonably assured of the measurement properties of their OM scale, Inkeles and Smith then searched for the *antecedents* of psychological modernity, focusing mainly on the structural changes and processes that accompany societal modernization. In general, they discovered that, depending on the country, between 32 to 62 percent (with a median of 47 percent for the six countries) of the variance in modernity scores was accounted for by a set of ten social background variables that are linked closely to socioeconomic development. Among these variables, formal education was unmistakably the most powerful determinant of individual modernity, exerting an influence on the latter that was two or three times as great as that of any of the other background variables. Exposure to mass media and the individual's occupational experience were approximately equal in the size of their effect, and second only to education in their impact on modernity. While earlier studies had emphasized the role of education, urbanism, and mass media as the primary determinants of psychological modernity, the distinctive focus of Inkeles' team was clearly on the impact of occupational experience — specifically, work in a modern industrial factory. Inkeles's team viewed the factory as an exemplar of the complex, role-differentiated, technocratic organization of industrialization, and thus an effective school in modernity.

In a supplementary analysis, Inkeles estimated the contribution of a person's national (ethnic) background also contributes to his or her level of modernity. The unique contribution of nationality, however, was relatively small when compared with the social background variables just mentioned, accounting for only 4 percent of the variance in individual modernity scores beyond what could be explained on the basis of the other social background factors. Among several possible interpretations of this finding, Inkeles favored one that attributed the observed differences due to the nationality factor to the "contextual effects" of living in a social milieu in which one is surrounded by modern people and institutions. He did not see such differences as reflections of culture and national character per se.[23]

In general, Inkeles and Smith took the sizable effects of structural variables on individual modernity as strong support for their major theoretical propositions that: (1) exposure to modernizing institutions, and in particular to large-scale productive enterprises, engender in the individual a set of attitudes, values, and behaviors that are best delineated in their so-called "syndrome of psychological modernity"; (2) individuals remain susceptible to the impact of modernizing experiences and institutions well beyond the periods of childhood and adolescence;[24] and (3) the underlying dimensions along which psychological modernity occurs largely transcend ethnic, cultural, and national differences.

Nearly 90 percent of the items on the OM scale pertain to the respondents' attitudes, opinions, values, or extent of knowledge about their social environment (the remaining items deal mainly with their retrospective self-reports of behavior). Therefore, the question of whether modernity is merely a state of mind, or whether persons with a modern orientation do in fact *behave* in ways that are more congruent with the institutional demands of a modern society, is of crucial interest to the evaluation of the concept of psychological modernity. Analytically, this question can be broken down into two parts. The first part concerns the degree of correspondence between modern attitudes and behaviors in individuals; the second relates to whether modern dispositions and behaviors are likely to facilitate economic and political development to any significant extent. With respect to both queries, Inkeles and Smith's position is characteristically confident:

> We affirm that our research has produced ample evidence that attitude and value changes defining individual modernity are accompanied by changes in behavior precisely of the sort which we believe give meaning to, and support, those changes in political and economic institutions which lead to the modernization of nations.[25]

However, the results of several other studies that have examined the linkage between modern values and behavior are more equivocal. In a study designed specifically to explore this issue, Michael Armer and Larry Isaac examined the relationship between psychological modernity, as measured by a short form of the OM scale, and different forms of modern behavior representative of those described in the modernity literature. The findings indicated that of some fifteen types of behavior considered, only three (frequency of newspaper reading, frequency of prayer, and involvement in political discussions) were significantly influenced by the respondents' level of psychological modernity. Hence, the respondents' OM scores increased the amount of explained variance in a composite index of modern behaviors by less than 1 percent (from 40.5 to 41.4 percent) over what could be explained on the basis of their socioeconomic status characteristics such as education, age, and income.[26]

In the absence of any cross-national and longitudinal studies of development, including data on both psychological and structural variables, the extent to which psychological modernity can help promote economic and political development continues to be a matter of conjecture and controversy. However, since most researchers in this field have treated this construct as a mediating rather than a causal factor, its value as a theoretical construct is fairly independent of its *consequences* for development.[27] In the following sections, I shall try to juxtapose modernity and tradition as two competing cultural systems and then explore some of the political ramifications of these concepts for understanding change in a concrete sociocultural context.

*The dialectics of tradition and modernity*  The place of tradition in the study of development has been a matter of much controversy and subject to shifting interpretations over the past three decades. In the modernization studies of the 1950s and 1960s, tradition never received the kind of analytic attention that was given to modernity, in spite of its inclusion in the then-popular tradition-modernity dichotomy. The belief that traditional institutions, customs, and modes of thought — often construed as impediments to social change and development — would give way to, and be eventually supplanted by, their modern counterparts turned the problem of tradition into a somewhat esoteric subject, one of interest mainly to the antiquarian or the ethnographer. For those interested in the dynamics of social and political change, it was not tradition, but modernity, which, as heir to the idea of progress, held genuine intellectual appeal and promise.

This asymmetry between the two poles was especially evident in the way in which the contents of tradition and modernity were delineated. While the defining characteristics of modernity were derived from the premises of the modernization theory, traditional traits were defined in mostly residual or negative terms, either as those characteristics that could not be considered modern, or as the hypothetical opposites of modern attributes. Moreover, while the term "modern" evoked an idealized image of the contemporary Western, industrialized, and liberal-democratic society, its opposite, "traditional" — used as both a descriptive and a diagnostic label — referred to an assortment of people and societies in the third world for whom entry into the ranks of the civilized depended mainly on their ability to emulate the ways and means of the moderns. The essential elements of the tradition-modernity dichotomy were described eloquently by Lloyd and Susanne Rudolph, who, in spite of some reservations, found it heuristically useful:

> "Modernity" assumes that local ties and parochial perspectives give way to universal commitments and cosmopolitan attitudes;

that the truths of utility, calculation, and science take precedence over those of the emotions, the sacred, and the non-rational; that the individual rather than the group be the primary unit of society and politics; that the associations in which men live and work be based on choice not birth; that mastery rather than fatalism orient their attitude toward the material and human environment; that identity be chosen and achieved, not ascribed and affirmed; that work be separated from family, residence, and community in bureaucratic organizations; that manhood be delayed while youth prepares for its tasks and responsibilities; that age, even when it is prolonged, surrender much of its authority to youth and men some of theirs to women; that mankind cease to live as races apart by recognizing in society and politics its common humanity; that government cease to be a manifestation of powers beyond man and out of the reach of ordinary men by basing itself on participation, consent, and public accountability.[28]

The portrayal of tradition as a conservative and stabilizing social force was consistent with the modernization theory's broadly functionalist orientation, according to which a society's pattern of commonly shared norms and values helped maintain a state of equilibrium among its various institutions and social elements. Under normal circumstances, the impetus for change came either directly from the outside or through the activities of those individuals or groups that, by virtue of their education, technical skills, occupational backgrounds, political style, and values, could break away from the bonds of tradition and act as "change agents." These included, depending on one or another version of the theory, the entrepreneurs, the modernizing elites, the technocrats, the new middle class, the military, and so forth.

In spite of its initial popularity, however, the tradition-modernity contrast did not go unchallenged for long. By the late 1960s, what Samuel Huntington later characterized as a "small-scale corrective reaction" took place against the prevailing conceptualizations of tradition and modernity as a polarity.[29] Almost in unison, several influential critics argued cogently against unitary, static, and homogeneous conceptions of tradition and its expected obsolescence in the course of modernization.[30] The resilience and plasticity of traditional forms and institutions and their capacity to provide a meaningful basis for political integration and legitimation, according to these critics, militated against the view of modernity and tradition as mutually exclusive; they were to be seen, rather, as two interpenetrating and mutually reinforcing features in all cultures.

At the psychological level, the archaic "traditional man" image proved to be considerably more resistant to conceptual revision. Traditional orientations and values continued to be described in stereotypic and mostly negative terms, suggesting irrationality, lack of independence, mental rigidity, and stagnation — qualities that can clearly impede a person's effective functioning in a modern society. Whereas considerable empirical attention was focused on the delineation of psychological modernity, traditionality, as a state of mind or constellation of individual attitudes and behaviors, remained largely unexplored. Even in *Becoming Modern,* a work distinguished for its rigorous empirical methods and analytic sophistication, one finds Inkeles and Smith's description of the "traditional man" to be essentially a list of opposites of modern traits, reflecting mainly their own assumptions — in the context of studying individual *modernity* — about the psychic requirements of modern social institutions, rather than an empirically based exploration of the psychological dynamics of traditional thought and action:

> Passive acceptance of fate and a general lack of efficacy; fear of innovation and distrust of the new; isolation from the outside world and lack of interest in what goes on in it; dependence on traditional authority and the received wisdom of elders and religious and customary leaders; preoccupation with personal and family affairs to the exclusion of community concerns; exclusive identification with purely local and parochial primary groups, coupled to feelings of isolation from and fear of larger regional and national entities; the shaping and damping of ambition to fit narrow goals, and the cultivation of humble sentiments of gratitude for what little one has; rigid, hierarchical relations with subordinates and others of low social status; and undervaluing of education, learning, research, and other concerns not obviously related to the practical business of earning one's daily bread.[31]

In general, what resulted from the "corrective reaction" of the late 1960s was a liberalized — or in Reinhard Bendix's terms, a "de-ideologized" — view of the relationship between tradition and modernity, one that downplayed any inherent contradiction between the two. Traditional institutions and practices were no longer regarded as obstacles to be overcome, but as features compatible with the demands of a modernizing society so long as its members were able to make the appropriate psychic and ideological adjustments to their changing circumstances. As one author put it:

> The desire to be modern and the desire to preserve tradition operate as significant movements in the new nations and developing economies. It is our basic point here that these desires, functioning as ideologies, are not always in conflict; that the quest for modernity depends upon and often finds support in the ideological upsurge of traditionalism.[32]

Today, two decades after the "corrective reaction" of the late 1960s, the pendulum seems to have swung further toward the side of tradition. Even within those intellectual disciplines whose past attitudes toward the concept was less than hospitable, there is a somewhat greater appreciation of tradition in its own right and of the immense potential of traditional ideas and institutions for social mobilization and change. As Edward Shils put it recently, "A slight turn in moral sentiment and in the intellectual credit of the past is perceptible. There is a little less unease in the presence of the idea of 'tradition,' but its long exile from the substance of intellectual discourse has left its meaning hidden in obscurity."[33] In the third world, too, the myriad "traditionalist" ideologies, which find their clearest expression in religious and ethnic movements, are presenting a far more serious challenge to many incumbent regimes than are secularist ideologies.

The term "traditionalism," as used in the present context, however, should not be taken to imply a mere *return* to indigenous patterns of thought and actions belonging to some earlier period in a society's idealized past. Rather, it represents a self-conscious, ideologically fashioned embrace (or imposition) of beliefs, values, and symbolic structures — particularly when they are overwhelmed by competing values — that are deemed essential to the preservation of the integrity and coherence of a culture. Traditionalist thought and behavior, therefore, can be as reflective, creative, and responsive to individual and collective needs as their modern counterparts can. And as Abdallah Laroui reminds us in his perceptive and stimulating essay, in order to survive and flourish,

> Tradition . . . demands as much activity as "progress," but in a different direction. . . . The maintenance of a tradition is the work of a politico-cultural elite whose activity, which may seem deviant to others, brings them as many satisfactions as would action of a modernist orientation.[34]

*The return of tradition: Islamic revival and revolution in Iran*     One of the more dramatic examples of contemporary traditionalist movements is the "Islamic resurgence" that has been smoldering in Muslim societies from Morocco to Indonesia since the early 1970s. Whether it is in the vehement rejection of Western values and lifestyles, in the strict observance of Islamic codes of personal conduct, in calls for enforcement of the *shari'a* (sacred law) in place of Western-imported civil codes, in the rise of militant "fundamentalist" or radical "Islamic-socialist" groups, or in efforts by incumbent regimes to enhance their political legitimacy and popular support by "Islamizing" their public policies and programs — there is hardly a Muslim country in the Middle East, or in the whole Islamic world, in which the strident voices of Islamic revival have not already had a noticeable impact on the vocabulary, form, and content of politics.[35]

   Islamic resurgence movements have been portrayed frequently by the Western media as extremist, anachronistic, and retrogressive, seeking to turn the already slow historical clock of their societies back to a medieval social order bereft of such quintessential achievements of modern civilization as secularism, rationality, science and technology, and respect for the rights of the individual. Students of political development have tended to view the rise of these movements as indicative of a "breakdown" in the critical and often precarious process of institution building under the strains of mass politics and rapid social mobilization. Their consequences, it is feared, may well include a new surge of authoritarian-populist regimes, escalation of ethnoreligious conflicts, and political disintegration and internecine warfare as in the case of present-day Lebanon. Furthermore, it is believed that these movements appeal primarily to the "multitude of alienated individuals who have lost their social-spiritual bearings"[36] by offering them not only an ideology of protest, but also a sense of dignity and a spiritual refuge.

Considering the diversity of the groups, movements, and organizations that are subsumed under the rubric of "Islamic resurgence" and the dearth of reliable information on the sociodemographic, ideological orientations, and personality characteristics of their members, any broad generalizations concerning their cultural and psychological dynamics must surely await further research.[37] Meanwhile, it might be useful to briefly examine some pertinent aspects of the Iranian revolution of 1977–79, about which relatively more is known, as illustrative, though not necessarily typical, of such movements. What makes the Iranian case especially noteworthy is that it presents the only example of a revivalist movement that has actually brought to power a fundamentalist Islamic regime, and one that has remained committed to its promise of a total "Islamization" of all spheres of social and political life.[38]

In reflecting on the causes and peculiarities of the Iranian revolution, many observers have found it paradoxical that a relatively stable, modernizing regime, with a vast and well-equipped army and internal security force, enjoying broad international support, could be brought down so swiftly by a nonviolent, religiously inspired revolution led by traditionalist clerics seeking to establish a theocratic Islamic government. A common explanation for this paradox is that the revolution came chiefly as a consequence of the all-too-rapid and far-reaching modernization program of Mohammad Reza Shah (reigned 1941–79); it represented a backlash by such reactionary elements as the ulama (Islamic clerics; literally, "learned men"), the bazaar merchants and the petty bourgeoisie, and the socially disoriented new urban migrants who had been disfavored, threatened, or passed by during the shah's ambitious modernization drive. There is undoubtedly some truth to such an explanation. However, to equate the opposition to the shah with a general, defensive reaction against modernity reflects a simplistic understanding of the nature of Iran's socioeconomic development during the final decades of the Pahlavi rule and a misapprehension of the character and dynamics of the mass-based social revolution that succeeded in toppling it.

To be sure, in the period from the early 1960s to the late 1970s, in particular, Iran did undergo extensive modernization, including substantial investments in heavy industry and infrastructure, urbanization, expansion of literacy and formal education, growth of communications and mass media, extensive social mobility, greater sexual equality, and higher rates of participation by women in paid labor, etc. But the uneven nature of the country's capitalist-oriented development, spurred and financed by dramatically increased revenues from oil, favored mainly the Westernized, predominantly urban, upper and middle strata and a growing "labor aristocracy" in the modern industrial sector — thus exacerbating long-standing structural inequalities in the country. Politically, the shah's real or perceived subservience to the United States, his contempt for the traditional Islamic culture of the masses, the endemic corruption, and, above all, the increasingly autocratic and repressive nature of the shah's rule led to growing resentment against his regime by virtually every segment of the population, including those very sectors that had benefited substantially from its various economic and social policies.

Furthermore, the ardently secularist and Western-oriented vision and policies of the country's "modernizing elite" created a profound *cultural* division between two segments of the Iranian society: on one side, a small "modern" segment composed of a Western-educated elite, the secular intelligentsia, and members of the "new middle class"; on the other, a "traditional" segment consisting of peasants (about half the population), the urban poor, small merchants, artisans, and the like — as well as others who, irrespective of their socioeconomic circumstances, adhered to traditional Islamic values, life-styles, and behavior.

For the traditional segment, encompassing the vast majority of the Iranian population, the "politico-cultural elite" that could best articulate their discontents and grievances was the Shi'ite ulama. A combination of historical, cultural, and political factors had prepared the ulama for playing such a role in Iran. These factors included: (1) their prior active participation in nearly every major opposition movement in the country over the past century, (2) their long-standing and close economic and personal ties with the traditional urban lower and middle strata, particularly the bazaar community, (3) their relative financial and political independence from the state, made possible by religious taxes and various charitable allowances and contributions from their devout followers, and (4) their control of an extensive network of mosques, religious shrines, and religious associations through which they could recruit and cultivate new followers, bolster existing ties, voice public grievances, and criticize the regime with relative impunity.[39] This latter political-agitational function was of special importance in view of the regime's total control over the mass media, its silencing of all forms of secular political dissent, and its disbanding or otherwise neutralizing political parties, labor unions, or other groups that refused to toe the official line.

The clerics' domination of the revolutionary movement in its later stages and their political hegemony over their secular counterparts in the postrevolutionary period, however, should not obscure the fact that the Iranian revolution represented a coalition of social forces and political ideologies that was unmatched among twentieth-century revolutions in its breadth. At the ideological level, in spite of the predominance of Islamic symbols and slogans, there was no single, monolithic "Islamic ideology," but a number of Islamic and secular ideologies. Each of these ideologies appealed to a particular social class or group that played a role in the revolutionary struggle. On the Islamic side alone, four principal variants could be distinguished:

"Radical Islam" was primarily the ideology of the young intelligentsia who were looking for a this-worldly revolutionary transformation of Iran into a classless Islamic society.... "Militant Islam" became the ideology of a segment of the ulama, the petty bourgeoisie, and the dispossessed, groups who were looking for both this-wordly and other-wordly redemption by establishing "God's Government" on earth. "Liberal Islam" was an "ideology of contest," appealing mainly to the bourgeoisie and the middle classes who vied for a larger share of political power within an Islamic-nationalist form of government to be created by nonviolent means. And, finally, "traditionalist Islam" was an "ideology of protest" for the old middle strata, including the majority of the ulama and the old petty bourgeoisie, who, reacting with increased moral indignation against the forces of social change, yearned for the return of the old order.[40]

Each of these variants, with the exception of "traditional Islam," represented an amalgam of Islamic and secular elements, and each represented a unique adaptation of traditional Islamic concepts and ideals that fitted the interests and proclivites of a particular group. In this respect, it is difficult to imagine a more encompassing, integrative, and elastic system of ideals and values than Islam for purposes of ideological articulation and revolutionary mobilization.

Beyond the level of ideology, both Islam and the ulama had a significant impact on the breadth and the ultimate success of the revolutionary coalition as well. Shi'ism in Iran never lost its inherently oppositional potential vis à vis temporal power, however much its more established and conservative leaders had adopted a quietist or even collaborationist stance toward incumbent governments. Its powerful symbolism of steadfastness, suffering and self-sacrifice in pursuit of truth and justice displayed in its various dramatic rituals; its remarkable capacity for redefining political conflicts in religious terms; its populist logic and vocabulary of pitting the "disinherited" against the "oppressors"; and its messianic promise of a just social order with the return of the "Hidden Imam" make it an unusually powerful religion of protest.[41] With Ayatollah Rouhollah Khomeini's innovative concept of *velayat-e fagih* (guardianship of the jurisconsult), which provided for the direct rule of the ulama for the first time in Shi'ite history, he and his militant followers acquired not only a potent ideology for inspiring the masses to revolution, but also a blueprint for replacing the "corrupt" and "satanic" Pahlavi regime with an "Islamic government."

Perhaps the most significant contribution of the ulama to the revolution was to provide it with a leader who, by combining his enormous personal popularity and charisma with the charisma of his office as *marja'-e taqlid* (source of imitation), was able to bring together the many disparate social forces of opposition into a single revolutionary coalition. The secularists, including those with a liberal-nationalist ideology, the leftist forces, and the modern intelligentsia, were gradually drawn into this coalition with the false hope that, once the common goal of bringing down the shah's regime was achieved, they — rather than their traditionalist clerical partners — would be shaping the country's political future. For their part, to forge the grand alliance, Khomeini and his militant followers launched a well-coordinated revolutionary mobilization, using every traditional as well as modern form of communication, agitation, and revolutionary propaganda, eschewing potentially divisive issues, bullying their ideological rivals (including the generally conservative and apolitical majority of the ulama themselves), and incorporating into the inner circle of the movement's leadership secular-minded individuals who could extend its appeal to the more educated and Westernized segments of the society to which the ulama still represented a reactionary social force. In all these respects, then, the clerics — their "traditional" lifestyle, cloak, and behavior notwithstanding — acted as supremely capable coalition builders and obviously possessed all the political acumen and flexibility of mind that such a task required.

What relevant conclusions, then, can be drawn from the case of the Islamic revolution for our discussion of the role of tradition in the study of development and social change? The first such conclusion, though hardly a novel one, is that the structural changes accompanying modernization do not necessarily bring about secularism, either at the level of political institutions and processes or in the attitudes and values of individuals who have been exposed to modernizing experiences.[42] But more significant than simply stating that the revolution presented a challenge to the secularization thesis is to specify the conditions under which religion played a critical role in the revolutionary movement itself. According to the argument presented here, the revival of religion must be understood with reference to the particular historical, socioeconomic, political, and cultural conditions within which it takes place. This is very much the same conclusion that was reached by Ali Dessouki in his integrative essay on the Islamic resurgence in the Arab world: "Islamic movements have to be seen in relation to the specific process of social change taking place in their societies, in particular to the issues of the changing position of classes and groups, political participation, identity crisis, the stability of regimes, and distributive justice."[43] In the case of Iran, as suggested, the unpopularity of the regime, the social inequalities produced and/or exacerbated by the country's particular path toward economic development, the cultural dualism created by the intensely Western-oriented Pahlavi regime and its overzealous modernizing elite, its severe curtailing of the institutional interests and prerogatives of the ulama in various spheres, and the inherent oppositional character of Shi'ite Islam vis à vis the state and its extensive mobilizational resources were among the more critical factors in the Iranian case.

Second, compared with their modern counterparts, traditionalist actors on the political stage, as leaders, strategists, propagandists and agitators, and simple cadres of a revolutionary movement, do not seem to be hampered by their presumably "traditional" syndrome of traits, such as a lack of personal efficacy, passivity, fatalism, preoccupation with personal and family affairs, and sense of isolation from the outside world. Similarly, traditional ideologies seem to be at least as efficacious in articulating the demands of a movement for social change and in inducing collective action of a radical nature as any of their modern, secular counterparts.[44] In this respect, there is nothing unique about Shi'ite Islamic ideologies, as essentially the same inference can be drawn from such diverse religiopolitical movements as ultra-Orthodox Judaism in Israel, "liberation theology" in Latin America, and the workers' resistance movement in relation to the Catholic church in Poland.

Thirdly, contrary to a rather prevalent notion that traditionalist religiopolitical movements appeal primarily to socially dislocated and anomic individuals (for example, recent rural migrants, the urban poor), a detailed analysis of the social bases of the Iranian revolution shows that such groups "made only a minor contribution to the movement (and that only in the later stages of the revolution) when compared to other, better established old and new social classes."[45] In other words, a traditionalist, religious movement can have as much, or even more, appeal to those individuals with a secure footing in their culture as it does to marginal social elements. Further, it appears that, at least insofar as the Iranian example is concerned, even those individuals with extensive exposure to modernizing institutions can be induced to radical political action by the powerful sentiments, if not the values and goals, of a traditionalist political movement.

And finally, in the conditions prevailing in *post*revolutionary Iran we can see some of the consequences of the triumph of a traditionalist movement. Since the revolution in 1979, the clerical leadership, in its quest to consolidate and expand its power, has tried, and by and large has succeeded, in eliminating virtually all other groups that had participated in the revolutionary coalition. Branding its real and perceived enemies as "hypocrites," "warriors against God," "corrupters of the earth," "counterrevolutionaries," or "liberals," the regime has treated them with severe and often brutal punishments from imprisonment to torture to death. Furthermore, the government's relentless "Islamization" campaign has extended its control (often through the use of gangs of thugs and "Party of God" troopers) into all spheres of public and private life. This has led to some of the greatest abuses of human rights, particularly toward women and members of religious minorities. While for the more dogmatically fundamentalist members of the regime the main objective remains the implementation of an absolutist vision of Islam through a "cultural revolution," for others, and perhaps the majority within the regime, the objective is simply to hold on to power at whatever cost. Whether such radical and coercive retraditionalization can succeed in a complex society is not possible to predict. If the serious economic and social problems that are now plaguing Iran, and the response of hundreds of thousands of Iranians who have chosen a life of exile, together with many more who continue to resist within the country, is any indication, the "Islamization project" will indeed be extremely costly both in human and in material terms. Thus, once again, a genuine and potentially constructive dialogue between tradition and modernity, in which the liberal-minded theorists of the modernization school had placed so much stock, has been silenced ruthlessly — this time in the name of tradition.

## NOTES

1.  For critical reviews of the modernization literature, see Andre Gunder Frank, "Sociology of Development and Underdevelopment of Sociology," in *Latin America: Underdevelopment or Revolution*, by Andre Gunder Frank (New York: Monthly Review Press, 1969); Samuel P. Huntington, "The Change to Change: Modernization, Development, and Politics," *Comparative Politics* 3, no. 3 (1971):283–322; Dean C. Tipps, "Modernization Theory and the Comparative Study of Societies: A Critical Perspective," *Comparative Studies in Society and History* 15 (1973):199–226; and Alejandro Portes, "On the Sociology of National Development: Theories and Issues," *American Journal of Sociology* 28, no. 1 (1976):55–85. For a recent wide-ranging and perspicacious critique of the postwar political development studies and their ideological premises, see Irene L. Gendzier, *Managing Political Change: Social Scientists and the Third World* (Boulder, Colo.: Westview Press, 1985).

2.  For the "world-system" approach, see Immanuel Wallerstein, *The Modern World-System: Capitalist Agriculture and the Origins of the European World-Economy in the Sixteenth Century* (New York: Academic Press, 1974), and its sequel, *The Modern World-System II: Mercantilism and the Consolidation of the European World-Economy, 1600–1750* (New York: Academic Press, 1980). For the "dependency" theory, see Fernando Henrique Cardoso and Enzo Faletto, *Dependency and Development in Latin America*, translated by Marjory Mattingly Urquidi (Berkeley: University of

California Press, 1979), and Samir Amin, *Imperialism and Un-equal Development* (New York: Monthly Review Press, 1977). For a useful and brief overview of this general perspective, see Thomas D. Hall, "World-System Theory," in *Annual Review of Sociology*, edited by Ralph H. Turner and James F. Short, Jr., vol. 8 (Palo Alto, Calif.: Annual Reviews, Inc., 1982), 81–106. Two recent attempts to effect a rapprochement between the "developmentalist" (modernization) and the world-system approaches are: Alejandro Portes, "Convergencies between Conflicting Theoretical Perspectives in National Development," in *Sociological Theory and Research: A Critical Appraisal*, edited by Hubert M. Blalock (New York: Free Press, 1980), and Tony Smith, "Requiem or New Agenda for Third World Studies?," *World Politics* 37, no. 4 (July 1985):532–61.

3. Immanuel Wallerstein, "Modernization: Requiescat in Pace," in *The Uses of Controversy in Sociology*, edited by Lewis A. Coser and Otto N. Larsen (New York: Free Press, 1976), 131–32.

4. For a probing though sympathetic review of this tradition, see Robert A. LeVine, *Culture, Behavior and Personality,* 2d ed. (Hawthorne, N.Y.: Aldine, 1982), especially chaps. 1–3.

5. For an extensive and critical survey of these studies, see Alex Inkeles and Daniel J. Levinson, "National Character: The Study of Modal Personality and Sociocultural Systems," in *The Handbook of Social Psychology*, edited by Gardner Lindzey and Elliot Aronson, 2d ed., vol. 4 (Reading, Mass.: Addison-Wesley, 1969), 418–506.

6. For a critique of this orientation in American social psychology, see Henri Tajfel, "Experiments in a Vacuum," in *The Context of Social Psychology: A Critical Assessment*, edited by Joachim Israel and Henri Tajfel (New York: Academic Press, 1972), 69–121.

7. Gordon W. Allport, "The Historical Background of Modern Social Psychology," in *The Handbook of Social Psychology*, edited by Gardner Lindzey and Elliot Aronson, 2d ed., vol. 1 (Reading, Mass.: Addison-Wesley, 1968), 59.

8. For a recent expression of such a viewpoint, see Lawrence E. Harrison, *Underdevelopment Is a State of Mind: The Latin American Case* (Lanham, Md.: University Press of America, 1985). The author, who spent many years in Central America as an official of the U.S. Agency for International Development, states that "more than any other of the numerous factors that influence the development of countries, it is culture that principally explains, in most cases, why some countries develop more rapidly

and equitably than others. By 'culture' I mean the values and attitudes a society inculcates in its people through various socializing mechanisms, e.g., the home, the school, the church" (xvi).

9.    This scheme of classification is similar to the one proposed by R. Kenneth Godwin, "Two Thorny Theoretical Tangles: The Relationships between Personality Variables and Modernization," *Journal of Developing Areas* 8, no. 2 (January 1974):181–98; my assignment of different studies to one or another of these three categories, however, differs somewhat from Godwin's. For a more general review of some of the conceptual problems in relating individual dispositions to change processes at the macrosocial level, see Herbert C. Kelman and Donald P. Warwick, "Bridging Micro and Macro Approaches to Social Change: A Social-Psychological Perspective," in *Processes and Phenomena of Social Change*, edited by Gerald Zaltman (New York: Wiley, 1973), 13–59.

10.   David C. McClelland, *The Achieving Society* (Princeton, N.J.: Van Nostrand, 1961); Everett E. Hagen, *On the Theory of Social Change: How Economic Growth Begins* (Homewood, Ill.: Dorsey Press, 1962); Lucian W. Pye, *Politics, Personality, and Nation-Building: Burma's Search for Identity* (New Haven, Conn.: Yale University Press, 1962).

11.   Daniel Lerner, *The Passing of Traditional Society: Modernizing the Middle East* (1958; Glencoe, Ill.: The Free Press, 1964). Rejecting explanations of modernization that are couched exclusively in terms of individual traits or structural determinants, Lerner argued that "either individuals and their environments modernize together or modernization leads elsewhere than intended. . . . We conceive modernity as a participant style of life; we identify its distinctive personality mechanism as *empathy*. Modernizing individuals and institutions, like chicken and egg, reproduce these traits in each other" (78).

12.   See, for example, John H. Kunkel, "Values and Behavior in Economic Development," *Economic Development and Cultural Change* 13, no. 3 (April 1965):257–77, and George M. Guthrie, *The Psychology of Modernization in the Rural Philippines* (Manila: Ateneo de Manila University Press, 1970).

13.   For an elaboration of this distinction, see James S. House, "Social Structure and Personality," in *Social Psychology: Sociological Perspectives*, edited by Morris Rosenberg and Ralph H. Turner (New York: Basic Books, 1981), 525–61.

14. Findings of this research have appeared in a series of articles and monographs since the mid-1960s. The first comprehensive account of the project's findings was presented in Alex Inkeles and David H. Smith, *Becoming Modern: Individual Change in Six Developing Countries* (Cambridge, Mass.: Harvard University Press, 1974); a sequel to that book, containing an overview of the findings of the original project, as well as a number of significant (though previously published) studies of individual modernity, is Alex Inkeles, with David H. Smith et al., *Exploring Individual Modernity* (New York: Columbia University Press, 1983). All subsequent references to the work of Inkeles and his associates in the present chapter will be made to these two volumes, rather than to the earlier reports of the project.

15. These include Leonard W. Doob, *Becoming More Civilized: A Psychological Exploration* (New Haven, Conn.: Yale University Press, 1960); J. L. M. Dawson, "Traditional versus Western Attitudes in West Africa: The Construction, Validation, and Application of a Measuring Device," *British Journal of Social and Clinical Psychology* 6 (1967):81–96; Joseph A. Kahl, *The Measurement of Modernism: A Study of Values in Brazil and Mexico* (Austin: University of Texas Press, 1968); Allan Schnaiberg, "Measuring Modernism: Theoretical and Empirical Explorations," *American Journal of Sociology* 76 (1970):399–425; Michael Armer and Robert Youtz, "Formal Education and Individual Modernity in an African Society," *American Journal of Sociology* 76 (1971):604–26.

16. Inkeles and Smith, *Becoming Modern*, 5.

17. While for practical reasons the study included only men in all six countries, Inkeles has maintained that the results would have been the same had women been included: "We are firmly convinced that the overwhelming majority of the psychosocial indicators we used to identify the modern man would also discriminate effectively among women. And we are quite certain that the same forces that make men modern — such as education, work in complex organizations, and mass media exposure — also serve to make women more modern" (Inkeles, *Exploring Individual Modernity*, 123–24). The findings of a study of modernity in Brazil tend to confirm Inkeles's statement; see Bernard C. Rosen and Anita L. La Raia, "Modernity in Women: An Index of Social Change in Brazil," *Journal of Marriage and the Family* 34, no. 2 (May 1972):353–60.

18. Inkeles, *Exploring Individual Modernity*, 101.

19. Similarly high reliability coefficients have been obtained for other scales of psychological modernity. See, for example, Michael Armer and Allan Schnaiberg, "Measuring Individual Modernity: A Near Myth," *American Sociological Review* 37, no. 3 (June 1972):301–16.

20. Inkeles, *Exploring Individual Modernity*, 102–3.

21. Pauline A. Jones, "The Validity of Traditional-Modern Attitude Measures," *Journal of Cross-Cultural Psychology* 8, no. 2 (June 1977):216.

22. Inkeles and Smith, *Becoming Modern*, 7.

23. Inkeles, *Exploring Individual Modernity*, 164–83.

24. This conclusion was seen by the Inkeles and Smith as a challenge to the widely prevalent viewpoint in personality theory, particularly its Freudian variety, "that everything important in the development of personality has happened by the age of six, and certainly by the age of sixteen" (Inkeles and Smith, *Becoming Modern*, 9). On this point, see an interesting exchange between Hagen and Inkeles in Everett E. Hagen, "Becoming Modern: The Dangers of Research Governed by Preconceptions," and Alex Inkeles, "Remaining Orthodox: A Rejoinder to Everett Hagen's Review-Essay of *Becoming Modern*," *History of Childhood Quarterly* 3 (1976), 411–21 and 422–435, respectively.

25. Inkeles and Smith, *Becoming Modern*, 312.

26. Michael Armer and Larry Isaac, "Determinants and Behavioral Consequences of Psychological Modernity: Empirical Evidence from Costa Rica," *American Sociological Review* 43, no. 3 (June 1978):316–34.

27. That the opposite interpretation is often made is to some extent the result of statements made by the modernity researchers themselves. For example: "To break out of that iron grip [of the outmoded and oppressive institutions of the less-developed societies] requires, among other things, that people become modern in spirit, that they adopt and incorporate into their personalities the attitudes, values, and modes of acting which we have identified with the modern man. Without this ingredient, neither foreign aid nor domestic revolution can hope successfully to bring an underdeveloped nation into the ranks of those capable of self-sustained growth" (Inkeles and Smith, *Becoming Modern*, 315). Such occasional lapses notwithstanding, Inkeles has stated firmly in more than one place that he considers the notion that individual change must precede societal

change to be a most serious misrepresentation of the views of most researchers in this field. (See, for example, Inkeles, *Exploring Individual Modernity*, 25.)

28. Lloyd I. Rudolph and Susanne Hoeber Rudolph, *The Modernity of Tradition: Political Development in India* (Chicago: University of Chicago Press, 1967), 3–4, n. 1. For an early, influential statement of the dichotomy and its ramifications for the study of development, see Edward Shils, *Political Development in the New States* (The Hague: Mouton, 1962).

29. Samuel P. Huntington, "The Change to Change," 293.

30. The most influential among these were Reinhard Bendix, "Tradition and Modernity Reconsidered," *Comparative Studies in Society and History* 9 (April 1967):292–346; S. N. Eisenstadt, *Tradition, Change and Modernity* (New York: Wiley, 1973); Joseph R. Gusfield, "Tradition and Modernity: Misplaced Polarities in the Study of Social Change," *American Journal of Sociology* 72 (January 1967):351–62; Rajni Kothari, "Tradition and Modernity Revisited," *Government and Opposition* 3 (1968):273–93; and Ali A. Mazrui, "From Social Darwinism to Current Theories of Modernization: A Tradition of Analysis," *World Politics* 21, no. 1 (October 1968):69–83.

31. Inkeles and Smith, *Becoming Modern*, p. 315. In a study exploring the deeper personality correlates of modernity, Richard Michael Suzman purported to demonstrate that "in comparison to traditional men, modern men are, in *general*, more field independent and differentiated, more conceptually abstract, and have higher levels of ego development" (see Suzman, "Psychological Modernity," *International Journal of Comparative Sociology* 14, nos. 3–4, 1973:275.

32. Gusfield, "Tradition and Modernity," 358.

33. Edward Shils, *Tradition* (Chicago: University of Chicago Press, 1981). See also E. J. Hobsbawm and Terence Ranger, eds., *The Invention of Tradition* (New York: Cambridge University Press, 1983).

34. Abdallah Laroui, *The Crisis of the Arab Intellectual: Traditionalism or Historicism?*, translated by Diarmid Cammell (Berkeley: University of California Press, 1976), 40.

35. According to a leading Egyptian student of the problem, "By the late 1970s, Islamic resurgent movements constituted the major ideology of dissent in the Arab world regardless of the type of political system or its declared ideology. Whether in revolutionary Syria or pro-Western Egypt, in Islamic-oriented

Saudi Arabia or secular Tunisia, the generalization holds true" (see Ali E. Hillal Dessouki, "The Islamic Resurgence: Sources, Dynamics, and Implications," in *Islamic Resurgence in the Arab World*, edited by Ali E. Hillal Dessouki (New York: Praeger, 1982), 3. The literature on the revival of Islam is quite extensive and growing rapidly. In addition to the volume edited by Dessouki, several other useful collections of papers on the subject have appeared in the past few years; particularly noteworthy among these are the following: Said Amir Arjomand, ed., *From Nationalism to Revolutionary Islam* (London: Macmillan, 1984); Juan R. I. Cole and Nikki R. Keddie, eds., *Shi'ism and Social Protest* (New Haven, Conn.: Yale University Press, 1986); John L. Esposito, ed., *Voices of Resurgent Islam* (New York: Oxford University Press, 1983); and James P. Piscatori, ed., *Islam in the Political Process* (New York: Cambridge University Press, 1983). For a recent study focusing on the "radical" Sunni revivalist groups in Egypt, Syria, and Lebanon, see Emmanuel Sivan, *Radical Islam: Medieval Theology and Modern Politics* (New Haven, Conn.: Yale University Press, 1985).

36.  R. Hrair Dekmejian, *Islam in Revolution: Fundamentalism in the Arab World* (Syracuse, N.Y.: Syracuse University Press, 1985), p. 52; see also Ismail Serageldin, "Individual Identity, Group Dynamics, and Islamic Resurgence," in Dessouki, *Islamic Resurgence in the Arab World*, 54–66.

37.  A widely cited study, based on actual interviews conducted in the fall of 1977 with members of two militant Islamic groups in Egypt, is, to my knowledge, the only empirical account of such groups published to date; see Saad Eddin Ibrahim, "Anatomy of Egypt's Militant Islamic Groups: Methodological Note and Preliminary Findings," *International Journal of Middle East Studies* 12, no. 4 (December 1980):423–53. See also Eric Davis, "Ideology, Social Class and Islamic Radicalism in Modern Egypt," and Farhad Kazemi, "The *Fada'iyan-e Islam:* Fanaticism, Politics and Terror," in Arjomand, *From Nationalism to Revolutionary Islam*, 134–57, and 158–76, respectively; and Serif Mardin, "Youth and Violence in Turkey," *Archives for European Sociology* 19, no. 2 (1978):229–54.

38.  For the historical background of the Iranian revolution of 1977–79, see Ervand Abrahamian, *Iran between Two Revolutions* (Princeton, N.J.: Princeton University Press, 1982), and Nikki R. Keddie, *Roots of Revolution: An Interpretive History of Modern Iran* (New Haven, Conn.: Yale University Press, 1981). The

course of events in the first five years of the Islamic Republic are reviewed best by Shaul Bakhash, *The Reign of the Ayatollahs: Iran and the Islamic Revolution* (New York: Basic Books, 1984). Of particular interest in the context of the present discussion are Said Amir Arjomand, "Traditionalism in Twentieth-Century Iran," in Arjomand, *From Nationalism to Revolutionary Islam*, 195–232; Michael M. J. Fischer, "Islam and the Revolt of Petit Bourgeoisie," *Daedalus* 111, no. 1 (Winter 1982):101–25; Ali Reza Sheikholeslami, "From Religious Accommodation to Religious Revolution: The Transformation of Shi'ism in Iran," in *The State, Religion and Ethnic Politics: Afghanistan, Iran and Pakistan* edited by Ali Banuazizi and Myron Weiner (Syracuse, N.Y.: Syracuse University Press, 1986), 227–255; and Majid Tehranian, "The Curse of Modernity: The Dialectics of Modernization and Communication," *International Social Science Journal* 32, no. 2 (1980):247–63.

39. For the position of the ulama in modern Iranian society and their relation with the Pahlavi state, see Shahrough Akhavi, *Religion and Politics in Contemporary Iran: Clergy-State Relations in the Pahlavi Period* (Albany: State University of New York Press, 1980); Hamid Algar, "The Oppositional Role of the 'Ulama' in Twentieth-Century Iran," in *Scholars, Saints, and Sufis: Muslim Religious Institutions in the Middle East since 1500*, edited by Nikki R. Keddie (Berkeley: University of California Press, 1972), 231–255; Michael M. J. Fischer, *Iran: From Religious Dispute to Revolution* (Cambridge, Mass.: Harvard University Press, 1980); Willem M. Floor, "The Revolutionary Character of the Ulama: Wishful Thinking or Reality?," and Azar Tabari, "The Role of the Clergy in Modern Iranian Politics," in *Religion and Politics in Iran: Shi'ism from Quietism to Revolution*, edited by Nikki R. Keddie (New Haven, Conn.: Yale University Press, 1983), 73–97 and 47–72, respectively.

40. Ahmad Ashraf and Ali Banuazizi, "The State, Social Classes and Modes of Mobilization in the Iranian Revolution," *State, Culture and Society* 1, no. 3 (Spring 1985):40.

41. For a discussion of the significant role of religious metaphors and rituals in Iran, see Mary Hegland, "Ritual and Revolution in Iran," in *Political Anthropology*, vol. 2: *Culture and Political Change*, edited by Myron J. Aronoff (New Brunswick, N.J.: Transaction Books, 1983), pp. 75–100; and Gustav Thaiss, "Religious Symbolism and Social Change: The Drama of Husain," in Keddie, *Scholars, Saints, and Sufis*, 349–66.

42.   See Cheryl Benard and Zalmay Khalilzad, "Secularization, Industrialization, and Khomeini's Islamic Republic," *Political Science Quarterly* 94, no. 2 (Summer 1979):229–41.

43.   Dessouki, "The Islamic Resurgence," 8.

44.   On the role of traditional values and relations in revolutionary mobilization, see Craig Jackson Calhoun, "The Radicalism of Tradition: Community Strength or Venerable Disguise and Borrowed Language?," *American Journal of Sociology* 88, no. 5 (March 1983):886–914.

45.   Ashraf and Banuazizi, "The State, Social Classes and Modes of Mobilization," 36.

# PART III

# The State and Development

PETER B. EVANS

# Foreign Capital and the Third World State

## INTRODUCTION

Sovereignty entails jurisdiction over economic activities within a state's geographic boundaries while the economic power of transnational corporations (TNCs) and international capital more generally is global, extending beyond the jurisdiction of any particular state. The contradiction between the geographic character of state power and the transnational character of economic power has consequences for political development across a range of historical periods and geographic regions, but nowhere is it more acutely felt than in the contemporary third world. In third world countries, the commanding heights of the private economy are pervaded by capital that is not only international in character but definitively foreign in the sense that its ultimate owners are generally domiciled in a different region of the world. The fact that private economic power is more clearly foreign gives the question of the relationship between capital and the state, a fundamental issue in any capitalist society, an additional salience for third world countries. How should the presence of

This essay represents a revised version of one segment of a larger argument originally published as "Transnational Linkages and The Economic Role of the State: An Analysis of Developing and Industrialized Nations in the Post-World War II Period," in Evans, Rueschemeyer, and Skocpol, eds., *Bringing the State Back In*.

foreign capital be assumed to affect the role of the third world state? Does the predominance of economic actors whose power escapes the state's jurisdiction undercut the economic role of the state?

This question is fundamental to any analysis of political development in the third world and a great deal of scholarly attention has been directed toward it during the past two decades. Before trying to summarize the results of that scholarship, however, it is worth noting that credit for drawing the attention of mainstream North American social science to such issues belongs to an initially quite marginal aggregation of third world scholars (especially Latin Americans) and heterodox (usually Marxist) North Americans who propounded what became known as the "dependency approach."

The issues of international political economy that were inserted into the agenda of the study of development by the *dependencistas* in the late sixties and early seventies have now become so integral to mainstream social science that it is easy to forget how neglected they were in the earlier modernization approach. Now that attacks on the "simplistic" early formulations of the dependency approach have become fashionable it is important to remember that the best of the dependency approach, the "historical-structural" approach advocated by Cardoso and Faletto, was anything but simplistic. As they put in the introduction to the belated English translation of their seminal work:

> We conceive the relationship between external and internal forces as forming a complex whole whose structural links are not based on mere external forms of exploitation and coercion, but are rooted in coincidences of interests between local dominant classes and international ones, and, on the other side, are challenged by local dominated groups and classes.[1]

The dependency approach was sufficiently provocative and challenging to push new generations of scholars into a variety of reflections on the ways in which capital accumulation and class formation in the third world were distinctive by virtue of the international political economy into which they were inserted. The rich panoply of theoretical debates and empirical investigations that it helped stimulate was fundamental to recent progress in the study of development and this work in turn generated new formulations and positions.

The lines of thinking that are summarized in this essay provide one example of the research that has sprung out of the dependency tradition. Few of the authors discussed would identify themselves as *dependencistas*. A number of them disagree violently with some of the hypotheses associated with dependency formulations, but all of them have been profoundly influenced in their research agendas and methodologies by the dependency approach.[2] Because it brings the dependency approach's traditional sensitivity to the impact of international factors and a new appreciation for the state as an institution and social actor together with the classic concerns of political economy, on-going work in this tradition might be labeled "the new political economy."[3]

What follows then, is an exercise in the new political economy. It is a tendentious essay in that it attempts to argue against the position, until recently common among *dependencistas* and others working on the consequences of the internationalization of production, that the penetration of foreign capital should result in the contraction of the economic role of the state in the third world.[4] Before trying to make the argument, however, its boundaries need to be made clear. First and most important, it examines in detail only one factor that affects the expansion of the state's role — the presence of foreign capital. Obviously, a variety of other factors influence the expansion of the state's role. On the one hand, the existence of some degree of previously acquired bureaucratic capacity and institutional coherence within the state apparatus is a precondition for the kind of expansive response to the challenge of foreign capital. State response also depends fundamentally on the configuration of domestic class forces and the degree of political support enjoyed by the regime. Finally, the effects of the transnational economic relations discussed here are often modified by the geopolitical considerations involved in the relations among states themselves.

A second kind of caveat is equally important. Expansion of

the state's role cannot be equated with the achievement of developmental aims. Economically active third world states continue to find their developmental projects thwarted by the adverse movement of international markets. In addition, there is no necessary connection between the expansion of a state's capacity to shape local capital accumulation and increased attention to the welfare of the mass of its population. The expansion of the state is, in short, not a panacea for development problems. It is rather a fact of the contemporary political economy of third world countries that must be understood and appreciated if problems of either development or dependence are to be effectively attacked in the future.

The discussion is organized on an analysis of the effects of different types of foreign capital: direct investment extractive activities, direct investment in manufacturing, and loan capital. Insofar as each type of foreign capital seems associated with an expansion of the economic role of the state, the general proposition can be considered reinforced, but variations in response to different types of capital also provide important clues to understanding the determinants of state expansion. The ultimate aim is a more subtle and realistic understanding of the ways in which the role of the state in the third world has changed in recent decades and the role of foreign capital penetration in stimulating those changes.

## TNC PENETRATION AND STATE ENTREPRENEURSHIP IN EXTRACTIVE INDUSTRIES

The classic characterization of TNC extractive investment in the third world is the foreign-owned enclave, exporting its output, relying on the local environment only for unskilled labor and the mineral resources themselves and able to count on the passive acquiescence of a compradore state apparatus. The state remained content with token tax revenues while the TNC was allowed to reap the lion's share of the benefits from the country's nonrenewable resources without contributing to its long-term development. Such an image is firmly grounded in the past experience of most third world mineral exporters but is now anachronistic.

Instead of a relationship between extractive enclaves and

supine compradore states, current research suggests that foreign-owned extractive sectors have increasingly provided sites for the expansion of nationalist and entrepreneurial activities on the part of third world states. Quantitative cross-national analysis suggests a positive relation between government revenues as a proportion of national income and the share of extractive industries in the national income.[5] Numerous case studies have documented the historical processes that explain the difference between this finding and the traditional image.

Tugwell[6] outlines nicely the way in which the unavoidable necessity of monitoring the activities of the international oil companies gradually produced a Venezuelan state apparatus with the bureaucratic capacity to operate the oil industry for itself, albeit with the continued profitable collaboration of the TNCs. A similar sequence can be observed in North Africa and the Middle East. Exploitative relations in which TNCs reap the overwhelming share of the returns from local oil production are gradually replaced by more symbiotic relations in which the state receives both a larger share of the returns and a larger share of the control over local production facilities.[7]

A sequence has been documented even more thoroughly in mining. Moran's classic study of copper in Chile[8] is a fine example. It shows how having transnational actors sitting astride the most important sources of government revenue and foreign exchange generates organizational development within the state apparatus even in the context of politics oriented almost completely toward accommodating the TNCs. In the case of Chile, the 1955 "Nuevo Trato" legislation, otherwise a model of state passivity in the face of transnational economic power, provided for the establishment of a "Copper Department" to monitor the activities of the industry.[9] This, in turn, became the training ground for the state managers who would eventually make it feasible for Chile to take over ownership of the industry.

The state initiative stimulated by confrontations with transnational actors in the extractive sector is not limited to extractive activities themselves. As the share of extractive revenues channeled through the state apparatus increases, financial constraints on state intervention recede. In states where ideological and domestic political constraints are also lacking, extractive activities may provide the basis for a fully "statist" economy. In Algeria, for example, the state makes over 90 percent of the country's industrial investments and controls almost as large a proportion of the country's industrial assets.[10] Even where the ideological predilections of dominant political elites are less oriented toward intervention, there is an organizational logic that pushes the effects of extractive initiatives in the direction of industrial activity. Just as the development of bureaucratic, monitoring agencies within the state apparatus prepares the way for the creation of state-owned enterprises, these enterprises in the extractive sector tend to move with an entrepreneurial logic of their own into industrial activities.

The first and most obvious target of the state's industrial initiatives are the key forward linkages whose absence generates opposition to foreign ownership to begin with. MineroPeru's highly profitable copper refining project is one of the best illustrations.[11] But, in many instances, forward integration goes far beyond the requirements of refining the locally extracted raw materials. The highly developed petrochemical empires of Brazil and Mexico's state-owned oil companies (PEMEX and Petrobras) are an example.[12] The recent petrochemical initiatives of state-owned oil producers in the Middle East[13] confirm the generality of the trend. Nor are the entrepreneurial endeavors of extractive state enterprises limited to elaboration of downstsream products. Brazil's iron mining giant, the Companhia do Vale do Rio Doce, for example, has become involved in other extractive industries (e.g., paper products) and in a diversified range of manufacturing and service activities, including fertilizer production, railway construction, consulting, and engineering.[14]

There is then a plausible sequence that runs from transnational domination of a local extractive sector to a substantially increased state role in the economy in general. But do the transnational origins of the capital that initially dominates the extractive sector play a key role in stimulating state involvement, or does the explanation of the sequence have more to do with the technical/economic characteristics of the extractive industries themselves, the transnationals? In addition, are there not some more general political and social preconditions that must be fulfilled in order for the sequence to unfold?

## CONDITIONS OF STATE EXTRACTIVE INITIATIVES

The most well-known method of explaining the increasing power of the state vis à vis the TNCs in extractive industries is the "obsolescing bargain" model popularized first by Vernon[15] and then by Moran[16] in his Chilean case study. In this view, the state is in a very weak position prior to the initial TNC investment because without the inputs that only the TNC can provide, no returns can be reaped from the local resources involved. Once the TNC has sunk the substantial initial investments necessary to begin exploiting the raw materials, it has a great deal to lose, and the bargaining position of the state improves. The combination of high initial fixed costs and relatively stable technology works against the TNC, while the existence of a local "learning curve" as far as technological and organizational issues are concerned works in favor of the state.[17] The "obsolescing bargain" does not result simply from the economic and technical characteristics of the industry.

For the "learning curve" to work, the general bureaucratic capacity of the state apparatus must have reached a certain minimal level before it is in a position to advance along the specific "learning curve" involved in a given extractive industry and exploit the possibilities of the obsolescing bargain. Thus, changes in the bargain depend on the historical evolution of the state apparatus as a whole and not simply on a sequence of investment decisions. Even more important is the strong influence of historical changes in the context of state-TNC bargaining relations. Thus Chile, whose relation with the international copper industry began in the nineteenth century, required more than half a century to discover the possibilities of "obsolescence," whereas Papua New Guinea, with a state apparatus that must be considered much less developed than the Chilean one, but with the benefits of the experiences of other third-world mineral exporters, could begin bargaining with the onset of the companies' initial interest.[18] The logic of the relation between extractive investors and third-world states has changed historically in ways that are quite independent of either the logic of particular investments or the development of particular state institutions.

Is the fact of foreign ownership a key element in the tendency of the state to take control of extractive production? The economic and technical characteristics of extractive industries, in combination with the fact that these industries are so often of central economic importance to the national economy and the standard legal convention that subsoil rights are part of the "national patrimony," might easily be considered sufficient to produce state intervention in these industries, whether or not they were foreign owned. All of these factors unquestionably contribute to state involvement, but there is also reason to believe that the presence of foreign capital provides an additional stimulus. Nationalism is one of the few effective counterarguments to accusations of "statism." State takeovers of TNCs must be, and have been repeatedly, supported by groups strongly in favor of "private enterprise." It is hard to believe that such support would have been forthcoming for the nationalization of the same industries had they been locally owned. The Peruvian military regime not only refrained completely from entering those sectors of mining in which local capital was strong, it also undertook to strengthen private local capital in the sector.[19] In Chile, the conservative nationalist party backed the takeover of Anaconda despite protestations that they were against "estatismo."[20] Its moves against the bauxite TNCs were the Manley regime's most successful initiatives, in part because there was strong private-sector support for the project.[21]

Private-sector support for state initiatives against extractive TNCs comes, in part, from a motive that is also important to state managers: TNC behavior stands in the way of developmentalist goals, not always and everywhere, but in certain key instances that provide critical ammunition for those arguing that the state must move in. On these issues, the structurally defined priority that TNCs must place on global profit maximization must conflict with a priority on local accumulation of capital. The most common example is failure to aggressively pursue possibilities for forward integration locally and the use of returns generated locally for expansion elsewhere.

In the copper industry, the almost universal reluctance of TNCs to invest in local refining capacity epitomizes the former problem. Kennecott's construction of a $100 million refinery to refine Chilean copper in Maryland, immediately following Chilean attempts to demonstrate their commitment to a good "business climate" by initiating generous incentives, is a prime example of how channeling profits outside the country can be combined with failure to engage in forward integration locally.[22] A more ironic example of the latter problem is Cerro's $154 million investment in the Rio Blanco mine in Chile, which was seen as just as hostile *by the Peruvians*[23] as Kennecott's investment in Maryland was by the Chileans. Whether the discrepancies between local preferences and TNC investment choices are seen as generated by bias or simply by the greater range of options available to TNCs, they create serious conflicts with local elites, both public and private.

The examples and arguments could be multiplied, but it is the general point that is important: while economic/technical characteristics make state intervention easier in export-oriented extractive industries than in other sectors,[24] foreign ownership is a key factor in making state initiatives politically feasible.

The nature of the extractive investments, the general historical context, and the special vulnerability of transnational (as opposed to local) capital all go into generating the conditions under which the state is likely to be able to expand its role in the extractive sector. But the role of more specific political factors must also be brought into consideration. When the state apparatus is dominated by groups less closely tied to private capital in general, it is more likely to move against TNCs. From Mossadegh's brief rule in Iran to the Manley period in Jamaica, initiatives vis à vis extractive TNCs become more likely with the advent of a regime whose class base is not simply the dominant elite.

Cardenas's nationalization of the petroleum industry in Mexico is a nice example. The fact that the state was allied with and supported the militancy of the petroleum workers was critical in moving the state toward nationalization. Mexico's move was almost half a century ahead of its time in terms of the general international climate.[25] The Peruvian case offers a different kind of example. It was not until the advent of the "revolutionary" military regime in 1968 that the Peruvian state became aggressive in dealing with the copper TNCs. In this case it was a regime without significant working class allies[26] and with close relations to the local bourgeoisie,[27] but it was nonetheless a regime that was forced to confront (agrarian) private capital in pursuit of developmentalist ends and was therefore more willing to move against the copper companies.[28]

Jamaica provides the most recent example of how the political base and ideology make a difference. Jamaica's bargain with the aluminum TNCs suddenly "obsolesced" with Manley's election in 1972, not because the economic character of the investment had changed and not principally because Jamaica had moved up the "learning curve," but because Manley mobilized existing Jamaican expertise on the project of renegotiating the country's arrangements with the TNCs. His strong political base allowed him to put popular support together with considerable support from local economic elites around a dramatically new bargaining position.[29]

Political specifics change the pace and character of state extractive initiatives, but, for purposes of the present argument, what is striking is not that more "progressive" regimes are more likely to take over extractive TNCs. Rather it is that the tendency for increased state control seems to proceed, albeit perhaps at a different pace, regardless of the character of the political regime. The Saudis are hardly social democrats, Seaga campaigned as the champion of free enterprise, and Pinochet did his utmost to turn Allende's Chile into its opposite, yet these regimes have embraced state control over mineral resources formerly owned by transnational capital. The fact that such undertakings can be supported by even the most reactionary regimes also indicates that an expanded state role may not represent a movement toward either socialism or national autonomy, and thereby raises forcefully this question: What are the consequences of state initiatives in the extractive sector?

## CONSEQUENCES OF AN EXPANDED STATE ROLE IN EXTRACTION

As state managers have joined TNC executives in organizing the exploitation of third-world mineral resources, the way in which third-world states participate in the international markets for these commodities has changed. So has the character of the industries within the countries themselves. The expansion of the state's role has also had consequences for domestic class structures and the configuration of domestic power relations. Some of these changes have moved in the direction hoped for by those who instituted them. Others have been cruelly in the opposite direction. Still other changes, including some very important ones, have moved along dimensions quite tangential to the aims and desires of those who promoted increasing state control.

In most cases, a substantial increase in the mineral rents available for local allocation has resulted, at least in the short to medium term. The massive shift in the geographic distribution of oil rents is only the most obvious example. Even in cases where the position of the state has been much more precarious, the shift in returns has been substantial. Manley's bauxite levy, for example, increased Jamaica's returns sevenfold.[29] The local infusion of resources does not come only from a redivision of rents between TNCs and the state. State entry into the extractive sector has also provided a basis for significant investments in the expansion of local output, as in Chile's buyout of Kennecott[30] and the Cuajone Projet in Peru.[31]

Perhaps even more significant for the developmental implications of state extractive initiatives have been new investments in key linkage activities. Peru's Ilo Copper refinery, "an unquestioned success in policy and economic terms,"[32] exemplifies the potential benefits of state involvement. Prior to the creation of MineroPeru, Peru had suffered from the general tendency of TNCs to resist forward integration of extractive investments. Cerro was not about to expand the limited capacity it had built earlier, and even the generally cooperative Asarco was steadfastly opposed to investment in refining. State entry broke the bottleneck. Petrobras's entrepreneurship in petrochemicals is a similar case.[33] Likewise, Brazil's CVRD, while it is not a steel producer itself, originated out of Brazil's difficulties in getting foreign capital to link the exploitation of mineral resources to the development of downstream activities.[34]

It is also important to underline these positive consequences of state initiatives in the extractive sector because it is all too obvious what does *not* result from state initiatives. Nowhere has increased state control over local productive facilities provided escape from the negative features of dependence on international markets. An expanded state role has not only been unable, with the temporary exception of OPEC, to force favorable raw material pricing changes, it has also failed to reduce price variability. To the contrary, it has been persuasively argued that the increasing involvement of third-world states increases the volatility of international mineral markets and ultimately places third-world exporters at a more disadvantageous position within these markets.

Moran set out the basic argument ten years ago:

> They [state-owned mineral enterprises] may come to inhabit the worst of all possible worlds: a fast weakening international copper oligopoly, with themselves relegated to the position of a spill-over market onto which has been shifted the burden of market uncertainty and instability for the entire industry.[35]

Looking over events since Moran's prediction, Shafer[36] supports the original analysis. Focusing on copper, Shafer notes the essential role of *the vertically integrated* (at least informally) oligopoly and points out that countries cannot provide informal vertical integration in the same way that TNCs can. In addition, the creation of state-owned enterprises increases the number of actors in the industry, further fragmenting what was (at least in the case of copper) already a deteriorating oligopoly. The effects of this fragmentation are exaggerated by the inability of state-owned companies to engage in effective cartel behavior. Not only have international organizations like CIPEC (Intergovernmental Organization of Copper Exporting Countries) and the IBA (International Bauxite Association) proved ineffective, but state-owned enterprises have proved much less capable than TNCs of cutting back output in the face of inadequate demand.[37] Finally, TNC perceptions of increasing political risk in third-world mineral operations (caused in part by expanded state involvement) have led them to expand capacity by developing deposits with lower ore concentrations in "safe" center countries, thus increasing glut at the expense of traditional third-world suppliers.[38]

The inability of state-owned producers to find a place for themselves in oligopolized mineral markets should not be exaggerated. The problems of the producing countries have been severely exacerbated by sluggish world economic growth. In a tighter world market third-world producers would be more able to take advantage of their lower cost operations. In addition, not all state-owned enterprises are in as difficult straits as the African copper producers that are the focus of Shafer's analysis. CVRD (Brazil's state-owned iron exporter), for example, is reputed to act as the price leader in international iron markets.[39] In a few cases state enterprises have gone so far as to set up vertically integrated subsidiaries in their developed country markets.[40]

Eventually state enterprises may learn to construct international networks comparable to those constructed by TNCs in the past. For the present, the fact remains that international commodities markets cannot be regulated from a purely national base, and state actors have proved, not surprisingly, highly unsuited to transcending their national bases. In the absence of effective international organization, dependence on unmanaged global markets can be an extremely disadvantageous position, regardless of whether the state owns or controls local production.

Just as increased state initiatives have not been able to favorably alter the operation of international markets, state entry has not meant the exclusion of TNC actors, even at the local level. TNCs remain involved either as owners operating in the context of arrangements negotiated with state managers (e.g., Asarco in Peru), as joint venture partners, or on the basis of management contracts (e.g., Venezuelan oil, copper in Zaire). In many instances, TNCs have found a useful local partner in the form of the state, one that is more predictable and more willing to bear risks than any other available local partner. In Peru, for example, Asarco has managed to substantially increase its share of the world copper market by cooperating with the Peruvian state.[41]

Conflicts over the expansion of the state's role in extraction are inevitable, but they should not be taken as indications that TNCs and third-world states are engaged in a "zero-sum" struggle over control of third-world mineral resources. It may be more accurate to see recent turmoil as a normal accompaniment to a restructuring of international oligopolies in extractive industries, a restructuring that will involve the construction of alliances between state apparatuses and TNCs. Over the long term, the symbiotic interests shared by all large producers of a given commodity may prove more important than the divisions that separate state managers and TNC executives. From this perspective, it makes sense to argue, as Becker does, that TNCs have preference for, and indeed a vested interest in, the development of "a more knowledgeable, competent host state — one administered by persons who understand the national interest in resource exploitation, write it into access agreements, and see to it that those agreements are observed over time."[42]

A more balanced view of the impact of increasing state involvement on relations with TNCs is also useful in trying to understand the effects of an expanded state role on domestic class structures and power relations. On the one hand, it is clear that the state, not local capital, is the principal heir and partner of the extractive TNCs. Local control of local production will not mean the triumph of "free private enterprise." Local private capital, having developed initially in an economy dominated by foreign capital, will now have to learn to operate in an economy dominated either by the state or by the state in alliance with TNCs.

Effective operation of the most important sector in an extractive economy requires a state apparatus that is both bureaucratically competent and "relatively autonomous" in the sense of being insulated from particularistic political pressures that could undercut efficiency. Mineral exporters that lack such a state apparatus will suffer accordingly.[43] At the same time, the more active role of the state in extractive enterprise will almost unquestionably lead to a more "capitalist" orientation within the state apparatus. Successful state managers will be those who have learned the "rules of the game" by which international oligopolists bargain. Because it now commands or at least shares control over economically vital activities, the entrepreneurial side of the state apparatus is likely to become more powerful, and the state apparatus as a whole is likely to become more thoroughly permeated by entrepreneurial or "bourgeois" attitudes.

We are now in a position to summarize the overall argument with regard to the consequences of transnational extractive investments for the role of the third-world state.

However effective foreign capital may have been initially in eviscerating the state apparatuses of the countries in which they operated, their long-run consequence has been to stimulate the development of more bureaucratically competent, relatively autonomous states more extensively involved in shaping the process of local accumulation. TNCs have done this, first of all, by promoting the development of industries that because of their economic and technical characteristics lend themselves to state control. They have also stimulated state action by engaging in strategies that clearly run counter to local interests in development and by forcing even conservative governments to deal first with problems of regulation and later with problems of inadequate (from a local point of view) investment. Finally, and somewhat paradoxically, they have promoted the growth of the state apparatus because they have found third-world states useful partners.

If foreign capital has helped to stimulate the expansion of the role of the third-world state, it has also helped to shape this expansion in a direction that makes the growing state apparatus more thoroughly capitalist in its orientation. The perennial problems of equity and distribution that have confronted third-world countries whose economies are dominated by multinationals are unlikely to be resolved or even ameliorated by the expanded state apparatuses that have emerged around extraction. Nor have these states escaped the problems of dependence that came with the externally oriented economies generated by foreign mineral investments. To the contrary, those in control of the state may find that controlling local production has made them more rather than less vulnerable to the vagaries of international markets.

The classic image of the state in mineral exporting countries as the supine creature of foreign mine owners should have been shelved a decade ago. The revisionist image of the "ascendance of host countries"[44] is also misleading in that it ignores the weakness of the state apparatus vis à vis international markets and the continued power of TNCs even with respect to local production. But a clear, albeit carefully qualified, argument for a connection between the penetration of transnational capital and the expansion of the role of the state can definitely be made in the case of extractive investment.

## MANUFACTURING TNCs AND THE ROLE
## OF THE THIRD WORLD STATE

The traditional argument with regard to the consequences of TNC manufacturing investment for the role of the third-world state is that the leverage created by the global power and flexibility of TNCs leaves the state unable to exercise influence over manufacturing investment. Because TNC investments in any given country are discretionary from the point of view of the corporation, TNCs may exact whatever concessions they desire in return for their support of local industrialization. The expectation generated by this traditional view is that the higher the share of TNCs in the formation of manufacturing capital, the less the state's ability to shape the process of capital accumulation.

The logic of the obsolescing bargain doesn't work in manufacturing. Fixed investment in plant and equipment may in principle be held hostage, but the importance of product innovation, changing process technology and new marketing techniques gives TNCs an ever-renewed advantage in most industries. Learning curve arguments do, however, still apply. Given a sufficient initial level of coherence and expertise, the bureaucratic apparatus of the state is still likely to improve its ability to regulate and control TNCs.

One of the best examples of a "learning curve" in manufacturing is provided by Bennett and Sharpe[45] in their analysis of the evolution of bargaining between the Mexican state and the major automotive transnationals. In the early sixties, when Mexican state managers began their first serious attempts to shape a denationalized automotive industry, they had a number of ideas as to how TNC behavior might be modified to increase their contribution to Mexican development. But the bureaucracy lacked the experience, technical expertise, and unity necessary to outmaneuver the TNCs. Over the course of the next fifteen years, experience and expertise were accumulated and behavioral controls grew more sophisticated. In addition, the different actors within the state apparatus developed a more unified approach.

By 1977, the state had decided to focus on the firm's balance-of-payments contribution as the key item of behavior to be changed. State managers were able to take the initiative in trying to force the automotive TNCs to stop being part of Mexico's balance-of-payments problem and become part of the solution. State managers were able to structure their proposals in such a way as to break the companies' united front and get them to agree that their exports would more than match their negative contributions, including both imports and profit remittances, to Mexico's balance of payments. In addition, a large proportion of the agreed-upon exports would be parts exports from Mexican-owned firms.

Bennett and Sharpe's analysis provides more than a nice example of TNC challenge and state response in manufacturing. It also illustrates the way in which third-world states may develop the capacity to enlist TNCs as allies against their own home states. While the auto companies were confident that they could not only adjust to but profit from the deal they made with Mexico in 1977, the U.S. government, which saw increased unemployment in Detroit as a primary aspect of the bargain, was unhappy with the bargain. In the U.S. case, however, conflicts between different segments of the state bureaucracy and deference to the preferences of the companies undercut the possibility of forcing an arrangement that appeared more in U.S. interests. If ability to realize national interests in the face of the competing interests of other nations is an indicator of "state strength," then the strength of the Mexican state would seem to have increased substantially in response to the necessity of learning to deal with manufacturing TNCs.[46]

Questions of national sovereignty, which are central to state expansion in extractive industries, have also proved important in manufacturing. No given manufacturing industry is likely to play the dominant role in third-world economies as extractive industries often do, but state intervention may still be justified on the grounds that certain industries hold the key to future industrial development and must not therefore be left completely in the hands of foreign capital.

The extensive state interventions that have occurred in both the Indian and Brazilian computer industries provide excellent examples of this process. The computer industry is typical of the high technology industries in which the position of the TNCs seemed to be impervious to assault from either local capital or the state. Yet in both India and Brazil, nationalist technocrats operating from inside the state apparatus managed to convince policy makers that having some indigenous control of the industry was so important to both future national security and future development that the state must act, regardless of the apparent technological difficulties.[47]

In both countries agencies were created that limited TNC participation. State enterprises were formed that embarked on the creation of indigenous computer designs, and state agencies and regulations began to play a fundamental role in shaping the development of the industry. Skeptical observers may question the developmental efficacy of these policies, but the fact remains that at the opposite end of the industrial spectrum from extractive activities the presence of foreign capital has once again served as a stimulus to the expansion of the state's role.

Challenges to sovereignty are not the only way in which TNCs stimulate the expansion of the state's involvement in manufacturing activities. The possibility of alliances between TNCs and the entrepreneurial side of third-world state apparatuses is as important in expanding the role of the state in industrial activities as it is in extractive ones. Pressure to include the state as a partner may come from managers of state enterprises themselves who for either nationalistic or opportunistic reasons do not want to see multinationals operating key ventures without a state presence. It may also come from the multinationals who see the state presence in a venture as valuable both because it is a source of capital and because it is a political insurance policy against nationalist attacks from other quarters. For the TNCs in search of a local partner a state enterprise may well offer greater financial strength, stability, and even technical expertise than any local private partner. Finally, the state may be brought in at the behest of local capital that is reluctant to enter into a joint venture with transnational capital without the mediating presence of the state.

For a variety of reasons, then, TNC presence in an industry may well lead to a state presence. The motivations for the alliance will vary from industry to industry.[48] They will also vary from country to country. In Brazil, the main thrust for state equity in manufacturing ventures came after almost a century of intensive penetration by transnational capital and must therefore be seen as a response to the challenge created by TNC domination of leading sectors. In Taiwan, some of the most important initial investments by U.S. TNCs included the state as a partner and the motivation may have been to assuage TNC fears created by the political uncertainty of the environment more than anything else. According to Gold,[49] "American investments in the fifties were generally joint ventures with the only enterprises that could offer the large markets and production scale to justify the effort, the state corporations."

Another, quite different logic linking the expansion of the state's role to TNC penetration is illustrated by the contrast between Hong Kong and Singapore, as described by

Haggard and Cheng.[50] Singapore stands out among the gang of four as the country whose manufacturing sector is most thoroughly dominated by TNCs. At the same time, its state apparatus is, like those of Taiwan and South Korea, "characterized by 'strong' dirigist bureaucracies capable of extracting and channeling resources."[51] In Hong Kong, on the other hand, "MNCs came to occupy a small but not insignificant position in an economy largely dominated by local firms." Yet the state apparatus is exceptional in its lack of intervention. The government of Hong Kong takes a "pure laissez faire approach," and there are no parastatals involved in manufacturing.[52]

There are, of course, a number of factors independent of the degree of penetration by TNC capital that would have to be taken into account in any fuller explanation of the contrasting role of the state in the two countries, most notably the colonial character of the government of Hong Kong. In addition, it would be a grave error to generalize too broadly on the basis of these two cases. TNC penetration means something quite different in the case of Singapore than it would in a Latin American case in which the relative dominance of foreign vis à vis local capital was similar. The TNCs arrived in Singapore in the era of the "ascendance of host governments," not in the era of traditional gunboat diplomacy, and they arrived at the behest of a well-organized authoritarian regime that had put together a conscious industrial policy, not in the context of a loose oligarchic regime dominated by agrarian interests. Nonetheless, these two cases are very difficult to account for in a model that argues that the more extensive the DFI in manufacturing, the more restricted the role of the state. They suggest, to the contrary, that under at least certain historical circumstances there may be a positive relation between TNC dominance of manufacturing and the emergence of a dirigist state.

As in the case of the extractive sector, it would be a mistake to confuse an expansion of the state's role in manufacturing with an ability to overcome the logic of global markets. Gereffi's[53] analysis of the steroid hormone industry in Mexico offers a good illustration. Between the mid-fifties and the mid-seventies, Mexico watched what had been a locally owned industry with a near monopoly on one of the most commercially successful new families of drugs in the post-World War II era become transformed into a denationalized industry dominated by North American and Western European TNCs. One response to this discouraging transformation was the creation of a state-owned firm, Proquivemex, designed to at least control the processing of the local raw material (barbasco root) that went into steroid hormones. This state initiative could not, however, prevent the dramatic further deterioration of Mexico's position vis à vis the international industry. Like the copper-mining companies, the pharmaceutical TNCs looked for new sources of raw materials that could be produced in "safe" locations. Because they were manufacturing rather than extractive companies, they did not have to go to higher-cost alternatives but could rely on technological innovation. By 1980, Mexico, which had supplied 75 percent of the raw materials for steroid hormones in 1963, accounted for only 10 percent.[54] State initiative and an expanded state role were not sufficient to counter the logic of the global evolution of the industry, which followed instead a path dictated by the TNCs.[55]

The steroid hormone example is a very specific case of the difficulties of counteracting dependency simply on the basis of an expansion of the role of the state. The more important general argument is slightly different. Even when the state "wins" as in the auto example with which this section began, winning does not necessarily mean the realization of national goals broadly conceived. For example, one of the reasons that the Mexican state became more "effective" in its dealings with the auto TNCs was that state managers focused increasingly on national goals that were compatible with the goals of the TNCs themselves. Ideas for mandating production of simple, low-cost standardized vehicles — instead of allowing TNCs to engage in their usual product differentiation — were dropped. Rather, the focus was on export promotion, which was quite compatible with the plans of the TNCs for internationalizing the industry in order to take better advantage of low-wage, non–U.S. labor.

Manufacturing and extractive interventions are similar in their failure to escape the constraints imposed by global markets or deal with welfare issues. But they are quite different in other respects. The logic of rapid technological change and constant product differentiation has not prevented state intervention but it has changed its character. State-owned enterprises have been less common and less effective when they exist in manufacturing. Intervention is more likely to take the form of regulation and oversight and when state enterprises are involved they are more likely to be joint ventures.

State intervention in manufacturing is much more likely than intervention in extraction to have the effect of creating space for the local bourgeoisie. The consequences of Brazilian and Indian intervention in the computer industry illustrates the point. In both cases, the state-owned enterprises that were formed were not particularly successful from a commercial point of view. State intervention did, however, have the effect of powerfully protecting a host of profitable and dynamic locally owned computer companies. By making it more difficult for TNCs to enter the computer industry, state intervention also increased the propensity of TNCs to license their technology to local firms. Bennett and Sharpe's analysis of the Mexican auto industry shows a similar effect. One of the central features of the Mexican government's policy was to force TNCs to expand their use of local parts suppliers, creating an important locally owned industry around the foreign-owned final assembly plants.

In manufacturing as in extraction, the initial absence of a strong local bourgeoisie is an important part of the link between the presence of TNCs and the expansion of the state's role, but the forms and consequences of the expansion of the state's role are different. State expansion in manufacturing seems to create space for local private firms to a much larger degree than interventions in extractive industries. Moving from extraction to manufacturing generally supports our initial hypothesis, but also adds an important variation on the theme.

## FOREIGN LOAN CAPITAL AND THE ROLE
## OF THE THIRD-WORLD STATE

Just as manufacturing investment came to replace extractive investment as the most dynamic segment of transnational capital flows after World War II, flows of transnational loan capital replaced direct investment, both extractive and industrial, as the most rapidly expanding form of transnational capital in the seventies. Finding the hard currency necessary to service foreign debt has become a central issue for most third-world countries. There are also a number of compelling case studies available demonstrating how foreign creditors can use the leverage they have acquired, usually concretized in the form of negotiations with the International Monetary Fund (IMF), to constrict the actions of third-world states and effectively exclude a range of policy options.[56] Generally, the external constraints associated with debt are extremely negative in their distributional and welfare consequences as well as in their limitations on the developmentalist aspirations of third-world regimes.

It is not surprising then that loan capital would be seen as undermining the autonomy of third-world state managers and undercutting the possibility of a more activist state role. Indeed, it unquestionably has this effect. But, even more than the two other kinds of capital that have been examined here, the consequences of transnational capital for the role of the state are double-edged. Without denying the eventual problems created for the state by flows of loan capital, it is also necessary to examine the ways in which the flood of foreign loans in the seventies underwrote or reinforced an expansion of the state's role to an extent unlikely to be reversed by the hard times of the eighties.

While transnational loan capital became increasingly private during the seventies as private commercial banks expanded their third-world portfolios and official assistance receded in importance, they had the effect of making state managers ever more crucial intermediaries between private bankers in the core and productive investments on the periphery. According to Frieden,[57] 80 to 90 percent of commercial bank

Eurocurrency lending to third-world countries are loans to
various public-sector entities — central governments themselves, central banks, state-owned enterprises, national development banks, and state-owned public utilities. The rest
are likely to carry state guarantees. Burgeoning flows of transnational loan capital propelled state apparatuses in major borrowing countries into "the central roles of overseer of
industrial growth and intermediary between foreign finan-
ciers and domestic productive investment."[58]

Like the TNCs, the banks seem to have generally considered
the state the least risky third-world borrower available. Consequently, the flow of foreign loans substantially increased the
power of the state vis à vis the local bourgeoisie. The regime
of Park Chung Hee in South Korea offers one of the best
illustrations of the latter possibility. In the late sixties, the role
of foreign debt in South Korea's industrialization was of a
magnitude almost unprecedented in the third world. According to Haggard and Cheng,[59] foreign capital accounted for
almost 40 percent of total savings and loan capital accounted
for more than 95 percent of foreign capital. This pattern
continued, though in slightly less extreme form, into the seventies. In the view of most analysts, one of the primary motivations for Korea's exceptional preference for debt was the
leverage that it gave the state over local industrialists. Foreign
loans required government approval and repayment guarantees, and so local capitalists needed the favor of the state
apparatus in order to obtain them. Since the cost of foreign
loans was substantially less than the cost of domestic loans,
access to them was a critical competitive advantage. Haggard
and Cheng[60] assert that "the preference for foreign borrowing
had a political motivation" and go on to say, "Foreign loans
provided an additional instrument of control to the government, while allowing it to extend greater assistance to local
enterprises." In Lim's view, "The most potent instrument for
influencing local capitalists, particularly those engaged in
large scale enterprises, was control of bank credit and foreign
borrowing."[61]

Transnational loan capital was not only useful to the Korean
state in controlling the local bourgeoisie. It also offered the

possibility of dependent development with less reliance on the TNCs, which the Park regime clearly considered a more threatening form of foreign capital. Because of the availability of loan capital, Korea was able to accept TNC investments on its own terms. As a result, "It is a distinctive feature of South Korea's dependent development that the state had the upper hand over both local capitalists and multinationals."[62]

Stallings' analysis of the role of international loan capital in Peru provides a nice complement to the Korean case.[63] She shows how two, relatively autonomous, authoritarian regimes (Augusto Leguia — 1919–1930; and the military under the initial leadership of Velasco — 1968–1980) were facilitated in embarking on their transformative projects by the availability of international loan capital. In both cases, the state was able to undertake projects that were opposed by the traditional local oligarchy and that incipient elites with a more strictly capitalist orientation were too weak to carry through because it had access to foreign resources in the form of loan capital.

While Stallings states clearly that she sees "foreign capital as facilitating an increased state role,"[64] she is equally clear in insisting that the Peruvian cases demonstrate the contradictory results of relying on foreign capital. As she puts it, foreign bankers "are unreliable allies since the interests of international banks, like those of multinational corporations, stretch far beyond the borders of any given country."[65] In the case of the two regimes she studied, "however much foreign resources may have helped Leguia and the military, their decline ... had catastrophic consequences for both governments."[66]

The Peruvian cases in combination with Korea reinforces the earlier suggestion that while foreign capital of all types may stimulate an expansion of the state's role, each type has distinctive consequences of the nature of state expansion. Extractive foreign capital tends to lead the state into directly productive activities and not strengthen the position of local private capital. Manufacturing TNCs tend to lead the state to make space for and strengthen the local bourgeoisie. Loan capital is much more ambivalent in its consequences for the relation between the state and the local bourgeoisie. It may either put the state in the position of being the principal supplier of capital to the local bourgeoisie, as in the Korean case, or it may provide the state with the possibility of undercutting a major segment of the local bourgeoisie, as in the Peruvian case.

**CONCLUSION**

Third-world states have clearly not shrunk as a result of the penetration of their economies by transnational capital, regardless of the specific form of that penetration. Instead, our survey of the literature has suggested that the state apparatus in a number of third-world countries has widened its role as a result of its interaction with transnational capital. In some instances, the challenge of dealing with the sovereignty-threatening intrusions of the TNCs has stimulated the development of a countervailing state bureaucracy. In other instances, the state apparatus has become the ally and local partner of the TNCs. In still others, it has become the crucial intermediary between transnational capital and the local economy. Based on the evidence considered here, the expansion of the state's economic role seems more likely in cases where transnational capital is the most powerful private actor than in cases where the state confronts a powerful, dynamic local bourgeoisie.

Is this overall result theoretically plausible? Not unless the circumscribed nature of what is being argued is clearly understood. What is *not* being debated here is the relationship between the penetration of transnational capital and the ability of the countries involved to develop. It is not being argued that increased reliance on transnational capital enhances the ability of the state apparatus to realize its own economic goals. Nor is it being argued that a symbiotic relation between the state and transnational capital enhances the welfare of the mass of the citizenry. What is in question is the scope of the state's economic role, the extent of its ability to shape the pattern of domestic capital accumulation, the range over which it is able to influence the decisions of private firms, and the degree of its direct, entrepreneurial involvement in the process of accumulation.

Once the restricted nature of the argument is made clear, it becomes quite plausible. J. P. Nettl reminded us almost twenty years ago[67] that regulating relations with the external world is the classic locus of state power. It follows that being able to define actors in the domestic economy as part of the external world makes state intervention in their affairs more legitimate. If the state's main competitors for economic power are not full citizens, then the state can bring its legitimacy as the unique representative of the "nation" to bear on the contest. The issue then becomes one of nationalism and political legitimacy versus the sanctity and efficiency of free (private) enterprise. Thus, despite the fact that transnational capital can bring to bear greater economic power than any local capitalist is likely to possess, the state has leverage and motivation that it lacks in contests with domestic capital. Thus, it is not so surprising as it might at first appear that the presence of foreign capital is associated with the expansion of the state's role.

Even if the hypothesis is considered confirmed, and there is obviously ample room for debate over whether sufficient evidence has been presented, its confirmation is hardly a conclusion. Cardoso and Faletto pointed out some time ago that it is "useful to remember that forms of dependency can change and to identify the structural possibilities for change."[68] Clearly, in the more advanced third-world countries a sizeable portion of those possibilities for change will involve the future operation of an expanded state apparatus. Identifying them should be a priority on the research agenda of the "new political economy."

One point of departure is the range of variation in the consequences of state expansion for the domestic bourgeoisie. Nothing in the evidence presented here suggests that the state's expansion is anti-capitalist. To the contrary, where state intervention was directed against the local elite it seemed to be directed against a fraction of the dominant class whose power was an impediment to capitalist development (e.g., the Peruvian oligarchy). Even where the state filled space that might conceivably have been filled by local private enterprise (e.g., in mining), the result is, at least in Becker's interpretation, the creation of one segment of a "corporate national bourgeoisie" within the state apparatus itself.[69] In a wide variety of cases from the Indian computer industry to the Mexican auto industry, the consequences of state intervention were to spawn collections of aggressive new profit-oriented private firms.

What all of this suggests is that the conventional dichotomy between increased state intervention and the promotion of capitalist development is misplaced, at least in the cases we have been discussing here. Perhaps the expansion of the economic role of the state is best viewed as a route to a more indigenously controlled capitalist development.[70] If so, the question of what this state-promoted third-world capitalism might look like must be confronted.

Is such a route to capitalist development viable? Certainly the striking success of Brazil and the East Asian NICs would suggest that it may be. What are its political concomitants? Can the democratization that is now sweeping the southern cone of Latin America prevail and serve as a model for the East Asian NICs? Must these countries remain at the mercy of the vagaries of international markets? Certainly, the evidence presented here suggests no route for escaping dependence on international markets. Can they move in the direction of more egalitarian social structures and thereby deal with the overwhelming welfare issues that are endemic in even the most successful third-world countries? The evidence here is mostly negative.[71] In short, it remains incumbent on the new political economy to deal with most of the items that were on the old *dependencista* research agenda, but to re-examine them in the light of the assumption that an active, interventionist third-world state will be one of the central actors in the struggle to determine which of the potential historical alternatives contained in the current situation of the third world are actualized.

## NOTES

1. F. H. Cardoso and E. Faletto, *Dependency and Development in Latin America*. (Berkeley: University of California Press, 1979, xvi.) For an excellent review of the dependency approach see Gabriel Palma, "Dependency: A Formal Theory of Underdevelopment or a Methodology for the Analysis of Concrete Situations of Underdevelopment," *World Development* 6, nos. 7/8 (1978) :881–924.

2. For a discussion of the relationship between some of these authors and the dependency tradition, see Peter Evans, "After Dependency: Recent Studies of Class, State and Industrialization," *Latin American Research Review* 20, no.2 (1985): 149–160.

3. For an elaboration of this characterization see P. Evans and J. Stephens, "Development and the World Economy," in R. Burt and N. Smelser (eds.) *Handbook of Sociology* (Beverly Hills: Sage, forthcoming).

4. Others have argued, of course, that transnational capital undercuts the capacity of third-world states. Perspectives that stress the positive contributions of transnational corporations (TNCs), as well as perspectives that emphasize the negative effects of TNC expansion, such as the "global reach" approach, have argued for a negative relation between the strength of the third-world state and the increasing penetration of transnational capital. But it was the *dependencistas* who most dramatically focused attention on the consequences of foreign capital in third-world countries. For the positive version of the argument, see George Ball, "The Promise of the Multinational Corporation," *Fortune* 75, no. 6 (1967):80; and Robert Gilpin, *U.S. Power and the Multinational Corporation: The Political Economy of Foreign Direct Investment* (New York: Basic Books, 1975), 220. For the "global reach" approach, see Richard Barnet and Ronald Müller, *Global Reach: The Power of the Multinational Corporation* (New York: Simon & Schuster, 1974).

5. Richard Rubinson, "Dependence, Government Revenue and Economic Growth 1955–1970," in *National Development and the World System: Educational, Economic and Political Change, 1950–1970,* edited by John W. Meyer and Michael T. Hannan (Chicago: University of Chicago Press, 1979), 213.

6. Frank Tugwell, *The Politics of Oil in Venezuela* (Stanford, Calif.: Stanford University Press, 1975).

7. John Blair, *The Control of Oil* (New York: Pantheon, 1976); and Steven A. Schneider, *The Oil Price Revolution* (Baltimore: Johns Hopkins University Press, 1983).

8. Theodore H. Moran, *Multinational Corporations and the Politics of Dependence: Copper in Chile* (Princeton, N.J.: Princeton University Press, 1974).

9. Ibid., 123–25.

10. Jeff Frieden, "Third World Indebted Industralization: International Finance and State Capitalism in Mexico, Brazil, Al-

geria, and South Korea," *International Organization* 35, no. 3 (1981):407–31.

11. David G. Becker, *The New Bourgeoisie and the Limits of Dependency: Mining, Class, and Power in "Revolutionary" Peru* (Princeton, N.J.: Princeton University Press, 1983), 217–18.

12. See Peter Evans, *Dependent Development: The Alliance of Multinational, State, and Local Capital in Brazil* (Princeton, N.J.: Princeton University Press, 1979); Evans, "Collectivized Capitalism: Integrated Petrochemical Complexes and Capital Accumulation in Brazil," in *Authoritarian Capitalism: Brazil's Contemporary Political and Economic Development,* edited by Thomas C. Bruneau and Philippe Faucher (Boulder, Colo.: Westview Press, 1981); and Evans, "Reinventing the Bourgeosie: State Entrepreneurship and Class Formation in Dependent Capitalist Development," *American Journal of Sociology* 88 (1982): S210–47.

13. David Isaak, "Basic Petrochemicals in the 1980s: Mideast Expansions and the Global Industry," Working Paper WP-82-3 (Honolulu: Resource Systems Institute East-West Center, 1982).

14. See Evans, *Dependent Development,* 249–54, and Silvia Raw, "A Case Study of the Companhia Vale do Rio Doce" (unpublished manuscript, 1983).

15. Raymond Vernon, *Sovereignty at Bay: The Multinational Spread of U.S. Enterprises* (New York: Basic Books, 1971).

16. Moran, *Multinational Corporations.*

17. C. Fred Bergsten, Thomas Horst, and Theodore H. Moran, *American Multinationals and American Interests* (Washington, D.C.: Brookings Institution, 1978).

18. See "Bougainville Copper Ltd.," Harvard Business School Case, 1974.

19. See Becker, *The New Bourgeoisie,* 221–22, 230.

20. Moran, *Multinational Corporations,* 212.

21. Evelyne H. Stephens and John D. Stephens, *Democratic Socialism in Jamaica: The Political Movement and Social Transformation in Dependent Capitalism* (Princeton: Princeton University Press, 1986).

22. Moran, *Multinational Corporations,* 102–3.

23. Becker, *The New Bourgeoisie,* 142–43.

24. L. P. Jones and E. M. Mason, "The Role of Economic Factors in Determining the Size and Structure of the Public Enterprise Sector in Mixed Economy LDCs," (Paper presented at the Second Annual Boston Area Public Enterprise Group Conference, Boston, 1980).

25. The Mexican nationalization was not only ahead of general international norms, it also helped in itself to push these norms forward. Other Latin American countries, in which the industry was more oriented to distribution and sale than to extraction, followed the Mexican example and nationalized. Venezuela, the most important third-world producer at the time, was able to significantly improve its share of returns (Nora Hamilton, *The Limits of State Autonomy: Post-Revolutionary Mexico* (Princeton, N.J.: Princeton University Press, 1982), 220.

26. Alfred Stepan, *The State and Society: Peru in Comparative Perspective.* (Princeton: Princeton University Press, 1978).

27. See Becker, *The New Bourgeoisie.*

28. In the case of the Cerro de Pasco Corporation the two types of confrontation fortuitously collapsed into one (see Becker, *The New Bourgeosie,* 142).

29. This figure for the increase in returns, which represents revenues of about $150 million additional, equal to 25 percent of the Jamaican government's previous *total* revenues from all sources, holds up even if one conservatively attributes *all* post-1974 decreases in Jamaican output to the negative effects of the levy on the "business climate" (see Stephens and Stephens, "Democratic Socialism").

30. Moran, *Multinational Corporations,* 133.

31. Becker, *The New Bourgeoisie,* 97–131.

32. Ibid., 218.

33. See Evans, *Dependent Development,* "Collectivized Capitalism," and "Reinventing the Bourgeoisie."

34. See Werner Baer, *The Development of the Brazilian Steel Industry* (Nashville, Tenn.: Vanderbilt University Press, 1969), and Raw, "A Case Study."

35. Moran, *Multinational Corporations,* 241.

36. Michael Shafer, "Capturing the Mineral Multinationals: Advantage or Disadvantage?" *International Organization* 37, no. 1 (1982):93–119.

37. The early success of OPEC at restricting output and raising the real price of oil looks in retrospect like the exception that proves the rule.

38. Raymond Vernon, "Uncertainty in the Resource Industries: The Special Role of State-owned Enterprises" (unpublished manuscript, 1982), 19.

39. Raw, "A Case Study."

40. Vernon, "Uncertainty in the Resource Industries," 20–21.

41. Becker, *The New Bourgeoisie,* 127.

42. Ibid., 325.

43. See Shafer, "Capturing the Mineral Multinationals," 119.

44. See Bergsten, Horst, and Moran, *American Multinationals,* 369–85.

45. Douglas Bennett and Kenneth Sharpe, *Transnational Corporations versus the State: The Political Economy of the Mexican Auto Industry* (Princeton: Princeton University Press, 1985).

46. The issue of whether TNCs, extractive or manufacturing, generally behave as agents of "U.S. national interests" is, of course, a topic for debate in itself (see Bergsten, Horst, and Moran, *American Multinationals;* Gilpin, *U.S. Power and the Multinational Corporation;* and Stephen D. Krasner, *Defending the National Interest: Raw Materials, Investments and U.S. Foreign Policy* (Princeton, N.J.: Princeton University Press, 1978). But there certainly have been in the past instances of U.S. TNCs behaving in ways that aided the U.S. economy at the expense of their host economies. Moran's discussion of the willingness of U.S. copper companies to accept U.S. price controls during World War II at Chile's expense (*Multinational Corporations,* 61–63) is one of the most clear-cut examples.

47. For the Indian case, see Joseph Grieco, *Between Dependency and Autonomy: India's Experience with the International Computer Industry.* (Berkeley: University of California Press, 1984). For the Brazilian case, see Emanuel Adler, *The Power of Ideology: The Quest for Technological Autonomy in Argentina and Brazil* (Berkeley: University of California Press, forthcoming) and P. Evans, "State, Capital and the Transformation of Dependence: The Brazilian Computer Case," *World Development* 14, no. 8 (1986). For a review of policies in both countries as well as several others, see F. W. Rushing and C. G. Brown (eds.), *National Policies for Developing Countries in High Technology Industries: International Comparisons* (Boulder, Colo.: Westview Press, 1986).

48. The most common location for such partnerships is the industrial downstream activities created by strong state enterprises with extractive origins, e.g., petrochemicals. But they may also be found in other industries. As noted by Thomas Gold (*Dependent Development in Taiwan,* Ph.D. dissertation, Department of Sociology, Harvard University, Cambridge, Mass., (1982, 290–91), for example, the government of Taiwan is using the joint ventures of state, local and TNC capital model in its new attempts to attract more technological advanced enterprises to the Hsinchu Science Industrial Park.

49. Gold, *Dependent Development in Taiwan*, 192.

50. Stephan Haggard and Tun-jeng Cheng, "State Strategies, Local and Foreign Capital in the Gang of Four," paper presented at the Annual Meeting of the American Political Science Association, Chicago, Ill., 2 September 1983.

51. Ibid., 36.

52. Ibid., 51, 37, 45.

53. Gary Gereffi, *The Pharmaceutical Industry and Dependency in the Third World* (Princeton, N.J.: Princeton University Press, 1983).

54. Ibid., 152.

55. The story is, of course, more complicated than this abbreviated version indicates. Had the state developed a clear vision of its goals earlier (Gereffi, *The Pharmaceutical Industry*, 125–28), and had the TNCs not been able to use local private-sector allies to create conflicts within the state apparatus and undermine the position of Proquivemex (ibid., 147–53), Mexico might have fared better. Nonetheless, even the most effective state action could not have changed the basic logic of the search for alternative sourcing.

56. Cheryl Payer, *The Debt Trap* (New York: Monthly Review Press, 1975); Barbara Stallings, "Peru and the U.S. Banks: Privatization of Financial Relations," in *Capitalism and the State in U.S.-Latin American Relations*, edited by Richard R. Fager (Stanford, Calif.: Stanford University Press, 1979), 219–53; Roberto Frenkel and Guillermo O'Donnell, "The 'Stabilization' Programs of the IMF and Their Internal Impacts," in Fager, *Capitalism and the State*, 171–216; Stephens and Stephens, "Democratic Socialism in Dependent Capitalism."

57. Frieden, "Third World Indebted Industrialization," 411.

58. Ibid., 429.

59. Haggard and Cheng, "State Strategies," 22.

60. Ibid., 58.

61. Hyun-Chin Lim, *Dependent Development in the World System: The Case of South Korea, 1963–1979*, Ph.D. dissertation, Department of Sociology, Harvard University, Cambridge, Mass., 1982, 147.

62. Ibid., 139. It should be noted, as in the case of Singapore, that the ability of the Korean state to undertake the strategy it did was contingent on the particular historical circumstances in which it found itself. Had it not been the case that the multinational corporations "were entirely absent in the local scene" when Park came to power (ibid, 139), the Korean state would

have had a much more difficult time controlling their expansion. The Korean experience, like the case of Singapore, cannot, for example, be generalized to Latin American or African cases.

63. Barbara Stallings, "International Lending and the Relative Autonomy of the State: A Case Study of Twentieth Century Peru," *Politics and Society* 14, no. 3 (1985): 257–288.

64. Ibid., 263.

65. Ibid., 283.

66. Ibid., 281.

67. J. P. Nettl, "The State As a Conceptual Variable," *World Politics* 20, no. 4 (July 1968): 559–92.

68. Cardoso and Faletto, *op. cit.,* xi.

69. Becker, *op. cit.*

70. This is hardly a novel proposition. It is essentially the one advanced by Gerschenkron twenty-five years ago. See A. Gerschenkron, *Economic Backwardness in Historical Perspective.* (Cambridge: Harvard University Press, 1962).

71. Falling *gini indeces* in Taiwan and Korea provide the best grounds for optimism on this score and even here the recent evidence from Korea is disappointing. See H. Koo, "The Impact of the State's Industrialization Policies," *World Development* 9, no. 10 (1984): 1029–37.

Parts of this essay are excerpted and adapted from "Transnational Linkages and the Economic Role of the State: An Analysis of Developing and Industrialized Nations in the Post-World War II Period," from *Bringing the State Back In*, edited by Peter Evans, Dietrich Rueschmeyer, and Pheda Skocpol. Copyright © 1985 Cambridge University Press. Reprinted by permission of Cambridge University Press.

ERIC A. NORDLINGER

# Taking the State Seriously

## TOWARD A STATE-CENTERED PERSPECTIVE

The study of the state is justified first and foremost because its authoritative actions, its public policies broadly conceived, are patently consequential for the many-times-larger society in which it is embedded. The state's authoritative actions are directly and indirectly implicated in the distribution (and loss) of enormous swatches of highly valued political, ideological, social, and economic goods and opportunities. This statement also applies to those many states that do not feature impressive extractive, distributive, and regulatory capacities. Not only do the more limited authoritative actions of such states constantly elicit widespread subjective and behavioral reactions, the possible expansion of their policy activities is itself a critical concern of numerous societal actors.

The fundamental question to be asked about the state thus becomes: How are its authoritative actions and inactions to be understood? This overarching question can be transformed into two that are more nearly manageable. First, is the state — that is, public officials writ large — acting upon its own policy preferences, translating them into public policy, or are its authoritative actions shaped and constrained by the expectations, demands, and pressures of some larger or smaller number of societal actors? Second, whatever the variations in autonomy and societal constraint, are they to be

For their suggestions and critical comments on an earlier draft of this chapter I am grateful to Jorge I. Domínguez, Stephan Haggard, Peter Hall, Sidney Berba, and Van Whiting, Jr.

explained endogenously, by relying upon the internal features of the state, or exogenously, by focusing upon the contours of civil society?

One approach to these questions in the case of first and third-world states has been decidedly society centered. The state is taken to be a largely manipulated, dependent, constrained, and responsive entity, little more than an arena in which the "representatives" of contending societal interests come together to hammer out their differences. With public officials being heavily dependent upon political support, with societal actors controlling and effectively deploying an armory of political and politically fungible resources, policy formation is understood as a response to the expectations and demands of those who control the largest armory of effective resources. Working on these assumptions, the basic issue becomes the double-barreled one of determining which resources in the hands of which societal actors are most effective in constraining the state. In any one society or type of society, are the especially effective resources to be found in politicized numbers, votes, clients, organization, social status, professional expertise, wealth, control over industrial, financial, and landed property, or in certain combinations of these resources? Once the differential effectiveness of these resources is known and their broader or narrower, dispersed or cumulative distribution is determined, it becomes possible to identify the private actors that predominate in having public officials translate their interests into public policy. These actors may turn out to be large landowners, large or small business firms, trade unions, specialized interest groups, ethnic and linguistic segments, churches, the national bourgeoisie, small numbers of party activists, the great majority of politically aware individuals, or some combination.

According to society-centered analysis, both the constraint of the state and the identity of the private actors that predominate in this regard are to be understood in terms of variables that reside outside the state's perimeters. Many of them refer to such political variables as the type and rate of political participation, the level of working-class mobilization, the amount of party competition, the number and organizational depth of political and quasi-political associations, the membership density of trade unions, the strategies of political movements, and mass political attitudes. Other variables, at the same or at a deeper level of explanation, include such distinctly nonpolitical ones as socialization within the family and school, class structure, economic growth rates, educational levels, mass communications networks, levels of urbanization, land distribution patterns, import-substitution phases, the export of different types of products, and the requisites of a capitalist economy.

According to the rival perspective, the state is treated as an independent actor and an independent variable. The state is seen to be frequently autonomous in turning its own policy preferences into authoritative actions, and markedly so by acting autonomously even when these conflict with the preferences of the politically best-endowed private actors. Treating the state as an independent variable is to look to its internal characteristics — from the recruitment and socialization of its officials to the arrangements of their offices — as commonly applicable explanations for variations in its autonomy.

The single most influential effort to rectify the imbalance between state- and society-centered analyses was carried out without ever using the term "state," although hardly ignoring it. Huntington's 1968 work[1] is most broadly significant in turning scholarly attention back to the political; in some respects it parallels Machiavelli's great assertion on behalf of the empirical and normative autonomy of the entire political realm. Huntington focuses upon the extent to which the state and other political organizations and their procedures are institutionalized as "stable and valued patterns of interaction." In conjunction with the level of participation, the latter accounts for a broad set of state and societal patterns falling under the heading of political stability. While autonomy is featured as one of the components of institutionalization (along with adaptability, coherence, and complexity), its variations are simply said to be due to an institution's coherence and an "environmental" or societal factor: a substantial "degree of competition among social forces" makes for a triangular relationship with the state positioned advantageously at its pinnacle.[2]

Starting circa 1970, a resurgent neo-Marxism has also contributed to state-centered analyses. In fact, much of the revival of neo-Marxism is related to the new-found prominence it accords the state in capitalist societies. Despite the strong society-centered thrust of its two major variants, neo-Marxism now offers a more fully elaborated and persuasive political economy by bringing the state into the analysis. According to the instrumental version, state actions are consistently shaped and constrained (depending upon the national setting) by industrial and financial capital, the commercial middle class, and the nascent bourgeoisie; in the structural version, state policies are driven by the "requisites" of capitalism as an economic system. Yet what has become a critical proposition turns neo-Marxism into the only macro theory that not only allows for but insists upon state autonomy. The capitalist state is "relatively autonomous" when it acts contrary to the exceptionally powerful demands of a short-sighted, narrow-minded capitalist class. It chooses, or is structurally compelled to do so, whenever this becomes necessary to safeguard capitalist relations of production and maintain political stability.

Still, the proposition does not move very far in a state-centered direction. The explanations for variations in autonomy are found exclusively within society; the capitalist state can overcome the opposition of the economically and politically dominant class when the latter is divided and when its political strength is nearly balanced by that of the nonpropertied class. These were the only autonomy-enhancing conditions identified by Marx and Engels, to which a bevy of neo-Marxists who have dealt with the "relative autonomy" proposition[3] has not added any other. Moreover, the state is said to be autonomous only "on occasion," only during those few times when the reproduction of capitalism is seriously threatened.

Neo-Marxists may well leave the theory of the state in capitalist society as it stands. But if not amended, it will continue to miss out on large slices of political reality, and allow "relative autonomy" to be brought into empirical inquiries as a way of "saving" the society-centered hypotheses, as it is otherwise very difficult to account for the adoption of reformist policies that are opposed by the bourgeoisie. Alternatively, the proposition may be expanded, starting perhaps by taking a leaf out of a non-Marxist study — one that relies entirely upon neo-Marxist writings to argue that the capitalist state does, in fact, act autonomously vis à vis capital with considerable frequency. On a straightforward reading of neo-Marxist writings, it turns out that there are four conditions that induce or structurally require state autonomy: (1) the capitalist class is itself sharply divided on major political economy issues, (2) the state's legitimacy as a class-neutral institution is in decline, (3) social peace is seriously at risk or has already broken down, and (4) capitalism's economic contradictions and irrationalities are intensified. With neo-Marxist scholars also claiming that one or more of these conditions obtain with some frequency, the syllogism is complete: the capitalist state acts autonomously with some frequency.[4]

During the last decade, a handful of studies have appeared that, taken together, underscore the autonomy of the state in diverse settings, concomitantly showing that civil society, social structure, and economic patterns provide sorely incomplete, if not misleading, accounts. The array of state actions that are explicated in a state-centered manner includes the formulation and adoption of social welfare policies in Sweden and Britain,[5] the installation of exclusionary versus inclusionary corporatist regimes in Latin America,[6] the success of military bureaucrats in eliminating the political and economic bases of the dominant landed classes in Japan, Turkey, Egypt, and Peru,[7] the pursuit of foreign economic policies contrary to the interests of American multinational corporations,[8] and the democratic state's adoption of public policies when its preferences diverge from those of varying combinations of voters, pressure groups, trade unions, and corporations.[9] Most recently, a collection entitled *Bringing the State Back In*[10] features studies of culturally and politically disparate countries that highlight how the state's autonomy is affected by its capacities for intervention in the economy and by societal contours that have themselves been purposefully or unintentionally shaped by state institutions.

Despite their ambitious claims, each of these studies exhibits at least two, and some all four, of the following limits and limitations. The critical concepts, including autonomy itself, are not defined, and if defined, not clearly so. Neither the findings nor their implications are generalized; they are not applied to all states, to certain types of states, to different kinds of policy issues, or to generalized situations and conditions. The writers do not apply a full-blown statist perspective insofar as some society-centered explanations are immediately introduced without first examining the possibility of the most important, necessary, or sufficient ones being located entirely within the state. A few state- and society-centered hypotheses are simply adopted, whereas a questioning posture could discover some serious difficulties, as with the proposition that a state's policy capacities or instruments almost necessarily heighten its autonomy.

In her overview of the state-centered literature, Skocpol[11] goes so far as to say that it represents a "paradigmatic reorientation." In reviewing several statist studies, Krasner says that they pose a "challenge to the analytic traditions that have dominated political science in the United States. They see a different political universe, ask different questions, investigate different political phenomena, and offer different kinds of answers."[12] These characterizations implicitly raise an issue about the past and the future.

With respect to earlier works in comparative politics, are such claims much exaggerated, or are we actually witnessing a fundamental shift in research and theory building? In this volume, Almond insists that the state has hardly been ignored; Migdal suggests that its impact has simply been taken for granted and that its presence has been conceptually melded into the "center" and "modern" sectors of third-world countries. Although the issue of state autonomy has not been explicitly analyzed previously, there is a good deal to be said on behalf of this view, especially in light of the limits and limitations of the statist writings that were just noted. Perhaps a position that splits the difference represents the most accurate assessment. This is one that agrees with Krasner's depiction of statist studies as constituting a broad "challenge" to earlier ones, and then adding that they have carved out an empirically attractive and analytically secure site that has yet to be extensively developed.

This assessment can be phrased differently to get us into the issue of the future. The title of Skocpol's essay — "Bringing the State Back In" — which features the claim of a "paradigmatic reorientation," is the perfectly appropriate one for characterizing recent developments. It should now be possible to take the state seriously, as seriously as it deserves to be treated given the recent studies that have underscored and illuminated its consequentiality. Doing so involves the adoption of four "positions" with respect to future research and theory building.

(1) Having established that state actions do not consistently involve public officials striving to win societal support or being constrained by private actors, taking the state seriously involves more than being on the lookout for additional instances of autonomy. It means making purposeful efforts to establish the outer limits of its occurrence and the conditions under which it obtains. How often do states manage to act autonomously when the cards are stacked against their doing so because of unpropitious circumstances and conditions? For example, we might attempt to determine the incidence of autonomy where the politically best-endowed actors are arrayed against the state rather than divided among themselves, with respect to democratically structured states as opposed to authoritarian ones, in instances in which elected rather than bureaucratic officials constitute the relevant decision makers, in cases of local-level officials alone having their hands on the policy levers in contrast to those in which the "central decision makers" are involved, with respect to domestic issues rather than national-security issues, and under day-to-day circumstances in contrast to crisis conditions.

(2) Given the numerous and ambitious claims of society-centered explanations, in absolute terms and relative to what statist studies have produced, taking the state seriously as an independent variable involves considerably more than search-

ing for state-specific accounts of high and low autonomy. To allow for the full development of the state as an independent variable means raising fundamental questions about the validity and relative explanatory power of society-centered claims. At the same time, state determinism should be extended as far as persuasive reasoning and evidence allow; societal explanations for variations in autonomy should not be introduced until it is evident that statist ones are insufficient. The critical and wide-ranging importance of the state as an independent variable may be appreciated by recognizing that it bears upon autonomy in four distinct ways. According the state the "full treatment" thus involves a four-fold inquiry into what may loosely be termed its institutional weight — the impact of its recurring activities, decision rules and processes, organizational arrangements, and structural features upon both public and private actors.

First, variations in the state's institutional contours give more or less firm shape, and impart substantive content, to the policy preference of individual officials and their organizations, as well as helping to determine which officials will prevail in having their own preferences adopted as the state's. Second, institutional patterns go a long way in determining whether public officials decide to translate state preferences into public policy, especially when these diverge from societal preferences. Public officials recognize that institutional patterns sharply affect the possibilities of altering societal preferences, counteracting societal opposition, circumventing societal sanctions after acting autonomously, as well as impinging upon the likelihood of adopted policies achieving their intended goals or outcomes. Institutions provide the information, so to speak, that public officials use in assessing the efforts, costs, and risks involved in the pursuit of autonomy. Third, whether or not correctly perceived in any given instance, institutions offer public officials differentially advantageous positions and opportunities to transform, neutralize, and overcome societal opposition. The effectiveness of public officials in these respects, and thus their autonomy, very much hinges upon the state's internal features. Fourth, whether or not intentionally designed with this in mind, institutions make for differentially effective opposition to the state. They help pattern societal preferences and resources due to their impact upon political beliefs and attitudes; the level of political awareness and participation; the divisiveness within and alignments between classes, ethnic segments, and interest groups; the organizational contours of political and quasi-political organizations; the specialization of interest groups; and the proliferation of patron-client relations.[13]

(3) As a whole, societal determinism is hardly unpersuasive. The state *is* more or less deeply embedded in society. Taking the state seriously thus entails the bringing together of state- and society-centered analyses in a meaningful manner, in ways that parallel the coexistence and interrelationships between the state and society. State autonomy will be fully explicated only after the interactions of the two kinds of variables and their joint impact have been understood and, if possible, brought together in the form of theoretically integrated propositions. On the latter possibility, there is good reason to focus first upon the state and then work out from there. Since the dependent variable refers to the behavior of public officials, the immediately relevant explanations are to be found among the subjective factors that directly determine their more or less autonomous actions. The most common and salient explanations are likely to be officials' beliefs and perceptions concerning the opportunities, risks, and costs involved in the pursuit of autonomy. If these can be analytically delineated, it then becomes possible to inquire into the state *and* societal realms to identify those variables that impinge sharply upon the subjective ones.

(4) Taking state autonomy seriously, indeed doing so with respect to any "big" concept and issue, means more than plunging into research and formulating hypotheses. It entails at least a measure of analytical self-consciousness — in this instance, a delineation of the problématique of state autonomy.

## THE *PROBLÉMATIQUE* OF STATE AUTONOMY

A state is autonomous to the extent that it translates its own preferences into authoritative actions. A totally autonomous state, if there is such an entity, invariably acts as it chooses to act, and does not act when it prefers not to do so. Adumbrating the problématique of state autonomy involves more than clarifying the central concepts. Since the "state" and "state autonomy" have been used in different ways, the definitional choices need to be justified via an elaboration of their implications. A discussion of the state's interests and goals is also required — for any explanatory statement in the social sciences, be it an account of a single event, an elucidation of an institution's impact, or a wide-ranging theory of the state, requires some motivational component if it is to be complete and meaningful. And with the state being simultaneously separate from and embedded in society, how are the major variations in these relations to be depicted analytically? Addressing these issues should generate some useful by-products, some pointed questions for research and theory.

Of the several ways in which the state has been conceived, it is well to embrace a modified Weberian definition, all the more so when analyzing its autonomy. The state refers to all those individuals who occupy offices that authorize them, and them alone, to make and apply decisions that are binding upon any and all parts of a territorially circumscribed population. The state is made up of, and limited to, those individuals who are endowed with societywide decision-making powers.

The emphasis upon individuals is justified not only because so much of the state's importance derives from the societal significance of the officials' purposefully undertaken actions. This emphasis also helps avoid the all-too-common anthropomorphic fallacy that Weber had in mind. "For sociological purposes there is no such thing as a collective personality which 'acts.' When reference is made in a sociological context to a 'state' . . . or similar collectivities, what is meant is . . . *only* a certain kind of development of actual or possible social actions of individual persons."[14] Only individuals act, thereby obviating exclusively legal, juristic, and normative order definitions of the state, which was Weber's intention.

This consideration also rules out other much-used definitions that focus upon "public institutions," "institutional arrangements for rule," and "administrative and coercive systems," at least if they do not also refer to individual actors. Institutions, rules, and systems do not engage in authoritative or any other kind of action. Even an appreciation of the weightiness or manifold impact of state institutions does not justify their inclusion. They are either vacuous or variable as definitional components. If used loosely to refer to patterned interactions among state officials and units, virtually all states can be characterized as ensembles of different institutions. But this kind of characterization does no more than (superfluously?) remind us to inquire into their impact upon public and private actors, which then varies considerably depending upon the degree to which the state is genuinely "institutionalized."[15] If the definitional component is used in a stricter sense to refer only to institutionalized structures, it becomes a variable element that is not applicable to all states.

Following Weber's conception of the state as a compulsory territorial entity, it has commonly been defined in terms of the individuals who have a monopoly of coercive means at their disposal, often with the additional stipulation that the monopoly be a legitimate one. These definitional components are problematic. They refer to variable rather than universal elements. While most states enjoy a coercive monopoly, and while it is often a legitimate one, since states differ and change in these respects they should not find their way into a definition of the entire universe of states. Further, a central definition should minimize the objections of scholars working in different research traditions; it should be as analytically and ideologically neutral as possible so as to minimize prima facie objections to the theory in which it is employed, while allowing for the addition of more controversial and variable components at the appropriate points in the theory-building enterprise. This means not defining the state in terms of the bases of its authority, given the stark disagreements about the relative importance of coercive sanctions and legitimacy.

The state has also been defined exclusively in terms of its so-called "core," which is taken to mean only one or two of its most salient parts — the "central decision makers," the executive, the higher reaches of the permanent bureaucracy, and/or the "administrative, legal, and coercive apparatus." But even where such officials do constitute the centerpiece of the state, they are not consistently the only ones involved in the making of public policy. Where does such a definition leave influential, independent, and occasionally dominant legislatures? Surely they are not part of civil society, and their members are hardly deserving of being "conceptualized" as public employees. And since we are concerned with all authoritative actions we cannot leave out the officials of the municipal sewer commission if they do, in fact, play a significant policy-making role.

Just as our definition of the state is intended to be devoid of variable components, analytically neutral, and maximally inclusive without unnecessarily detracting from its meaningfulness, so too is the definition of state autonomy. According to the alternative definitions, the term becomes almost synonomous with a state's "strength" or "power" in relation to society, which is not surprising since the terms imply and overlap with one another.

According to one alternative definition, a strong state — an autonomous one — is able to negate societal demands; the greater the private resources standing behind the demands and the greater the resistance that the state is able to overcome, the greater its autonomy. This is how the term is used in neo-Marxist writings on the capitalist state. The state is "relatively autonomous" when it overcomes the opposition of the capitalist class that is taken to be dominant within civil society. Without elimiting the definition to one particular class, this is also how Skocpol defines the term: an autonomous state is one that prevails when its interests conflict with those of whichever class is economically and politically dominant.[16] Krasner also adopts this usage. But he does not restrict the definition unnecessarily to a dominant class, presumably because such an entity is not invariably present, and even when present, there are often other powerful actors pressuring the state. And Krasner adds a second, equally important dimension — the degree of societal change successfully engineered by the state. The state is increasingly autonomous or powerful to the extent that it is not only able to resist societal pressures, but also goes on to change private behavior patterns, and even alters the social and economic structure.[17] Both conceptions are meaningful in that they embrace demanding criteria that are difficult for most states to satisfy. Yet their very ambitiousness unnecessarily restricts the applicability of the autonomy concept and partly distorts its meaning.

To define autonomy in terms of the state acting on its interests only when these conflict with those held by the politically dominant private actors is analytically to exclude, or substantively to distort, those cases in which the state does so in the absence of a divergence in state-society preferences. There is no a priori reason to think of such states as weak or lacking in autonomy. To find that public officials are making public policies that derive from their own preferences is patently significant. And their doing so with societal support behind them is not necessarily less significant than their doing so in the face of societal opposition. Both intuitively and analytically, the former kind of state may be seen to be at least as "strong" as the latter — all the more so if (as is sometimes the case) it succeeds in purposefully reinforcing the political position or beliefs of those private actors whose societal preferences converge with its own. The state then has its own "strengths" to rely upon in addition to those stemming from the support given by societal actors.

There is another problem. What is one to make of a state that translates its preferences into public policy after having altered divergent societal preferences in accordance with its own? Surely this is a strong, autonomous state even though its authoritative actions are not taken in the face of societal opposition. The distinction between states that act on their preferences with and without societal support is undeniably crucial. But it is advisable, all the more so since nothing is to be lost, to use the term autonomy inclusively. Having done so, particular and generalized distinctions can be drawn among autonomous states on the basis of the societal support they enjoy and the opposition they encounter and overcome.[18]

There are also reasons for not defining autonomy in terms of the degree of societal change that the state has engineered, its success in purposefully altering behavioral patterns and structural contours. For one thing, state preferences do not regularly encompass such goals. Where they do not, the concept at best would be inapplicable and, at worst, would be used to define away the autonomy or strength of a large number of states. Those that act upon their ideological beliefs in circumscribing policy interventions and in re-privatizing public enterprises are surely "deserving" of being recognized as autonomous. In addition, the rationale for equating the strength of the state with the amount of change it brings about is at least partly off the mark. The critical measure of power is not the scope of change, but the amplitude of societal support the state enjoys and the degree of opposition it overcomes, whatever its objectives happen to be, including the preservation of the status quo. A state that succeeds in its aim of preserving an unbearable disparity in the distribution of social and economic values is not demonstrably weaker than one that brings about vast societal changes in the face of equally potent opposition. Nor is it unreasonable to depict a state that has enormous support in preserving the status quo as being as strong overall as one that has engineered great changes despite enormous opposition.

Compared with these alternative definitions of autonomy, the one offered here is thus at least as meaningful, avoids some untenable assumptions, has the advantage of being more encompassing, and encourages the introduction of narrower, more demanding criteria as the bases for distinguishing among types of autonomous actions.

How then are we to conceive of the preferences of the state, whose translation into authoritative actions constitutes its autonomy? Given the encompassing definition of autonomy, state preferences are necessarily conceptualized in a corresponding manner. In fact, the justification of an inclusive notion of state preferences would largely overlap with what has just been said about autonomy.

Although the term preference may imply unity or consensus, it should certainly not be taken to mean that all those officials who manifest a preference with respect to the issue at hand are in agreement. State preferences are usually the product of at least some internal conflict, competition, pulling and pushing, bargaining, compromise, and coalition building. In the absence of agreement, the aggregation of individual preferences obviously involves far more than a counting of heads. State preferences should thus be viewed as the resultant of the interested official's resource-weighted preferences. "Weight" is based on the number of officials on different sides of the issue, the powers of their offices, the distributable rewards and punishments they control, their strategic position with respect to the issue at hand, as well as the information, expertise, and political skills at their disposal, as these in turn are mediated by institutional decision rules and informal norms.

Substantively, state preferences refer to authoritative actions and inactions with respect to any and all objects and relations. These "targets" of public policy include not only all aspects of society and economy, the collective and noncollective values of private individuals and their behavioral interactions. They also encompass state-society relations, the regime structure and its rules and penalties for pressuring and replacing public officials, as well as intrastate relations, such as the distribution of responsibilities, missions, and budgets among state units and changes in the latter's hierarchically ordered and functionally specific powers. Since all of these constitute potentially or currently salient issues for at least some public (and private) actors, they bear upon the state's autonomy.

If possible, state preferences should have considerable analytical "bite." Ideally, we would identify a small number of motivations that consistently, if not invariably, impart substantive content and directionality to these preferences. But is there an inclusive motivational component, one that encompasses all the prominent values, interests, and goals that shape the state's preferences?

Several candidates come to mind immediately. These include the state's collective interests in preserving itself, maintaining political order, and securing its territory and population. In addition, there are the officials' interests in continuing to occupy their offices and maintaining the prerogatives of the organizations within which they are situated.

These constitute a powerful, invariably present set of motivations. However, even taken all together they are not consistently relevant, not regularly activated in reacting to policy issues. Nor are these interests fully inclusive. Can we afford to ignore the policy-salient motivations of some public officials to further the public interest as they see it, to view themselves and the state as legitimate actors, to maintain a positive public identity and self-image, to gain a sense of professional competence, to attain a feeling of solidarity, to carry out their responsibilities in a routine or generally convenient manner, to advance their careers, and to fulfill their "private" interests?

With the ideal of substantive inclusiveness being unrealizable, a second-best alternative might still prove useful — that of delineating a motivational component that is consistently salient, regularly related to the fulfillment of whatever substantive interests underlie the state's preferences. One of these is the state's capacities for autonomous action. These are clearly valued since the translation of state preferences into public policy entails a partial to complete fulfillment of the interests from which the preferences are derived. So too is societal support — the noncoerced behavior of societal actors that is on balance politically supportive of the state's preferences and the "corresponding" public officials. Societal support not only goes a very long way in making for autonomy, but when achieved via societal support, the efforts, costs, and risks of autonomous actions are minimized, in many instances approaching zero. With these points in mind, a quick review of the large handful of collective, organizational, and individual interests that shape the state's preferences should indicate that they are substantially, often fully, realized when the state has the capacity for autonomous action and enjoys societal support.

To say that autonomy and societal support are consistently salient and valued does not mean that both are present, simultaneously achievable, or equally salient and valued. There is, of course, a fundamental, frequently activated contradiction between them. For like all authoritative and directive entities, the state is situated in a societal environment but not fully of it. Being separate from society by virtue of the authoritative positions they occupy, even the officials of an open, highly permeable state commonly subscribe to distinctive interests and beliefs that make for policy preferences that diverge from those of society's. And being embedded in society and subject to the state's directives, private actors commonly hold preferences that diverge from the state's, concomitantly prompting a variably activated interest in influencing and constraining its actions. Understanding how the trade-offs and offshoots of these contradictions are viewed and addressed by the state, and whether they are "resolved" in favor of the state, society, or both, constitutes an encompassing issue in the study of state-society relations.

There are, then, compelling reasons to bring autonomy and support together as the two dimensions of a classificatory scheme that is applicable to the universe of states, to any of its subsets, to any single state over time, and (with some modification) to any one action or inaction on the part of a given state. The typology depicted in Figure III.1 roughly distinguishes among strong, independent, responsive, and weak states. These are the ones that rank high or low on the autonomy and support dimensions; much of the classificatory space is left empty even though many states exhibit a moderate ranking in one or both respects.

Strong states are those that enjoy high autonomy and support. They are doubly strong in that they regularly act on their preferences and have societal support in doing so. Independent states rank high in autonomy and low in support. They frequently translate their preferences into public policy despite divergent societal preferences. Acting in accordance with societal preferences, responsive states are characterized by low autonomy and high support. Weak states are doubly so. They strive to act autonomously despite divergent societal preferences, but failing to do so, they rank low in both autonomy and support.

The typology implicitly raises, and can be used to address, the fundamental issues of state autonomy and many involving state-society relations. With what kind of frequency do public officials act autonomously as societal support varies? How is the convergence and divergence of state-society preferences

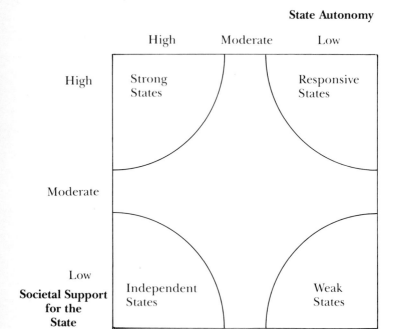

**State Autonomy**

|                                | High | Moderate | Low |
|--------------------------------|------|----------|-----|

High — Strong States — Responsive States

Moderate

Low
**Societal Support
for the
State** — Independent States — Weak States

FIGURE III.1.  *A Typology of States*

to be understood? Do some states place a demonstrably higher value upon autonomy relative to support, or are the values roughly equivalent, with the differences in the rankings relating primarily to the opportunities for acting autonomously? Under conditions of divergence, why do some states attempt and succeed in transforming societal preferences? Where preferences diverge, why are some states autonomous while others are constrained? Are the answers to these questions to be found primarily in the public or the private realm?

The four-fold typology also helps generate a somewhat narrower set of questions. Do independent states that rank high in autonomy and low in support tend to rule in a consular manner, governing from above by ignoring society, or do they rely upon their resistance capacities to overcome societal opposition? Over and above being constrained by the expectation of societal sanctions, might not some responsive states with low autonomy and high support constitute instances of public officials allowing their preferences to be shaped in accordance with those of certain societal actors, the officials dissuading themselves from acting on their preferences in the belief that authoritative actions will not produce the desired policy goals or outcomes? Do authoritarian states regularly turn out to be independent and democratic states responsive, or are they not all that dissimilar in these respects, their more salient differences relating to the kinds of societal resources and actors who are effective in influencing their policies? Can democratic states be accurately characterized as being at least as strong as totalitarian ones? When one kind of regime structure is about to give way to another, is the state at that time usually a weak one, or is it just as likely to be independent or responsive?

It is no mere understatement to say that all these questions cannot be answered here, even if they could be addressed fully at this juncture in research and theory building. Still, the aim of the next section is hardly unambitious. The attempt to develop a theoretical account of variations in state autonomy that relies exclusively upon the attributes of the state for its independent variables speaks to several of the questions that were just raised, and does so precisely because state determinism is taken as seriously as it deserves to be.

## THE STATE AS AN INDEPENDENT ACTOR
## AND AN INDEPENDENT VARIABLE

A full explication of just about any political phenomenon features both subjective and structural variables, with pride of analytical place being assigned to one or the other depending upon what is being interpreted or theorized. The analysis of state autonomy may profitably begin at the subjective level. As a behavioral phenomenon state autonomy is immediately explicable in terms of the officials' beliefs and perceptions — those relating to the value, costs, risks, and opportunities of autonomous action. After identifying and delineating the salient subjective variables, they can be put to good use in identifying the most common and important structural variables that impinge upon them, concomitantly illuminating the ways and paths along which they do so. In addition, the clear-cut distinction between the two kinds of variables helps give the analytical end product an internally coherent form at different levels of explanation.

Variations in autonomous behavior are shaped by four subjective variables that exhaust all the possibilities at this level of analysis. Most briefly, autonomy varies in accordance with the degree to which public officials are susceptible to expressions of societal interests in forming and modifying their preferences; the greater or lesser importance that they attribute to active societal support in assessing how much of it they can forgo in acting on their own preferences; the extent to which public officials believe themselves capable of counteracting the societal opposition that is likely to precede and follow the adoption of their preferred public policies; and the officials' more or less optimistic expectations that their preferred policies will produce the intended outcomes. When these subjective attributes of the relevant public officials are considered together, we can refer (respectively) to the malleability, insulation, resilience, and vulnerability of the state. In short-hand fashion, the extent to which the state is MIRVed constitutes an exhaustive explication of its autonomy at this level of analysis: malleability and vulnerability are negatively, and insulation and resilience are positively, related to autonomy.

This fourfold proposition does not take us nearly far enough, even after it is elaborated. For it is not an especially "deep" explanation of state autonomy; the literal and figurative "distance" between the subjective variables and autonomous actions is less than impressive. The issue then becomes one of identifying those structural features of the state that (do and do not) impinge sharply upon each of the MIRVed properties — those structural patterns that shape the officials' perceived opportunities and risks, their calculations of likely costs and benefits, and the beliefs and interests that bear upon autonomous actions. The subjectively conceptualized malleability, insulation, resilience, and vulnerability of the state thereby come to be intervening attributes standing between the state's structural features and autonomous actions.

*Malleability*

A fully autonomous state not only translates its preferences into public policy, they are very much its own preferences. Two states may be equally successful in acting upon their preferences, but if one of them has allowed them to be shaped by the known interests of societal actors it is substantially less autonomous than the one that has acted upon its own preferences.

Malleable states are decidedly susceptible and receptive to societal interests in forming and altering their preferences — and this quite apart from the constraining impact of societal demands, pressures, and leverage. At the extreme, some public officials simply adopt the preferences of certain societal actors as their "own"; others are positively disposed to "private tutoring" in forming their preferences; still others are willing to look to private actors for some guidance and cues. This is not to suggest that a minimally malleable state ignores society. Indeed, its preferences may be affected by any and all aspects of society, including a full awareness of the interests of particular private actors. However, the information is treated as "data" that officials interpret, assess, puzzle through, and otherwise react to according to their own lights. The preferences of a minimally malleable state are shaped within its precincts — by what public officials do, where they sit, whom they intereact with, what they see and know, along with the individual, organizational, and collective interests that regularly emerge in the course of "serving" the state.

Two structural variables go a long way in accounting for variations in the state's malleability — its boundedness vis à vis society and its internal differentiation. Like any other social unit, states are more or less bounded relative to the actors in their environment; literally and figuratively, the separating walls vary enormously in height and porousness. A well-bounded state is made up of state careerists at all levels. Officials remain within the public sector throughout most of their careers, middle- and high-ranking positions are filled from within the state, and length of service is an important criterion for elevation into them. In a poorly bounded state, officials move back and forth between the public and private sectors, lateral entry is commonplace at all levels, and ascent to its higher reaches is fairly rapid.[19]

There are several connections between boundedness and malleability. State careerists have a bevy of issue-relevant memories and experiences to draw upon in reacting to alternative policy options; they have little need to go looking for "private tutors." Given their length of service, they tend to hold their preferences firmly, all the more so since they have long-standing incentives and psychological reasons to convince themselves that the promotion of their individual, organizational, and collective interests tends to be congruent, if not consonant with, the fulfillment of the "public interest." Moreover, low boundaries usually make for a shallow socialization into state mores and values. With officials spending only short terms within the state and new recruits being brought in at middle and high levels, political learning is limited and conformist pressures are minimal, and less than effective when exerted. Over and above any material inducements, "in and outers" may well identify so closely with the private actors whom they have worked with, for, and under, and with whom they expect to establish similar relationships in the future, that they allow themselves to be guided by these actors' preferences.

Variations in malleability are also due to the state's differentiation — the number of its separate units and their spatially and functionally diverse responsibilities. The differentiated state is a corpuscular and specialized state. With specialization comes expertise and a substantial measure of subjectively experienced competence, which is to say that officials tend to subscribe to their preferences with much conviction. Experts are neither disposed to being guided by societal actors nor readily impressed by their interpretations of all sorts of hard and soft data. A corpuscular state tends to generate its own preferences. Councils, committees, departments, bureaus, agencies, commissions, and boards react to policy alternatives in accordance with their organizational routines, strategic vantage points, and collective interests, notably the maintenance of their budgetary allotments, formal powers, and programmatic missions. The internal features of well-bounded and differentiated states thus come to have a pronounced and durable impact upon policy preferences.

To underscore the pronounced impact of these two structural variables, it is worth considering a seemingly plausible alternative explanation — the availability of easy and frequent access to the state on the part of private actors. Where access is commonly granted, the preferences of public officials are likely to be shaped by expressions of private interests; to be heard face-to-face, usually in an informal setting, is conducive to persuasion and frankness. Although often attributed to a state's decentralized structure, access itself is not an internal feature of the state, but rather a dimension of state-society relations. To suggest that the state's openness to society barely impinges upon malleability is thus an especially telling point on behalf of the relative explanatory power of boundedness and differentiation.

The significance of access is partly misconceived in that it is often granted for reasons unrelated to the officials' receptivity to societal interests. Private actors are welcomed so that officials can obtain information, elicit societal preferences so as to deflect or alter them, and gain societal support by giving some recognition and a sympathetic hearing to (the leaders of) private associations. The significance of access is overrated because it is often limited to its literal meaning — the opening of doors, entry into vestibules and offices, meetings in corridors. To be seen and heard does not necessarily make for persuasion, given the considerable gap between them. Access is frequently superfluous and face-to-face meetings irrelevant, since public officials are often well aware of particular private interests. They can readily know of or can surmise their content from newspaper reports, editorials, petitions, demonstrations, election results, opinion surveys, and the private actors' socioeconomic characteristics and past actions. It is only the detailed aspects of private preferences and publicly embarrassing concerns that need to be expressed face to face.

## Insulation

The autonomy of any social unit is very much a function of its dependence upon the actors in its environment. The autonomy of public officials is maximized (at least in the short run) when they believe themselves to have little need for active societal support. With politically supportive behavior having little importance for such an insulated state, it can afford to act on its own preferences when these diverge sharply from latent societal interests and manifest preferences.

The most thoroughly insulated of states are well represented by "sultanism," Weber's extreme type of absolutist rule. The ruler is so little concerned with the supportive behavior of his subjects that he treats them almost as if they were his personal property. The ruler's authority over them is appropriated just as he would "any ordinary object of possession," allowing him "to sell it, to pledge it as security, or to divide it by inheritance."[20] A fully insulated state is concerned with only one kind of societal behavior — that relating to the maintenance of "law and order," compliance with public laws, regulations, and directives. A poorly insulated state has a perceived need for some combination of several kinds of active support — such as the votes cast for incumbent officials and political parties, the turnout and the number of "yes" ballots in state-sponsored referenda, contributions of all sorts to the incumbents' electoral campaigns, public words of endorsement and demonstrations on behalf of the government and its policies, high turnouts at state-sponsored rallies, enthusiastic receptions for the government's leading figures, and the calling and calling off of politically inspired strikes and work stoppages.

Variations in the state's insulation can largely be accounted for with a single variable: the state's position on the cohesiveness-divisiveness continuum. The public officials of a highly cohesive state assign similar priorities to the issues on (and off) the agenda, hold substantively similar policy preferences, and resolve those issues on which preferences differ according to widely agreed-upon decision rules. A thoroughly divided state exhibits just the opposite characteristics, with divisions over the decision rules extending to the hierarchical position and responsibilities of state units and offices.

There are two connections between cohesiveness and insulation. Dependence upon private actors and their political resources is lessened to the extent that the state's resources are maximized. In a cohesive state any one set of officials has the resources of others to rely on in freeing itself from a dependence upon societal actors. In the case of divided states, public officials find it difficult to circumvent or mitigate the impact of societal support and opposition since private actors are advantageously situated to play them off against one another. And officials who do not have adequate intrastate resources to prevail in the formulation of state preferences have an incentive to turn to sympathetic private actors for additional support, quite possibly followed by an "escalating" dependence as other officials also turn to private actors to buttress their positions within the state.

In addition, cohesive states can better insulate themselves through the use of force, choosing to rely upon the application of coercive measures rather than upon more or less freely given support. The decision to employ force is an exceptionally consequential one; it has the potential for extensive and divisive repercussions within the state. Divided states are consequently more reluctant to resort to force than are cohesive ones whose intrastate bonds serve to mitigate or at least partially offset the more or less likely divisions. The repression of potential and active opponents may well run counter to the attachments of some officials to the targeted societal actors, if not also to their political values and regime norms. Coercion sometimes contradicts institutional interests, including those of the officer corps whose professional and heroic self-image is often tarnished when soldiers are transformed into policemen and force is used against unarmed nationals. The turn to force threatens the standing of those officials whose offices and institutions would be downgraded as the state's center of gravity shifts toward the security forces. And there may be a diffuse concern that the repression of private actors will spill over into the state, that public officials will suffer its unintended consequences as they too become potential targets. Of course, some divided states also opt for repressive rule, but because they are divided the case for repression usually has to be a far stronger one, perhaps bordering on a rationale of self-preservation. As such, divided states turn to force less often.

Quite apart from this connection between cohesiveness and a reliance upon coercion, there is the possibility that insulation varies with the state's coercive capacities. Public officials can afford to ignore or downplay the importance of low support levels to the extent that they control numerous armed personnel, in absolute terms or relative to population size. A state with abundant military, paramilitary, and police forces can dissuade opponents from actively challenging its authoritative actions and can put down outlawed opposition if it does arise. Being able to deter and defend against opposition efforts, such a state sees itself as being little affected by low or declining support levels, while a state with minimal coercive capacities might even put its survival at risk if it is politically inattentive.

This rationale may appear persuasive. There is, however, no more than a weak relationship between the absolute or relative number of armed personnel and its coercive significance. The decision of disaffected actors who might well turn to prohibited forms of opposition is a function of the probability of being identified, arrested, or captured, and of the severity of the consequent sanctions they would suffer. Yet the number of armed personnel is totally unrelated to the latter and has a barely discernible impact upon the former. In most societies, even a small security force can reasonably be expected to deter illegal opposition since it places the vast majority of private actors at risk; opponents of the state cannot easily evade detection, arrest, and capture unless they move into the (frequently nonexistent) hills, and even there they are rarely able to stave off the military. Only when small- to large-scale violence has already appeared is the size of the security forces critical. The state's dependence upon its societal supporters increases with the spread of armed opposition, which is related to the size (and effectiveness) of the security forces.

## Resilience

The autonomy of any social unit is enhanced to the extent that it can free itself from the constraints that the actors in its environment seek to impose upon it. Autonomy is maximized when a social unit can deal effectively with those actors whose divergent preferences prompt them to try to control its actions. The resilience of the state refers to its perceived capacities for counteracting potential and actual societal opposition — opposition whose aims may range from the implementation of an administrative ruling to the overthrow of the state.

A highly resilient state believes itself to be exceedingly well endowed with resistance capacities. These capacities can be used to counteract divergent preferences in and of themselves, their translation into determined opposition activities, and/or the impact of such activities upon the state. Public officials see themselves as being capable of altering, perhaps transforming, societal preferences to make them convergent with their own; dissuading and restraining the challengers from (fully) employing their resources and capitalizing upon their points of leverage; and/or neutralizing the effectiveness of the constraining resources that are deployed. A minimally resilient state believes itself to be largely incapable of altering societal preferences, mitigating opposition efforts, or diminishing their impact.

We have already encountered the two structural variables — differentiation and cohesiveness — that explain most of the variation in the resilience of states. The officials of a well-differentiated state are advantageously situated to alter societal preferences that diverge from their own. They might capitalize upon their status as experts to articulate and justify their preferences in a politically neutral, nonpartisan idiom, emphasizing their consideration of the policy options in a thoroughly rational, technical, legalistic, or otherwise professional manner. The specialization of offices and units fosters a diversity of skills — from the skillful interpretation of technical data supplied by well-staffed interest groups to the agile manipulation of public symbols — that can be put to effective use in mitigating the constraining efforts of private actors and their impact upon the state. Out of their well-focused, specialized activities, public officials develop a storehouse of experiences in dealing with particular private interests and pressures that are useful in determining how best to counteract them. With an abundance of councils, agencies, departments, boards, committees, and commissions, the differentiated state is a complex, opaque entity; its decision sites, processes, and responsibilities are hard to pinpoint from outside its precincts, as well as being potentially manipulable by public officials bent upon circumventing societal constraint efforts. It thus becomes very difficult for the many private actors who reside at some "distance" from the state to bring their resources to bear upon its salient parts.

Variations in the resilience of states are also explained by their cohesiveness. The possibility of altering divergent societal preferences is viewed more optimistically by public officials who can profit from high cohesiveness in appearing to speak for the state as a whole. The articulation of a consistent and coherent message is of critical importance in shaping societal preferences; where public officials aim to transform widespread societal beliefs, values, and preferences, cohesiveness comes close to constituting a necessary condition for the "activation" of this strategy. Cohesiveness also encourages efforts to counteract societal opposition. At the extreme, the officials of a cohesive state view themselves as so advantaged that they are fully confident of their ability to deal with all manner of societal opponents, if not also expecting the latter to take the same view of the matter and thus be deterred from mounting a challenge. At a rather consequential minimum, the officials of a cohesive state are fully aware of their ability to marshal the resources and coordinate the actions of the state in fragmenting, neutralizing, and otherwise offsetting and countering the deployment of private resources.

It is commonly said that the degree of state centralization — the concentration or dispersion of decision sites — bears sharply upon the stength, power, and autonomy of states. One connection between the centralization and resilience of states runs through their cohesiveness: the resources of a centralized state can be pooled and its actions coordinated, thereby sharply negating private pressures. However, this connection is already covered by the cohesiveness variable; the concentration-dispersion of decision sites does not add anything in this regard. In fact, a focus upon centralization would weaken the proposition since it does not regularly make for cohesiveness; the occupants of one or two decision sites may well be as sorely divided as are the occupants of five or six. For policy divisions among the occupants of different decision sites *and* of any one of them are frequently the product of differences in the officials' generational ages, professional training, factional affiliations, partisan loyalties, ideological beliefs, and ethnic identities. And there is no reason to suppose that their impact is any less than that of the officials' organizational and decisional locations. Moreover, decentralized states are especially cohesive with respect to "low" policy issues. In spatially and functionally segmented states, different sets of officials tend to deal separately and exclusively with narrow bands of public policy. The many units usually have little or no interest in one another's policy activities; where overlapping interests do make for different policy positions they are poorly situated to influence the actions of other units.

The other connection between centralization and resilience looks like this: when a state's formal powers and policy instruments are dispersed among numerous decision sites, any one of them is sorely weakened in its ability to resist societal pressures; even those private actors who are not well endowed with political resources can exert effective pressures upon the separate, small, and thus nonresilient state units. However, in this reasoning what matters most is not the internal structure of the state, but the position of the salient public and private actors *relative* to one another. The critical factor is not the concentration-dispersion of decision sites: it is the fit between this variable and the size and resources of societal groups. A decentralized state would be disadvantaged in confronting a few large groups, and a centralized state would be well placed in countering the pressures of many weak ones. Yet neither pattern is especially common. State and societal actors have a habit of adapting to one another organizationally when they regularly engage in cooperative, bargaining, or conflictual relations. Of the two common patterns — a centralized state facing a few large groups of societal actors and a decentralized state confronting many small ones — there is little reason to suppose that the centralized state is better able to resist societal demands than is its decentralized counterpart.

One other proposition should be considered. Perhaps the most often heard explanation for state autonomy, power, or strength relates the number of policy means or instruments at the state's disposal to what is, in effect, its resilience. Public officials who have their hands on numerous policy levers for extracting societal resources, distributing public resources, and regulating private behavior can use these levers as carrots and sticks with which to counteract societal demands and opposition. Jobs and promotions within the public sector, contracts, licenses, exemptions, the speed with which laws are implemented, the strictness with which they are enforced, and all manner of administrative rulings, legal interpretations, and discretionary behavior can be used to deter, discourage, and coopt societal challengers.

This reasoning is eminently persuasive. It also happens to be incomplete: there is another side to the proverbial coin. A state that is well endowed with policy instruments invariably takes authoritative actions that are patently consequential for a panoply of private interests. It thereby generates wants, expectations, and deprivations whose number and intensity motivate private actors to exert, mobilize, and organize themselves on behalf of their own preferences. A wide range of policy instruments simultaneously enhances the state's resilience and multiplies the societal demands and pressures that are to be resisted if the state is to act autonomously. The political activism inspired by the state's policy instruments might not fully offset their enhancement of the state's resilience. But their neutralizing impact is sufficient to warrant our not relying upon policy capacities in this respect.

*Vulnerability*

A social unit with sufficient wherewithal to act upon its preferences may yet be disinclined to do so; the likely results of pursuing its preferred course of action, the probability of its intended goals being realized, are assessed less than optimistically. The vulnerability of the state speaks to the choice of acting more or less autonomously depending upon the expected success or failure of the policy ventures embodied in its preferences.

A vulnerable state is dissuaded (more precisely, it dissuades itself) from translating its preferences into authoritative actions in the expectation that the intended goals will probably not be realized, the desired policy outcomes not achieved, the policies not successfully implemented. An invulnerable or minimally vulnerable state's translation of its preferences into public policy is not negated by an expectation of likely policy failure.

Variations in the vulnerability of states are explicated by their policy capacities — the variable that was just said to be problematic with respect to their resilience. Public officials realize that some policy goals cannot be realized by offering material incentives, by making other-regarding appeals, or by simply issuing laws and regulations. These means are (respectively) in short supply, ineffective, and not adequately fine tuned. The attainment of some goals requires structures of implementation — formal powers and organized personnel — to direct and regulate private behavior, distribute public resources, and extract societal resources. In the absence of an appropriate and presumptively effective policy instrument, the state is disinclined to act upon its preferences. While any one instrument may be seen as suitable, it may also be seen as procedurally cumbersome, be overly inclusive or narrow in scope, be tainted with a poor track record, or be held in disrepute by the relevant societal actors. The existence of several policy capabilities that are potentially adaptable, expandable, or suitable for the goal at hand clearly increases the likelihood of an appropriate and effective capability being available. And in these instances there will invariably be "interested" officials attempting to persuade skeptical ones that their organizations are indeed capable of effective policy implementation.

Still, this generalization is limited in its explanatory range. Its applicability is circumscribed, limited to those policy preferences that involve heightened state intervention for their realization and a change in interventionist strategies and means. The number of available policy instruments does not bear significantly upon the state's vulnerability with respect to preferences involving the contraction or continuation of interventionist policies, of numerous foreign policy and defense issues, of most of the rules governing state-society relations, and of the allocation of powers, resources, and budgets within the state.

This explanatory gap might, of course, be filled with another yet "undiscovered" state-specific variable. However, it is more likely that those aspects of a state's vulnerability that cannot be accounted for, in terms of its policy capacities, can be explained largely by one or more society-centered variables — a possibility that leads into the concluding section of this essay.

### BACK TO THE BEGINNING AND A LITTLE BEYOND

To summarize, state autonomy is immediately understood in terms of four subjective properties of the state: its malleability, insulation, resilience, and vulnerability. Their variations are in turn explained by four structural features: the state's boundedness, differentiation, cohesiveness, and policy capacities. These features account for state autonomy along the paths and in the ways identified by the intervening subjective variables. We also found that easy and frequent access to the state, the size of its coercive forces, the concentration-dispersion of its decision sites, and its policy capacities (in connection with the state's resilience) have no more than a marginal impact upon the subjective MIRVed variables. As such, the relative explanatory power of the four structural features is concomitantly heightened; the latter may even exhaust the general features of the state at this level of analysis. Here then is a reasonably parsimonious, integrated, and coherent theory of the state as an independent actor based exclusively upon the state as an independent variable.

The next step in taking the state seriously gets into a "deeper" level of explanation and moves from the heuristically prior static analysis of autonomy to its "dynamics." How are changes and variations in the four structural variables to be explicated? How can we account for their development, maintenance, and alteration over time, their variations among states, and, certainly not to be ignored, their differential appearance within certain types of state institutions? These questions can readily be pursued while continuing to take the state seriously as an independent actor and an independent variable. Whatever the specific accounts of changes and variations in the structural variables, we should simultaneously be asking whether these entail more or less autonomous actions and whether the explanations are state or society centered. There is, moreover, this distinct possibility: less than fully autonomous officials manage to alter the state's structural features so as to enhance their capacities and opportunities for autonomous action.

This possibility may even be a pattern with respect to externally inspired issues — which would hardly be surprising since the state is commonly first and foremost in dealing with external actors and international exigencies. At times it confronts other states, at others it is compressed and constricted by them, with respect to security, the economy, and other issues of the greatest salience for state and society. According to Tilly's historical account of European state building, the impetus came from the international arena as it engendered a perceived need for a larger and larger military establishment on the part of the state, which in turn necessitated higher levels of taxation, followed by the expansion and differentiation of the bureaucracy so as to endow the state with the policy instruments to collect them.[21] International circumstances and the dominant officials' foreign policy preferences combined to highlight the latter's problematic realization, which then prompted structural changes that enhanced the state's autonomy. A broadly similar account applies to some Latin American states in their encounters with the transnational actors of the wealthy, industrialized countries. In attempting to control and benefit from these dealings, the states expanded their technocratic elements and policy instruments for directing the domestic economy. Even a Chilean state that readily accommodated transnational capital created a "Copper Department" to monitor the foreign-owned industry. The newly trained officials subsequently made it possible for the state to act on its preferences in taking over and operating the copper mines as public enterprises.[22]

Cameron's analysis[23] of the "openness" of the industrialized countries' economies to the international economy also fits into this kind of explanatory framework: the state acts autonomously in reacting to the international environment, its authoritative actions concomitantly enhancing its capacities and opportunities for other autonomously undertaken actions. Here the connections between the percentage of GNP made up of exports and imports and the growth of public expenditures occur along a statist and societal path. Where the economy is heavily trade dependent the state is limited in its capacity to manage the domestic economy. The state is vulnerable with respect to preferences involving the management of aggregate demand, unemployment levels, and capital formation. In order to gain more managerial leverage when confronted with fluctuations in the international economy public officials purposefully extract and allocate a larger proportion of economic resources. The societal path begins with openness to the international economy resulting in an above-average concentration of industry. The latter makes for high rates of unionization and strong labor confederations, which in turn lead to the frequent election of left-dominated governments that are given to increasing public expenditures.

These society-centered explanations bring us back to the beginning of the essay. Although state autonomy was purposefully not defined relative to societal preferences and resources, there is no doubt that its full explication will involve relational hypotheses — explanations that focus upon the relations (e.g., ratios, congruity, consonance) between state and societal variables. Taking the state seriously involves bringing statist and societal accounts of state autonomy together in empirically meaningful, mutually illuminating, and analytically integrated ways. What makes for considerable difficulty in doing so at the outset is certainly not a shortage of societal condidates; there is rather an *embarras des richesse* to contend with in attempting to determine which hypotheses at widely differing levels of explanation enjoy the most plausibility. There is another difficulty. The impact of many of the societal variables upon state autonomy has not been clearly spelled out; much has been left unsaid, implicit, and vague about the reasons, channels, and ways in which they affect the state.

This essay offers the beginnings of a "solution." With the subjective MIRVed variables constituting the immediate explanations of behavioral autonomy, and they being exhaustive of the possibilities at this level of analysis, the question becomes: What are the societal variables that account for variations in state autonomy via their impact upon the state's malleability, insulation, resilience, and vulnerability? These MIRVed variables may be used as a theoretical beachhead from which to reconnoiter and then to move into the societal interior in search of the critical variables. They could also be used as an analytical sieve to sort out the societal "nuggets," simultaneously identifying the channels through which they impinge upon state autonomy.

By way of briefly showing something of what might be accomplished, consider the oft-heard generalization that the state's autonomy is markedly heightened when the contending societal actors are equally balanced in their political and politically fungible resources. The MIRVed variables suggest precisely how and why one variable impinges upon the other. An equal balance heightens both the state's insulation and its resilience. Its dependence upon societal support is sharply diminished since the contending groups, classes, or ethnic segments substantially neutralize the significance of one another's constraining resources, perhaps leaving public officials free to act on their own preferences — at a minimum, allowing them to choose whom to rely upon for support. The state also becomes more resilient in being advantageously situated to counteract societal pressures and leverage by playing off the rivals against one another. This "finding" may then be used to suggest that the balance of contending resources is a more powerful explanation for state autonomy than is the overall level of political mobilization, for the proportion of politically aware and active individuals bears only upon one of the MIRVed variables. The state is less resilient in that far more is required of it to counteract the demands of a politically mobilized population.

As another illustration of the analytical usefulness of the MIRVed variables, take the numerous statements that have related the number and organizational depth of a society's intermediary associations to state autonomy. Starting with de Tocqueville, and extending through political pluralism and theories of mass society, to current work on societal corporatism in Western Europe, some very different kinds of connections have been drawn between intermediary associations and the state. They could be profitably disentangled, assessed, weighed, and elucidated by relying upon the MIRVed variables. Take the conflicting assertions found in recent corporatist studies. It is said that state autonomy is limited by the "representational monopolies" enjoyed by highly organized peak associations of employers and workers. It is also said that state autonomy is enhanced insofar as the existence of national, hierarchically organized trade unions allows the state to impose unwanted economic policies upon the rank-and-file membership.[24] But might it not be that both claims are partly valid? The former relates to autonomy via the state's limited resilience in counteracting the well-populated and highly organized associations; the latter affects autonomy via the state's low vulnerability in being able to implement its policies successfully.

Despite the demonstrable significance of society, an essay on taking the state seriously should not conclude on this note. We can bring the state back for an encore by noting that when the explication of societal phenomena is taken one step further, it often leads squarely back to the state — to its institutions and recurring policy activities. To continue with intermediary associations, the state can help explain their greater or lesser proliferation, as in de Tocqueville's "modernistic" interpretation of their scarcity in prerevolutionary

France. The state's autonomously undertaken fiscal policies featured the collective or communal, rather than the individual, assessment of taxes in each village. "Every taxpayer [consequently] had an urgent and unfailing motive for spying on his neighbors and promptly notifying the collector of any increase in their means."[25] Recurring state policies thereby gave the French political culture a decidedly suspicious cast, thereby inhibiting the formation of voluntary associations that impinge upon the state's autonomy — a statist impact that extended into the nineteenth century and the first half of the twentieth.

**NOTES**

1. Samuel P. Huntington, *Political Order in Changing Societies* (New Haven, Conn: Yale University Press, 1968).
2. Ibid., 20.
3. Ralph Miliband, *Marxism and Politics* (New York: Oxford University Press, 1977); Alan Wolfe, *The Limits of Legitimacy: Political Contradictions of Contemporary Capitalism* (New York: Free Press, 1970); Goran Therborn, *What Does the Ruling Class Do When It Rules? State Power and State Apparatuses under Feudalism, Capitalism, and Socialism* (London: New Left Books, 1978); Ernest Mandel, *Late Capitalism,* translated by Jarus DeBres (Atlantic Highlands, N.J.: Humanities Press, 1975); Erik Olin Wright, *Class, Crisis, and the State* (London: New Left Books, 1978); Claus Offe, "Structural Problems of the Capitalist State," in *German Political Studies,* edited by Klaus von Beyme (Beverly Hills, Calif.: Sage, 1971); Nicos Poulantzas, *Political Power and Social Classes* (London: New Left Books, 1973).
4. Eric A. Nordlinger, *On the Autonomy of the Democratic State* (Cambridge, Mass.: Harvard University Press, 1981), 174–81.
5. Hugh Heclo, *Modern Social Politics in Britain and Sweden* (New Haven, Conn.: Yale University Press, 1974).
6. Alfred C. Stepan, *The State and Society: Peru in Comparative Perspective* (Princeton, N.J.: Princeton University Press, 1978).
7. Ellen Kay Trimberger, *Revolution from Above: Military Bureaucrats and Development in Japan, Turkey, Egypt, and Peru* (New Brunswick, N.J.: Transaction Books, 1978).
8. Stephen D. Krasner, *Defending the National Interest: Raw Materials Investments and U.S. Foreign Policy* (Princeton, N.J.: Princeton University Press, 1978), 55–57.

9. Nordlinger, *Autonomy of the Democratic State.*

10. Peter B. Evans, Dietrich Rueschemeyer, and Theda Skocpol, eds., *Bringing the State Back In* (Cambridge: Cambridge University Press, 1985).

11. Theda Skocpol, "Bringing the State Back In," in ibid., 3–37.

12. Stephen D. Krasner, "Approaches to the State: Alternative Conceptions and Historical Dynamics," *Comparative Politics* 16, no. 2 (January 1984), 226.

13. Cf. the "new institutionalism" literature as synthesized by James G. March and Johan P. Olsen, "The New Institutionalism: Organizational Factors in Political Life," *American Political Science Review* 78, no.3 (September 1984): 734–49.

14. Max Weber, *The Theory of Social and Economic Organization* (New York: Free Press, 1947), 102.

15. Huntington, *Political Order.*

16. Theda Skocpol, *States and Social Revolutions* (Cambridge: Cambridge University Press, 1979), 29–30; Skocpol, "Bringing the State Back In," 4.

17. Krasner, *Defending the National Interest,* 55–57.

18. See Nordlinger, *Autonomy of the Democratic State,* 27–31, for such a typology.

19. Compare the formulation in Nelson W. Polsby, "The Institutionalization of the U.S. House of Representatives," *American Political Science Review* 62, no. 1 (March 1968):144–68.

20. Weber, *Theory of Social and Economic Organization,* 347.

21. Tilly, 42, 54, 73–74.

22. Theodore H. Moran, *Multinational Corporations and the Politics of Dependence: Copper in Chile* (Princeton, N.J.: Princeton University Press, 1974); Peter B. Evans, *Dependent Development: The Alliance of Multinational, State, and Local Capital in Brazil* (Princeton, N.J.: Princeton University Press, 1979); David G. Becker, *The New Bourgeoisie and the Limits of Dependency: Mining, Class, and Power in "Revolutionary" Peru* (Princeton, N.J.: Princeton University Press, 1983); Evans in this volume.

23. David R. Cameron, "The Expansion of the Public Economy: A Comparative Analysis," *American Political Science Review* 72, no. 4 (December 1978):1243–61.

24. Leo Panitch, *Social Democracy and Industrial Militancy: The Labour Party, the Trade Unions and Incomes Policy* (Cambridge: Cambridge University Press, 1976).

25. Alexis de Toqueville, *The Old Regime and the French Revolution,* translated by Gilbert Stuart [1856] (Garden City, N.Y.: Doubleday Anchor, 1955), 183.

# PART IV

# Conclusion

GABRIEL A. ALMOND

# The Development of Political Development

DURING THE TWO decades between the mid-1940s and the mid-1960s, comparative politics and development studies were growth industries. Based primarily in the United States and taking off at the same time that important developments were occurring in the social sciences, these studies sought to make sense out of the reconstruction of governments and economies in postwar Europe and the explosion of nations and the search for modernization in the third world.

## DEVELOPMENT STUDIES

Development studies of the third world enlisted the efforts and made the reputations of a whole generation of political scientists, economists, sociologists, anthropologists, and other social scientists. An early research wave in the 1950s and 1960s swept into the new nations of Africa and Asia. It consisted of young Ph.D. candidates and postdoctoral researchers — David Apter (1955, 1961), Leonard Binder (1961, 1962), Henry Bienen (1967), James Coleman (1958), Lucian Pye (1956, 1962), Dankwart Rustow (1957), Richard Sklar (1963), Robert Ward (1959), Crawford Young (1965), Myron Weiner (1957,

This paper was prepared for and presented in first-draft form at a meeting of the Joint Seminar on Political Development; Harvard-M.I.T., on 26 October 1983. It has been revised in the light of criticisms and suggestions of Peter Smith, Jorge Domínguez, Tony Smith, David Collier, and Robert Packenham.

1962), Aristide Zolberg (1963), and many others. These then-young scholars gave us our first theoretically informed monographic studies of Ghana, Uganda, Nigeria, the Ivory Coast, the Congo, Tanzania, Turkey, Iran, India, Pakistan, Japan, Malaya, and Burma, to list some of the more important ones.

During this same period, a group of political sociologists and quantitatively inclined political scientists, working with statistical data on contemporary nations, developed and tested hypotheses regarding the relationship between aspects of modernization such as industrialization, urbanization, education, and the spread of the mass media, on the one hand, and political mobilization and democratization, on the other. These included Daniel Lerner (1958), Seymour Martin Lipset (1959), James Coleman (1960), and Karl Deutsch (1961), who presented these "social mobilization" hypotheses in a number of versions in the late 1950s, followed by Philips Cutright (1963), Deane Neubauer, Donald McCrone, Charles Cnudde, (1967), and others, who brought precision and statistical sophistication to bear on these relationships.

Economic historians and economists were especially challenged by third-world problems and prospects and produced a substantial literature, including studies by Alexander Gerschenkron (1953, 1962), Simon Kuznets (1955, 1959), Bert Hoselitz (1952), Max Millikan (1961, 1967), Edward Mason (1958), W. A. Lewis (1955), Hollis Chenery (1955), Gerald Meier (1957, 1964), Walt W. Rostow (1960), Albert Hirschman (1958), Everett Hagen (1962, 1968), and others. The economic historians were concerned with the implications of Western experience with industrialization for third-world development, while the economists dealt with questions of development strategy and planning, international trade and development, the problems of technology transfer, the economics of agricultural development, entrepreneurship in the third world, and the like.

The "new," the "emerging," the "underdeveloped" or "developing" nations, as they were variously called, challenged the classificatory talents and theoretical imaginations of Western social scientists. They brought to this effort to illuminate the prospects of the third world the ideas and concepts of the enlightenment and nineteenth- and early twentieth-century social theory, which had sought to make sense out of European and American modernization. The "progress" promised by the enlightenment — the spread of knowledge, the development of technology, the attainment of higher standards of material welfare, the emergence of lawful, humane, and liberal polities, and the perfection of the human spirit — now beckoned the third world, newly freed from colonialism and exploitation, and straining against its own parochialisms. The challenging question confronting the scholars of the 1950s and 1960s was how these new and developing nations would find their way into the modern world.

The social and political theorists who contributed to this literature included sanguine Condorcets and skeptical Voltaires. Some thought, as Robert Packenham (1973) put it, that all good things go together, that science, technology, industry, and democracy were part of a seamless web, while others like Hirschman (1958), Samuel Huntington (1965), S. N. Eisenstadt (1964), and Packenham himself anticipated disequilibria, decay and breakdown, and a long groping process. The insights, the hypotheses, the analytic categories that these theorists brought to their work came from Karl Marx, Sir Henry Maine (1883), Max Weber (1918), Ferdinand Toennies (1887), Emile Durkheim (1893), and other nineteenth- and early twentieth-century writers. A group of students of development followed in the historical sociological tradition of Weber, emphasizing structural specialization and cultural secularization. These included Eisenstadt (1964), Reinhard Bendix (1964), and Gunther Roth (1971).

Talcott Parsons as a codifier of much of this literature was influential in the conceptual efforts of development theorists (1937, 1951). His grandiose plans for the unification of the social sciences, his conceptions of system and function, of the interaction of culture and personality, and his categories of orientation to action entered into the work of both micro and macro development theorists. Some of these writers gave special emphasis to psychological factors in modernization processes — attitudes, values, and personality characteristics. These included David McClelland and his students (1953, 1961), Pye (1962, 1965), Hagen (1962), Lerner (1958), and more recently, Alex Inkeles (1974). Others stressed the importance of institutions in development processes, either specific institutions such as bureaucracy (Braibanti 1966; Eisenstadt 1962) or interactions among institutions (Sutton 1954; Riggs 1957; Shils 1960; Almond 1956, 1960, 1963; Apter 1965; and other). Though these writers may have stressed the macro or the micro aspect of development and modernization, most acknowledged the importance of both levels.

Some writers proposed and tested specific development hypotheses, such as Huntington's "mobilization-institutionalization" explanation of political order and breakdown (1968); Rustow's theory of historical transitions to democracy (1967, 1970); Robert Dahl's theory of the conditions of polyarchy (1971); and Robert Holt and John Turner's (1966) explanation of economic growth in England and Japan in contrast to France and China, in terms of the counterproductive economic consequences of powerful regulatory states in the latter two countries. A group of writers presented linear theories of economic and political modernization. Walt W. Rostow was the pioneer in this genre with *The Stages of Economic Growth* (1960), followed by the socio-economic-political "phases of modernization" schema of Cyril Black (1966) and by A. F. K. Organski's *The Stages of Political Development* (1965). Rostow (1971) published a later expanded version of his argument that included the political preconditions of economic growth (1971). Most of these various approaches to political development are well summarized in a paper by Samuel Huntington and Jorge Dominguez (1975).

In an appraisal of the intellectual productivity of these decades, Francis X. Sutton (1982), an officer of the Ford Foundation since 1954, spoke of "the exciting expansion of international scholarship that has been one of the academic glories of our time." As a result of these efforts, he stated, "The academic world has become a great storehouse of what had hitherto been rather scattered pockets of expertise throughout this country, and a great flowering of intellectual effort on far places has resulted."

## THE POLITICAL DEVELOPMENT SERIES

In midcourse of this outpouring of creative work, the Committee on Comparative Politics of the Social Science Research

Council (SSRC) embarked on a program of conferences and publications designed to bring together existing knowledge and expertise on development problems and patterns. The planning of this series grew out of the conviction that development in the third world called not only for a mix of economic policies but for political institutions with the capacity for mobilizing and upgrading human and material resources. Political variables were viewed as important as economic ones; indeed, it was the assumption of the committee's program that there could be no economic development without political development. The first program in this series was on communications media and processes and political development. It began with a conference directed by Lucian Pye in 1961 and culminated in the first volume of the Political Development Series (Pye 1963). This book contained theoretical discussions of the relationships of communications and political development, as well as case studies of communications patterns in Japan, Turkey, Iran, Thailand, and Mainland China. Among the themes developed in the volume were the role of the mass media in transforming attitudes, communications patterns in third-world areas, and the role of intellectuals in modernizing processes.

The second volume, edited by Joseph LaPalombara (1963), treated the place of bureaucracy in modernization and development, containing theoretical, historical, regional, and country chapters. The themes covered included the tensions between bureaucratization and democratization, the place of bureaucracy in European political development, and third-world experience in the recruitment and training of government personnel. The third volume, edited by Robert Ward and Dankwart Rustow (1964), took two relatively successful cases of development outside of the European–North American area — Japan and Turkey — and compared them historically, institutionally, and culturally. The fourth volume, edited by James Coleman (1965), dealt with the central process of modernization — education — examining its significance for economic and political development in various types of societies pursuing different educational and developmental strategies.

The fifth volume, edited by Lucian Pye and Sidney Verba

(1965), focused on political culture and political development, comparing the attitude patterns of some ten European and third-world nations and considering the consequences of these cultural patterns for industrial development and democratization. The sixth volume, edited by LaPalombara and Myron Weiner (1966), dealt with political parties, party systems, and interest groups in Western Europe, the United States, and some third-world countries, exploring the role and potentialities of political groups in economic and political developmental processes.

The goals of these first six volumes were modest: simply to draw on available knowledge and expertise in the United States and abroad and to present a "state-of-the-art" analysis of the role of these political institutions and processes in developed and developing societies. For students of comparative politics and political development in the 1960s and 1970s these volumes became the authoritative, world-scale codifications of knowledge on comparative institutions — bureaucracy, parties, political culture, and educational and communications institutions and processes.

The last three volumes of the committee series had more ambitious purposes. Two of them — Volumes 7 and 9 — were parts of a theoretical project intended to present and test a particular theory of political development. Volume 7, *Crises and Sequences in Political Development,* was written by six of the then-committee members: Leonard Binder, James Coleman, Joseph LaPalombara, Lucian Pye, Sidney Verba, and Myron Weiner (Binder et al. 1971). This group proposed that developmental patterns could be explained by the way in which nations and societies encountered and solved a common set of state- and nation-building problems. The form that these problems and challenges took, and the sequence in which these "crises" occurred, would constrain, if not determine, the structural and cultural development of political systems. The five problems, or "developmental crises," as they came to be called, were national identity, legitimacy, participation, penetration, and distribution. The central chapters of Volume 7 treated these individual crises, drawing on historical and contemporary experience to elaborate them. In addition there were three more general chapters (contributed by Binder, Coleman, and Verba) presenting, analyzing, and evaluating the "crisis and sequence" hypothesis from a number of perspectives.

Volume 9 contained the work of some ten historians who were asked to test the crisis and sequence hypothesis against the historical experience of most of the countries of Europe as well as the United States (Grew 1978). Given the methodological differences between historians and political scientists, Volume 9 of the committee series must be considered an unusually successful interdisciplinary experiment. The historians who participated included distinguished practitioners of their craft. They took their obligations seriously and produced an unusual volume on comparative state and nation building, concluding that the theoretical framework presented in Volume 7 was illuminating and useful in describing the historical developmental patterns of the nations or groups of nations that they analyzed. In a lucid introductory essay Raymond Grew summarized and reformulated the "crisis and sequence" approach and suggested a research agenda growing out of this enterprise. The notion of a sequential order in these crises had to be rejected, a proposition that had already been questioned in Volume 7.

Volume 8 approached the theme of political development from an empirical historical perspective (Tilly 1975). Since third-world countries were in most cases involved in the process of seeking to create centralized states out of congeries of tribal and traditional structures, the European historical experience with state building might serve to illuminate these contemporary problems and processes. A historian-cum-sociologist, Charles Tilly, was commissioned to lead this undertaking with the support of a number of European historians and social scientists. As in Volumes 7 and 9, state building was seen as the consequence of historical efforts to cope with a series of critical problems, such as defense against external aggression, the maintenance of internal order, the supply of food and other essential goods, and the extraction of resources for these and other purposes. The building of the state apparatus through the recruitment and training of civilian and military personnel, and their organization into bureaucracies, grew out of efforts to cope with these problems of defense, domestic order, revenue extraction, and expenditure control. The way in which these problems were encountered and dealt with helped explain the differences among political institutions in Britain, France, Germany, Italy, Spain, and other countries treated in the volume. The authors of Volume 8 concluded that European historical experience may illuminate some aspects of third-world state-building prospects and that state building tends to be a generic process requiring the concentration of extractive, regulative, and distributive capacities. In Europe these developments occurred in the context of almost continuous civil and international warfare — with coercive power requiring resource extraction and the regulation of behavior, and these in turn requiring trained personnel and bureaucratic organizations.

## POLITICAL DEVELOPMENT RESEARCH AS IDEOLOGY

This substantial literature did not lend itself easily to simple characterizations. It was methodologically variegated, including Weberian historical sociological studies as in Eisenstadt (1962), Bendix (1964), and Roth (1971); Parsonian analysis as in Sutton (1954) and Riggs (1957); statistical methods as in Neubauer (1967) and McCrone and Cnudde (1967); psychological methods as in McClelland (1953); and rational choice modeling as in Harsanyi (1969) and much later as in Popkin (1979). Politically it included scholars with relatively naive expectations of democratization in the third world, as well as skeptics and pessimists who foresaw authoritarian regimes. It included "hawks" and "doves" as the Vietnam War divided American academic circles. Over time, as the new and developing nations encountered difficulties and turned largely to authoritarian and military regimes, the optimism and hopefulness faded, and interest, productivity, and creativity abated.

In the mid-1960s an attack on development research began that assimilated mainstream social science and comparative politics to American imperialism and neocolonialism. It was described as an inhumane "positivist" literature, as a Cold War literature, as an ideology that could not be separated from Vietnam. The political standpoint of the critics varied from that of a Mark Kesselman with a moderate left perspective to the more principled Marxism of Suzanne Bodenheimer (now Jonas), to the "dependency" theorists, Fernando Cardoso, Andre Gunder Frank, and others.

In a review article appearing in 1973 Mark Kesselman described the political development literature of comparative politics as preoccupied with order and stability and as predicting an ethnocentric American pattern of economic growth, democratization, and de-ideologization in the new nations of the third world. Kesselman reviewed Huntington's *Political Order in Changing Societies* (Huntington 1968) and Binder et al., *Crises and Sequences in Political Development* (Binder et al. 1971), of the SSRC series, as major exemplars of these propensities. But he included the much larger literature of political development. He stated that "one approach (with many variations) has dominated comparative politics; the search for order" (1973, 153).

In a much more sweeping critique Suzanne Bodenheimer (Jonas) wrote of the "ideology of developmentalism" (1970) that suffused the literature of comparative politics, sociological theory, and behavioral political science. She attributed to the political development literature four epistemological sins leading it to four errors in theory. The epistemological sins were the beliefs (1) in the possibility of an objective social science free of ideology, (2) in the cumulativeness of knowledge, and (3) in universal laws of social science, and the belief that (4) these versions of social science were exportable to third-world countries. These epistemological sins led to the theoretical errors of belief in incremental and continuous development, the possibility of stable and orderly change, the diffusion of development from the West to third-world areas, and the decline of revolutionary ideology and the spread of pragmatic and scientific thinking.

This characterization of the development literature as ethnocentric, projective, quietistic, and unilinear and as the intellectual handmaiden of capitalism and imperialism stemmed from the work of Marxist theorists, mostly in Latin America.

In an article that appeared in the mid-1960s entitled "The Sociology of Development and the Underdevelopment of Sociology," Andre Gunder Frank reviews the American development literature from Weber through Parsons, Hoselitz, Rostow, McClelland, and many others. Frank "examines the North American emperor's social scientific clothes and exposes the scientific nakedness behind his ideological sham" (1969, xi). It is a theory, he alleges, that imputes a set of modern properties to the West and bases third-world modernization on the diffusion of these characteristics to the non-West; "one part of the system, Western Europe and Northern America, diffuses and helps the other part, Asia, Africa, and South America, to develop" (1969, 76).

Cardoso and Faleto argue that "in almost all theories of modernization it is assumed that the course taken by political, social, and economic systems of Western Europe and the United States, foretells the future for the underdeveloped countries. The 'development process' would consist in completing and even reproducing the various stages that characterized the social transformation of these countries" (1979, 11).

This characterization of modernization theory is repeated in the writings of American students of Latin American development. Thus, Ronald Chilcote and Joel Edelstein describe the "diffusionist model" of the American literature as depicting a process in which "progress will come about through the spread of modernism to backward, archaic, and traditional areas. Through the diffusion of technology and capital, these areas will inescapably evolve from a traditional toward a modern state" (1974, 3). And Samuel and Arturo Valenzuela in a recent article impute to the development literature the view that "in the process of modernization all societies will undergo by and large similar changes. . . . " and that the history of the presently modern nations is taken as the source of universally useful conceptualizations" (1978, 538). This view of the political development literature of these earlier decades as simplemindedly ethnocentric is canonized in a paper of Joel Migdal (1983) on the state-of-the-art in political development studies. Again, in a recent article Tony Smith characterizes the developmentalist paradigm "as 'unilinear' or 'ethnocentric' in its concept of change; that is, it projected a relatively inflexible path or continuum of development in which social and political forms would tend to converge, so that the developmental path of the West might well serve as a model from which to shed light on transformations occurring in the South" (1985, 537).

The claim that the primarily American literature presented a monolithic and unilinear model of political development and projected Anglo-American and capitalist values on the outside world cannot survive an even casual reading. Confining ourselves to the Political Development Series, which was one of the most visible products of this literature, it is instructive that in the first volume of the series, and in the first effort to specify the content of modernization and development, Pye presented a most circumspect treatment, which bears repeating in the light of the "ethnocentric-unilinear" image presented by these critics:

> In recent years there has been a conspicuous and uneasy search for satisfactory words to identify and describe the non-industrialized societies of the world which have now become or are shortly to become sovereign nations. We have sought to use, but with only varying degrees of satisfaction, such terms as "backward," "non-Western," "underdeveloped," "developing," and "emerging." In large measure the problem, of course, stems from our concern over possibly offending those being identified. But it also arises from our own uncertainty as to the nature of these societies, their future prospects, and the appropriateness of our even suggesting that possibly they should change their character to be more in accord with the industrially advanced societies. A generation of instruction in cultural relativism has had its influence, and social thinkers are no longer comfortable with any concept which might suggest a belief in "progress" or "stages of civilization." In the meantime, however, as the West has gradually learned to appreciate and sympathize with cultural differences, many of the spokesmen for the non-Western world have become increasingly impatient with their own traditions and have insisted that it is their right and duty to change their societies to make them more like the industrial world. Yet there is a note of qualification in even the most insistent of these calls

for change, for there is the realization that more respect is to be gained from being distinctive than from being an inferior version of a foreign culture. Everyone seems to sense that some forms of difference are acceptable while others are not (1963, 14).

LaPalombara in that same year speaks in the most unqualified terms of the dangers of applying a unilinear Anglo-American model to the analysis of third-world developments.

It is apparent, for example, that rapid economic change leading to industrialization can be effected without conformance to the social and institutional patterns that we might ascribe to the Anglo-American model. Indeed, it may very well be that rapid change in the economic sector is much more meaningfully related to what we might call an undemocratic pattern of social and political organization. In any event, if any kind of clarity is to emerge from our use of such concepts as modernization and development, it will be vitally necessary to specify what we mean by the concepts and to indicate explicitly when a shift in meaning occurs. Failure to do this is certain to encumber our discussions of political change with confusion and with culturally limited and deterministic baggage (1963, 10).

And Ward and Rustow in their comparative study of Japan and Turkey state unequivocally:

Democracy and representative government are not implied in our definition of modernization. Czar Peter of Russia, Sultan Mahmud of Turkey, and Emperor Meiji of Japan were modernizers, but decidedly not democrats or conscious forerunners of democracy. Germany was more modern in the 1930's than in the 1880's, though its government was less representative and less liberal. Classical Marxists believed that all societies move along a single path, though not at equal pace, toward one preordained goal. This artless and simplistic notion does not gain in validity as we change the sign at the finish line from "Communism" to "Democracy."

There are nonetheless certain definite political characteristics that modernizing societies share. Commonly modernization begins under autocracy or oligarchy and proceeds toward some form of mass society — democratic or authoritarian. Under whatever regime, the hallmarks of the modern state are a vastly expanded set of functions and demands. Public services come to include education, social security, and public works while civic duties involve new forms of loyalty, tax payment and, in a world of warring states, military service. The very concepts of public service and civic duty, indeed, are among the vital prerequisites of modern politics (1964, 5).

In a similar mood, Coleman tells us that the dangers of "ethnocentrism, teleological bias, and the absence of a single objective measuring rod complicate the conceptualization of 'political development' " (1965, 15). He proposes that modernization is an open-ended process consisting of trends toward increasing structural differentiation leading to increased governmental capacity and trends toward equality in the legal, participatory, and distributive senses. The movement might be in a liberal democratic direction, but it might with equal probability be in an authoritarian direction. In my own work I argue explicitly against the simple diffusionist notion of unilinearity in the early 1960s (Almond 1970, chaps. 5 and 6). Huntington argues the improbability of democratic outcomes in third-world political systems (1968, 1970). And Dahl takes a similarly pessimistic view (1971).

The attribution of the view to mainstream comparative politics that the modernization of the third world implied a capitalist and democratic outcome simply cannot be sustained by evidence. The great theorist of modernization, Max Weber, was most pessimistic about the prospects of democracy and capitalism and foresaw a future dominated by bureaucracy. Alexander Gershenkron (1962), a leading European economic historian, emphasized that the later the industrialization, the greater the probability of a major role for state authority. Recognizing the fragility and superficiality of democratic institutions in third-world countries, Edward Shils (1960), in one of the early and influential classifications of third-world polities, spoke of "tutelary democracies" and "modernizing oligarchies" as being the most common forms that third-world political development was taking at the time that he was writing. Whether and how soon genuine democratization would occur depended on fundamental changes in social structure and culture, processes drawn out in time and uncertain in outcome. LaPalombara and Weiner in their conclusions as to the role of political parties in modernizing processes are quite skeptical about the prospects of competitive party systems in third-world nations (1966, 433 ff.).

## THE DEPENDENCY MOVEMENT

The unanimity of dependency writers — North American as well as Latin American — in this egregious misrepresentation of mainstream comparative politics, and the acceptance of this view on the part of others, looks more like a conversion phenomenon than a genuine and critical literature search. Indeed the dependency writers rarely cite the "modernization" literature in detail, and when they do, they often quote out of context, exaggerate, and otherwise distort the literature. Peter Smith (1983) refers to some of this dependency literature as "guerrilla-intellectual work" and to the dependency movement as an "ambush." The dependency literature in this sense has to be seen as a political-intellectual activity, as scholarship in the support of political goals. Indeed, dependency writing rests on the Marxist theory of knowledge, the view that political knowledge above all is essentially class struggle based, is inextricably ideological. Thus, the modernization and development literature cannot escape its association with capitalism and imperialism; it is a defense of capitalism and imperialism. The dependency perspective, on the other hand, is a defense of the interests of the exploited peasants and workers on the periphery of the capitalist world. With the intellectual choice formulated in these terms, with the aspiration to social science and objectivity denigrated as an inhumane status quo supporting "positivism," scholars are excused from serious searches of the literature. The social science of capitalism is procapitalist by necessity; the only alternative is a prosocialist social science. The dependency school could fortify its position by drawing on Thomas Kuhn's (1960) theory of scientific revolutions, a philosophy of science that rejected the assumption of scientific cumulation in favor of a discontinuous conception of paradigm change. This became the epistemological position for many social scientists in the 1960s, and it gave their metamethodological discussions a certain philosophy of science chic.

How can we explain this intellectual ambush, this intellectual-guerrilla movement? For the Latin American scholars who led this movement, there was for the most part no special change in viewpoint. They were Marxist intellectuals who in the mid-1960s acquired much greater resonance as expectations of increased growth and welfare were disappointed and as repressive military and authoritarian regimes replaced the populist ones of the 1950s and early 1960s.

The American *dependencistas,* on the other hand, came largely from a generation of Ph.D.'s in Latin American politics or history in the mid-1960s. Their formative years as intellectuals were overshadowed by the black rebellion, the Vietnam War, Watergate, and the campus-based cultural revolution of the 1960s. Their views were also shaped by the failure of development hopes in the third world and particularly in Latin America. These American Latin Americanists adopted the Marxist framework of their Latin American colleagues at a time when the bona fides of American civilization and American scholarship were widely questioned. In doing so, however, they cut their ties with the tradition of neutral social science scholarship even as an aspiration. For while it may be said that full objectivity, full detachment from one's social and cultural biases, is an impossibility, the constant search for ways of minimizing ideological and cultural bias, of bringing them under control, is very much alive. The American *dependencistas* had given up the injunction of Thomas Huxley to "sit down before fact as a little child, be prepared to give up every preconceived notion, follow humbly wherever and to whatever abysses nature leads, or you shall learn nothing." It was this scholarly norm of aspiration toward value-free social science that these then-young scholars rejected.

Dependency theory, elaborated in the work of Fernando Henriques Cardoso (1969), Andre Gunder Frank (1969), Osvaldo Sunkel (1967), Theotonio Dos Santos (1970), and others, came out of the Marxist-Leninist intellectual tradition. It was Marxist in its emphasis on class struggle in political-economic explanation; it was Leninist in its emphasis on imperialism. The analytic structure of dependency theory is

relatively simple and straightforward. World capitalism consists of four interrelated classes — the capitalist center (the
capitalist classes in the United States, Western Europe, Japan,
etc.); the periphery of the center (the exploited underclasses
of the advanced capitalist world); the center of the periphery
(the dependent bourgeoisie in Latin American, African, and
other third-world countries); and the periphery of the periphery (the rural peasant and Indian populations, the *favela*
dwellers, and the like in Latin American and other third-world
countries). Capitalist political economy creates and maintains
a coercively exploitative and extractive process, drawing resources from the periphery to the center and condemning
the periphery to a state of underdevelopment or distorted
development. This vicious circle can be broken only by fundamental change in the periphery and the center, the elimination of capitalism, and the introduction of socialism.

By comparison with Marxism and Leninism, dependency
theory is incomplete and inconclusive. While it speaks of revolution and socialism as alternatives to the capitalist world
system, the strategy, whether Marxist, Leninist, or some other,
is left to implication. Marxist and Leninist theories are predictive theories. In Marx the dialectic of class struggle leads
to the dictatorship of the proletariat by an economic-socio-
logical-psychological logic; in Lenin mature capitalism leads
to imperialism and war, and these in turn give way to the
dictatorship of the proletarian vanguard as social breakdown
occurs and an increasingly disciplined revolutionary vanguard
seizes power.

The *dependencistas* tell us only part of the story. In the place
of the allegedly complacent notions of the modernization theorists, they affirm as political reality this fourfold exploitative
scheme. From the dependency point of view, all the work of
the development economists, political scientists, sociologists,
social psychologists, and anthropologists was elaborate win-
dow dressing concealing the underlying stark confrontations
of exploiter and exploited in the capitalist center, in the periphery of the center, in the dependently developed periphery, and in the underdeveloped periphery of the periphery.

The most authoritative version of this schema was first presented by Cardoso and Faletto in the first edition of their book *Dependency and Development in Latin America* (1969). A later writing of Cardoso (1973) takes into account the extraordinary growth rates in Latin America in the late 1960s and early 1970s by describing this growth as "associated dependent" development. "Associated dependent" development refers to third-world economies in the age of the multinationals when there is economic growth in dependent countries, a form of growth that is distorted, which redounds to the benefit of the exploiting classes, particularly in the capitalist metropole; the condition of the peripheral lower classes is left unimproved or worsened. In later writings Cardoso (1979; Cardoso and Faletto 1979) seems to be backing off a bit from this extreme pessimism and its revolutionary implications. But only a socialist *transformation* can eliminate dependency, as Cardoso and Faletto spell it out in the concluding paragraphs of the most recent edition of their book. They explicitly exempt socialist societies from dependency theory. They write: "Although there are forms of dependent relationships between socialist countries, the structural context that permits an understanding of these is quite different from that within capitalist countries and requires specific analyses" (1979, xxiv).

Dependency theory is not very good Marxism (or very good Leninism). Marx was far too good a historian and social scientist to have treated the world political economy as divisible into four class formations. The social periphery of metropolitan capitalism would not qualify as a Marxist proletariat, nor would the peripheral social groups of the dependent countries. A Marxist revolution would have to occur in the capitalist industrialized world, and not in the backward, predominantly rural, agricultural periphery. That part of the world would have to wait its turn, its own capitalist, industrial maturation.

Dependency theory is not very good Leninism in that for Lenin imperialism and war were necessary conditions for proletarian revolution, but the development of a conscious, disciplined Communist party was the *sufficient* condition, and dependency theory has no category for internal political variables. The internal politics and policies of hegemonic and dependent nations have no explanatory power, except by implication. The entire historical process, from the dependency perspective, is driven by hegemonic capitalism, its agents the multinationals and the dependent indigenous bourgeoisies, motivated by an unremitting appetite for profits and capital accumulation. Internal politics is present either in the passive mood of a politics dominated by the imperialist hegemon, or by implication in the active revolutionary socialist mood.

The dependency approach can best be characterized as a propaganda fragment of an ideology, a polemic against mainstream development theory. Having attributed a simpleminded interpretation of third-world development to the social sciences of the advanced capitalist countries, the *dependencistas* proposed an alternative, almost reciprocal interpretation of third-world development. If, as alleged, capitalist social science posited a benign, tutelary relationship between the first and the third worlds, the dependency interpretation posited a malign, exploitative relationship. If, as alleged, capitalist social science posited the effective diffusion of capitalist and democratic institutions and processes from the first to the third world, the dependency writers posited penetrated and distorted economies, and suppressive political institutions doing the dirty work of the hegemonic classes.

### Dependency As a Research Agenda

The test of any research approach is its productivity. Does it generate novel ways of looking at the subject matter? Does it increase our knowledge and make it more reliable? Are its concepts and theories open to modification by experience? What impact has dependency theory had on third-world and particularly Latin American studies? A number of points have to be made in this connection. First, Latin American social science studies in the United States were in their infancy at the time that the dependency approach became popular. There was rapid growth in the number of third-world and particularly Latin American specialists in the 1950s and 1960s, but Latin American area studies had not had sufficient time to develop traditions and professional norms. Second, conditions of research in Latin America (and in Africa and Asia as well) changed in the 1960s and the early 1970s. The collapse of popular regimes in much of Latin America made research access much more difficult for both American and indigenous scholars. Third, the wave of repression in Latin America and other third-world areas tended to radicalize the indigenous intellectuals. Indeed, it was this situation of repressive military regimes, more or less supported by the United States, that made the dependency scenario plausible. Hence, along with the restrictions on research freedom characteristic of authoritarian regimes, the climate for research became heavily politicized in Latin America and among American students of Latin America (Dominguez 1982).

These circumstances may explain the fact that a substantial proportion of the students of Latin America in the United States adopted the dependency perspective, abjuring "positivist" social science and its separation of the study of politics from its conduct. Surely not all of the Latin Americanist profession moved in this direction. Some converted to it; some flirted with it. But all of the Latin Americanists had to take this approach seriously since it had such powerful and influential advocates in the countries where they did their research.

We should not blink at the fact that the adoption of a dependency perspective was a backward step, a movement away from the hard-won rule of evidence and inference in social studies. It gave up the battle for science in the study of society on the grounds that a complete victory could never be won. It involved the adoption of unfalsifiable concepts of the state as a part of class domination, of politics as struggle and that alone, and of society as a complex of exploiting and exploited economic classes.

But if the dependency portrait of American development research was distorted, and if the dependency approach in itself was flawed as we suggest that it was, there are still two questions to be considered that, positively answered, might result in some favorable evaluation of the consequences of the dependency movement. First, was there any merit at all in the critique of modernization research? And second, did the dependency perspective produce creative research itself, and did it have a constructive impact on mainstream political science?

With regard to the first question we would have to acknowledge that dependency theory stressed variables that development theory in its earlier stages tended to neglect. The dependency approach is based on two causal propositions: (1) economics in the sense of the structure of production and the associated economic class structure causes politics and (2) the hegemonic capitalist nations cause the "underdevelopment" of the dependent nations. Mainstream political development theory in the 1950s tended to confine itself to national and political variables. It focused on the internal politics of the nation-state, neglecting the international context.

These were biases that grew out of the world situation that development research sought to capture in the years after World War II. Eastern and Western Europe were in the throes of boundary changes and constitutional transformations. There were new governmental institutions, new electoral arrangements, new party and interest group systems taking shape against a background of political catastrophe and destruction. In the Middle East, Africa, and Asia new nations were emerging by the dozen. Comparative politics of the 1950s and 1960s was a massive, enthusiastic, primarily American effort to encompass this novel and heterogeneous reality. That it tended to be synchronic rather than diachronic, that it was concerned with order and a low-cost approach to social change, were the consequences of the political reality and intellectual challenges confronting us in those years. The big political story in those decades was the emergence of political order out of the conflictual disorder of war and the collapse of empires. It is true that the view of development and change was one that stressed cost. No group of scholars coming out of the background of the 1930s and 1940s could minimize the issue of cost in human life and material destruction of violent and revolutionary change. It is also true that there tended to be a pluralist bias in these developmental theories. But this again calls for no apology in view of the tormented search for the reintroduction of pluralism in those societies which have sought to eliminate it. The hope for a low-cost and pluralist approach did not blind this generation of scholars. We have already pointed out that the notion of an incremental, low-cost developmental future for third-world countries was sharply challenged in early work of Huntington (1965) and by Eisenstadt (1964), Packenham (1966, 1973), and many others. Indeed, this naivete was more characteristic of politicians than it was of academics. It was part of the packaging accompanying requests for appropriations for foreign aid programs.

Systematic account of the role of international variables in national development was already being taken in the 1960s, and the best of this work does not draw at all from the dependency literature. A number of papers (including one by Karl Deutsch) in Harry Eckstein's (1963) collection on "internal war" dealt explicitly with the role of international factors in civil and guerrilla wars. James Rosenau edited a volume appearing in 1964 that dealt with international aspects of civil strife. The contributions included papers by Rosenau himself, Morton Kaplan, George Modelski, Andrew Scott, Karl Deutsch, and Richard Falk. Later work of Rosenau (1980) dealt with national-international linkages in more general terms. An early article of this writer's (1970, chap. 6) placed national development in the context of international interaction. This was elaborated in a later article (1971) that examined the ways in which national political development influenced the international system in which the international environment affected national development. A later book (1973) treated the role of international variables in national development theoretically and through a set of historical case studies. Several of the chapters in Volumes 8 and 9 of the SSRC Political Development Series (Tilly 1975; Grew 1978) emphasized the importance of international events for political development; in particular, see Samuel Finer's chapter on the role of war and the military in Volume 8 and Tilly's introduction and conclusion to that volume. More recently Gourevitch (1977) has done interesting research on the internal political consequences in Europe and America of international economic crises such as the depressions of 1870–90 and the 1930s. Peter Katzenstein's recent book *Small States in World Markets* (1985) is a most significant analysis of the interaction of national and international variables in the explanation of political-economic development.

One may argue that more theoretical and empirical work is necessary on the national-international linkage. But it is doubtful that the dependency view of these relationships, which reduces them to class concepts, is a constructive way out of this neglect. Similarly, the "world system" treatment of the national-international relationship, like the dependency approach, offers a spurious solution to the problem by denying causal significance to internal national variables (see Thompson 1983, passim).

From the very beginning of development research, the interaction of politics and economics was stressed. Lerner (1958), Lipset (1959), Coleman (1960), and Deutsch (1961) all emphasized the political consequences of industrialization. Industrialization, associated with the spread of education and the emergence of the mass media, resulted in political mobilization. An earlier, somewhat naive version of this hypothesis related industrialization to democratization. But by the mid-1960s the sober view was that industrialization and the other components of social mobilization produced political mobilization that might constrain development in an authoritarian populist direction *or* in a democratic direction. Thus, mainstream political development studies tested Marxist and other hypotheses as open propositions regarding the relations among changing organization and control of production, changing class structure, and changing political tendencies. As evidence accumulated, a more complex and finely grained theory of the relation between economics and politics supplanted the earlier cruder and simpler ones.

The economists and economic historians dealt with aspects of economic and political interaction from other perspectives as well. As we have already suggested, Alexander Gershenkron (1953) at a quite early time pointed out that the later the industrialization, the greater the likelihood of strong state intervention. Simon Kuznets (1955) in early work showed that in the first stages of industrial growth there was a tendency toward increasing income inequality. At higher levels of industrialization there is greater equality. The Kuznets or "U-shaped curve" hypothesis has been tested and elaborated a number of times in the last few decades (Adelman and Morris 1967; Chenery et al. 1974, 1979).

Thus, it is not correct to say that the "dependency" emphasis on political economy and on international variables had significant impact on mainstream development studies. The movement toward the inclusion of international variables and in the direction of political-economic analysis was internally generated in both international relations and comparative politics studies, and was not the result of the dependency polemic. The best of this recent work in international political economy shows little evidence of having been influenced by the dependency literature. At most we may say that the dependency critique gave some accent to already strong tendencies in mainstream research.

While the "dependency" perspective may in some sense have become the most salient perspective in Latin American and African studies, there has been a lively polemic over its merits among students of the third world, and the balance now seems to be moving toward its critics. Robert Packenham (1976, 1983) from the beginning has been critical of dependency theory as being based on a set of unfalsifiable assumptions. Recognizing the importance of international interaction in constraining the choices of developing countries, Packenham suggests that dependency ideas be viewed as hypotheses to be tested against data on political and economic exchanges between the advanced capitalist countries and the developing ones. He calls this "analytic" dependency, by contrast with the "holistic" dependency of Cardoso and the others of the dependency school. Tony Smith (1979, 1981a, 1981b) views the development literature from the perspective of his important study of the variety of different historical imperialisms and their consequences for postimperialist development. He sharply criticizes dependency theory on the ground that it denies explanatory power to the specific characteristics and experiences of individual countries.

James Caporaso (1978), in a special issue of *International*

*Organization* on "Dependence and Dependency in International Relations," concludes his comments on a critical note:

> With respect to dependency I am both less certain and more cautious about fruitful directions to take. Our impulses to quantify and test are so strong that we often miss nuance and complexity, which I am afraid we have already done in our premature efforts to test dependency theory. These dangers are all the more real because semantic precision and syntactical clarity are not the strong points of dependency theory. Instead of measurement and testing, I would expect that a sober assessment of the kinds of knowledge claims made by dependency theory would be a first order of business. If dependency theory can be expressed as a body of testable propositions, the next steps would be similar to those outlined for dependence. I suspect there will be great controversy at this first stage and that severe disagreement will exist between those who want to move dependency theory in the direction of verifiable theory along positivist lines and those who see it as an interpretive device. At this juncture, different scholars may have to part company and go different ways" (1978, 43).

In a later review article (1980), Caporaso gives unqualifiedly favorable treatment to two dependency publications (Cardoso and Faletto 1979; Evans 1979). At the end of his review, however, he gently chides the dependency writers for their resistance to the notion that there can be degrees of dependency. Caporaso cannot quite swallow the Cardoso argument that dependency is an all-or-nothing situation. He wonders why Cardoso and Faletto present so little evidence to support their conclusions, relying rather on assertions backed up by illustrative examples. Caporaso applauds Cardoso and Evans for their stress on political economy and international variables, without questioning the determinist ways in which politics and economics are related and in which the international arena is portrayed with its remarkable omission of the "second world."

Efforts to test the validity of dependency propositions include cross-national statistical studies and case studies of various kinds. It should be pointed out that the moment empirical testing is adopted as a standard for validating or invalidating dependency propositions, we are in mainstream social science territory. Thus, Bruce Russett (1983) in his report on statistical efforts to test dependency propositions is careful to describe the ideas of such writers as Cardoso, Dos Santos, and Gunder Frank as the "dependency perspective," reserving the term "dependency theory" to describe the findings of scholars using "quantitative statistical methods to create rigorous theories and sub-theories that are derived from the conceptualizations of the dependency perspective" (1983, 562).

Russett summarizes the quantitative literature dealing with two of the principal themes of the dependency perspective, the negative effect of penetration of foreign capital on rates of growth in peripheral countries and the effect of such penetration on patterns of inequality. Russett finds, on examining almost a dozen cross-national statistical studies carried out in the 1970s and early 1980s, that there is almost unanimous agreement that short-term penetration by foreign capital is associated with higher rates of GNP per capita growth. For the longer term, the relationship between growth and capitalist penetration is less clear. Some writers find a deteriorating rate of growth. Other more recent work, including Russett's own research, suggests a positive relationship. The view of some *dependencistas* that the effect of capitalist penetration is negative on growth has not survived these empirical tests. The relationship would seem to be complex, positive in some times and places and negative in others, with local conditions, size, resources, and historical experience having substantial impact.

The larger empirical study (Sylvan et al. 1983) from which Russett reported some results presents an unconvincing defense of dependency theory. It demonstrates that the greater the capitalist penetration, the greater the degree of concentration on a few export commodities. There also seems to be a tendency to concentrate trade with a few trade partners. Beyond this the findings of this statistical study of third-world trade and cultural exchange patterns are inconclusive. The effects of foreign penetration on patterns of growth and distributive tendencies vary widely according to specific circumstances. To quote the report: "We refute relatively simplistic formulations of *dependencia* theory and reinforce the arguments of those noted theorists, steeped in the experience of their own countries and regions, who have consistently emphasized the importance of contextual variables and have resisted broad brush generalizing" (Sylvan et al. 1983, 106).

The general relationship between economic growth and equality is described by the Kuznets "U-shaped" curve. Studies summarized in Chenery (1979, chap. 11) now show that the original insight of Kuznets (1955) based on European experience — to the effect that inequality increases in the early stages of economic development and then declines at higher levels — has been substantially confirmed. The dependency perspective would suggest that given these larger trends, the more penetrated a less developed country by foreign capitalism, the greater the inequality in income distribution. Russett's review (1983) of the research testing this hypothesis is inconclusive. But the dependency argument that this deterioration in income equality is an inevitable consequence of capitalism — built in, so to speak — does not survive the counterexamples of such countries as South Korea, Taiwan, Malaysia, Singapore, and Thailand, where income distribution has improved along with growth. Deliberate development policies involving the introduction of labor-intensive industries, infrastructure improvements, manpower training, land distribution, and agricultural policies may mitigate the negative impact of growth on distribution. In other words, the Kuznets curve may be mitigated by deliberate development policy choices.

One of the most sophisticated dependency studies so far produced is Peter Evans's (1979) analysis of the "triple alliance" of multinational corporations, elite local capital, and what he calls the "state bourgeoisie" in Brazil. By the indigenous private business elite he does not mean to include the entire bourgeoisie, but only that part that is involved in the larger and more modern economic enterprises. And by the "state bourgeoisie" he refers to that part of the bureaucracy that manages public enterprises and oversees the economy. He acknowledges that in "semi-peripheral" dependent countries such as Brazil where industrialization has already taken root, economic growth even of substantial proportions is possible. In addition, the relation between the multinationals and the private and state bourgeoisie is not hierarchic, but pluralistic, a relationship that can and is modified by bargaining. But this domestication of the multinationals is capable of only one kind of redistribution, according to Evans: "redistribution from the mass of the population to the state bourgeoisie, the multinationals, and elite local capital. The maintenance of the delicate balance among the three partners militates against any possibility of dealing seriously with questions of income redistribution, even if members of the elite express support for income redistribution in principle" (1979, 288).

Though Evans claims to be dealing with Brazilian politics and public policy, he barely touches on political forces outside of the "triple alliance" such as the military, the Church, the industrial working class, and the larger part of the middle class not included in "elite local capital." His "triple-alliance-semi-periphery" model (which he extends from the Brazilian case to include countries at economic levels or with potentials like that of Brazil — for example, Mexico and Nigeria) is dependent for its effectiveness on the economic, political, and military support of the capitalist powers (principally the United States) and the support, tolerance, or passivity of those internal power groups not included in the "triple alliance." The Brazilian model, according to Evans, cannot survive without its allies from the center and without the support, ineffectiveness, and passivity of domestic political forces. Though he acknowledges the vulnerability of the triple-alliance model to external as well as internal power and to policy changes, Evans nevertheless asserts that "despite all that has changed, the essential features of imperialism as it was described by Hobson and Lenin remain" (1979, 50).

The weakness in Evans's analysis lies in his ideological assumptions. The power structure of international capitalism and semiperipheral dependent development is vastly oversimplified so that the only possible alternatives are the continuation of the triple alliance or its collapse as a consequence of internal or external transformations. For Evans as well as

for Cardoso and other dependency writers there are no degrees of dependency. There is dependency or socialism.

Another theoretically sophisticated study in this broad tradition was Guillermo O'Donnell's work on "bureaucratic authoritarianism" (1973). In this study, O'Donnell sought to
explain the trend toward authoritarianism in Latin American
politics during the 1960s and 1970s by the dynamic of "dependent capitalist development." As dependent economies
moved from import-substitution strategies to the introduction
of capital goods industries and consumer durables — as these
economies sought to "deepen" and industrialize under conditions of international dependency — the requirements for
capital accumulation, investment, and the control of populist
pressures called for a repressive and technically sophisticated
state apparatus. Hence the alliance of the military and the
economic technicians in bureaucratic authoritarian regimes.

The advantage of the O'Donnell formulation was that the
proposition was presented as an empirically testable hypothesis. Unlike most dependency propositions it was not simply
asserted and illustrated; it was asserted and tested tentatively
by O'Donnell himself in the two cases of Brazil and Argentina.
More important, it was tested in a volume edited by David
Collier and published under the auspices of the Social Science
Research Council (1979). The volume included contributions
from O'Donnell and Cardoso as well as a number of other
Latin American and American scholars. The results of this
test by and large were a rejection of the purely economic
explanation or "industrial deepening" theory of bureaucratic
authoritarianism. Albert Hirschman questions whether such
a monocausal theory should ever have been seriously enter-
tained (Collier 1979, chap. 3). Julio Cotler challenges the hypothesis from the perspective of a number of country
experiences (chap. 6). Neither O'Donnell (chap. 7) nor Cardoso (chap. 2) seriously defends the theory. James Kurth, in
an impressive examination of European historical experience,
demonstrates the looseness of the connection between industrialization and authoritarian political institutions in the Europe of the late nineteenth- and twentieth-centuries (chap. 8).
Collier, in an excellent summary chapter, disaggregates the

concept of bureaucratic authoritarianism and points out the direction for more productive research on Latin American political economy. What is constructive about this "bureaucratic authoritarianism" intellectual episode is that through simply following the rule of scientific evidence and inference, we have succeeded in escaping from a sterile polemic and have moved into solid and productive research on the interaction of political and economic variables in development processes.

In addition to statistical and country studies, there have been a number of specific industrial case studies intended to exemplify dependency or to test the validity of its propositions. Among these, two very recent case studies make serious claims to having tested the dependency approach. Gary Gereffi (1983), in an analysis of the pharmaceutical industry in Mexico, argues that he has made a crucial case study testing the validity of the dependency argument. By a "crucial case study," in Harry Eckstein's (1975) sense, Gereffi means that a demonstration of the validity of dependency propositions in the case of pharmaceuticals in Mexico would constitute proof of their general validity since Mexican pharmaceuticals constitute a "least likely case" for dependency. That is, as Gereffi puts it, in Mexico after World War II, conditions were most favorable for the indigenous development of world leadership of a dynamic and technologically sophisticated segment (steroid technology) of the pharmaceutical industry. Mexico had exclusive access to the most efficient raw material, and a local firm (Syntex) was a world leader in steroid technology, with a high volume of output. Even given these favorable conditions, multinational pharmaceutical corporations invaded and largely took over the Mexican industry with two consequences supportive of the dependency approach: indigenous growth in Mexico was distorted by "an inequitable distribution of industry benefits favoring the central capitalist economies and the transnational corporations (TNCs) more than Mexico, and by a restriction of Mexico's choices in pursuing its development options . . . " (1983, 155).

These are not, properly speaking, the principal dependency propositions on growth and distribution. Dependency propositions are global, not industry specific. Even if Gereffi had proven these propositions in the Mexican pharmaceuticals case, they could not be generalized across economies and across nations. There are far too many variables and too much variation to be captured in a single case. By his own claims Gereffi has not proven the dependency argument. The third phase of his case study describes the efforts of the Mexican state after 1975 to protect Mexican interests vis à vis the multinational corporations by the establishment of a state corporation to control the production, pricing, and supply of the steroid raw material. While the maximum program of this state corporation failed to be fulfilled, the program was able to increase the price paid for the raw material and the rate of return to Mexican farmers. Furthermore, Gereffi views the entrance of the state into the pharmaceuticals picture in Mexico as a relatively open and potentially productive one from the point of view of domestic interests. In other words, he does not exclude the possibility of a reversal of dependency trends through state decisions in Mexico and other third-world countries. In the second part of his book Gereffi examines the pharmaceutical industry cross-nationally and comes to conclusions in conflict with Evans's "triple alliance" thesis. Thus, he finds private pharmaceutical companies capable of acting in support of societal goals, and state pharmaceutical companies and government regulators in some third-world countries intervening effectively in the interest of a more equitable distribution of access to pharmaceuticals.

As we have just seen, Gereffi does not claim to validate the dependency perspective as advanced by such writers as Cardoso and Evans. It is an open, varied, and changing phenomenon that he describes. And, in contrast to the pessimism of Cardoso, Evans, and others, he concludes, "The continuing dilemmas of development most be understood, then, as generating not just constraints, but also opportunities for national actors" (1983, 253).

In his case study of the mining industry of Peru, David Becker (1983), employing a more classical Marxist social democratic approach, views the emergence of a national bourgeoisie out of the development of the Peruvian mineral industries in progressive terms. The corporate national bourgeoisie, in his judgment, is not simply a creature of the multinational corporations. It pursues a more progressive social, economic, and political policy than the old oligarchy. It has been responsible for growth and greater distributive equity and enjoys substantial legitimacy. Becker argues that given the present situation in Peru a socialist alternative does not exist: "The ascent of the corporate national bourgeoisie has not arrested what would otherwise have been a broadly based movement of popular liberation and has led to some noteworthy gains for the popular sectors" (1983, 334).

Becker also points out that the state in Peru, while substantially influenced by the corporate national bourgeoisie, is not its creature. It has autonomy and can act in the interests of other sectors of society. The Peruvian trade union movement is relatively robust and supportive of the bourgeois democratic regime. This picture of power and policy in Peru is in contrast to Evans's "triple-alliance" model of Brazil. Becker gives short shrift to the dependency ideas of such theorists as Cardoso, on the grounds that empirical investigation "consistently fails to verify them" (1983, 341). These are his concluding comments:

> Deficient in explanatory power and unable to stand up to empirical tests, the "theory" of dependency as a systemic outcome of relations with international capitalism is, in reality, an ideology. Dependencista ideology has been useful to political and economic elites striving to free themselves and their nations from subjugation to neocolonialism. That goal has been largely attained. Now the task is to focus on the national basis of elitism and domination — which an ideology that blames all evil in the Third World on the metropoli cannot do. The ideology depreciates the drive to institute local participatory democracy (a step forward even in its less-than-perfect bourgeois incarnation) and to extend it beyond formal politics; one searches in vain for a dependencista appreciation that democracy is the only meaningful check on elite power. Accordingly, dependencismo no longer furthers, as it once did, the cause of general human liberation. It is time, therefore, for progressives to lay it to rest" (1983, 342).

When we deal with case studies like that of Becker or even Gereffi, or with the statistical tests summarized by Russett, we are really beyond the dependency approach. We are back in mainstream social science and political science research, where we are governed by professional criteria of evidence and inference.

## THE PRODUCTIVITY OF MAINSTREAM COMPARATIVE POLITICS

While third-world research continues on a substantial scale, it no longer is the "growth industry" of the 1950s and 1960s. This is in part a consequence of restricted access for research in repressive regimes, but it is also a consequence of an abated excitement. Development has turned out to be a brutal slog-ging process. There have been more economic growth suc-cesses than democratization ones. Nevertheless, the integral pessimism of the late 1960s and early 1970s has turned out to be inappropriate. The relationship between politics and economic development turns out to be more complex than expected. The authoritarian regimes of Brazil, Argentina, Uruguay, and others seem to have run their course and have given way, or are giving way, to popular regimes favoring "turning the rascals out," just as popular regimes were turned out in these countries in earlier decades. Development and modernization seems to produce enough disappointments to discredit both popular and authoritarian regimes in turn.

The accomplishments of area studies in the last decade have been substantial. Aside from the distortions produced by the dependency movement, primarily in Latin American and Af-rican studies, much good work has been done. It would not be an exaggeration to claim that area studies have come to interact creatively with one another and have both drawn upon and contributed to political theory in the last few dec-ades. The concept of "clientelism" has proven to be particu-larly fruitful in third-world area studies. The recognition of the importance of patron-client relations in politics has roots in sociological and anthropological theory. The earliest con-tribution to this literature was that of Carl Lande (1965), who interpreted Philippine politics almost entirely in terms of a factionalism based on patron-client relations. Within a few years, applications of the patron-client concept appeared in Keith Legg's study of Greek politics (1969), James C. Scott's (1972) studies of Southeast Asia politics, and Rene Lemarchand's (1972) work on African politics. Jackson and Rosberg (1984) make effective use of the patron-client concept in their recent study of personal rule in Black Africa. Clientelism has also proven to be a useful concept for the analysis of Middle Eastern political processes, as is suggested in the work of James Bill and Carl Leiden (1983) and of Robert Springborg (1982). The general theoretical implications of patron-client relations and their intellectual history are treated in an excellent symposium edited by Steffan Schmidt et al. (1977). Eisenstadt and Lemarchand (1981) have also drawn together a cross-area collection of patron-client studies, and Eisenstadt (1984) more recently have presented a sociological theory of clientelism.

Despite the difficulties of access to field research, Communism studies have produced distinguished work in recent years. The application of analytic models and concepts from comparative politics and political sociology has illuminated Communist politics in important ways. The polemic among Gordon Skilling (1971, 1983), T. H. Rigby (1980), Jerry Hough (1983), and others over the applicability of interest group theory and pluralism to Communist political processes has been unusually productive of insight. Similarly, Rigby and his associates (1982, 1983) have made good use of the concepts of legitimacy and patron-client relations in analyzing Soviet and Communist politics. The concepts of bueaucratic politics (Dawisha, et al. 1980), political participation (Friedgut 1979), and political culture (Brown and Gray 1977; White 1979) have also been applied in Soviet and Communism studies. Jan Triska (1977, 1981) has pioneered in utilizing political development and political sociology concepts in Eastern European studies.

There has been a similar effort to illuminate Chinese politics through the application of Western social science notions. Harry Harding (1984), in a review of Chinese political studies, divides Chinese political science scholarship in the post–World War II period into three generations. The first generation of studies was primarily descriptive of the emerging institutions and processes. The second generation, based primarily on materials brought to light in the Cultural Revolution, was a more specialized literature dealing with such themes as the bureaucracy, various areas of public policy, and geographic regions. More recently Western social science concepts and models have been applied to Chinese data. Thus, there are applications of factional models, interest group models, bureaucratic politics models, belief system models, and generational models. Harding concludes his analysis by projecting the prospects of future work on China, based on, at least for the moment, more accessible data. He sees great promise in this combination of more open access for field research and a closer integration of Chinese studies into comparative politics.

The significance of this three-decade-long interaction between political theory and area studies has not been fully appreciated. Giovanni Sartori (1970), in his celebrated "concept misformation" article, and some of the contributors to the Robert Ward and Lucian Pye symposium on political science and area studies (1975) would seem to have missed the point of this intellectual experience when they criticize it for "concept stretching" or ethnocentrism. Surely Hugh Skilling, T. H. Rigby, and Jerry Hough when they debated about interest groups in Communist political systems were not so naive as to believe that they would discover chambers of commerce, farm bureaus, Leagues of Women Voters, and the like in the Soviet Union, Poland, Hungary, etc. They were dissatisfied with the totalitarian model and tried the interest group model for fit. What came out of this exercise was a sharper delineation of the power-policy structure in Communist political systems. The same might be said of the patron-client model, the bureaucratic politics model, the issue network and "iron triangle" model, and the other conceptual models taken primarily from American political studies that have proven so useful in bringing out the similarities and differences among "first-," "second-," and "third-" world countries. Creative model fitting has been the essence of the game. The critique of this work as ethnocentric or as violating methodological rules stems from an ideological bias or from an extreme ideographic methodological position.

In the 1970s, there was a renewed interest in Western Europe. In the "new nation" excitement of the 1950s and early 1960s, training and research in European studies had declined. In the 1970s, the advanced industrial societies (now including Japan) began to develop "interesting" problems — the environment and the "quality of life," a slowdown of growth, inflation, unemployment, party realignment and dealignment, and "ungovernability." There were interesting movements, issues, and solutions in the wind — tax rebellions, neocorporatism, neoeconomic classicism, neoconservatism. The accessibility of these countries for research and the availability of reliable quantitative data challenged the theoretically adventurous and methodologically sophisticated scholars in comparative politics.

There have been a number of solid accomplishments in comparative and development studies in the last decade or so.

## 1. Political Economy Studies

The political economy of development continues to be a productive research field. Hollis Chenery (1974, 1979) and his collaborators in World Bank-sponsored research continue to produce important studies illuminating the issues of growth, distribution, and public policy in third-world countries. Albert Fishlow and his collaborators (1978), as well as Howard Wriggins (1978), have made important contributions to our understanding of important third-world welfare and growth issues within the framework of the research program of the Council on Foreign Relations.

## 2. Comparative Political History

The field of comparative political history has been particularly productive of insight into developmental patterns in the last decade. Over the longer time span this approach to history as a way of generating hypotheses about political development has been influenced by three intellectual currents: (1) Weberian political sociology, (2) neo-Marxist ideas, and (3) more general social scientific hypotheses and methods. The influence of Marxism has been pervasive in comparative historical sociology. Since his work, no serious political scientist or sociologist can afford to neglect the role of economic forces in the explanation of social reality. The important difference has been between those who insist on a primacy for economic forces and class structure in historical explanations and those who attribute explanatory significance in addition to religion, ethnicity, political processes, personality, and the like.

Weber's sociology of religion was in some sense a polemic against the Marxist view of economic causality, though social class and status continue to play important explanatory roles in his sociological theory and research. In the postwar period there have been noteworthy contributions to comparative political history by Weberians, primarily in the earlier decades. Eisenstadt's *The Political Systems of Empires* (1963) was in direct continuity with Weber's theory of types of "domination." Eisenstadt's study of bureaucratic empires filled in a theoretical and empirical gap in Weber's monumental work, and his later work continued to develop Weberian themes. Reinhard Bendix in 1964 published his *Nation-Building and Citizenship,* which contrasted nation-state developments in Western Europe, Russia, Japan, and India utilizing Weber's political sociological concepts of rationality and traditionality, patrimonialism, bureaucratization, plebiscitarian democracy, and the like. Guenther Roth (1968) got significant explanatory mileage out of Weber's concept of patrimonialism in the analysis of third-world development.

The neo-Marxist trend (if one can still properly call it that) has been quite productive, beginning with Barrington Moore's *Social Origins of Dictatorship and Democracy* (1966), including Perry Anderson's *Lineages of The Absolutist State* (1974) and Immanuel Wallerstein's *The Modern World System* (1974, 1980), and culminating in Theda Skocpol's *States and Revolutions* (1979). While all four of these writers would characterize themselves as in some sense drawing on Marxism, they display a wide variety of explanatory logics. Thus, Wallerstein's *World System* theory is a simple monocausal world capitalism logic with three actors — a capitalist core, a semiperiphery, and a periphery. Barrington Moore's *Social Origins* presents two causal logics — an explicit parisimonious "bourgeousie-rural social structure" explanation of the historical origins of capitalist democracy, fascism, and Communism, embedded in a much more complex and dense series of historical case studies reflecting cultural and political as well as economic explanations. Anderson rejects a warfare theory of the origins of the European absolutist state and proposes a more orthodox Marxist logic of peasant-nobility class struggle in the late feudal period in Western Europe. Finally, Skocpol's study of the classic social revolutions in France, Russia, and China is related to Marxism mainly by self-characterization. Class structure and conflict are not Skocpol's powerful variables in explaining these great social revolutions. They are more in the nature of background factors, while serious military defeats and collapsing state structures are the sufficient causes. Skocpol refers to herself as a "structuralist," viewing history as largely explained by the interplay of international, social, and state structures, and with politics and leadership definitely soft-pedaled.

The more eclectic social science-influenced comparative historical current began in the early 1970s with the SSRC volumes edited by Binder (1971), Tilly (1975), and Grew (1978), discussed earlier. Two symposia deal with the theme of the collapse and reinstitution of democracy in the last few decades. Juan Linz and Alfred Stepan (1978) attempted to distill generalizations from our historical experience with the collapse of democracies in Europe and Latin America in the last half century. Philippe Schmitter, Guillermo O'Donnell, and their collaborators (forthcoming) have attempted to codify more recent experience with transitions to democracy from authoritarian regimes in Europe and Latin America.

The international political economy school has produced a series of comparative historical studies linking politics and economics and national and international factors. This fruitful interdisciplinary work has produced, among others, such interesting studies as Gourevitch's (1977, 1984) two analyses of the consequences of major depressions — that of 1870–90 and that of the 1930s — for European and American political development; Kurth's (Collier, 1974) analysis of the interaction of industrialization and democratization in Europe during the late nineteenth century; Peter Katzenstein's symposium (1978) comparing and explaining the foreign economic policies of the major democratic capitalist nations; and Katzenstein's recent brilliant *Small States and World Markets* (1985).

### 3. Comparative Survey Research

Comparative survey research has made major progress in the last few decades. Sidney Verba (1978) and his associates, Ronald Inglehart (1975), Samuel Barnes and his associates (1979), and Robert Putnam and his collaborators (1973, 1981) have vastly improved our understanding of the structure, conditions, and consequences of political participation and of the political culture of mass and elite groups in advanced industrial societies. The cross-national accummulation of electoral results and of survey data on partisanship and attitudes on issues has made possible increasingly accurate analyses of political trends. Contributions such as Richard Rose's *Electoral Behavior: A Comparative Handbook* (1974) and Dalton, Flanagan, and Beck's *Electoral Change in Advanced Industrial Democracies* (1984) have provided us with more rigorous explanations of changing political behavior.

### 4. Comparative Public Policy Studies

Comparative public policy has been established as an important field in political science under the leadership of Arnold Heidenheimer (1983), Peter Flora (1981), Hugh Heclo (1974), and Richard Rose (1984). It has generated a set of empirically validated propositions about the economic, political, and cultural conditions affecting differences in the public revenue and expenditure policies, and in income maintenance, health, and education policies in Europe and North America in the last century.

## 5. Econometric Studies

In the econometric tradition, important statistical work has been done on the relationship between economic growth, the volume and composition of governmental revenue and expenditure, the ideological composition of governments, the level and structure of trade union organization, strike levels, inflation, and unemployment rates. This literature, in which the work of Douglas Hibbs (1977, 1978), David Cameron (1978, 1982), Roger Hollingsworth (1982), and James Alt (1983) has been of particular importance, along with the comparative public policy literature and the historical political economy literature cited earlier, represents substantial responses to the challenge of a political economy of comparative politics.

## 6. Comparative Interest Groups and Neocorporatist Studies

A comparative interest group and neocorporatist literature has developed in the past decade, contributed to by Philippe Schmitter (1979), Gerhard Lehmbruch (1982), Suzanne Berger (1981), John Goldthorpe (1984), and others. This literature deals with the interesting problem of the interaction of interest groups and bureaucracies in the contemporary crises of political economy. A major investigation of trade associations and the political economy of advanced industrial societies is currently under way under the leadership of Schmitter.

## 7. Comparative Political Party Studies

The classic tradition of comparative political party studies is being carried on by Giovanni Sartori (1976), Arend Lijphart (1977, 1984), and G. Bingham Powell (1982), among others. This work has brought our understanding of electoral engineering and of the conditions and consequences of different varieties of party systems to higher levels of rigor.

## 8. Methodology

Finally, mainstream comparative politics has generated a useful methodological literature, dealing with problems of linguistic equivalence in cross-national research, setting standards in conceptualization, and exploring the explanatory power of different comparative strategies. Adam Przeworski and Henry Teune (1970), Robert Holt and John Turner (1970), Sidney Verba (1967), Giovanni Sartori (1970, 1975), Arend Lijphart (1971), and Mattei Dogan and Dominique Pelassy (1984), among others, have all made important contributions to this literature.

The ideological battle has not had the "chilling" effect in studies of advanced democratic nations that it has had on third-world area studies, particularly Latin America. This is due to the fact that the intellectual tradition of European and American area studies is older and better established. The professional corps is larger; there are more publication outlets. The neo-Marxist literature of Europe and America is not as simplistic as the *dependencia* literature. Neo-Marxist and mainstream comparative studies meet in a common interest in social class and economic variables as explanatory of political phenomena. They move apart when class becomes the primum mobile of political explanation and when the concept of the state becomes a set of unspecified and unverified coercive relations among classes.

A new research thrust concerned with reaffirming the importance of the state in political explanation has still to prove its productivity. Eric Nordlinger's (1981) argument urging the importance of the state and government as initiating policy, as having autonomy even under great societal pressure, makes a useful contribution to research strategy. On the other hand, the concept of the state in the recent volume edited by Evans, Rueschemeyer, and Skocpol (1985) seems to have metaphysical overtones. This neo-statist movement seems to have overlooked the fact that the pluralist and structural-functional movements in political science were efforts, largely successful, to demystify the state concept, to disaggregate and operationalize it, so that it could be accurately observed and measured. It surely will serve no useful purpose to remystify the state concept, to reintroduce its Hegelian reification and ambiguity (Krasner 1984; Lentner 1984). In addition, these neo-statists have not as yet done a good search of the literature. Though evangelists of a new comparative history, they caricature the historical background of the pluralist movement. Far from demeaning the state, the pluralists were powerful advocates of the mobilization of the less advantaged elements of the population in order to gain access to the state and to increase state power for welfare objectives. The pluralists were not only New Dealers; they were also engineers in the construction of what later became the "imperial presidency." Charles Merriam, Pendleton Herring, V. O. Key, and others all served apprenticeships in the work of the National Resources Planning Board, the President's Committee on Administrative Management, and the early Bureau of the Budget — all of which were concerned with strengthening the state. The allegation that the pluralists reduced the state and government to a simple arena where societal interests compete with one another simply does not bear a close scrutiny. We must ask if the neostatists have ever examined the last chapters of Truman's *The Governmental Process* (1951); or E. Pendleton Herring's *Federal Commissioners* (1936) and *Presidential Leadership* (1940); or V. O. Key's *The Administration of Federal Grants to States* (1937) and *Politics, Parties, and Pressure Groups* (1949). Indeed there are, in any university library, many shelves of books dealing with political and governmental institutions strongly influenced by pluralism, which would challenge this caricature of the pluralist treatment of the state.

The neostatists do not make clear what they propose to pack into the state concept, but they seem to resist the thought of unpacking it for analytic and empirical research purposes. As this neostatist impulse takes tangible form in empirical studies of one kind or another, will it not lead to research on executives, bureaucracies, military institutions, parliaments, political parties, interest groups and electorates, or relations and interactions among them? Will it avoid studies of comparative public revenue and expenditure, comparative public policy, comparative political culture? Indeed, if this neostatism is more than semantic juggling, it will surely be disaggregated into these specific research themes. And it is difficult to see what new insight, what new research programs will have been stimulated by "Bringing the State Back In."

This account of comparative politics and political development studies in the last few decades makes the case that the field is not in "crisis," as some have argued. If there has been a crisis it has been a political rather than an intellectual one. This essay also makes the case that the characterization of the literature of comparative politics as an ideological defense of imperialism and capitalism simply is not borne out by evidence. The dependency writers who have been responsible for this portrayal of the field have failed to search the literature; where they cite it, they often misrepresent its content and meaning. The dependency research program has not made its case. Its principal propositions have failed to be confirmed or have been disconfirmed. Insofar as the dependency approach has become a serious research program involving rigorous case studies and quantitative tests of the relations between carefully operationalized variables, it has become part of mainstream comparative politics. The argument that the *dependencistas* directed our attention to the importance of the international environment for economic and political development and brought political economy perspectives to bear on these processes cannot be sustained. These tendencies were already present in the mainstream literature, and they continue with great vigor today. And if one examines the literature cited in these international and political economy studies there is little evidence of impact of the dependency perspective. One cannot escape the conclusion that the dependency movement was a political movement, and that its net effect may have been intellectually counterproductive.

Mainstream comparative studies, rather than being in crisis, are richly and variedly productive. If there is no single paradigm today, it may be said that there never was one. In the four decades since World War II, the level of rigor has been significantly increased in quantitative, analytical, and historical-sociological work. It has not escaped cultural and ideological bias, but it aspires to and attains an ever-greater honesty and detachment.

**REFERENCES**

Adelman, Irma and Cynthia Taft Morris. 1967. *Society, Politics, and Economic Development: A Quantitative Approach*. Baltimore, Md.: Johns Hopkins University Press.

Almond, Gabriel A. 1956. "Comparative Political Systems." *Journal of Politics* 18, no. 3 (August).

Almond, Gabriel A. and James Coleman, eds. 1960. *The Politics of The Developing Areas*. Princeton, N.J.: Princeton University Press.

Almond, Gabriel A. and Sidney Verba. 1963. *The Civic Culture*. Princeton, N.J.: Princeton University Press.

Almond, Gabriel A. 1970. *Political Development: Essays in Heuristic Theory*. Boston: Little, Brown.

Almond, Gabriel A. 1971. "National Politics and International Politics." In *The Search for World Order*, edited by Albert Lepawsky et al. New York: Appleton-Century-Crofts.

Almond, Gabriel A., with Scott Flanagan and Robert Mundt. 1973. *Crisis, Choice, and Change*. Boston: Little, Brown.

Alt, James E. and K. Alec Chrystal. 1983. *Political Economics*. Berkeley: University of California Press.

Anderson, Perry. 1974. *Lineages of the Absolutist State*. New York: Humanities Press.

Apter, David E. 1955. *The Gold Coast in Transition*. Princeton, N.J.: Princeton University Press.

Apter, David E. 1961. *The Political Kingdom in Uganda: A Study in Buceaucratic Nationalism*. Princeton, N.J.: Princeton University Press.

Apter, David E. 1965. *The Politics of Modernization*. Chicago: University of Chicago Press.

Barnes, Samuel H., Max Kaase, et al. 1979. *Political Action: Mass Participation in Five Western Democracies*. Beverly Hills, Calif: Sage.

Becker, David. 1983. *The New Bourgeosie and the Limits of Dependency*. Princeton, N.J.: Princeton University Press.

Bendix, Reinhard. 1964. *Nation Building and Citizenship: Studies of Our Changing Social Order*. New York: Wiley.

Berger, Suzanne D., ed. 1981. *Organizing Interests in Western Europe: Pluralism, Corporatism, and the Transformation of Politics*. New York: Cambridge University Press.

Bienen, Henry. 1967. *Tanzania: Party Transformation and Economic Development*. Princeton, N.J.: Princeton University Press.

Bill, James A. and Carl Leiden. 1979. *Politics in the Middle East*. Boston: Little, Brown.

Binder, Leonard. 1961. *Religion and Politics in Pakistan.* Berkeley: University of California Press.

Binder, Leonard. 1962. *Iran: Political Development in a Changing Society.* Berkeley: University of California Press.

Binder, Leonard. et al. 1971. *Crises and Sequences in Political Development.* Princeton, N.J.: Princeton University Press.

Black, Cyril E. *The Dynamics of Modernization.* 1966. New York: Harper & Row.

Bodenheimer, Suzanne. 1970. "The Ideology of Developmentalism." *Berkeley Journal of Sociology* 95–137.

Braibanti, Ralph, ed. 1966. *Asian Bureaucratic Systems Emergent from the British Imperial System.* Durham, N.C.: Duke University Press.

Brown, Archie and Jack Gray, eds. 1977. *Political Culture and Political Change in Communist States.* New York: Holmes & Meier.

Cameron, David. 1978. "The Expansion of the Public Economy: A Comparative Analysis." *American Political Science Review* 72, no. 4 (December).

Cameron, David. 1982. "Social Democracy, Corporatism, and Labor Quiescence: The Representation of Economic Interest in Advanced Capitalist Society." In *Order and Conflict in Contemporary Capitalism: Studies in the Political Economy of Western European Nations,* edited by John J. Goldthorpe. Oxford: Oxford University Press.

Caporaso, James. 1978. "Dependence, Dependency, and Power in the Global System: A Structural and Behavioral Analysis." *International Organization* 32.

Caporaso, James. 1980. "Dependency Theory: Continuities and Discontinuities in Development Studies." *International Organization* 34, no. 3 (Autumn).

Cardoso, Fernando Henrique and Enzo Faletto. 1969, 1979. *Dependencia y desarrollo en America Latina.* Mexico City: Siglo Veininno Editores.

Cardoso, Fernando Henrique. 1973. "Associated Dependent Development: Theoretical and Practical Implications." *Authoritarian Brazil: Origins, Policies, and Future,* edited by Alfred Stepan. New Haven, Conn.: Yale University Press.

Cardoso, Fernando Henrique. 1979. "On the Characterization of Authoritarian Regimes in Latin America." In *The New Authoritarianism in Latin America,* edited by David Collier. Princeton, N.J.: Princeton University Press.

Cardoso, Fernando Henrique and Enzo Faletto. 1979. *Dependency and Development in Latin America,* Berkeley: University of California Press.

Chenery, Hollis. 1955. "The Role of Industrialization in Development Programs." *American Economic Review Papers and Proceedings* 45 (May): 40–57.

Chenery, Hollis, et al. 1974. *Redistribution with Growth*. New York: Oxford University Press.

Chenery, Hollis. 1979. *Structural Change and Development Policy*. New York: Oxford University Press.

Chilcote, Ronald and Joel C. Edelstein, eds. 1974. *Latin America: The Struggle with Dependency and Beyond*. Cambridge, Mass.: Schenkman.

Coleman, James S. 1958. *Nigeria: Background to Nationalism*. Berkeley: University of California Press.

Coleman, James S. 1960. "Conclusion: The Political Systems of the Developing Areas." In *The Politics of the Developing Areas*, edited by Gabriel A. Almond and James Coleman. Princeton, N.J.: Princeton University Press.

Coleman, James S. 1965. *Education and Political Development*. Princeton, N.J.: Princeton University Press.

Collier, David, ed. 1979. *The New Authoritarianism in Latin America*. Princeton, N.J.: Princeton University Press.

Collier, Ruth Berins and David Collier. 1979. "Inducements versus Constraints: Disaggregating 'Corporatism.'" *American Political Science Review* 73 (December).

Cutright, Philips. 1963. "National Political Development: Measurement and Analysis." *American Sociological Review* (April).

Dahl, Robert A. 1971. *Polyarchy: Participation and Opposition*. New Haven, Conn.: Yale University Press.

Dalton, Russell J., Scott C. Flanagan, and Paul Allen Beck, eds. 1984. *Electoral Change in Advanced Industrial Democracies*. Princeton, N.J.: Princeton University Press.

Dawisha, Karen, Graham Allison, Fred Eidlin, and Jiri Valenta. 1980. *Studies in Comparative Communism* (Winter).

Deutsch, Karl W. 1961. "Social Mobilization and Political Development." *American Political Science Review* 55, no. 3 (September): 493–514.

Dogan, Mattei and Dominique Pelassy. 1984. *How to Compare Nations: Strategies in Comparative Politics*. Chatham, N.J.: Chatham House.

Dominguez, Jorge I. 1978. *Cuba: Order and Revolution*. Cambridge, Mass.: Harvard University Press.

Dominguez, Jorge I. 1980. *Insurrection or Loyalty: The Breakdown of the Spanish American Empire*. Cambridge, Mass.: Harvard University Press.

Dominguez, Jorge I. 1982. *LASA Newsletter* 13, no. 2 (Summer).

Dos Santos Theotonio. 1970. "The Structure of Dependence." *American Economic Review* 60, no. 5:235–46.

Doran, Charles F. and George Modelski, eds. 1983. *North-South Relations: Studies of Dependency Reversal.* New York: Praeger.

Durkheim, Emile. [1893] 1933. *The Division of Labor in Society.* New York: Macmillan.

Eckstein, Harry, ed. 1963. *Internal War.* Glencoe, Ill.: Free Press of Glencoe.

Eckstein, Harry. 1975. "Case Study and Theory in Political Science." In *Handbook of Political Science,* vol. 7, edited by Fred I. Greenstein and Nelson W. Polsby. Reading, Mass.: Addison-Wesley.

Eisenstadt, S. N. 1963. *The Political Systems of Empires.* Glencoe, Ill.: Free Press of Glencoe.

Eisenstadt, S. N. 1964. "Breakdowns of Modernization." *Economic Development and Cultural Change* 12, no. 4 (July):345–67.

Eisenstadt, S. N. and Rene Lemarchand. 1981. *Political Clientelism, Patronage, and Development.* Beverly Hills, Calif.: Sage.

Eisenstadt, S. N. *Patrons, Clients, and Friends: Interpersonal Relations and the Structure of Trust in Society.* Cambridge: Cambridge University Press.

Evans, Peter. 1979. *Dependent Development: The Alliance of Multinational, State, and Local Capital in Brazil.* Princeton, N.J.: Princeton University Press.

Evans, Peter B., Dietrich Rueschemeyer, and Theda Skocpol, eds. 1985. *Bringing the State Back In.* New York: Cambridge University Press.

Fishlow, Albert, et al. 1978. *Rich and Poor Nations in the World Economy.* New York: McGraw-Hill.

Flora, Peter and Arnold J. Heidenheimer, eds. 1981. *The Development of Welfare States in Europe and America.* New Brunswick, N.J.: Transaction Books.

Frank, Andre Gunder. 1969. *Latin America: Underdevelopment or Revolution.* New York: Monthly Review Press.

Friedgut, Theodore H. 1979. *Political Participation in the USSR.* Princeton, N.J.: Princeton University Press.

Gereffi, Gary. 1983. *The Pharmaceutical Industry and Dependency in the Third World.* Princeton, N.J.: Princeton University Press.

Gerschenkron, Alexander. 1953. "Social Attitudes, Entrepreneurship, and Economic Development." *Explorations in Entrepreneurial History* 6 (October).

Gerschenkron, Alexander. 1962. *Economic Backwardness in Historical Perspective: A Book of Essays.* Cambridge, Mass.: Harvard University Press.

Goldthorpe, John J., ed. 1984. *Order and Conflict in Contemporary Capitalism: Studies in the Political Economy of Western European Nations.* Oxford: Oxford University Press.

Gourevitch, Peter. 1977. "International Trade, Domestic Coalitions, and Liberty: Comparative Responses to the Crisis of 1873–1896." *Journal of Interdisciplinary History* 8:281–313.

Gourevitch, Peter. 1984. "Breaking with Orthodoxy: The Politics of Economic Policy: Responses to the Depression of the 1930's." *International Organization* 38, no. 1.

Grew, Raymond, ed. 1978. *Crises of Political Development in Europe and the United States.* Princeton, N.J.: Princeton University Press.

Hagen, Everett E. 1962. *On the Theory of Social Change: How Economic Growth Begins.* Homewood, Ill.: Dorsey Press.

Hagen, Everett E. 1968. *The Economics of Development.* Homewood, Ill.: Richard D. Irwin.

Harding, Harry E. 1984. "The Study of Chinese Politics: Toward a Third Generation of Scholarship." *World Politics* 36, no. 2 (January):284–307.

Harsanyi, John. 1969. "Rational-Choice Models of Political Behavior vs. Functionalist and Conformist Theories." *World Politics* 21, no. 4.

Heclo, Hugh. 1974. *Modern Social Politics in Britain and Sweden: From Relief to Income Maintenance.* New Haven, Conn.: Yale University Press.

Heidenheimer, Arnold J., Hugh Heclo, and Carolyn Adams. 1983. *Comparative Public Policy: The Politics of Social Choice in Europe and America.* New York: St. Martin's Press.

Herring, E. Pendleton. 1936. *Federal Commissioners.* Cambridge, Mass.: Harvard University Press.

Herring, E. Pendleton. 1940. *Presidential Leadership.* New York: Farrar & Rinehart.

Herz, John, ed. 1982. *From Dictatorship to Democracy: Coping with the Legacies of Authoritarianism and Totalitarianism.* Westport, Conn.: Greenwood Press.

Hibbs, Douglas. 1977. "Political Parties and Macroeconomic Policy." *American Political Science Review* 71 (December).

Hibbs, Douglas. 1978. "On the Political Economy of Long Run Trends in Strike Activity." *British Journal of Political Science*, 8 (April):165–66.

Hirschman, Albert O. 1958. *The Strategy of Economic Development.* New Haven, Conn.: Yale University Press.

Hirschman, Albert O. 1963. *Journeys toward Progress: Studies of Eco-*

*nomic Policy-Making in Latin America.* New York: Twentieth Century Fund.

Holt, Robert and John Turner. 1966. *The Political Basis of Economic Development.* Princeton, N.J.: Van Nostrand.

Holt, Robert and John E. Turner, eds. 1970. *The Methodology of Comparative Research.* New York: Free Press.

Hollingsworth, Roger. 1982. "The Political-Structural Basis for Economic Performance." *Annals of the American Academy of Political and Social Science* (January).

Hoselitz, Bert F. 1952. *The Progress of Underdeveloped Areas.* Chicago: University of Chicago Press.

Hough, Jerry. 1983. "Pluralism, Corporatism and the Soviet Union." In *Pluralism in the Soviet Union,* edited by Susan Gross Soloman. London: Macmillan.

Huntington, Samuel P. 1965. "Political Development and Political Decay." *World Politics* 17, no. 3:386–430.

Huntington, Samuel P. 1968. *Political Order in Changing Societies.* New Haven, Conn.: Yale University Press.

Huntington, Samuel. 1984. "Will More Countries Become Democratic?" *Political Science Quarterly* 99, no. 2.

Huntington, Samuel P. and Jorge I. Dominguez. 1975. "Political Development." In *Handbook of Political Science,* vol. 3, edited by Fred I. Greenstein and Nelson W. Polsby. Reading, Mass.: Addison-Wesley.

Huntington, Samuel P. and Clement H. Moore, eds. 1970. *Authoritarian Politics in Modern Society: The Dynamics of Established One-Party Systems.* New York: Basic Books.

Inglehart, Ronald. 1975. *The Silent Revolution: Changing Values and Political Style among Western Publics.* Princeton, N.J.: Princeton University Press.

Inkeles, Alex and David Horton Smith. 1974. *Becoming Modern: Individual Change in Six Developing Countries.* Cambridge, Mass.: Harvard University Press.

Jackson, Robert H. and Carl G. Rosberg. 1984. *Personal Rule in Black Africa: Prince, Autocrat, Prophet, Tyrant.* Berkeley: University of California Press.

Katzenstein, Peter J. 1978. *Between Power and Plenty: Foreign Economic Policies of Advanced Industrial States.* Madison: University of Wisconsin Press.

Katzenstein, Peter. 1985. *Small States and World Markets.* Ithaca, N.Y.: Cornell University Press.

Kesselman, Mark. 1973. "Order or Movement? The Literature of Political Development As Ideology." *World Politics* 26, no. 1.

Key, V. O., Jr. 1937. *The Administration of Federal Grants to States.* Chicago: Public Administration Service.

Key, V. O., Jr. 1949. *Politics, Parties and Pressure Groups.* New York: Crowell.

Krasner, Stephen D. 1984. "Approaches to the State: Alternative Conceptions and Historical Dynamics." *Comparative Politics* 16, no. 2.

Kuhn, Thomas S. 1960. *A Theory of Scientific Revolution.* Princeton, N. J.: Princeton University Press.

Kuznets, Simon. 1955. "Economic Growth and Income Equality." *American Economic Review* 4, no. 5.

Kuznets, Simon. 1959. *Six Lectures on Economic Growth.* New York: Free Press.

Lande, Carl H. 1965. *Leaders, Factions, and Parties: The Structure of Philippine Politics.* New Haven, Conn.: Southeast Asia Studies, Yale University Press.

LaPalombara, Joseph. 1963. *Bureaucracy and Political Development.* Princeton, N.J.: Princeton University Press.

LaPalombara, Joseph and Myron Weiner, eds. 1966. *Political Parties and Political Development.* Princeton, N.J.: Princeton University Press.

Legg, Keith, R. 1969. *Politics In Modern Greece.* Stanford, Calif.: Stanford University Press.

Lemarchand, Rene. 1972. "Political Clientelism and Ethnicity in Tropical Africa: Competing Solidarities in Nation-Building." *American Political Science Review* 66, no. 1.

Lentner, Howard H. 1984. "The Concept of the State: A Response to Stephen Krasner." *Comparative Politics* 16, no. 3.

Lerner, Daniel. 1958. *The Passing of Traditional Society: Modernizing the Middle East.* Glencoe, Ill.: Free Press.

Lewis, W. Arthur. 1955. *The Theory of Economic Growth.* London: George Allen & Unwin.

Lijphart, Arend. 1971. "Comparative Politics and Comparative Method," *American Political Science Review* 65, no. 3.

Lijphart, Arend. 1977. *Democracy in Plural Societies: A Comparative Exploration.* New Haven, Conn.: Yale University Press.

Lijphart, Arend. 1984. *Democracies: Patterns of Majoritarian and Consensus Government in Twenty-one Countries.* New Haven, Conn.: Yale University Press.

Lindblom, Charles E. 1977. *Politics and Markets.* New Haven, Conn.: Yale University Press.

Linz, Juan J. and Alfred Stepan, eds. 1978. *The Breakdown of Democratic Regimes.* Baltimore, Md.: Johns Hopkins University Press.

Lipset, S. M. 1959. "Some Social Requisites of Democracy." *American Political Science Review* 53:69–105.

Maine, Henry. 1883. *Ancient Law.* New York: Holt.

Mason, Edward. 1958. *Economic Planning in Underdeveloped Areas.* New York: Fordham University Press.

McClelland, David C. et al. 1953. *The Achievement Motive.* New York: Appleton-Century-Crofts.

McClelland, David C. 1961. *The Achieving Society.* Princeton, N.J.: Van Nostrand.

McCrone, Donald and Charles Cnudde. 1967. "Toward a Communication Theory of Democratic Political Development: A Causal Model." *American Political Science Review* 61, no. 3.

Meier, Gerald M. and Robert E. Baldwin. 1957. *Economic Development: Theory, History, Policy.* New York: Wiley.

Meier, Gerald M. 1964. *Leading Issues in Development Economics: Selected Materials and Commentary.* New York: Oxford University Press.

Migdal, Joel S. 1983. "Studying the Politics of Development and Change: The State of the Art." In *Political Science: The State of the Discipline,* edited by Ada Finifter. Washington, D.C.: American Political Science Association.

Millikan, Max F. 1967. *National Economic Planning.* New York: Columbia University Press.

Millikan, Max F. and Donald L. M. Blackmer. 1961. *The Emerging Nations: Their Growth and United States Policy.* Boston: Little, Brown.

Moore, Barrington, Jr. 1966. *Social Origins of Dictatorship and Democracy: Land and Peasant in the Making of the Modern World.* Cambridge, Mass.: Harvard University Press.

Nelson, Joan M. 1979. *Access to Power: Politics and the Urban Poor in Developing Nations.* Princeton, N.J.: Princeton University Press.

Neubauer, Deane. 1967. "Some Conditions of Democracy." *American Political Science Review* 61, no. 4.

Nordlinger, Eric A. 1981. *On the Autonomy of the Democratic State.* Cambridge, Mass.: Harvard University Press.

O'Donnell, Guillermo A. 1973. *Modernization and Bureaucratic Authoritarianism: Studies in South American Politics.* Berkeley: Institute of International Studies, University of California.

Organski, A. F. K. 1965. *The Stages of Political Development.* New York: Knopf.

Packenham, Robert. 1966. "Political Development Doctrines in the American Foreign Aid Program," *World Politics* 18, no. 2.

Packenham, Robert A. 1973. *Liberal America and the Third World: Political Development Ideas in Foreign Aid and Social Science.* Princeton, N.J.: Princeton University Press.

Packenham, Robert A. 1976. "Trends in Brazilian National Dependency since 1984." In *Brazil in the Seventies,* edited by Riordan Rhett. Washington, D.C.: American Enterprise Institute.

Packenham, Robert A. 1983. "The Dependency Perspective and Analytical Dependency." In *North-South Relations,* edited by Charles F. Doran and George Modelski. New York: Praeger.

Parsons, Talcott. 1937. *The Structure of Social Action.* New York: McGraw-Hill.

Parsons, Talcott, and Edward A. Shils, eds. 1951. *Toward a General Theory of Action.* Cambridge, Mass.: Harvard University Press.

Popkin, Samuel. 1947. *The Rational Peasant.* Berkeley: University of California Press.

Powell, G. Bingham, Jr. 1982. *Contemporary Democracies: Participation, Stability, and Violence.* Cambridge, Mass.: Harvard University Press.

Przeworski, Adam and Henry Teune. 1970. *The Logic of Comparative Social Inquiry.* New York: Wiley.

Putnam, Robert D. 1973. *The Beliefs of Politicians: Ideology, Conflict, and Democracy in Britain and Italy.* New Haven, Conn.: Yale University Press.

Putnam, Robert D., Joel D. Aberbach, and Bert A. Rockman. 1981. *Bureaucrats and Politicians in Western Democracies.* Cambridge, Mass.: Harvard University Press.

Pye, Lucian W. 1956. *Guerrilla Communism in Malaya: Its Social and Political Meaning.* Princeton, N.J.: Princeton University Press.

Pye, Lucian W. 1962. *Politics, Personality, and Nation Building: Burma's Search for Identity.* New Haven, Conn.: Yale University Press.

Pye, Lucian W., ed. 1963. *Communications and Political Development.* Princeton, N.J.: Princeton University Press.

Pye, Lucian W. and Sidney Verba, eds. 1965. *Political Culture and Political Development.* Princeton, N.J.: Princeton University Press.

Rigby, T. H., ed. 1980. *Authority, Power and Policy in the USSR.* New York: St. Martin's Press.

Rigby, T. H. and Ferenc Feher, eds. 1982. *Political Legitimation in Communist States.* New York: St. Martin's Press.

Rigby, T. H. and Bohdar Harasymiw, eds. 1983. *Leadership Selection and Patron-Client Relations in the USSR and Yugoslavia.* London: Allen & Unwin.

Riggs, Fred W. 1957. "Agraria and Industria." In *Toward A Comparative Study of Public Administration,* edited by W. J. Siffen. Bloomington: University of Indiana Press.

Rose, Richard. 1974. *Electoral Behavior: A Comparative Handbook.* New York: Free Press.

Rose, Richard. 1984. *Comparative Policy Analysis.* Glasgow: Centre for the Study of Public Policy, University of Strathclyde.

Rosenau, James N., ed. 1964. *International Aspects of Civil Strife.* Princeton, N.J.: Princeton University Press.

Rosenau, James N. 1980. *The Study of Global Interdependence: Essays on the Transnationalization of World Affairs.* London: Frances Pinter.

Rostow, Walt W. 1956. "The Take-Off into Self Sustained Growth." *Economic Journal* 66:25–48.

Rostow, W. W. 1960. The *Stages of Economic Growth: A Non-Communist Manifesto.* Cambridge: Cambridge University Press.

Rostow, Walt W. 1971. *Politics and the Stages of Growth.* Cambridge: Cambridge University Press.

Roth, Gunther. 1968. "Personal Rulership, Patrimonialism, and Empire Building in the New States." *World Politics* (January).

Russett, Bruce. 1983. "International Interactions and Processes: The Internal vs. External Debate Revisited." In *Political Science: The State of the Discipline,* edited by Ada Finifter. Washington, D.C.: American Political Science Association, 541–68.

Rustow, Dankwart A. 1957. "Politics and Islam in Turkey 1920–1955." *Islam and the West,* edited by Richard Frye. ('S-Gravenhage, Netherlands), 69–107.

Rustow, Dankwart A. 1967. *A World of Nations: Problems of Political Modernization.* Washington, D.C.: Brookings Institution.

Rustow, Dankwart. 1970. "Transition to Democracy: Toward a Dynamic Model." *Comparative Politics* 2, no. 3.

Sartori, Giovanni. 1970. "Concept Misformation in Comparative Politics." *American Political Science Review* 64, no. 4.

Sartori, Giovanni. 1976. *Parties and Party Systems: A Framework for Analysis.* Cambridge: Cambridge University Press.

Sartori, Giovanni, Fred W. Riggs, and Henry Teune. 1975. *Tower of Babel: On the Definition and Analysis of Concepts in the Social Sciences.* Pittsburgh, Penn.: International Studies Association.

Schmidt, Steffan W., James C. Scott, Carl Lande, and Laura Guasti, eds. 1977. *Friends, Followers and Factions: A Reader in Political Clientelism.* Berkeley: University of California Press.

Schmitter, Philippe and Gerhard Lehmbruch, eds. 1979. *Trends towards Corporatist Intermediation.* Beverly Hills, Calif.: Sage.

Schmitter, Philippe, Guillermo O'Donnell, and Laurence Whitehead, eds. Forthcoming. *Transitions from Authoritarian Rule: Southern Europe and Latin America.* Baltimore, Md.: Johns Hopkins University Press.

Scott, James C. 1972. "Patron-Client Politics and Political Change in Southeast Asia." *American Political Science Review* 66, no. 1.

Shils, E. A. 1960. *Political Development in the New States.* The Hague: Mouton.

Skilling, H. Gordon. 1983. "Interest Groups and Communist Politics Revisited." *World Politics* 36, no. 1 (October).

Skilling, H. Gordon and Franklyn Griffiths, eds. 1971. *Interest Groups in Soviet Politics*. Princeton, N.J.: Princeton University Press.

Sklar, Richard. 1963. *Nigerian Political Parties: Power in an Emergent African Nation*. Princeton, N.J.: Princeton University Press.

Skocpol, Theda. 1979. *States and Revolutions: A Comparative Analysis of France, Russia, and China*. Cambridge: Cambridge University Press.

Smith, Peter H. 1979. *Labyrinths of Power: Political Recruitment in Twentieth-Century Mexico*. Princeton, N.J.: Princeton University Press.

Smith, Peter H. 1983. "Unpublished Discussion." Joint Seminar on Political Development, Harvard-M.I.T., Cambridge, Mass.

Smith, Tony. 1979. "The Underdevelopment of Development Literature." *World Politics* 31, no. 2.

Smith, Tony. 1981a. "The Logic of Dependency Theory Revisited." *International Organization* (Autumn).

Smith, Tony. 1981b. *The Pattern of Imperialism: The United States, Great Britain, and the Late-Industrializing World since 1915*. New York: Cambridge University Press.

Smith, Tony. 1985. "Requiem or New Agenda for Third World Studies." *World Politics* (July): 537.

Springborg, Robert. 1982. *Family, Power and Politics in Egypt*. Philadelphia: University of Pennsylvania Press.

Stepan, Alfred. 1971. *The Military in Politics: Changing Patterns in Brazil*. Princeton, N.J.: Princeton University Press.

Stepan, Alfred, ed. 1973. *Authoritarian Brazil: Origins, Policies, and Future*. New Haven, Conn.: Yale University Press.

Stepan, Alfred. 1978. *The State and Society: Peru in Comparative Perspective*. Princeton, N.J.: Princeton University Press.

Sunkel, Osvaldo. 1973. "Transnational Capitalism and National Disintegration in Latin America." *Social and Economic Studies*, 22:132–36.

Sutton, Francis X. 1954. "Social Theory and Comparative Politics." Unpublished paper, Social Science Research Council Conference, (June) Princeton N.J.: Princeton University.

Sutton, Francis X. 1982. "Rationality, Development, and Scholarship." Social Science Research Council. *Items* 36, no. 4.

Sylvan, David, Duncan Snidal, Bruce M. Russett, Steven Jackson, and Raymond Duvall. 1983. "The Peripheral Economies: Penetration and Economic Distortion." In *Contending Approaches to World System Analysis*, edited by William Thompson. Beverly Hills, Calif: Sage.

Thompson, William R., ed. 1983. *Contending Approaches to World System Analysis*. Beverly Hills, Calif: Sage.

Tilly, Charles, ed. 1975. *The Formation of National States in Western Europe*. Princeton, N.J.: Princeton University Press.

Toennies, Ferdinand. [1887] 1957. *Community and Society*. East Lansing: Michigan State University Press.

Triska, Jan F. and Paul Cocks, eds. 1977. *Political Development in Eastern Europe*. New York: Praeger.

Triska, Jan F., and Charles Gati, eds. 1981. *Blue-Collar Workers in Eastern Europe*. London: George Allen & Unwin.

Truman, David. 1951. *The Governmental Process*. New York: Knopf.

Valenzuela, Samuel and Arturo Valenzuela. 1978. "Modernization and Dependency." Comparative Politics (July).

Verba, Sidney. 1967. "Some Dilemmas in Comparative Research." *World Politics* 20, no. 1.

Verba, Sidney, Norman H. Nie, and Jae On Kim. 1978. *Participation and Political Equality: A Seven-Nation Comparison*. London: Cambridge University Press.

Wallerstein, Immanuel. 1974, 1980. *The Modern World-System*. 2 vols. New York: Academic Press.

Ward, Robert and Dankwart Rustow, eds. 1964. *Political Development in Japan and Turkey*. Princeton, N.J.: Princeton University Press.

Ward, Robert E., Richard Beardsley, and John W. Hall. 1959. *Village Japan*. Chicago: University of Chicago Press.

Weber, Max. [1918] 1979. *Economy and Society: An Outline of Interpretive Sociology*, edited by Guenther Roth and Claus Wittich. Berkeley: University of California Press.

Weiner, Myron. 1962. *The Politics of Scarcity: Public Pressure and Political Response in India*. Chicago: University of Chicago Press.

# Notes on Contributors

GABRIEL A. ALMOND taught at Yale, Princeton, and Stanford Universities until his retirement. Among his many works are *The American People and Foreign Policy*; *The Politics of Developing Areas* (coeditor); *The Civic Culture: Political Attitudes and Democracy in Five Nations* (coauthor); *Comparative Politics: System, Process and Policy* (coauthor); *Crisis, Choice, and Change* (coauthor); and *The Civic Culture Revisited* (coeditor). He is a Past President of the American Political Science Association, and was Chairman of the Committee on Comparative Politics of the Social Science Research Council from 1954 to 1963.

ALI BANUAZIZI is Professor of Social Psychology at Boston College. He served as the editor of the journal *Iranian Studies* from 1968 to 1982, and is currently on the editorial board of the *International Journal of Middle Eastern Studies*. His publications include "Iranian 'National Character': A Critique of Some Western Perspectives," in *Psychological Dimensions of Near Eastern Studies* (edited by L. C. Brown and N. Itzkowitz); and *The State, Religion and Ethnic Politics: Afghanistan, Iran and Pakistan* (coedited with Myron Weiner).

ROBERT H. BATES is the Henry R. Luce Professor of Political Science at Duke University. His most recent work is *Essays on the Political Economy of Rural Africa*. He is currently at work on two other books: one is tentatively entitled *Commodities and Contention in Kenya*; the other is *Toward a Political Economy of Development: A Rational Choice Perspective*.

WALKER CONNOR is the John R. Reitemeyer Professor of Political Science at Trinity College in Hartford, Connecticut. Recent publications include *The National Question in Marxist-Leninist Theory and Strategy* and *Mexican Americans in Comparative Perspective*.

WINSTON DAVIS is Professor of Religion at Southwest University, Texas. He is the author of *Dojo: Magic and Exorcism in Modern Japan* as well as articles and monographs on Japanese religion and society. These include "Towards Modernity: A Development Typology of Popular Religious Affiliations in Japan"; and Ittoen: The Myths and Rituals of Liminality." He is working on a study of economic development and the transformation of religion in Japan and England.

JORGE I. DOMÍNGUEZ is a Professor of Government, and a member of the Executive Committee of the Center for International Affairs, at Harvard University. A former President of the Latin American Studies Association, he is the author of *Cuba: Order and Revolution* and *Insurrection or Loyalty: The Breakdown of the Spanish-American Empire*. He is coauthor of *Central America: Current Crisis and Future Prospects* and *The Caribbean: Its Implications for the United States*, and editor of several books dealing with Mexico and South America. In 1986 he won a Peabody Award as Series Editor for "*Crisis in Central America*," a four-part television series aired by the Public Broadcasting System in 1985.

PETER B. EVANS is Professor of Sociology at Brown University and Associate Director of the Center for the Comparative Study of Development. He is also Co-Chair of the Research Planning Committee on States and Social Structures of the Social Science Research Council. He is the author of *Dependent Development: The Alliance of Multinational, State, and Local Capital in Brazil* and numerous articles on the political economy of development. He is currently engaged in research on the growth of the computer industry in Latin America and East Asia.

SAMUEL P. HUNTINGTON is Eaton Professor of the Science of Government and Director of the Center for International Affairs at Harvard University. He is also President of the American Political Science Association. During 1977 and 1978 he served at the White House as Coordinator of Security Planning for the National Security Council. In 1970 he was a founder of the quarterly journal, *Foreign Policy*, and was its co-editor until 1977. He has studied, taught, and written widely in three areas: (1) military policy, strategy, and civil military relations, where his principal books include: *The Soldier and the State: The Theory and Politics of Civil-Military Relations*; *The Common Defense: Strategic Programs in National Politics*; and *Living With Nuclear Weapons* (co-author); (2) American and comparative politics, where his principal books include: *Political Power: USA/USSR* (co-author); *The Crisis of Democracy* (co-author); and *American Politics: The Promise of Disharmony*, 1981; (3) political development and the politics of less developed countries, where his books include: *Political Order in Changing Societies* and *No Easy Choice: Political Participation in Developing Countries* (co-author).

JOEL S. MIGDAL is Professor and Chairman of the International Studies Program in the Henry M. Jackson School of International Studies at the University of Washington. He is the author of *Peasants, Politics, and Revolution* and *Palestinian Society and Politics*. Recently, he finished writing *Strong Societies and Weak States: State-Society Relations and State Capabilities in the Third World*. Professor Migdal spent the 1985–86 academic year in Israel on a Fulbright-Hays Research Award.

JOAN M. NELSON is a Fellow at the Overseas Development Council in Washington, D.C. Her major publications on political participation are *Access to Power: Politics and the Urban Poor in Developing Nations* and, jointly with Samuel P. Huntington, *No Easy Choice: Political Participation in Developing Countries*. Other research interests include migration and migration policies, and foreign aid. Her recent and continuing focus is the politics of economic stabilization and adjustment in developing nations.

ERIC A. NORDLINGER is a Professor in the Department of Political Science at Brown University, and an associate of the Center for Foreign Policy Development at Brown and the Center for International Affairs at Harvard University. He has been the recipient of grants from the Ford Foundation, the National Science Foundation, and the National Endowment for the Humanities. His publications include *On the Autonomy of the Democratic State*, *Soldiers in Politics*, and *Conflict Regulation in Divided Societies*. He is currently studying some issues of grand strategy with special reference to American foreign policy.

MYRON WEINER is Ford International Professor of Political Science and Research Associate of the Center for International Studies at the Massachusetts Institute of Technology. He is the author of numerous books on India, including *Party Politics in India*, *Politics of Scarcity*, *Party Building in a New Nation*, *India At the Polls: The Parliamentary Elections of 1977*, *India At the Polls, 1980*, *Sons of the Soil* and *India's Preferential Policies* (co-author with Mary F. Katzenstein). His co-edited publications include *The State, Religion and Ethnic Politics: Afghanistan, Iran and Pakistan* (with Ali Banuazizi); and the forthcoming *Competitive Elections in Developing Countries* (with Ergun Özbudun). He is currently writing a book entitled *Nimble Little Fingers: Public Policy and Child Labor in India*.

# Name Index

# Subject Index